WHO
NEEDS
LIGHT?

WHO
NEEDS
LIGHT?

KATHRYN E. MAY, PSYD

authorHOUSE®

AuthorHouse™
1663 Liberty Drive
Bloomington, IN 47403
www.authorhouse.com
Phone: 1-800-839-8640

First published by AuthorHouse   12/02/2011

ISBN: 978-1-4685-0701-0 (sc)
ISBN: 978-1-4685-0700-3 (hc)
ISBN: 978-1-4685-0699-0 (ebk)

Library of Congress Control Number: 2011961388

Printed in the United States of America

THE SNAKE

I am a snake
I slither and slink
And into the shadows I slide.
I hide under cover
And wait for my prey,
I flash my bright colors
And gracefully glide,
I lure them
They trust me
I flatter and bribe.
Bedazzled, besotted,
They open their heart
And then when they're sated
I silently dart
I poison, betray;
That is my way
I am a snake.

To Amos, who was an explorer of life's deepest mysteries, and who taught that truthfulness is the essence of good character.

TABLE OF CONTENTS

THE SNAKE 5

TABLE OF CONTENTS 9

ACKNOWLEDGMENTS 13

THE HURT CHILD by Amos Gunsberg 15

INTRODUCTION 17

PART I: BECOMING A SELF: THE WAR WITHIN **21**

THE VELVET ASSASSIN 22

YOU CAN'T MAKE ME 23

Chapter One A NEW-BORN LIGHT 25

THE REJECT I 38

REJECT II 39

Chapter Two THE ROOT OF OUR MISERY 40

PART II: LIFE IN THE CULTURE OF UNHAPPINESS **61**

I AM GOD 63

Chapter Three A SUFFERING SOUL 65

PASSIVE-AGGRESSIVE 74

WORKAHOLIC 75

Chapter Four HOW A SIT-DOWN STRIKE BECOMES

A WAY OF LIFE 76

POISON POLLY 86

SADIST 87

Chapter Five A TEACHING GUIDE FOR THE ADULT CHILD:

HOW TO TRAIN YOUR ABUSIVE PARENT.............. 88

PART III: THE DEVELOPING MIND **97**

Chapter Six ENCODING THE CHILD.................................99

    NEAT FREAK..106
    MACHO 107

Chapter Seven FEELING LIKE A CHILD...........................108

Chapter Eight LEARNING TO BE BLIND.........................121

    SPARKLE PLENTY...132
    GLUTTON 133

Chapter Nine WHAT YOU SEE IS NOT WHAT YOU GET.............134

Chapter Ten CLAIMING YOUR BODY,
        PUTTING DOWN ROOTS........................148

    WE DO WHAT OUR PARENTS DID.................................156

Chapter Eleven THE FORKED PATH................................158

PART IV: DANGEROUS LIAISONS.............................. **165**

    ON LIVING INSTEAD OF ADDICTION 166

Chapter Twelve THE MOTHER OF ALL ADDICTIONS...................168

    THE RAT 182
    THE LAMB 183

Chapter Thirteen KILLING MARIA 184

    THE SNAKE'S REWARD 193

Chapter Fourteen CHILDREN OF DARKNESS.........................194

    RAPE STAR..230
    KITTEN 231

Chapter Fifteen...232

    WHY BE A WANNABE?..232
    CONFESSIONS OF A SOUL KILLER 237

Chapter Sixteen TO BE OR NOT TO BE............................238

THE SNAKE 256

by Oscar Brown, Jr. 256

Chapter Seventeen *LESSONS WE LEARN IN A REALLY*
BAD RELATIONSHIP................................257

PART V: THE LOVE WARS: TAKING CHILDHOOD INTO RELATIONSHIPS 265

THE THERAPIST'S CHALLENGE 267

Chapter Eighteen *LOVESICKNESS* 268

Chapter Nineteen *THE GOODNESS AND MERCY TRAP*.................274

SADIST..286

THE NURSE..287

Chapter Twenty *HOW TO RAISE AN ABUSER*.....................288

Chapter Twenty-One *PLAYING ON THE DARK SIDE* 303

IGNIS FATUUS By Aline Kilmer.............................303

PART VI: ABUSIVE INSTITUTIONS 309

GOING CRAZY 311

Chapter Twenty-Two *HOW SCHOOLS, POLITICS, SCIENCE,*
RELIGION AND DESCARTES LED US
ASTRAY..312

THE UPWARDLY MOBILE PRINCESS...........................334

COMMANDANT..335

Chapter Twenty-Three *AYN RAND AND MACHIAVELLI:*
APOLOGISTS FOR GREED AND POWER....336

GOD'S MESSENGER 352

THE SHEEP'S SAGA 354

Chapter Twenty-Four *VIOLENCE IN THE STREETS*.........................356

AGAINST THE WALL By Aline Kilmer 364

Chapter Twenty-Five THE CHRIST WE NEVER KNEW 372

PART VII: TRANSCENDING THE PAST.........................**379**

Chapter Twenty-Six START A PEACE MOVEMENT 380

AN APOLOGY By Oscar Brown, Jr. 381

MY NATIVE COSTUME By Martin Espada 387

DEPRESSION 390

OBSESSIVE-COMPULSIVE 391

Chapter Twenty-Seven HOW CAN I GET OVER IT? 392

THE WINDS OF FATE By Ella Wheeler Wilcox.................415

Chapter Twenty-Eight LEARNING FORGIVENESS 416

Chapter Twenty-Nine ALL YOU NEED IS LOVE 426

SONNET XIV 427

Chapter Thirty LEAD WITH AN OPEN HEART...............................429

OVER THERE by Makarta 440

Chapter Thirty-One AWAKENING 442

Chapter Thirty-Two EARTH AS MOTHER..466

EARTH MOTHER SINGS by Makarta 484

Chapter Thirty-Three CREATING A NEW SOCIETY...........................485

BIBLIOGRAPHY 493

ACKNOWLEDGMENTS

I wish to thank the people without whom this book would not have been possible.:

My mother, who is much maligned in this book, but without whose influence I would not have learned to fiercely defend my inner self, and to learn the life-preserving value of following my heart. It was this process which led me to become a champion for the growth and expression of the unique people we each are. I know she approves now.

Diane Bradford and Sukyong Suh, who read the manuscript and made valuable comments and corrections.

Laura Gardner, whose artistic vision expressed mine so clearly on the cover she designed.

My clients and friends whose stories appear here as examples of hope and personal triumph. I write this for them and because of them.

The scientists, researchers and intuitive psychologists who came before me, opening new frontiers.

My muses, Ernest Hemingway, Emily Bronte, Freida and Eric Fromm, and e. e. Cummings.

Max and Annette Finestone, who have provided me with the kind of family support that anyone would be lucky to have.

Amos Gunsberg, my therapist, mentor and friend, without whose inspiration, constant support and guidance I could not have carried on the work he began.

THE HURT CHILD
by Amos Gunsberg

It would have been so simple, my Mother,
I didn't ask for much
Just see me—just that,
And say I'm alright
Not great, even, just enough.
Anything but this blaming gaze,
Fixed somewhere beside me,
Before me, above me,
But never seeing me.
This harsh inner rasping
Against the grain
As you twist me to your needs,
Rent from myself, I cannot breathe
The world is a frigid plain,
Desolate, barren
Naked in the wind,
I see no warmth, no hope,
No mercy, no grace,
Your condemning refrain,
Sapping my strength,
Fragmenting my brain.
As I struggle to endure it,
You calously ignore it
My shivering denied,
In horror, I go numb
My screams belied,
In silence, I hide.
Driven into a prison,
Pale and hard-faced
Silent and docile,
My spirit has died.
Robot, machine-like
I bend to your will.
My dullness scorned,
You leave me alone
To my private grief
At last.
I just wanted to be born
I. just wanted to be me, Mama.
It wasn't too much to ask.

INTRODUCTION

Who needs Light? We all do. People have lost their grounding, to each other, to the Earth, and to Spirit. We have become overwhelmed by a culture in which people behave badly. Disrespect, selfishness and hatred fill the air. How did we get here? What can I do about it? "How could they do that to me?"

I have written this book to try to answer these questions. I also want to pass on the information I learned over a 25-year period with my therapist and mentor, Amos Gunsberg. He did not write anything about the techniques he developed. I have done my best to capture the essential elements of the work. The visual and brain-focusing method, the Gunsberg/May Technique, will be discussed in the first part of the book. I have also included some of the scientific explanations for why it is so effective.

Fortunately, brain scan studies and the use of MRI imaging can now identify emotional activity in the brain in new ways. These new discoveries provide visual evidence to expand and ground the clinical work. However, the neurological changes which the brain-focusing work accomplishes could be documented with MRI equipment. This has not yet been done. I invite collaboration for this purpose.

The book also contains some of the exercises which Amos and I have used in the individual brain-focusing work. Unfortunately, it is not possible to teach the focusing shift described here in a book. A companion teaching video will also be forthcoming. It will demonstrate how individual volunteeers are able to dramatically change the way they use their visual equipment. Behind the Gunsberg/May technique is the basic understanding that by changing the way you use your eyes, you change the way you see the world.

The later sections of the book are my own expression of the philosophy of life which Amos taught. I have added the spiritual emphasis to the work we did together. I offer my experiences as an invitation for others to discover and to pursue their own heart truths.

I also have a deep concern about the collision course with disaster our consumer economy and oil dependence have created. Our abuse of each other and our habitual abuse of the planet have threatened life on Earth for our children and grand-children. I address these social issues throughout the book.

In later chapters, I describe incidents in my own life which opened my eyes to a new way of seeing life on Planet Earth. I now see a spiritual adventure we all share. That spiritual adventure is deeply interwoven with a connection to the Earth. I have discussed some of these issues in the chapter "Earth as Mother."

Our educational systems have failed to teach children the most basic skills to sustain life on the planet. They must learn entirely new practices for building, planting, and developing community relationships. New schools will be needed to teach children how to work with Nature spirits, the nature beings who make our life on Earth possible. It will be a necessary shift in consciousness if we are to continue life on the planet.

The book is organized to tell the story of how a growing child experiences the effects of abuse in his relationship to himself, his family, his community, and the culture. These influences at every level have had a profound effect on our children. We have produced a culture of Darkness and selfishness which stifles Light and creativity. We have become what I have called Head People. Lost in imagination and fantasy, we are vulnerable to the seductions of Children of Darkness.

I have suggested that the Abusive Personality is an archetype, in the tradition of Carl Jung and Joseph Campbell. He or she is an anti-hero, the shadow side of the ancient hero myth which is repeated in story and song throughout the ages. Our character, the Abuser, is often as charismatic and intriguing as the hero, but his or her effect on others is the opposite. Where the hero acts to preserve and protect, the anti-hero does the opposite. In personal, financial or political relations, the anti-hero's actions always lead to pain and destruction.

For all those who have had a devastating brush with someone I have called an Abusive Personality Type, I have written Part Four, "Dangerous Liaisons," and especially the descriptive chapter on Children of Darkness and why you should avoid them. It is a practical guide for anyone who has been, or might be, blinded by the charm and animal attractiveness of the Dark Ones.

A dramatic human drama takes place in the interplay between seductive attractions to the Dark Ones and the struggle to free oneself from addictive relationships and habits. These impulses often seem to pull in both directions at once, creating an internal battle between light and dark, life and anti-life. This destructive battle is vividly and tragically enacted in people who have grown up under the influence of a parent who is a Child of Darkness. For these people, the undercurrents of anxiety and depression arise out of a primitive, unspoken fear—the fear of annihilation of the very threads which bind one together as a self. For these sufferers, I have included my best "tough love" two-week cures for overcoming depression, anxiety and stress.

Since every book on psychological trauma needs some levity, and to discourage maudlin self-diagnosis, I have included a number of my poems. Therapists will recognize them as portraits of various DSM IV[1] character disorders. Other readers will simply recognize them as your mother, your boss, or your brother-in-law. Mostly, they are arranged in pairs (or couples) as you might expect them to be in real life. I have also included a small play to illustrate how it feels to be an adult struggling with overwhelming feelings and compromises made because of a brutal childhood.

The stories I have included are all real, and told just as they happened. All the names are changed for privacy's sake, except my own family members.'

Early in the book, I addressed learned self-hatred, and how it is at the base of all forms of psychological human misery. In direct conflict with self-hatred is the human drive toward personal evolution that is driven by our free will and our spiritual desire to create and grow. Like a seed that needs to sprout and develop to its fullest potential, we each need to fulfill the Heart path we came here to live out. We must learn to love ourselves, our fellows and our God if we are to grow.

A groundswell of hope and spirituality is surfacing around the globe and at home. I feel the currents around me, as the proponents

---

[1]   *The Diagnostic and Statistical Manual* is the reference which therapists of all kinds must use to categorize psychological difficulties in medical terminology, especially for reimbursement by insurance companies.

of Light and of Darkness appear on the scene. I will add my voice to the struggle, because it is a part of my spiritual commitment to a path toward Light. I hope it may support and hearten others as they face their own challenges when they come to the universal fork in the road: the moment when the course of a human life will be changed by an individual's choice between Light and Darkness.

PART I.

BECOMING A SELF: THE WAR WITHIN

THE VELVET ASSASSIN

What? What are you crying for? Leave me alone
You're being a sissy, you know it.
Your father works hard and he really does love you
He just doesn't know how to show it.

So just mind your manners and don't be defiant
And things will work out for the best
You're always too sensitive; you know his temper
You'll give him those pains in his chest.

You can't always get what you want, you're so selfish
You're dwelling on unpleasant thoughts.
Take your anti-depressants and go to your room
With that video game you just bought.

Forget it, ignore him. You've been such a rebel
You'd take on the devil himself.
So just hold your tongue if you want to survive it
Like me, keep your thoughts to yourself.

YOU CAN'T MAKE ME

I am a diamond in the rough,
I tease them and mock them with promise.
They know something precious is in there
I flash just a hint of my prowess.

They try to inspire me; they urge me, "Try harder!
You'll triumph! You'll flourish. Compete!
There's a ladder to climb! It's the image that matters,
Your cup is half full, just get back on your feet!"

"Forget about music and poems and painting,
You'll get used to the stress and the tension.
A respectable job and grandchildren for us,
Thirty years and you'll have a good pension."

Every once in a while, I just flash them a smile,
Willing victims, they just don't conceive it.
I won't do it their way; they'll never believe it
They fall by the wayside, and still they don't see it.

But they'll never succeed, and what makes them think
That I should glow brilliant with splendor
What, give up my secret, my lure and my pride?
I'd rather go off on a bender.

Fools, have you forgotten what envy arises
The strong are attacked, and the stupid rewarded.
How, jealous and petty, the critics swoop in,
I'd rather pretend I'm retarded.

I am a diamond in the rough
I wasn't meant to win.

CHAPTER ONE

A NEW-BORN LIGHT

> From the swales in the dales of the Yorkshire trails
> To the swamps of the Southern bayou,
> The voice of disdain rings out in my brain,
> "Dim your light, Child. We deny you."

C hildren look up to the adults who raise them. It does not matter whether those adults are kind, honest and forthright, or whether they are mean, vicious abusers. A young child will hold a parent in awe, without judgment, even when the parent's actions may cause the child physical or emotional pain. A child simply tries to get along, to survive, and will do whatever necessary to accomplish it. Since their powers of analytic thinking do not begin to develop until after age six, children will simply do their best to make sense of their environment with the limited knowledge and brain power they possess. These childhood beginnings also determine the cultural lens through which they will later view the world. It is vital to understand the early beginnings which shaped our personalities when we view our later emotions and actions.

The Case Against Children

Every child comes into the world wanting to be accepted and welcomed. However, in the Western world, we have imposed an implicit philosophy which goes something like this: Children are unruly, selfish, destructive little creatures who must be disciplined, controlled, corrected and punished if they are ever to be acceptably civilized. If your parents don't do it, then your teachers will. Overlaying this authoritarian attitude toward children is an increasingly libertarian attitude toward adult behavior. This sometimes spills over into extreme indulgence toward children's needs. (Perhaps we can bribe this hopelessly unruly kid into behaving.) Thus, the average child is likely to be whip-lashed during a regular day between punitive and authoritarian discipline at school or in the neighborhood, and excessive indulgence in toys, technical devices, food treats and pampering at home. The contradiction is dizzying to children.

Our most intolerant attitudes toward children seem to have evolved from an amalgam of some of the most conservative and harsh elements which each of us brought with us from our own childhoods Perhaps these moralistic and controlling attitudes inspired the current American pendulum swing to physical overindulgence and pampering. Of course there are exceptions, glowing examples of creative and inspired parenting and teaching, but sadly, a large number of Americans tend to look at children with attitudes on a scale from subtle disapproval to outright dislike. Meanwhile, rude and aggressive children whose loud public conversations seem to consist of only seven dirty words (as defined by comedian George Carlin) fuel the notion that this generation is truly going to the dogs. I believe it is the conflicting, shifting lessons which have left them lost, rudderless and disturbed.

Let's look at some common childrearing techniques. One study found that the average toddler is subjected to some kind of negative command nine times every hour. Imagine: "Stop that! Don't do that! Don't touch that! Be quiet! Sit down! That's not nice! Don't! You can't have that! No!" Is it any wonder they are anxious, jumpy and stressed out?

This practice would plant the seed of self-doubt and self-hatred in even the most obedient and well-loved child. In spite of the psychological damage it wreaks, the philosophy dictating a controlling, crime-and-punishment approach to human development is maintained in the public school systems and in many families as if it were law, even though there has never been any real evidence that it's appropriate or effective in the long run.

The hypothesis that children are naturally unruly and in dire need of molding could easily be proven wrong. Logic requires that we need just one example of a culture where children are not disobedient and have never been punished or severely criticized. There are such cultures. For example, Inge Bolin, an anthropologist, spent time with a small tribe in the Peruvian Andes where harmony and friendliness were the everyday norm, where community cooperation and fun were shared by everyone, including the children.[2] These people were dumbfounded when Bolin described our American society where children are frequently disrespectful toward their parents and others. They could not comprehend why any child would do such a thing. There is no word in their language for "disobedience." In their culture there was no serious crime, everyone helped each other, and it was simply expected that the children would be valuable and contributing members as well. If they were asked to do something, of course they would do it, because that's just what everyone did. Why wouldn't they? Everyone's survival and well-being depended on it.

Bolin and many others before her have demonstrated the fallacy of our disciplinary approach and its polar opposite, massive indulgence, but we have remained mostly lodged in our traditional ways. Pandering to a child's every whim springs from the same fundamental philosophy as the crime and punishment approach, which is: They are useless, defective, lazy, and the most effective way to control them is through rewards rather than punishment. Thus, we reward them without the expectation that they will accomplish anything meaningful. The resulting mix of entitlement, shame and self-doubt has crippled generations of good and able individuals. Proponents of the crime and punishment approach will argue that shame and self-doubt encourage lawful behavior and more manageable citizens. This is true, in the short run. It has been used throughout the ages by despots (including parents) who wished to exercise absolute control over others. It has also historically led to rebellion and revolution.

On the other hand, there have always been leaders among us—Jesus, Buddha, Gandhi, to name a few—who had faith in the ability of the common people to behave with compassion and fairness toward their fellow humans. I have taken that position in this book, with an eye to the greater good: I believe we would advance more rapidly as an

---

2   Bolin, Inge, *Growing Up in A Culture of Respect*. This single volume demonstrates the radical differences between the traditional Andean childrearing traditions and our own, and will cause any conscientious parent to rethink many of the practices we take for granted.

evolving civilization if we learned to treat our children more kindly, and less indulgently.

There is an enlightened guide to how to raise a child to fulfill its true human potential. It is the story of Anastasia, written by Vladimir Megré. The third book of *The Ringing Cedars* series, called *The Space of Love* offers an entirely new perspective on how to raise a child with superior intelligence and spiritual awareness far beyond anything we have seen in our own children. It has been translated from the Russian, and is now available for all of us stunted Earthlings to savor and learn from. Once you have read the series, and you have gotten to know Anastasia and her life as a woman in partnership with Nature, your view of children, and your outlook on life will never be the same.

It is my belief that we are all here—each one of us—to live out a spiritual path, to evolve toward greater love and creativity, and to take actions to express those qualities. The challenges and obstacles of a difficult childhood offer us the opportunities to affirm our faith and develop greater resolve in the face of opposition, but the way through to free expression can be a difficult one. Many of us find it easier to achieve the sentiments of love, compassion and empathy than to act on those feelings. We have become paralyzed by fear, self-doubt and self-involvement. In this book, I offer examples of how the traumas and conflicts of childhood create deeply-rooted self-hatred. That self-hatred can create such feelings of alienation that many have abandoned any higher aspirations in favor of "looking out for Number One."

It takes determination to awaken to the truths of our own prejudices and misguided actions. It becomes easier if we work together, in our families and in our friendships, to grow toward the freedom which will encourage each of us to take our place as a force toward evolution and Light.

The barriers you meet, in yourself and in others around you, will serve to prove your mettle. It takes faith, and the strength of character which grows from faith, to hold fast to the qualities we think of as Light-actions: compassion, kindness, empathy, generosity, forgiveness, fairness, courage. You must first free yourself from the bonds of fear and uncertainty—the residue of having been raised amidst personal, cultural and historical cruelty. As Americans, we have also been raised with relative political freedom and material prosperity. This has freed most of us from the need to be preoccupied with the struggle for survival, although many of us still speak of "survival" when we are really talking about greater convenience or luxury. As a result of our material successes, we are now in the position as leaders of the planet to fulfill our path as a people by creating a new form of social contract, even if it means starting anew. We have done it before. The planet is changing, and humankind must change with it, or perish.

In the following chapter of this book, I will present a picture so that you can put yourself into it, look into your heart of hearts and absolve yourself of all the "crimes" of your childhood, whether they belong to you, your parents or elders, your schoolmates or siblings. You will never be truly happy and free as long as you still define yourself by what they thought, what they said, and how they felt about you. It doesn't matter. Once you are an adult, you begin anew, with your own intelligence, and the ability to decide what you choose to believe, how you choose to behave, and how you feel about yourself in your heart.

First, let's debunk some of these old myths about what children are really like.

The Truth about Children

1) *Children are far more sensitive and aware of their surroundings than we generally give them credit for.*

Moments after birth, infants begin scanning the environment for faces and voices. By three months of age, the child's sensory equipment is highly developed; vision and hearing are excellent, and they are able to pick up and respond to the emotional quality of the interactions between the adults in their environment. I have seen a six-month old infant repeatedly burst into tears when his parents, sitting nearby, expressed anger toward each other in restrained whispers. No matter how quietly they spoke, the infant picked up the emotional discord, and immediately screamed as if in pain. When an infant is faced with constant discord and abuse, as many children are, they will have to learn to dramatically turn down this sensitivity. They literally desensitize themselves in order to avoid living in a constant state of terror or screaming irritation. I believe this "numbing down" is the rule rather than the exception in our culture and possibly many others.

As we become numb, we lose our ability to "read" the environment accurately and to sense incipient danger. By adulthood, few people are as accurate at sensing vibrational cues in the environment as children and many animals are.

2) Children know they are weak and helpless, compared to adults.

They do not think they are "the boss," or that they are in charge of their families or communities. Their powers of observation do allow them to experience adults as huge, looming over them, and capable of wondrous activities which they, the children, have no ability to perform (like driving a car, reading a book, or using money). Regardless of their admirably active imaginations, normal children do not assume they really are Superman, unless they are repeatedly and specifically encouraged to believe so by the adults around them. Therefore, it is not necessary to "show them who's boss." Their own survival instincts allow them to perceive where their food comes from, and who provides shelter. They learn very early who they "belong" to. Like Konrad Lorenz's[3] geese who imprinted on the first lab assistant they saw, and followed him ever after, they will cling tightly to the one or two adults (in our nuclear family structured culture) who provide for their sustenance.

3) Children tend to look up to and bond with the adults that care for them.

It is part of the child's mental equipment at birth to form an attachment to those who feed them. None of us is exempt from this innate predisposition to search the faces we meet, and to listen for the all-important voice of the mother who will ensure our survival. We are all primed to love our parents, to look to them for safety and reassurance, and to be fed, emotionally and physically, by those closest to us.

4) Children want to please their parents.

---

[3] Konrad Lorenz found that new-born goslings would attach to the lab assistant who was present at their birth as readily as they would to their goose mother.

Their survival depends on it. They constantly check in with their caretaker to make sure they are being watched over, and that their actions meet with approval. Toddlers at play offer an especially vivid example of this tendency. They are able to toddle off to explore the world for a short time, but will return to lean against their mother's knee, or climb into her arms for "refueling" from time to time. Thus, children demonstrate their need and their recognition that the mother (or other primary caregiver) is, to them, "The Source."

5) *Children are easily frightened.*

Because of their limited experience and knowledge, much of what children come across is new and incomprehensible. They need an adult guide to hold them close, and as they get older, to hold their hand and to explain the mysteries of the world, step by step. A reassuring and steady presence creates a secure foundation for life, especially if that person teaches the child a deep sense of faith in a benevolent Higher Power. If the child feels frightened, she will search the faces of the adults around her for reassurance and comfort, and will seek physical contact to allay her fears, even if it is the parent she is afraid of.

6) *Whatever our parents do, however they treat us, we come to experience as "love," and as "relationship."*

If a child has a parent who is cruel, abusive and neglectful, the child will conclude that they are unlovable and defective, not that there is something wrong with their parent. There are a few notable exceptions to this unconditional love state of childhood, like children who perform deliberately cruel acts, but they usually occur when the child is either pushed to the brink of insanity by the family and community's cruelty, or one or both of the parents is secretly fueling a rebellion. It is our inclination as human children to take the blame for whatever happens in our relationships with our elders. Perhaps this has provided the evolutionary benefit of protecting the older generation from the rage of their sometimes patricidal offspring, thereby insuring the survival of the species. Nevertheless, in dysfunctional families, this tendency to let parents off the hook leads to a never ending downward spiral of self-blame and resentment which is then focused on each succeeding

31

generation. As the inmates I worked with told me repeatedly: "My mother beat me every day with a knotted clothesline (coat hanger, extension cord), but she never did it without a reason. My mother was a saint for putting up with me." More likely, these were the childrearing techniques the mother experienced herself.

7) *The less we are given by our caretakers in the way of stability, reassurance, and acknowledgment, the harder it is to leave home.*

We need the warmth, acceptance and ongoing experience of looking deeply into the eyes of a human who looks back with kindness and recognition. This intimate connection allows us to develop and strengthen the inner structure of a self among other selves, a sense of kinship. Loving treatment creates a bond between the child and his caregiver. Even more importantly, looking deeply into the eyes of an appreciative and interested parent allows the child to bond with himself. By absorbing the sense of goodness he sees in the parent's look, the child begins building a picture of life which includes his own competence and his ability to contribute to society, first the society of his small family, then that of his community. The conviction, "I count," allows the child to reach out, and to expect his contribution to be welcomed. Without this, the child will be reluctant to even try to make his way in what he experiences as a cold, cruel world.

Vision of Love

By about four weeks of age, an infant will look deeply into his mother's eyes, coo and smile, all the while kicking and waving its arms with excitement. This infant greeting, universal across all races and cultures, is the little person's communication of love to his mother and the others who care for him. It is a lucky infant whose mother responds in kind, with curiosity, pleasure, acknowledgement, and with the conscious awareness of the pleasure this new relationship offers.

Throughout infancy and early childhood, a healthy baby will continue to search deeply into the eyes of the people around her, but especially her mother, absorbing the quality, the tone and the emotional atmosphere she finds there. The infant whose gaze is met with pleasure and acceptance will feel nourished and satisfied, deep in the centers of her brain where relationship structures begin to form. The neurons begin to align into patterns which will strengthen and grow with each pleasurable encounter. The wordless feel of it is something like, "Mmm. Mommy-n-me. Mmm, good." As the infant grows, this will eventually generalize to "Mmm, good. People and me." Sometime around three years, the good feelings will evolve into the inner identity structures, "I feel good. I am good."

This nourishment the infant receives through its eyes is even more important than milk. With too little of this kind of connection, we are left with a deep sense of emptiness, longing and need. Most of us have received some emotional nourishment—enough to stay alive and to maintain our connection to other humans as a source of potential companionship and satisfaction, but our expectations are skewed by the fear of rejection. This leaves us focused ever on ourselves and our fears, rather than freeing us to jump into life with both feet.

Unfortunately, some of the lessons we absorb most completely are the feelings of disapproval and disdain from those who belittle us. These attitudes, transmitted to us before we are able to understand or fend off their toxicity, become imbedded deepest, lodged in the child's psyche to fester and grow, tainting our view of ourselves from our earliest awakenings. But this is just the beginning.

Learning to be an Abuser

Childhood becomes the breeding ground for whatever our parents and our culture pass on to us as attitudes, beliefs, religious practices and moral teachings, because the child/student is vulnerable, gullible, and eager to please. These are not simple academic exercises, like arithmetic learned at a desk. They are hard-earned lessons in how to treat each other, what to value, how to respond to conflict, and what to do when you don't like something. We learn by being the living object lesson—the focus of our parents' kindness, frustration or rage, as our parents themselves have learned.

Some among us have been so defeated by their childhood experiences that they come out of it without any hope for true bonding or any capacity for generosity of spirit toward their fellow humans. These become the predators, the con men and women, the "players," heartless betrayers and back-stabbing manipulators who then wreak havoc on those around them, continuing the cycle of inhumanity and abuse. Mental health professionals have become accustomed to referring to these people as psychopaths, or, when they are not physically violent, sociopaths. I will refer to them as Abusers, or Children of Darkness.

In an oppressive family, without mitigating influences, the child will unwitting agent of the very abuse which interfered with his unique self in the first place. Given license and cultural approval, he will go on to suppress others, to promote the religious or cultural ideas of his community. He will not, however, call it oppression. He will call it morality, or discipline, or Godliness, or what's good for you, as he was told when the mind-screws were put to his vulnerable little psychological thumbs. Thus, the child learns to identify with the aggressors—his powerful and dangerous parents, his grandparents and the leaders they look up to. It seems better than the alternative, which is to see himself as a weak and helpless victim.

Nevertheless, there are always some among us who are repelled by the brutality of being forced to give up one's individuality and originality. Whether by temperament or constitution or the intervention of a guardian angel, they resist becoming enthusiastic proponents of destructiveness. However, they are not unscathed by severe childhood abuse or neglect. Instead, they may harness the destructiveness by turning it inward against themselves, where it becomes an underground wellspring of self-hatred, along with its socially acceptable companions, self-doubt and fear.

Ironically, for many of us who make this move to resist becoming Abusers ourselves, we gravitate to the other end of the spectrum of our psychological template, recreating the childhood feelings and attitudes which defined us as victims in our relationships with powerful others. Thus, we tend to define ourselves as "good" by comparison to the "bad" Abusers. This interplay of good versus bad, light versus dark, unconsciously defined as Abuser versus victim becomes the unshakable, unexamined backdrop to our later relationships.

Shock and Awe

The worst part about a bad childhood is not the painful events themselves. Bruises heal, hearts mend. The worst part is the convictions we come away with. These are beliefs about our self-worth, what the world has to offer, and the limiting definitions about abusers and victims described above.

Childhood emotional deprivation (that awful sense of not being seen or respected) leaves us feeling empty and longing, convinced that what we didn't get has created a hole in ourselves where mother or father was supposed to be—an emptiness that love was supposed to fill. It is this very sense of emptiness, longing and need which becomes woven into our attraction to others, especially to those who hold out the promise of acceptance and affirmation to fill the hole in ourselves. Ironically, we are also trained through childhood deprivation to be most attracted to those who hold out promise while also treating us as coldly as those who hurt us in the past, because whatever our parents did, we feel as love. I call this the Shock and Awe Principle.

Thus, we may be most attracted to the person who promises much but delivers very little. The combination of push/ pull and seduction followed by abuse replicates the painful longing of childhood. This person simultaneously seems to offer a promise of greater love than we have ever known. That greater love is supposed to bring with it validation and wholeness. Finally, the hunger will be satisfied. It is no accident that popular love songs talk about the hope of being filled up, made whole, saved from despair, born anew.

The Children of Darkness learn (by instinctive predatory awareness or by trial and error) to read the signs of someone made weak from undernourishment. Like the lion stalking a herd of antelope, a Dark One will single out the one who is a little distant from the herd, or a little less robust than the others. Then he will pounce. The victim, in a state of need which overrides her own innate sense of self-defense, sees the lion coming and instead of acknowledging her fear, she is drawn to the lion's strength and cunning, which to her may look like sense of purpose. She may even admire his voracious single-mindedness. See how he circles, eyeing her hungrily. Her heart beats faster with the expectation: "He wants me! He needs me!" If the dark gleam in his eye matches the way she was looked at by one or both of her parents, she will vibrate, like a tuning fork, to the familiar frequency which resonates in her nervous system. It feels like love! No matter that his true motivation is to eat her alive—or in human terms, to take advantage of her, rob her, use her, and probably discard her mangled remains afterward.

Imagine the scene in reverse: the stalker is a woman. The man senses danger, but it feels like excitement. Having been seared by the cold and demanding look in his mother's eyes, this young woman's predatory look and animal attractiveness draw him like a magnet, and he's a goner. Warnings from friends about her past treachery are ignored. He rationalizes, "That was in the past," or, "She probably didn't love him the way she loves me." There are limitless versions of this scenario, across gender, age, and circumstances.

These besotted lovers are in for a disappointing, bumpy ride. They will be living out the lament so aptly described in the musical genre we call "You done me wrong" songs.

Open Your Self to Change

We learn from our experience. During the long years of childhood, we become imprinted with the atmosphere and attitudes of those who feed us. We may consciously embrace those values, or we may reject and fight against them. Either way, they become a part of the template we use to define life. Our definitions of right and wrong, light and dark, strong and weak are formed as acceptance or rejection of the most important themes and experiences of our childhoods. To a lesser degree, life shapes us as adults as well. We no longer live solely within the tribe of our origins. We are exposed to dramatically different attitudes about how life should be lived, and what good and evil really are. If we are open to it, we can examine the presumptions we came out of childhood with, and we can change them.

We can never know all the influences which shape another person. All the studies and theories in the world will never explain why one individual dedicates their life to love and service while another chooses darkness and self-promotion. These are individual choices, each of us exercising our free will, while inexorably influenced by the forces that have shaped us. The most effective tool we have at our disposal is compassion. If someone (including you) is leaning toward selfishness and destruction of others, we can be certain there were strong influences in that direction from the past. The quickest route to healing from the misunderstandings and self-destructive convictions from the past is through forgiveness, beginning with yourself and your own internalized dark ideas.

Whatever the damaging influences from the past might have been, what we do about them is up to each individual and his or her own conscience.

THE REJECT I

My body is gross and unwieldy
I sit here alone and afraid,
Too ugly too sorry too sad and dejected,
I'll never know why I was made.

I hate what I see in the mirror
I hate what I see in my face
My weak chin, my stupid grin,
My big feet, I ardently hate.

I scurry around after dark
I'm starving for something like food.
I fear them, they fear me
They don't see God's creatures
They don't know I've tried to be good.

Momma can't stand me, she shows it
Disgust shows all over her face
I can't help my nature, not really
I live on in endless disgrace.

I guess I'm just lucky
My Ma lets me stay here
Nowhere I could go
Can't make it out there.

Maybe someday I'll find
A bug misfit like me
A friend I can count on
A chance to be free.

But the years seem to pass by
And still nothing changes
No one comes, no one sees me
They must think I'm dangerous.

I yearn and I long
For a touch or a smile
But they grimace and shudder,
Condemn me to exile.

I don't want to scare them or hurt them
They don't know the ache in my heart
I lay low, just wishing and dreaming,
Oh, when will my sorry life start?

REJECT II

I hide in dark corners
My hard shell protects me.
I suffer their poison
(They always reject me).

Alone and afraid I creep out of my haven
They cringe and recoil at my presence.
They think I'm disgusting,
Repulsive, unclean,
As if filth and disease were my essence.

But I don't deserve this fervor and passion
I never attacked in a similar fashion,
I come out when they're sleeping
I can't help my hunger,
It's just for the crumbs I come creeping.

Hey, you over there!
Yes, you, fellow reject,
You have a nice tidbit?
Now that would be perfect.

And if we need more,
There are crumbs on the floor
Downtown in my favorite pub.
So if you're conceiving of spending the evening
Alone in your room in a pout,
Forget it my friend, there's a place round the bend
Where they serve up the best chips and stout
An onion ring is my favorite thing
What say, Cucaracha, it's time for a fling
Get your gladrags, I'm taking you out.

CHAPTER TWO

THE ROOT OF OUR MISERY

". . . But thou, contracted to thine own bright eyes,
Feed'st thy light's flame with self-substantial fuel,
Making a famine where abundance lies,
Thyself thy foe, to thy sweet self too cruel.
                    —From Shakespeare's Sonnet #1

After 40 years of studying psychological and social issues, I have come to a recent epiphany. I believe that psychology and psychiatry have gone needlessly far afield in their search for the causes and cures of psychological pain. Our scientific approaches have generated oceans of data, but little that is conclusive or helpful. We are taught to look at this behavior, examine that childhood event, study genetic influences and chemical imbalances, to no avail. We can describe and name our myriad difficulties, but we have yet to definitively identify what really causes emotional problems, or to design workable treatments. I believe our intellectualizations and earnest investigations have led us away from the obvious. In the absence of identifiable brain injury or severe malfunction, I am convinced that all emotional misery *in adults* arises from self-hatred. By "misery," I mean neurosis, depression, anxiety, compulsions, obsessions, addictions, and more.

Humans know how to pull together to overcome floods, fires, earthquakes and pestilence, but the single most misery-inducing life experience is to be at war with yourself. It never ends. Self-loathing leads us into hideous relationships in which we tolerate oppression and abuse, because we secretly believe we deserve it. It inspires foolhardy and risky behavior, because we feel compelled to disprove (or prove) its tenets, and it generates endless despair, anxiety, anger and discontent when we are unable to change it.

We have not seen this endemic self-hatred for what it is because it is so pervasive and so intimately familiar for most of us that it would not occur to us to identify it as the source of all kinds of misery. We see it in everyone we know, everywhere we look. Its common description—"beating up on yourself"—is often positively associated with higher performance and increased motivation. Can this attitude of disapproving of yourself be all bad? Would we not end up lazy and selfish if we stopped it?

I believe it is destructive, corrosive, and without benefit in the development of human potential, and I will make the case here that we will be better off as individuals and as a culture without it. It has never been shown to be true that anyone's character or performance was improved, in the long run, by humiliation and cruelty. Just the opposite. Yet, as a culture and as a race, we continue to belittle and attack ourselves and each other in the name of education, religion, culture, civilization, good manners, and even entertainment. Why do we do this?

The Enemy Within

Some of us believe that everyone should be given an equal chance; equal treatment under the law is a principle we embrace. Regardless of our religious or spiritual beliefs, we might even go so far as to admit that we feel protective of all living creatures, large and small. Our sense of reverence for life leads us to perform acts of kindness toward creatures we come across from an early age. (Remember burying your pet turtle?) Yet, people who would think twice about stepping on a bug think nothing of killing their own spirit in a barrage of harsh criticism.

I sincerely believe that to raise the level of happiness and well-being in the world, we need to address one issue: What does self-hatred look like, where does it come from, how does it affect our close relationships, our educational practices, our culture at large, our political institutions, and everything else that structures our world, and how can we eliminate it?

Let's start by noticing what self-hatred looks like in practice. We must have a reasonable definition for what we're looking for, so we don't miss its insidious but less virulent forms. For our purposes here, I will define it to include all its varied shades, on a continuum from self-deprecating humor to suicide. All its manifestations include some sort of disapproval of one's self. Behind the disapproval lurk long-accepted convictions:

"I am not worthwhile; I'm defective;
"I will never be enough;
"I am invisible;
"I am nothing;
"I don't deserve to live;
"I am unlovable; I'm unloving;
"I'm bad;
"I'm disgusting;
"I'm ugly;
"I'm stupid."

Whatever the individual shadings, the basic conviction always boils down to some variation on the idea that one's self is worthless and warrants rejection from others.

Before you dismiss this idea out of hand as too extreme or not applicable to you, stop to consider honestly which of the above comments you may have made to yourself in moments of frustration or impatience. What have you said to yourself, about yourself, when you're feeling low, or when life has dealt you a serious disappointment? Identify the shading and tone of the self-condemnation you most often indulge in. Write down your habitual accusations so that you will be able to remind yourself as you go through the reading and exercises later in the book.

Now, notice how you have lived your life in relation to these ideas. For most people, the fundamental idea of worthlessness carries nearly unlimited power because it operates "under the radar," as an unconscious backdrop rather than a conscious decision. If you ask a person directly whether they think they are truly worthless, they will often respond that no, they don't think so, but they still feel as if it's true. This leaves them in the completely untenable position of living a life based on an all-encompassing belief which is not of their own making. It then requires massive denial while simultaneously spending inordinate amounts of time and energy trying to compensate for it, disprove it, rebel against it, rise above it, counteract it, learn to live with it, or deny it.

For instance,

- Have you become a workaholic to disprove it?
- Are you anxious because you fear rejection?
- Did you develop addictions to ease the pain of it?
- Are you inclined to feel superior to others as a way of trying to rise above it?
- Have you become cranky and impatient with the futility of disproving it?
- Are you depressed because you believe it?

Let's imagine a typical day. You wake up in the morning, and think, "Oh, no, another day." You shuffle to the bathroom and look in the mirror. "Yuck. I look awful." Opening your closet, you think, "Agh, these clothes will never be good enough to make me look right, or cover up how inadequate I really am." You gulp down coffee or tea to get your reluctant motor started, to fortify you against what you think of as the day's difficulties and disappointments. You drop your keys on the way out the door, and think, "I'm such a klutz." Someone cuts in front of you driving, or grabs the cab you were signaling, and you think, "The world is conspiring against me," or "These people are all idiots."

You hate your body. Passing a store window on your way to work, you see your reflection and grimace. You could never exercise enough to be really satisfied with it. You tend to skip meals because you are distracted and inattentive to your body's needs, or you overeat because you feel dissatisfied and hungry even when you're full.

At work, you dread criticism from your superiors or colleagues. You think of it as "stress," and feel the need of a day off to "chill out" every time it happens. When you are asked a question and don't know the answer, you feel ashamed, stupid. Exhausted by a day of defensive denial and offensive self-recrimination, you leave with the hope of recharging for the next day.

At home, your partner asks in a matter-of-fact tone if you remembered to pay the phone bill, and you feel like jumping down his or her throat for treating you like an idiot. A small complaint can escalate into a name-calling conflagration, because you feel defensive and vulnerable.

Your sex life is disappointing or nonexistent, or you are obsessed with sex because you never feel adequate or fulfilled. You reject your partner because you believe he or she is inadequate too, if only because he is with you.

You watch television or surf the internet for hours, ignoring friends and family, reducing your social life to a wasteland, because making the effort to be with people is just too hard. You spend hours "hanging out" with acquaintances, without creating deep or lasting relationships.

You sleep badly and too little, worrying about whether you will be able to achieve anything, or accomplish what you need to, or be accepted. Instead of welcoming sleep, you replay past insults, imagining different outcomes in which you display greater confidence, better retorts, less "thin-skinned" responses. Alternatively, you imagine future disasters and spend hours planning to avoid them.

Misery, anxiety, despair: These are the emotional responses to deeply buried convictions, instilled in the earliest days and months of life, long before we had the intellectual capacity to understand or counteract them. How this happens is the focus of the next several chapters. Understanding why it happens—apparently to all of us, to one degree or another—is crucial to understanding ourselves, and our development as human beings.

Baby Steps

Let's start with the way we welcome children into the world. For several generations, infants in Western cultures were ushered into the world in the medically approved way, in a sterile, brightly lit operating room, surrounded by masked people wearing protective gloves. The baby was often removed directly from the mother's womb by Caesarian section as a matter of convenience for mother or doctor, depriving the baby of the gradual, stimulating entry process through the birth canal. Although this radical surgical procedure is rarely necessary, it continues to increase.

Under glaring lights, the baby would find itself suddenly in a cold, harsh environment, being jostled about by strange hands. The umbilical cord was cut immediately, suddenly removing the baby from the support system which had sustained it for nine months. Suction instruments were shoved into the baby's mouth and nose to clear breathing passages for the brand new experience of breathing on its own. (As far as I know, the tradition of holding the baby upside down and smacking it to make it cry fell out of favor some time ago.) However, other barbaric procedures remain.

In some cases, both the mother's and baby's systems were suppressed by the anesthetic given to the mother, making it impossible for them to have anything resembling a joyful greeting. The baby was tightly wrapped in a blanket, restricting normal movement. After a brief and groggy moment with the semiconscious mother, it was swept away to the nursery along with other crying infants. The new mother was taken away to recover. That is day one.

Joseph Chilton Pearce, in *The Biology of Transcendence* has commented on these barbaric childbirth practices, citing the astonishing research which shows that babies birthed this way frequently take 3 or 4 days to recover from the elevated stress response it causes. Millions of infants were subjected to scenarios similar to these, as we waited for scientific evidence to show we were torturing our infants in the name of cleanliness. Science brought those answers, as early as the 1970's, when research demonstrated that infants recognize faces at birth.[4] They must be stunned and terrified by inhuman-looking masked strangers looming over them. Science also finally confirmed what "primitive" mothers have always taken for granted: that skin-to-skin contact immediately after birth leads to far better bonding and attachment for years to come.[5]

Cultural practices change slowly, but fortunately, birthing centers close to hospitals have replaced the operating room for normal births. "New" techniques encourage an atmosphere of warmth, quiet, low

---

[4]   Numerous studies since the 70's have established that not only can an infant recognize human faces at birth, but within   hours the baby is able to distinguish a picture of his own mother's face from that of other women.

[5]   Klaus and Kennel. Since the 70's this team has published a number of excellent research-based books on mother-infant bonding.

light, and skin-to-skin physical contact with the conscious mother whose spouse, family and friends support her and take part in the joyful occasion. Fortunately, new babies are spared the traumatic beginnings many of their parents and grandparents experienced.

Once home, however, many infants continue to be subjected to stressful, inhumane practices which mothers for generations have been encouraged to follow. For instance, the baby is expected to sleep alone in a crib, separated from the mother, rather than snuggled at the mother's side, as is done in less "developed" countries. Deprived of the comforting intimacy of the mother's heartbeat and breathing which regulates and stabilizes the infant's immature systems, some infants succumb to the mysterious Sudden Infant Death Syndrome.[6] It has taken us decades to acknowledge that our standard practice with infants may have created a disease which is unknown in less rigidly controlled cultures where infants are normally held or carried for the first months of life. An infant sleeping at her mother's side would not be on her stomach, or flat on her back, but cradled comfortably in the crook of her mother's arm, eliminating uncomfortable pressure points or dangerous smothering crib corners. From a physical point of view, it would certainly be preferable. Psychologically, sleeping cuddled next to the mother would have a vastly different effect than having to endure the nightly loneliness of being suddenly without her familiar voice, breathing and heartbeat.

Cultural influences come to bear on the family in insidious ways. For instance, in America, we live in a culture where breastfeeding is seen as unseemly, even obscene. Bottle-feeding is not. The inference is that the mother's feeding the child is either sexual and therefore private, or that her breasts are primarily sexual objects which will be seen as seductive by men and must be hidden. More enlightened proponents of breastfeeding recognize that any attitude which separates the female from her crucial function as the baby's source of nourishment is downright perverse. Some women have felt so outraged at these puritanical attitudes toward breast-feeding that a new militancy has been spawned in the pro-breastfeeding movement. Young mothers

---

6   BMJ, (British Medical Journal) provides online commentary on published articles. October, 2000 featured discussion on the issues surrounding SIDS, smoking, and bed-sharing.

have staged public breast-feedings to make their case. Recently, young women have circulated a petition and flooded Facebook, the social network site, with photos of breastfeeding mothers after Facebook removed pictures of a proud breast-feeding young mother from her site on the basis that they were "obscene." The petition asks, "What, exactly, is obscene about breastfeeding?" The answer, of course is *nothing*, but it is a measure of how sex-obsessed and out of touch our culture really is that it would even occur to anyone to even make a connection between obscenity and breast-feeding.

Our childrearing practices have lacked empathy for the infant's most basic needs. Mothers who long to comfort a crying infant are commonly told to let the child cry himself to sleep. This is based on the belief that responding to the baby's cries will "spoil" him, and the sooner you show them who is boss and how they need to behave, the better. Picking up the crying infant is thought to set in motion a grossly oversimplified notion of conditioned response: It encourages more crying and constant demands for attention. This ignores the fact that children too prefer to sleep soundly and without interruption if they are comfortable, physically and emotionally. Secure children who have been attended to and comforted when they need it cry less.

Products of our own ancestral abuses, we cling to our insensitive practices and go on producing generation after generation of human beings who are overwhelmed by emotional trauma. The result is a mass dissociation from the physical and spiritual underpinnings which would otherwise guide us, leaving us in a state of pervasive desensitization which numbs our innate capacities for empathy and kindness.

Then we become parents.

The practices cited above are not considered abuse or neglect. So far, we have described a good childhood. However, the feelings of confusion, anxiety and loneliness which a "normal" infancy engenders begin laying down the tracks for a self-identity based in worthlessness, hopelessness and fear, and the endless compensations it requires.

These insensitive childrearing practices, because they have been shared by so many of us, have helped to shape what has become the American cultural identity, legitimizing and perpetuating trauma-producing traditions which might otherwise have been rejected long ago. Individuals who leave childhood with enough of their sensibilities intact to object to entrenched abusive practices may find themselves at odds with the people around them.

Insensitivity Breeds Contempt

In the quest to compensate for feelings of worthlessness and fear, many Americans have become swaggering braggarts. Many of the loudest voices glorify toughness, unwavering superiority, and rigid insensitivity to the concerns of any nation but our own or any person but ourselves. In our blind rush to feel special, to overcome insecurities, we have ignored ancient teachings warning against pride. Pride is one of the most virulent of all human failings. It can blind us to our own crass self-promotion and arrogant disrespect for others. Pride and hubris lead to aggression, and the self-gratifying sense of entitlement which makes physical and emotional abuse commonplace in modern families.

When the evening news brings stories of rape, child molestation and murder into every living room daily, the social mores against such behavior are loosened. What used to be strange and foreign has become familiar (as in family). It has the effect of creating the illusion that everyone is doing it, and pretty soon everyone is, because children are given the lesson that this is how people behave. They are much more likely than their parents, then, to take criminal behavior in stride, and even to indulge in it whimsically, without the boundaries of conscience and social constraints that former generations took for granted. As the standard of decent behavior has loosened in the cyber world, so has the behavior in the culture at large. We now find ourselves in the midst of a downward spiral into Darkness which escalates with every passing day.

A society's elders are influenced by current trends as well as by their own upbringing. Cultural values which are trumpeted in the streets, on TV, in movies and songs shape and influence elders and the ideals they wish to "instill" in the young. This in turn affects each young child's experience of himself and his relationship to the world, as the feedback loop of culture, family and self comes full circle.

Thus, the emotional foundations we lay down in our earliest years as a result of our interactions with the world will lay the groundwork for our relationship with ourselves. How we relate to ourselves in turn effects how we will relate to others, and how we will see and interact with the world, as individuals and as citizens. This is an ongoing, organically reciprocal interchange between self and others which is lifelong and changeable, but it cannot be open and free-flowing unless we understand the influences which shaped our first responses.

Early Fault-lines Lay the Groundwork

Traumatic beginnings are often followed by various forms of stress-producing abuse from family or school relationships. As a result, profound distortions take place in the way we relate to ourselves. We begin to disconnect from our bodies, and especially from our hearts, to go off into a dream state. In this way, we create an "alternate reality" for ourselves, one where our own thoughts and feelings reign, separate from the moment-by-moment experience of Earthbound reality. The child learns to daydream and fantasize rather than perceive and respond. Curiosity about the outside world wanes, and the child turns instead to her own thoughts for solace and entertainment. This is the beginning of a self-arrangement which suppresses the flow of information from the body—especially the heart—to the brain. The child's naturally responsive state is replaced by a compromised kind of intelligence, disconnected from direct sensory experience, and therefore disconnected from reality. The resulting configuration leaves us top-heavy: all brain and no heart. As long as we remain in this state of disconnectedness, we can think anything, imagine anything, and believe anything. Our feelings then become a response to our own thoughts, rather than a direct response to the environment. This is the start of a life as someone I will call a Head Person: still walking around, still behaving "normally," but detached from the heart and bodysoul and the deep connections to Earth and Spirit which are possible only through the heart.

In the beginning, babies delight in their own toes and fingers, giggle when they see a familiar face or a new animal. Their curiosity and awe is boundless, but it does not continue into adulthood for most of us. Even adults who were carefree as young children lose their capacity for lightheartedness and joy, and come to think of those qualities as "childish." Our language reveals our prejudice. Notice how the word we most often use for the condition of being like a child carries a pejorative meaning. What does that say about our feeling toward children? It reveals our unexamined prejudice against spontaneous feeling of all sorts. We no longer jump for joy or clap our hands in glee the way a child does at the sight of a puppy or a glittering soap bubble. Those kinds of emotional expression are reserved for sporting events and winning the lottery.

The next time you are at a mall, or on a busy street, notice how people become progressively heavy-footed as they get older. Teenagers show the signs of what is to come. Instead of skipping, they begin to shuffle. Girls especially begin to mince along, keeping their thighs pressed together and their arms stiff and constricted. Adults waddle, weighted down by their unpleasant thoughts and rolls of fat, and almost everyone's energy is flavored with a heavy mix of worry, disapproval and fear, the equivalent of a full-body furrowed brow. Americans are not a happy crowd.

Disconnection

The well-meaning fields of psychology and other helping professions have encouraged a focus on the self to the exclusion of practically everything else. This tendency is now so rampant in our culture we no longer even notice it. We referred to those who came of age in the 80's as the "Me Generation." The Me Generation was the first mass symptom of the shift to self-centeredness. It turns out they were the messengers of a coming era, rather than an anomaly. By the 80's, Americans had combined the hedonistic self-indulgence of the 60's (minus the love and peace message) with a massive fervor for material consumption previously unseen on the planet. Greed became elevated to an art form. Every subsequent decade has witnessed an ever-increasingly self-involved culture focused primarily on material gain, hedonistic pleasures and physical beauty. Colleges report huge increases in the educational programs which lead to the most lucrative careers in business, law and technology, while programs leading to a life of social service or the arts have lost enrollment at the same time their funds have been cut. Until very recently, a life of service was so uncool as to be completely off the radar for most young people.

I was present in a group of over-sixty women when the topic of cultural change came up, as it often does. They were commenting about what seemed to them to be a complete change in attitude in young people starting out. "We lived on practically nothing, right after college. We would have been terrified to have a debt of any kind. And these enormous houses some young people want. What do they do with all that space?" I asked what they thought were the most profound changes. One woman said, "We didn't have televisions in every room for starters. We had one, and we watched it at specific times, occasionally. When I was a kid, one or two people in the neighborhood had TV's, and they would invite people over for special events. It was a social event, not a solitary escape."

"We were pretty well off," said another woman, "but I still only had three pairs of shoes: play, school, and good. What more could you need? We didn't spend all that much time shopping. It had to be a pretty special occasion, one we would plan for, sometimes for weeks, like the back-to-school buying trip for new clothes to replace the ones we had outgrown over the summer. It was like a rite of passage, not an everyday indulgence. Of course, there weren't any shopping malls—just one or two department stores, and we always went to the local stores where they knew us."

As for modern conveniences, a home with one telephone in the hallway was not considered inconvenient, since a telephone was something you used occasionally, not something you wore. But, they reminded each other, those were the details of life that really don't capture the profound difference in the way life felt. The main difference is in how separate and disconnected people have become from one another. For young people who have swum in these waters most of their lives, it is difficult to explain that it does make a difference whether you talk to someone face-to-face or just text-message them. It makes a difference in the state of your heart, and theirs.

We all agreed that although it wasn't perfect, the role of women as the center of the home life helped to make it a simpler, more predictable time for most children. After school, children came home to a neighborhood and played together, often in physically active games, deepening their connections to one another while they developed competence, agility and strength. Having a mother at home meant that most people, from every economic group, ate some kind of home-cooked meal around a table every night, face to face. However meager or sumptuous that meal might be, it included intimate contact.

Living in a smaller house or apartment meant you were in closer proximity with the people you cared about. Whatever the emotional state of the others in the family, you knew who they were and how they were doing on an intimate day-to-day basis, because you all shared the same space, breathed the same air, and communicated constantly with one another, for better or worse. There was no escaping to your own room with a TV or internet connection. Everyone spent time in the same room together. Arguments were fought and resolved; feelings were expressed because they had to be, and relationships were clarified one way or another. For most people, there was more action in their interactions, and more potential for deep satisfaction.

Spending time together meant that children saw their parents interacting with each other. They modeled what marriage was in a moment by moment display which is rarely witnessed in today's loosely organized family life, where everyone comes and goes, and where parents rarely even share a bathroom with their children, much less a kitchen table. Life as a couple was on public display, without makeup or pretense or even much privacy. Everyone in the family knew if the parents disagreed, if the argument was settled, and if they made up. The cult of privacy and modesty has meant that children don't know that parents have sex, and that it forms a bond of love between them. From their point of view, they probably think that teenagers have sex, but grownups don't, and that sex is a furtive athletic event, disconnected from family life and mature love.

Children today have little of this modeling, and so are even more vulnerable to learning their lessons from the snarling, insulting and mocking television versions of what a marriage looks like.

Replacing Intimacy with Consumption

Notice the content of nearly every TV commercial. There are incessant reminders of what you should do or buy to make you happy. In one way or another, they involve hedonistic pleasures, material consumption and physical beauty. There is a constant focus on weight loss, exercise and physical self-improvement, playing into the implied agreement that there is something wrong with almost all of us. Makeover TV programs feature extensive plastic surgery as a route to improved self-esteem. We are encouraged to pursue these enhancements as if they were the antidote for all feelings of malaise or emptiness. Even the pursuit of a relationship is taken on as if it were something you can acquire and consume. We are expected to pursue, win over and capture someone to love us, rather than build trust and friendship through mutual connection and shared effort.

It has long been understood in the advertising industry that "sex sells." Generally, this idea has been applied to selling everything from toothpaste to beer, by implying their product will make you more sexually attractive. Recently, the ploy has been taken to its logical absurdity. A Cadillac ad suggests that your automobile should provide you with a sexual experience: "When you turn on your car, does it return the favor?" If it doesn't, you must be missing out.

At the end of the day, if shopping, exercising, drinking, eating, sex and driving have not lifted your mood or rebuilt your sagging self-esteem, you can "ask your doctor." Prescription drugs are promoted as an instant cure for depression, anxiety, sleeplessness, sexual dysfunction, and practically every other emotional bump in the road you might experience. We are encouraged to medicate our moods, as if our emotional state were solely an internal condition, rather than looking for the source of our problems in the family, social, economic or educational environment or our self-referential response to it.

One of the most common complaints I hear from clients is that they realize they are too much "in their heads," to the point where they lose contact with their feelings. This, combined with self-hatred means that they are the preoccupied and often sleepless because of a constant barrage of worries, planning and self-criticism. The running commentary in their heads is so annoying that a huge pharmaceutical industry has developed to provide relief for it. In later chapters I will address our tendency to be Head People, and the many unfortunate ramifications this has, especially to someone with a tendency for self-hatred. It means that the chatter in their heads will be a battlefield that leaves the person exhausted and discouraged even before they get out of bed. Being Head People also has an enormous impact on the way we organize our society, educate our children, and how we think about work, play and relationships. While self-hatred is the emotional source of misery, living in your brain (basing your decisions on thinking rather than feeling) is the physical source of misery. It is the living expression of a deep division in the self, the default operating system which relies on one small part of the human organism to the neglect of heart, soul and body. Later chapters will explore how we got this way, and how we can change. For now, let's look at the cultural expressions of our self-absorbed Head focus and the way it perpetuates our misery.

Our Sick Society

Try an informal sociology experiment as you watch television. Enlist friends and family in the project if possible. During a week of commercials, monitor and take notes on the content of the ads to identify the implied advantages each product offers. For instance, soap and shampoo are not presented simply as aids to cleanliness, but as something far more exciting. This simple exercise will help to increase your awareness and build your immunity to the barrage of commercialism you are being inundated with daily.

The important part about this exercise is that it can help to free us from the influences which have shaped our behavior, our attitudes, and even our basic philosophy of life and feelings about ourselves. Constantly bombarded with images of wealth, happiness and sensuous pleasure, the average consumer between shopping sprees is bound to feel inadequate and left out. Credit cards are offered as a means to material and sensual pleasures—the implied cure for self-doubt or unhappiness. We are constantly offered the non sequitur: You can buy something priceless. If the debt this promotes leaves you sleepless and harried, call your doctor immediately and get drugs to assuage the anxiety and depression you suffer as a result of your impulsive choices. Meanwhile, it has become nearly taboo to mention how your behavior and your self-centered consumption affect your own spiritual state, or what it does to other people and the environment. For several generations we have kept these concerns mostly at arm's length by referring to them as "political" issues.

It is impossible to heal our emotional conflicts without addressing the state of the environment we live in. To do so would be like taking pain killers to cure cancer. To heal the sickness-at-heart which has afflicted so many of us, we must also address the sickness at the heart of our culture.

The ecologically unsustainable consumer-driven system could not have been packaged and sold to us so effectively had we not all been steeped in the palliatives and philosophies that depend on a state of fear of insufficiency (in the presence of unprecedented plenty) and the sicknesses it creates in us. In 2006-7 The BBC aired a four-part television series called *The Century of the Self*, written by Adam Curtis. The series traces the origins of our current materialistic culture to the beginnings of the field of "public relations," the brainchild of Sigmund Freud's nephew, Edward Bernaise. Carefully documented and compellingly told, it provides a historical view of the way advertising changed from selling products based on their practical value to selling self-esteem as a way to manipulate and control the masses. It has been a cynical use of the concept of "id," the center of instinctual needs. By creating a sense of inadequacy and want for the glamorous products which were to increase popularity and happiness, public relations experts have been able to turn several generations of consumers into compulsive addicts. Our lives and our planet have never been the same.

It's All About Me

As normal human yearnings for meaningful connection with others are redirected toward self-centered consumption, we are left hungry and empty, as if we were trying to nourish ourselves with a steady diet of cotton-candy. It is never enough, and it can never wholly satisfy us. Feeling confused and inadequate, we think, "Why am I so miserable? Everyone else seems to be having so much fun!" They probably are, for the moment you witnessed, but they too go home alone or in uncomfortable, disconnected groups, imagining that if they only had won the lottery, everything would be better. The temptation is then to begin another round of consumption of food, alcohol, "recreational" drugs or sex, to try to fill the emptiness in their hearts and in their souls. A soul can't be satisfied with consuming. It can only be fed by taking actions of service to others. Our entire culture has it backwards, by encouraging taking in rather than giving out. It has stopped the energetic flow on the planet, which is referred to as the Universal Law of Flow. The result is a monumentally constipated people whose bloated condition is reaching explosive proportions.

Many people will turn to some form of counseling for help with their stoppages. Often they will find help solving problems and regaining their equilibrium, but the backdrop of gnawing dissatisfaction often remains to resurface another day. This is inevitable, because the approach we have all been taught focuses primarily on the individual and their inner workings. The difficulties, we are told, are caused by a lack of self-esteem. Self-esteem has become the well from which we are encouraged to drink our fill, the balm which will resolve all our personal difficulties, regardless of the state of our empty and meaningless lives.

The great flaw in this reasoning precludes the cure. Successes, flattery, love poured over us from every quarter does not lead to fulfillment. There can never be enough compensatory love to make up for childhood injuries or adult misfortunes, because it does not go to the source of the problem. As we will see later, an overabundance of self-esteem is a symptom of psychopathology: the state of caring for no one but yourself. The path to deep and lasting fulfillment of the sort that can carry us through thick and thin is being of service to others.

True healing takes place when we set aside our self-involved concerns to do something for another person. This takes us out of the realm of personal satisfaction and pride to an entirely different place. A life without service to others is by definition an empty and meaningless existence, regardless of the number of toys and hedonistic pleasures one can accrue, and regardless of how physically fit and beautiful one may be. By contrast, the fulfillment which comes from being of service to others, selflessly, without need for reward or ego satisfaction, taps into our sense of creativity and belonging. This is the cure for self-hatred.

Showing unconditional care for another is the polar opposite of self-hatred. The more you do it, the more your own self-hatred melts away. The effect cannot be defined in words, but must be experienced. This is a complete shift philosophically and behaviorally for most of us, but it is the way out.

This need to be of service to others will be expanded upon throughout the book. First, let's look at self-hatred, and how it is a fundamental expression of our self-involved life-style.

Ego's Battle Ground

I will use the term "Ego" in a different way from the Freudian id-ego-super-ego concepts which have become familiar in our everyday conversations. Briefly, Freud saw id as a seething cauldron of instincts in need of taming. I have done away completely with the idea of innate warring internal forces, in favor of a broader view of human beings which allows for innate spiritual potential, and an understanding that overly aggressive, anxious or depressed emotional states are often the result of problematic beginnings. In Freud's lexicon, ego was seen as the conscious intellect, and superego as conscience. Instead, I refer to "ego" as the agent of survival and intellectual self-promotion, the way popular usage implies a self-centered or bigheaded attitude.

Ego begins as the mechanism of self-preservation, an important and necessary element of the self, especially in a dangerous childhood world. Under duress, however, we can become excessively focused on survival issues to the neglect of creativity, love, and spiritual connection to something beyond ourselves. This emphasis on survival of the self encourages us to further separate from our bodies and hearts in favor of a mind-centered adaptation. Rather than follow our hearts, we analyze, ponder, figure out, weigh and measure every detail of life to control every outcome. Narrowing our focus to concentrate on minutiae removes us from the flow of life, into the realm of thinking, planning and fantasy. Although this adaptation may come as a relief to someone whose childhood reality brought chaos and pain, it carries an unintended disadvantage. We inevitably come to think about things using the ideas and language we were taught. The language itself carries implied values and judgments. (Think of all the underground meanings associated with the word "girl" for instance, or "success.") Ego, the agent of self-promoting ideas, becomes the carrier of these prejudices, values, and (mis)understandings. Voila, you unwittingly become the agent of your own culture of sadness.

First, we must recognize that our ego has grown powerful and willful as a result of having to put so much energy into issues of psychological or physical survival throughout a long childhood. These early conditioned responses lead us into an adulthood which becomes increasingly slanted toward greed and self-indulgence. Thus, our culture—and family-endorsed responses to early fear and deprivation become cemented into what we come to think of as our "self." This manufactured identity may not be an authentic reflection of who we really are in the deepest part of our being, our soul. This is the part of our self which longs to be expressed in creative acts and in service to others.

Nearly every client I see at one time or another mentions a tendency to "beat up" on themselves. With growing self-awareness, most of us become conscious to some degree of the connection between having been at war early on with parents, teachers, siblings, or the bullies on the playground, and our inclination to turn the battles inward as we grow older. Ultimately, any battle which is turned inward will eventually be expressed in our relationships with others. Knowing it is not enough. We must look further.

Ego, the protector of our very survival, is always on the lookout for danger, and does not take kindly to being set aside or displaced. Thus, Ego is the instigator and the recipient of the self-centered indulgence we have mentioned above, growing ever more bloated and acquisitive, paranoid and self-righteous. Now here's where the serious challenge comes. Can you admit to being self-centered and judgmental without taking it personally? If you are willing to acknowledge the influence of your family and the culture in having shaped you it makes it easier.

In spite of the encouragement from our culture, most of us don't really like to think of ourselves as self-centered and childishly indulgent. It sounds like such an unforgivable character flaw. Our first reaction would be to protest and deny it, but if we can be courageous enough to truly examine it, here lies great impetus to change. We do not want to be selfish. We want to be the best human beings we can be, so let's tackle it. Remember: this is not a criticism of you, it is just a fact of your acculturation.

Pervasive ego-centeredness is not a new phenomenon. What's new is its massive acceptance and glorification. Beyond the self-indulgence of constant talk about "I" and "me," and of opinions and pontifications (what *I* think about nearly everything, especially as it concerns *me)*, is our tendency to turn our Ego-based thought processes against ourselves. Considering what we have described here, beating up on yourself can be seen as the ultimate Ego-indulgence: "It's all about Me! Even beyond that, "It's all about the disapproving things I think about Me," and "It's all about what I think you think about Me," and "It's all about what I feel about what you think of Me, and "It's all about what I think you feel about Me." In other words, self-hatred is the ultimate All About Me. It is a festering expression of inward-focused meanness and pettiness.

Do you find it intolerable to think of yourself as mean and petty? Then vow to stop beating up on yourself. Cultivate instead an attitude of cordial acceptance and appreciation for the fact that we all come with a certain combination of talents, strengths, weaknesses and fears, and that is as it should be. We all are presented with challenges and difficulties, and the best we can expect is that we not make the same mistakes too many times. We are all here to learn, and we learn better without oppressive disapproval—our own or anyone else's.

Several of the following chapters describe the neurological/psychological process by which this excessively ego-centered development takes place. This is not a story of human suffering and psychological damage. As you will see, our brains are malleable, our hearts can heal, and our definition of what we call our "identity" can change.

Broken Heart Connections

Over long years of childhood, the separated-from-yourself arrangement is reinforced by adults who are already fully formed Ego-motivated Heads. They are out of touch with their hearts because of their own early traumas and acculturation. At their behest, we are encouraged to learn by rote memorization, take direction without question, and reflexively accept their directives and opinions as if they were our own. This is not the worst part. Losing the direct connection from our soul to our hearts and bodies deprives us of the natural instinct to love ourselves, and to feel comfortably one with the rest of humanity.

Optimal functioning has two key features: first, the ability to love oneself and others, and second, to lead with our hearts when taking action. I believe we have the power to evolve and grow in these ways every day we live. It is the path to finding meaning and purpose in our lives.

As beings with free will and the capacity for heart-based deep emotional and spiritual feeling, we can overcome entrenched prejudices. The result is a new sort of freedom, based in love and creativity, with strong connections to others of our own kind as well as to the Earth and all its life-forms.

PART II.

LIFE IN THE CULTURE OF UNHAPPINESS

I AM GOD

I am untouchable, indestructible
No struggle or trial affects me.
Sticks and stones may break my bones
But my iron will protects me.

I'm at the center of cosmic forces,
The flowering of my planet.
Others resent me, conspire against me
It's my destiny, I didn't plan it.

Fate haunts me, the gods are against me,
The traffic piles up on my highway
My tire went flat, the rain came down, but
My team won by doing it my way.

My secret powers, my matchless talents
Are a mystery behind the scenes.
Unheralded, humble, I mustn't reveal
My kid passed:'cuz I passed on my genes.

I control it; I will it, I deal the cards,
I cloak my power, I wield my sword
I could conquer, but I refrain.
I'm a benevolent Lord.

Poor human, you're unaware
I exterminate you in my mind,
But no, I forgive you, I let you live
This time I prefer to be kind.

CHAPTER THREE

A SUFFERING SOUL

We are born ready to learn about becoming human. Even as infants, we have some sense of ourselves, and we come into the world with the expectation of being welcomed. We are born open, expectant, eager. We have been prepared and formed for interaction with our fellow humans. Not just our bones and muscles and organs and blood, but also our eyes, ears, and our impressionable brains. Our capacity and readiness to smile—and to respond to another's smile—are developed inside the womb. We are born wired, ready to relate to human faces above all other objects, and to human eyes above all else in the human face. We are born ready to make contact, to learn and grow and love and thrive. Children are also instinctively spiritual creatures. We are born with an innate sense of awe toward the wonder of the world about us and beyond us. These qualities are inherent in the human soul, and would be our primary orientation for life if our deep connections were not interfered with.

In human experience, all that is important to us lies in the meaning and feeling of interaction with our environment. Our whole bodies are ready to be guided by our heart and soul. We would develop that way, heart-first, if we were allowed to. Heart and soul would permeate mind and body. As it is, this is not the way most of us begin, so we must work hard to recover, to restore ourselves to being open and loving. It helps to have a vision of what the ideal could give us.

It is every child's fundamental right to be welcomed into the human species. Each child should be accepted as a new member. He needs to be recognized both as human and as a unique individual. She needs to be loved and nourished, helped to grow into a fully human member.

Too often we are born into a hornet's nest of unfulfilled needs, desires, family politics and distorted perceptions. Our essential humanness is not seen, or is lost in the shuffle, or is deliberately, maliciously ignored and trampled upon. We are not appreciated or encouraged to be who we are.

Dina was a client who described the relentless family cruelty that drove her cousin to commit suicide and her sister to give up on life. Her only solace as a young child was to retreat to the walk-in closet in her room where she could hide from them. She said, "I used to go into the closet to visit myself. Until now (thirty years later) I had forgotten I did that." She was able to then begin to thaw from the icy stance she had developed in imitation of her family tone, and to reconnect with the admirable human qualities she remembered in that child.

There are no examinations for people to earn the privilege of becoming parents. Parents themselves may have been brought up in abusive situations. For example, in her own childhood a mother may have had to rely on grounding herself in fantasy. Today, she may handle the infant's physical being well enough, but her attention is directed elsewhere, in a vaguely hallucinatory dream state where the infant represents something which is known only to her. She may "adore" the infant, treating him as the be-all-end-all of her existence, but she is then dealing with a product of her own imagination, not the flesh-and-blood infant. Perhaps she sees him as a trophy, a bargaining chip, a savior, or a blessed distraction. Whatever she is envisioning, it is not the actual infant. If she saw him accurately, she would see he is not her possession, and he does not want to be spoiled or indulged or used. He does not want to have to play a role for his mother. He needs to be helped to grow into his own being.

"Spoiling" a child—giving him all manner of exceptional favors, material possessions, electronic gadgets and indulgences—literally does spoil him. It disrupts the child's natural learning process, which he requires to deal with the world and achieve independence. Instead, he is redirected to focus on things rather than people.

A mother at the other end of the emotional spectrum might be cold and punishing toward the child. Again, she is dealing with an image based on past hurt, resentment or hate. She is not dealing with the warm, lively person at hand.

The infant of a mother who is split off in these ways, hallucinating her baby's identity and needs rather than seeing them, cannot make contact. The baby searches her mother's eyes for feedback, communication, communion, and finds something else. Rather than someone who returns the child's searching gaze with recognition and appreciation, the infant sees a distracted, spaced-out blank, or a glaring and intrusive specter. The child is forced to come up with a devastating conclusion: She is not enough, in and of herself, to warrant being seen.

Eager, ready and rebuffed. Our essential humanness, our individuality, our very being is wounded. Thrown off balance, we come up with the only feeling/explanation we can. "I am defective." That is why my caretaker does not confirm me, or respond to my efforts to make contact. There is something fundamentally wrong with me.

The result is that we begin to function less effectively, and we then use that as support for the eventual conclusion that we are constructed badly.

It isn't true. The fact is that many of us were not given our birthright: the right to be welcomed into humanity. At first, it just feels bad, but we do sense that life has dealt us an unfair hand. When our brain develops to the point where we can perceive a separate "me," we conclude it is because we are defective. This conclusion—this blow to our self-esteem—puts us into a rage. Rage is a natural and appropriate response to such a situation, but we classify it as further proof that we are defective. We cannot act on the rage, and we can't stop feeling it. This puts us into a further rage, and so it escalates into festering self-hatred, and aversion to the world and all it holds. All we can do at this point is take pride in being something other than human.

Thus, we are pushed further and further from our original potentially unified human self into a being divided into warring parts: Ego against Heart, darkness against light. The most tragic part of this experience as a divided self is that we then begin to see everything in the world as two opposing forces warring against each other, like a mirror of our inner experience: black against white, men against women, gay against straight, good against evil, God against Satan, and us against them.

It becomes impossible to conceive of Oneness, because once you have separated mind from heart, you can no longer feel you belong as a part of All That Is. For a Heart person, everyone belongs, everyone has value. There are no divisions or separations between the living things on the planet. That's just the way it is. A Head person would read this discussion as if it's the Heart people against the Head people.

The Alien

Feeling we are not a member of our own species is quite a blow.

A child notices when his mother actively avoids seeing him. He wonders: "Why does she look away?" When she must look in his direction, when he calls to her repeatedly, she only pretends to be seeing him. Since children look up to their parents, the child is in no position to understand or declare that his parents are doing anything other than the appropriate best. The only conclusion available is this: Not only am I unimportant, not only am I some other species, but there must be something about me that is too horrible to look at.

With his child imagination he will develop a picture of what he must really be like. He may picture some kind of animal or insect, monster or alien. He believes he has "proof." Anger and outrage are normal and appropriate responses to not being seen, but a child has no perspective or knowledge about such things. He will classify his responses as ugly. That is the way he has been looked at when he expressed them. He is indeed hideous.

The conclusion the child reaches will be tailored to the intensity and frequency of disapproval or rejection in his life, and the mythology and cultural influences the child has available to him. The dynamic which ends in self-hatred is common to many children under duress. This is especially true for children who do not have the solace of a deep connection to Nature, and to teachings about a Higher Power whose influence transcends that of the people around him. There is great comfort in knowing that your parents do not have the last word when it comes to your own worth. Without that, a child is at the mercy of the people around him, no matter how cruel and opinionated they might be.

It is not unusual to see a beautiful woman look into the mirror and say something like, "I'm so ugly" (or so fat, or bony, or short, or blemished in some way). She is not commenting on what is there in the mirror; she is complaining about what she imagines to be her true characteristics. If she is asked to look closely at how she truly looks, she will say, "Oh, but that's not who I really am."

As children grow older and go to school, their thinking expands to take in concepts like the differences between species. Their exploration ranges far and wide in search of explanations for how they have been treated. Their reasoning might go something like this: "They treat me like a hideous bug or vile creature, like the way they react to a cockroach. Maybe I'm a cockroach, or maybe a rat." The child is disappointed to find that he has some pronounced differences from the other creatures he discovers here on earth. "The cockroach and the rat don't seem to recognize me either. Maybe I don't really belong here. Maybe I'm an alien from some other planet, or some strange and distant place that no one knows about, like ET. If I were among my own kind, it would be okay. They would love me. I'm only considered ugly here, like the ugly duckling who really was a swan." Because the child has been treated in inhuman ways, he assumes he anything but human.

At some point a horrible doubt creeps in. "Maybe I wouldn't be accepted on my home planet either. Maybe they rejected me too. Maybe that's why I'm here."

On and on, the child's vivid imagination searches for some explanation, any answer to explain his own feelings of rejection and pain. Thoughts about being a cosmic reject become completely intolerable, because he is left without self-esteem or hope. He has to make up a story about why he was sent here.

Some of us take the cloak and dagger route: We were sent here to spy, or to destroy. Others take the sainthood route: We were sent here to be a savior, or to bring special knowledge. Whatever scenario we work out, based on the stories and myths and television programs available to us, in it we are not just special. We are Super-Special.[7]

As a cover story, in order not to let on about our secret identity, we may present ourselves as being less-than, less than even the average level of human capabilities. The truth is, we consider ourselves more-than—exceedingly more-than. Given her feelings of superiority, the older child begins to feel contemptuous toward the values and activities of the adults around her. Why bother to try to prove

---

[7]   It is no accident that these superhuman themes are omnipresent in children's stories, TV shows and toys. In recent generations, enterprising adults have profited enormously because enormous numbers of children identify with them.

herself? These humans won't see her true value, so why try? She is not lazy; she is protecting herself from further disappointment and misunderstanding

Little by little, as we grow and learn more about the world, we embellish our identity. Depending on our imagination, we could be an exotic bird or fish or animal, or a cloud, a saint or a messenger from God. Whatever we imagine, it is not human, and it is more-than.

Superhumanness or inferiority seem to be nearly universal conclusions for children who have suffered emotional trauma early in life. The earlier it happens, the more deeply buried the convictions will be. Most of us come to it so early that it permeates our thinking and actions without our realizing it. Even if we were aware of the feelings, we would not share them, because each of us thinks we are the only one—the only superior alien living in human disguise.

This is a lonely, duplicitous existence. Once we have concluded we are more than human, humanity takes on the cast of being gray and boring. We see *them* as being limited, ordinary, common, and dull, dull, dull. We feel the burden of pretending to be one of them.

We have gone from warm-blooded, receptive infant to someone who fears and avoids other people. Love comes to mean disappointment and alienation. We shut down our hearts.

Although intelligence may remain seemingly intact, it is separate from the heart, leaving the person oddly "out of touch." Emotion, especially the emotions along the "warm" spectrum, are eliminated in favor of remaining separate, safe and out of danger. Thus, we become Head people, and proud of it. Once you are a full-fledged Head person, you see life differently than you did as a young child. Perhaps this is what we really mean by a loss of innocence.

I was discussing the idea of "the alien" with a group of young teenagers. I asked if they understood. Each of them gravely nodded their head. They began telling their stories about how being at odds with their parents had made them feel different from other kids. They saw themselves as aliens. One boy, well-known for annoying even the most tolerant teachers, said, "Yeah, but I always figured I had a destiny in life, like to do something special." I asked what that was. He said, "Oh, like blow up the world."

It all boils down to self-worth, and how we find ways to love our Egos, in the absence of loving ourselves.

In the process of leaving behind our precious humanity, we travel a lonely path which eventually leads us to do away with human considerations like conscience or feelings of brotherhood. Although we may proclaim otherwise, we behave in such a way as to erase human values such as honesty, decency and fair play. Our unspoken motto becomes: "I don't allow anyone in this world to be precious to me, including me."

This position of clandestine arrogance often takes on a religious cast, based on popular notions of God. For instance: God is all-powerful, God can do whatever he likes, God knows more than any human. I feel those things. I am a god, a god in my own image.

Believing we are God leads to behaving in a high-handed way. Our disconnectedness comes out in every facet of life, from the way we treat our friends or our pets to the way we recklessly despoil the Earth. We do not consider our behavior to be cruel or inhumane. The reasoning behind it is this: "I am superior, and because these humans have made me suffer, I have the right to do whatever I want."

At great cost.

Cut off from our human hearts, we remain angry and hurt, wounded and disappointed. These negative, self-pitying feelings take us deeper and deeper into Dark, insatiable need. We become predators, preying on our own kind, especially the children, never realizing they *are* our own kind. We walk like a stranger among strangers, feeling deep loss and loneliness. It is loneliness for our selves, our human hearts, our human souls—and for company.

With each turn in this downward spiral into Darkness, we are faced with a conflict about our own self-worth and our relationship to God. Having been deeply stung by disrespectful treatment, without any faith in a connection to a Higher Power, we are left without compassion or a sense of belonging. We must be either better or worse. We are left feeling that being human is worthless. The war within solidifies into hatred and contempt for our true, human self. Our alien-identified Ego feels superior and apart.

Intellectual (Ego) Strategies

You may be reluctant to see yourself this way. Open your mind. You may have an inkling that some of this applies to you, especially during those times when you are under stress, or "out of control." If you are a Head person, here are some of the characteristics you will notice about yourself:

1) Your first impulse will be to deny that any of these things happened to you, or if they did, it didn't affect you.

2) You have a running commentary in your mind. You go to great lengths to explain, justify or excuse any unkind behavior you may have seen in yourself. You may extend this justification to those you care about or identify with.

3) The running commentary in your mind is primarily judgmental. You constantly evaluate and criticize the people and things around you: "This is good, that is bad. This shows good taste, that is repellant. This is attractive, that is ugly. This deserves to live, that does not."

4) You find it difficult to identify with children, animals or the opposite sex. You rarely feel compassion about what they are feeling, especially when they are distressed. You will probably want to deny this, especially if you are a parent, but you will be able to notice it in your reaction to a child's "bad" behavior. Your first impulse will be to quickly try to suppress the child's complaints through disapproval or swift punishment. You will extend this strategy to relationships with the opposite sex if you can get away with it.

5) You will use the saying, "He really has a big heart" while describing someone whose behavior is frequently cruel or insensitive toward others.

6) You may believe you are a good judge of character, but you are frequently disappointed by friends, relations and acquaintances.

7) You may hear yourself saying you are afraid of commitment of some kind because you are afraid of getting your heart broken, but you prefer not to acknowledge that your heart is closed.

8) You frequently feel alone and beleaguered. You cannot trust in the Universe to provide what you need. You feel you must somehow do it all yourself.

9) You are uncomfortable in any situation you cannot control. You will go to great lengths to arrange, manage, orchestrate and define your relationships and interactions with others.

10) Add your own favorite avoidance strategy here.

This is a challenge many of us face as adults. We must find a way to reconcile the shards of self which result from unkind treatment in childhood, and how we think about ourselves as a result. It takes strong medicine to shake yourself loose from old habits and old ideas, especially when they saved your life as a child. As lonely as the Superior Alien identity might be, it is better than having been driven completely insane by the pain of childhood rejection.

The following chapter offers a day-by-day illustration of the innermost feelings and thoughts the adult uses to find grounding and solace after a childhood in an unwelcoming world. You may recognize yourself in parts of it.

PASSIVE-AGGRESSIVE

Oh my, did I spill that?
How clumsy of me.
Your new suit, your briefcase,
All sopping with tea.
I wish I were suave and
Well-ordered like you.
I just stumble along
And—oops—step on your shoe.

You're competent, worldly,
Not fearful like I am.
You're brave and secure,
You go forth like a lion,
While I'm so distracted,
My mind's left ajar . . .
Oh, yes, did I tell you
I totaled your car.

Oh, I'm so hopeless,
You'll hate me, you see,
I locked out the children
And misplaced the key.
But the neighbor was lovely,
The police were so gracious,
Now, where is my wallet?
I guess I've misplaced it.
I'll just have to borrow
A wee bit of money.
I'm so glad I could help
When you needed me, Honey.

WORKAHOLIC

I am a Worker Bee
I earn my keep.
The world could not function
If I were to sleep
Too long, or vacation
Before work is done.

They know they can count on
My dogged attention,
I sweat and I swear
And eschew all pretension;
The real goods, the best job –
That's what I require
Of myself, while the others
Can't help it; they tire.

They tell me to slow down;
There's no time for fun
My mission, my pleasure
Is getting it done.

I've done my best work
It's the most I can do
But I can't seem to please
The slave-driver in you.

And now I must answer
The call to be fair
To the standard I've set
And collapse in my chair.

From the time I was weaned
Till I find myself here,
I've been working myself
To the bone, I fear.

Now it's time to admit
To myself and be free
That the slave-driver here is
None other than me.

Chapter Four

HOW A SIT-DOWN STRIKE BECOMES A WAY OF LIFE

In order to tell this human story in more intimate terms, it is written in a form resembling a Greek drama. The narrative italicized paragraphs introduce the issues the child had to deal with from a sympathetic observer's point of view. Then, the adult's voice is presented in the left-hand column, crying out his or her deepest feelings, as the child who has suffered faces adulthood. In the right column, the explanation flows along side by side with the child's voice, like a Greek chorus commenting on the thoughts and rationale behind the emotions. The narrator and the chorus use the plural "we" to acknowledge that our "hero" is not alone in these child feelings of anguish and rage.

Brutal Beginnings

A difficult childhood has consequences. We make compromises we would not have otherwise considered. We come out of childhood with inaccurate convictions in place. This is the story of some of the ways we manage, after suffering through inauspicious beginnings.

I feel like a child.

In our anguished child brain, we are convinced that our true identity is the child we once were. We made the pledge to never grow up and desert him or her, no matter what.

People may leave us, hurt us. They don't understand. They don't care. They act as though we don't exist, but this child will always exist. We are not going to go on without a foundation, before we're ready. We're not going to budge until they recognize what they did, and apologize and make it right.

I won't.
I WON'T!
I WON'T!!!

You can't make me.
Nothing can make me.

I'm waiting until things are fair.
This is unfair

I'll have nothing to do with a world that humiliates and mocks me.

I will stop time until I'm good and ready.

I won't grow.

This isn't happening.

It's too awful if it's really happening.

No! It can't be!

Time is not passing!

I'm not growing, not really.

We swore we would refuse to deal with reality until reality relents and gives us what is rightfully ours.

We only wanted a loving, supportive environment in which to thrive and grow.

To honor our pledge, we must hold time still.

Drifting in a hypnotic suspended-animation state, we feel as if time stands still.

Time doesn't stand still.

We grow.

We make believe we really succeeded.

Again and again.

It's a desperate position. The last stand of an oppressed, helpless little being.

Once we have taken this position, we "prove" our convictions by reacting to life as if we really are physically and mentally tiny.

We relate to our bodies as if they were a child's—small and weak.

See, what you say isn't really real.
What's really real is what I believe,
what I decide!

I AM A CHILD!!!

I'm paralyzed without help.

I can't take much stress.
I can't take very much change.

They're not taking care of me.
It's too much.

I can't manage all these feelings.

I can't deal with the way things are.

I know in the back of my mind that
I'm grown up, but I *feel* tiny. That's
what's real.

I'm a tiny child perched in the control
room of a big robot.

All-powerful giants tower over me.
I must struggle against them to save
my life.

Everything seems to be up close and
larger than life.

I'm little.

Our arms and legs feel short.

It feels as if we can be taken
over, consumed, or maybe we
can consume others.

We feel no connection to
ourselves, other than noticing
the commands we give our
bodies.
We see parts of our bodies
doing things, but it's not US.
It's just a thing to maneuver
and use.

We feel it when something
touches our body. The sensors
are working, but that's all.

Our emotional reactions, our
thoughts and feelings are the
same as they were back then.

We feel easily hurt. We have
trouble managing our big
feelings.

We operate as if we were
that child in every sense, with
every sense.

It doesn't seem strange
because other adults describe
themselves the same way.

We focus our eyes the way
a child does, with awe and
wonder, even at things we
have seen many times before.

It's all too much, too big, too overwhelming.

We don't have an accurate sense of the distance between ourselves and objects in the world, especially people.

I'm right. I'm fine.

Criticism is intolerable.

I refuse to admit they got me. No! I'm fine. I held out!

We have been wrenched from our true selves, blocked from fulfilling our natural drive.

I'm stronger!

It was the only way to save our sanity, our self-esteem.

I was never helpless!!!

It hurts too much to feel the injustice of having been humiliated and oppressed, mocked, ridiculed, belittled and ignored, a vessel for others' needs.

I was NEVER helpless!

I didn't give in.

We gave up.

I fought!

We were not allowed to be, to grow in our own time in our own way.

I never begged!

We begged, we pleaded. We offered ourselves up as victim and sacrifice, because we had no other choice.

They didn't mean it.

The cruelty. We don't under-stand the wanton cruelty.

I'm indispensable to them.

It hurts too much to have done everything in our power to get what we needed, and to have failed.

And Then We Tell Ourselves

We tell ourselves stories to make it feel better: "He didn't mean that. She didn't really do that. They can't help it. It's probably my interpretation. They weren't being vicious. I must have done something to deserve it. I should have tried harder. It's not nice of me to think that. They were right. I'm not nice. Ungrateful. My mind must not work right. I must be a born troublemaker, emotionally unstable. Some kind of chemical imbalance. I must not be who I thought I was. I can't be seeing what I'm seeing. Yes, that's it. It must mean something else."

This isn't happening to me!

It might be happening to the body, but that isn't *me*.

That's just the boring, earth-bound part.

Weak. Vulnerable.

I'm above all that.

I float about, watching with contempt.

I can escape any time I want. I just go off in my imagination. I can sacrifice her. She's not important as long as *I'm* okay.

Look! I can punish her too.

I can do it just the way they did.

I'm not like them, I'm stronger and better. More cruel and cold. I can beat her better than they can.

We look about us for help in keeping our separated-off state. Friends offer drugs and alcohol.

Addictions are helpful to ease the pain and loneliness we feel for the self we left behind.

Once we have separated off from our unique human selves, we can no longer afford to value wholeness in ourselves or others.

It would be far too painful to acknowledge what we have lost.

We make compartments inside ourselves to pretend we don't know what we're doing.

In depriving ourselves we feel superior, above it all.

In our secret thoughts we feel *more-than* because we need less kindness or warmth than others.

They're nothing compared to me.
I can prevent her from succeeding,
deprive her of pleasure, mastery, *self*.

When we do self-destructive
things we don't evaluate it in
terms of the actual cost.

We know the body might
suffer, but it doesn't matter.

I hate that human stuff.

Nothing matters but
preserving the Ego's sense of
superiority.

I can keep her on starvation rations, or
stuff her with food to slow her down.

Drugs, alcohol, cigarettes,
obesity, promiscuity, none are
really bad because they help us
forget, and it's only the body
that suffers, not *us*.

Not let her breathe.

I think for her.

Who cares. We believe we
have stopped time. We can
procrastinate, put things off as
long as we like.

I don't give her a moment's peace.

I put her in terrible situations and
laugh as she tries to get out of them.

Watch TV, smoke dope,
daydream.

Make her crazy with anxiety.

We think we have to deal with
"stress" by escaping from life.

We may get a nasty shock
if we notice we've lost an
opportunity, but we don't
blame ourselves. We refuse
to acknowledge we are not
dealing *in reality*.

Watch her squirm.

See! I'm strong, tough, invincible.

Should anyone point out the
facts, we insist it's "just their
opinion" and disregard it.

Nothing can touch me.
I'm just lonely because I haven't found
the right person yet. That would make
everything better.

Love is something others are
supposed to give us, but we
don't want to return it.

Later.

It is better to be with someone who is cruel and indifferent than to have to open our hearts to someone who shows genuine love and expects us to behave as an equal and return their love.

I refuse to be hurt again.

We are in awe of people who are unaffected by feelings.

No one could blame me, after all I've been through.

We call it power, getting our way, being strong.

Whatever.

It's sensible, not being a sucker.

I am a very generous, giving person. I am always helping other people.

We may even make a display of magnanimously helping others.

People like me because I am always doing something nice for others.

We would not give without taking credit publicly for our generosity.

It makes me feel good.

Awards and accolades are good for business.

We Add Our Own Stamp of Approval

Once we have made the shift to accepting fragmentation and illusion as our own idea, we put time, energy and creativity into it. Thus, we make it our own. We dismiss our gut reactions. We install something imaginary, and respond emotionally to that. We feel we can never relax, never let down our guard against reality. We use television, alcohol or drugs or some other self-induced hypnotic state to distort our perceptions for us. All in all, it's a lot of work.

There are compensations. We take pride in how firmly we believe our imaginings in the face of all the evidence to the contrary. It is a measure of our control and mastery.

We pretend. Then we pretend we were pretending and say, "Of course, I know better."

Who's to say what's real and what isn't? This is MY reality.

As we were torn away from ourselves, we were forced to go against our natural growth, to violate ourselves, and to like it!

I am the center of my own Universe!

I know what's best!

We then "ground" ourselves in our brain-centered Ego, to give ourselves a sense of something substantial to hold onto.

I'm great!

I BELIEVE!

We invest in ideas, especially self-aggrandizement and dislike for others who are different from us, as a way to manage our feelings of alienation and anger.

Living in Your Head

We come to see any threat to our imaginings—our precious ideas—as a threat to our whole world, to our definition of who we are, to our feeling of sanity, security and self-worth. We're put into the position where we must constantly defend against reality, the most threatening thing in the whole world. Our fears extend to everything in the world a child might fear, and more. We fear others who are not exactly like us. Lost in our narrow, hallucinated world, we are strangers to unfamiliar plants or animals, to the night's darkness and the ocean's waves.

Shut off from our hearts and our bodies, we have nothing left but our racing minds to guide us. We live in constant fear that something might slip through and bring down our whole edifice. We turn to others for ideas on how to live—the same ones who ripped us away from the use of our senses and our body intelligence. We are now ready to become one of Them, our family, our security. We are prepared to make alien circuitry ours. We will never be alone. We have finally learned to think the way they do.

This accomplishment, letting go of our hearts, our intuition and our senses, prepares us to live in a world of thoughts and ideas, opinions, beliefs and convictions. Instead of feeling compassion, we are judgmental. Rather than love, we feel contempt, worry or indifference. Rather than faith, we turn to dogma. Instead of companionship, we have possessions. In place of community, we have entertainment. But at least we are no longer feeling the anguish and confusion of childhood.

Through no fault of our own, we have become the victims, the participants, and the budding future architects of a heartless and soulless society.

Note:

In later chapters, I will go on to describe the scientific underpinnings of how one learns the earliest lessons of becoming a self under the glare of an Abusive parent. Because of my own experience, I have a deep appreciation of the impact on the developing child, as well as the greatest hope that we can learn better ways to prevent suffering, to heal as individuals and as a culture. I offer my own story as a working example of how devastating the emotional effects can be, and how sweet the triumph of survival and recovery. In my life-long search to understand the mysteries of why there is such Darkness in the world, how to recover from it and what we can learn from it, I have found there are deep and valuable connections to be made on the way to freedom. Through a growing sense of faith in the positive forces of love and creativity in the Universe, I have learned to see Darkness as a potentially positive force as well. I have come to trust the homily, "If it doesn't kill you, it will probably make you stronger." That strength can be used to propel yourself toward Light, and with it the discovery of love and inner peace.

POISON POLLY

I am a toy, a doll
So sweet, I'm always smiling,
With glamorous clothes
And painted lips
I'm so fragile, so beguiling.

With my long, long eye lashes,
I poise on my high, high heels,
So gorgeous, so helpless, so cute.
You can almost pretend I'm real.

With my golden locks,
My tiny little voice,
My peals of silvery laughter,
I'll be whatever you want me to be.
Happily ever after.

Lift me, carry me, squeeze me, play with me,
You can have your way with me.
I never get bored and I never stray
I'll always be here for another day
Providing you never cross me.

My Daddy adores me,
Looks after my honor
My last boyfriend fell in the river.
I swear, they overcompensate
With their thoughtfulness and fervor.

But never mind,
With you I'm safe,
You're so suave and handsome and tall,
You're my perfect match,
My charming prince,
You're a living, breathing doll.

SADIST

I am a toy,
A rough and tumble toy,
A football made to be kicked.
I am here for a plaything,
A lonely dismay thing,
To be picked on,
Tossed and tricked.

They poke me,
I squeal; they laugh,
Then they lift me and let me fall
They roar with sadistic delight.
I beg them to give me the ball.

They love our game,
Teasing the foil,
I'm here for your torturing pleasure,
While I get better and better.
I play along, but they don't get it,
I am the buried treasure.

Will they? Won't they?
The bold titillation, the play
They aren't aware that I'm learning and growing,
And I will take over one day,
Then I will be gloating and sneering
With Power
While they grovel and whimper and pray.

CHAPTER FIVE

A TEACHING GUIDE FOR THE ADULT CHILD: HOW

TO TRAIN YOUR ABUSIVE PARENT

My younger brother, Tom, called me to say he had found our 92-year-old mother unconscious on the floor next to her bed, where she had been for some time. She was taken to the hospital, and was immediately given intravenous fluids. She had suffered a stroke and dehydration.

"She's conscious now. She's not saying much, but I can tell she's in there. She gave me The Look."

"You mean the beady-eyed look?" I said.

"Yeah, you know, the Rat Look."

I was stunned by the sudden and vivid picture his description evoked in my mind's eye: her small pale eyes, narrowed in the predatory glare she revealed only in private moments when she dropped her affable public face to show her true feelings. The look carried with it a threat, "Don't even try to cross me. I'll bite your head off" and a searing indictment, "You are beneath my contempt. You disgust me."

The memories from our years together washed over me as I contemplated the possibility of her death. It had been many years since I had come to the hard-won understanding that there would be no warmth, no comfort, and no genuine love possible in a relationship with this woman who had been my "mother." I knew my brother still sometimes longed for the approval that would never come. He had struggled all his adult life to be free of her but still he lived nearby, doing repairs on her house and running errands for her. When severe illnesses had threatened his life and made working impossible, she supported him financially, tightening her grip when he was most vulnerable.

It was her lifelong policy to reward dependence on her, while punishing self-reliance. When Tom had developed a drinking problem in his youth, she would refill the bottles in her liquor cabinet so "no one would know." In this way she secretly fed his addiction and his resulting dependence on her.

I was just nine years old when Tom went through his "terrible twos." It began the most traumatic period of my childhood, not because she tormented me, which she did frequently, but because I was forced to watch her torture him. I was helpless to do anything to stop it.

The summer he was two and-a-half, we went to stay at our remote cabin on a lake in the Michigan woods. There, without neighbors or friends to intervene, I watched the nightmare of our mother's mission to subdue Tom's spirit.

One afternoon after an especially enjoyable day at the nearby sand dunes, she announced that it was time to leave, and ordered us into the car to return to the cabin. Accompanied by our young aunt, my older brother and I obediently climbed into the car.

Tom, unwilling to leave his sand castle, said, "No!"

She reacted viciously, in her most threatening voice, "Get in the car! Now!"

He refused, so she got into the car and drove away. I was stunned as I watched my little brother through the rear window, screaming and crying, running after the car on the gravel road in his little bare feet.

Finally, she stopped, got out and said, "Get in the car!"

Instead of obeying, he sat down in the road. My heart stopped. Again she drove away. Again he ran, shrieking and crying. When she finally stopped the car for the third time, I said a silent prayer, "Please, Tom, stop fighting her." Then I realized what I had wished, and took it back. Fear and shock washed over me. I wanted the torture to stop, but I understood in the deepest part of my being that as long as he kept fighting against her, he was still there, still alive.

Finally, she picked him up and dragged him back to the car. She won by brute force, but he hadn't given in. I felt a sense of awe toward this little brother who had held out so bravely against such odds.

This incident stayed with me all my life. I was filled with guilt and sorrow for not being able to protect him. It forged a steely resolve in me to hold out against her cruelty, no matter what I had to do, until we could be free. It also seared the realization into my heart and soul that this woman who called herself our mother was never to be trusted, no matter how much she pretended to be charming and generous. I knew then that she was not like other people in some profound and deep way, and that most of them either did not know it, or pretended, like my aunt, that it was some temporary aberration when she behaved this way.

Having used her beauty and charm to marry and outlive a doctor and two wealthy businessmen, she accrued a considerable amount of money over the years, which she tended lovingly and spoke about often. The last husband had paid her handsomely as an incentive to marry him in spite of his advanced age, poor health, and cantankerous attitude. He contended it was better to give it to her upfront than to have her "waiting for me to die." This questionable union lasted ten long, combative years, during which she took her revenge on the stone-deaf old man by loudly insulting him in public: "You old goat!" when he made demands on her. However, she stayed for the money, which she squirreled away and invested for the time it could be used to entice her friends and relatives.

No one was spared the seduction of imagining great wealth to be left on her death. The promise of no more struggles; the final recognition of your worth in the form of a generous bequest . . . If only you were willing to show your loyalty, your admiration and gratitude, and to turn over your soul and your integrity in the bargain.

Numerous incidents revealed the depth of her heartlessness and ruthless control over the people around her, especially the most vulnerable ones, her children. Here are three examples of her characteristic style.

At one of Tom's lowest points, she bought him a house, but she kept the title in her name until her death. Certainly this discouraged him from leaving town. At the same time, I was facing the possibility of having to sell my home in order to finish graduate school. When I asked for her help with tuition, she said, "Why don't you just quit school and get a real job!"

As a returning student, after ten arduous years, I had finally completed my B.A. in psychology, then two Master's degrees and a PsyD, also in psychology. She showed up at my final graduation with the gift of a fire engine red Ford, a 2-seater fake sports car (I had three children), and asked, "What is this degree you're getting, again?"

My family nickname in childhood was "Katy." She used it to great effect when she wanted to diminish and degrade my intelligence or my competence. In a revealing moment with Tom, she sneered, "Katy and her psycho-business!"

"I couldn't just leave her there," Tom had said on the afternoon he found her. "It would have been a lot easier for everyone, probably for her too, but I couldn't. She was almost gone . . ." He knew I would understand. He is a good man, with an aching soft spot that never healed, and a conscious awareness of the especially virulent cruelty she had visited upon him all his life. She had misused his generosity and robbed him of his self-confidence, and still, he would help to save her life. In this way, he triumphed. He did not become like her.

Breaking the Spell

In the years after our childhoods, our mother mellowed, as energetic Abusers tend to do. She proved she could be "trainable" if the reward for good behavior was important enough for her. In her case, the loss of relationship with her only daughter, who was generally respected in the community, would have been an intolerable social embarrassment to her. She eventually learned to follow the rules of decent human behavior I set out for her in writing.

During one especially unpleasant exchange she had sneered at my intelligence, mocked my interest in the environment, and scoffed at my lack of racial prejudice. Fed up with her abuse, I sat down and wrote her a letter outlining what she could and could not say to me if she wished to have any contact with me in her life ever again. (I meant it.) I wrote two lists outlining exactly what she must do and what she must not do. They were my rules of decent behavior.

First, she must acknowledge my status as a competent adult—one who deserves treatment at least as cordial as she would offer toward an adult acquaintance or friend. I then listed the specific things she may and may not say to me or about me. I kept it simple and direct, outlining basic rules of decorum a 6-year-old would understand. I began with insisting on an attitude of positive acknowledgment befitting my status as a fully functioning adult, and included simple, appropriate comments for everyday use. I spelled out what she was to say in particular situations, for instance:

1) Upon my arrival, she was to offer positive greetings and comments, such as "I am happy to see you. I'm glad you were able to come," and "Thank you. I appreciate your effort."

2. Should I happen to be experiencing a difficulty in some way, she should offer simple empathic-sounding responses, such as "I'm so sorry to hear that." or in the case of triumphs, "Congratulations!" or "Good for you!"

3. Negative attitudes and insulting comments which are absolutely unacceptable include: "You always think you know everything," or "No wonder nobody likes you. You're always so—selfish,— messy,—scatterbrained,—stubborn,—opinionated,—liberal," and so on.

My instruction manual filled a page or two, leaving no doubt that I would apply a policy of zero tolerance toward insults and annoying comments.

I was surprised when Tom called to tell me she had posted my letter on her refrigerator, in full view for all visitors to see. She had apparently displayed it as an example of my audacity, but it seemed to have the opposite effect. Ever afterward, I noticed a distinct air of deference and respect from relatives who might have seconded her in the past.

By the time I saw her again, our relationship had changed. She never again treated me with the offhand cruelty which had been her stock-in-trade. At times I observed her literally biting her tongue, or stopping herself in mid-sentence, but she managed to comply rather admirably for several years, until the following brief incident.

We were sitting in front of the TV on a quiet post-Christmas day. As a commercial about the all-American values and principles of a particular giant agribusiness played, she rhapsodized about what a wonderful company it was, and how much profit she had made on its stock.

I said, "Yes, wonderful except it has just been indicted on seven counts of degrading the environment and abusing its employees."

She stiffened, took on The Rat Look, and hissed, "You're so smart, you think you know everything."

I very calmly turned to look directly into her eyes, allowing a long pause to hang in the air, then I said, "That's one."

A tiny gasp, and her mouth snapped shut. She gathered herself, then said in a voice an octave higher than usual, "Would you like a cup of tea?"

I said, "Yes, thank you," and she never showed her claws to me again.

Of course, this good behavior held true only in my presence. She didn't change. Behind my back she continued her campaign of alternately disparaging my character and bragging about my accomplishments. At least our time together was pleasant enough.

This can be an effective strategy for anyone who wants to compel difficult parents to behave tolerably. Complete your letter with all the typically hurtful things they may not say to you that are cruel or utterly inaccurate. Do not hesitate to demand positive regard, even if you believe there are areas in your life you may be less than satisfied with. That is your business to change or live with, not theirs.

I use the example of my own experience not because it is remarkable or unique. In my years of practice, I have become increasingly aware of how utterly typical these events were. Anyone growing up with an Abusive Personality Type, a Wannabe, or a Dysfunctional Aggressive parent is likely to have experienced nearly identical events. The details and the turn of phrase may vary, but the feeling of being relentlessly worn down, attacked and humiliated are the stuff of despair, misery, and ultimately, self-hatred. It is especially jarring when the attack comes out of the blue in moments that call for celebration and congratulations in a normal family.

I was lucky during childhood on three counts. First, I had a grandfather who was kind, attentive and available during my early years. Second, I grew up in a town where nearly everyone went to college, and I was swept along in the cultural expectation that all children would behave decently, study hard and succeed. Possibly best of all, throughout elementary and high school my teachers were generally inspiring, accomplished and very kind.

Without those mitigating influences, I would surely have turned out as the Abusive clone she wanted me to be. As it was, I felt the undertow from childhood in every area of my life. Repeatedly, through my teenage years and beyond, I was charmed and seduced by Abusers in the guise of friends, lovers, and business associates. Memories of my own rebellious and thoughtless behavior still make me blush for the confused and desperate young woman I was.

It was only after a long and healing therapy experience that I began to feel an internal immunity building. First I regained the neurological alarm system which warns of an Abusive Personality "vibe" nearby. I began to feel my skin crawl and the hair stand up on the back of my neck when I was in the presence of an Abuser. Next I began to see the emptiness in their eyes and the superficial quality of their emotionality. Little by little, I "came to my senses," until one day while crossing a room, I stopped dead in my tracks with the thought: "I will never have another bad relationship!" I was profoundly aware that the deepest reason for that change was the time I had spent looking into the kind, intelligent eyes of my mentor and therapist, Amos Gunsberg, as together we retrained my neurological circuitry.

No amount of drugs, or talking and analyzing alone could have had the same neurological effect as the experience of his calm presence and his steady gaze. I knew the effect of our work had been to literally rewire the innermost channels in my brain—those deep limbic connections where the meaning of how I experienced relationship had been formed. Much of our work had addressed just that—how my mother's early predatory gaze had seared my nervous system and left me jangled and disorganized in the deepest levels of my being. It was only afterward that I realized how profoundly my recovery had relied on absorbing the accepting gaze of this person I had come to trust and admire. I felt the change at the deepest levels. My reflexes were different. Colors were brighter. Hope returned.

Since I was professionally trained in the classic tradition which tends to discourage self-revelation, I have not written about these events before. However, I find that my own experience of having lived with a frequently abusive mother gives me a deep appreciation of the impact on one's neurological functioning that the experience brings with it. If not for those experiences, I would not have the empathic understanding I gained there.

I also have a real appreciation for how long the road back is for those of us who were the victims of destructive parents. How much simpler it would be and how much pain could be avoided if we could ensure that no child should be the captive daily recipient of a Dark One's bone-chilling gaze.

The undertow from childhood has a specific "feel" when you have been cannibalized psychologically by a parent. It leaves the victim mesmerized, as if in a hypnotic state. The child's normal feelings of helplessness are increased to the point of paralysis. It is no accident we are fascinated by the vampire genre. A parental Abuser leaves the child feeling as though they have been touched by an overwhelming force, drained of their own life-force, helplessly taken over by the powerful and awesome parent. These mind/body experiences in childhood create fertile ground for a particular kind of vulnerability. Helplessness and self-loathing frequently grow into self-destructiveness and an attraction to the same toxic interactions we have been entrained to. Thus begins the romance with The Dark Side.

If we are to change our attitudes and feelings, we must bring Light into those deepest channels, easing and reworking the feelings which were imbedded there. As the Light of love and healing eases and opens those channels, new possibilities for happiness will emerge.

The following chapters offer a way of understanding the impact of this kind of destructiveness on the developing child's personality and sense of self. They provide a neurological picture of how these interactions lay down channels in our brain where abuse and destructiveness merge into feelings of attraction and love at the deepest levels. However, this is just the beginning. We must call it what it is, then heal the toxic effects by truly absorbing the valuable human lessons we learn in a brush with a Dark One.

PART III.

THE DEVELOPING MIND

CHAPTER SIX

ENCODING THE CHILD

W e were not born feeling inadequate or guilty, and we would not have come to those feelings had they not been foisted on us from without. Healthy babies do not hang their heads, slouch, or worry. It takes time to develop those cringing responses to life. It also takes time and intellectual development to evolve toward the vengeful stance described in "Football" above. The following chapters will explore how and why the traumas of childhood are registered in the brain, and how they become the unique template through which each person interprets the world and acts on it in later life. This template becomes what the person thinks of as their *self* and forms the basis for adult values and beliefs.

The Triune Brain

The human adult brain is made up of three fairly distinct areas, which develop and evolve as we grow from infancy to adulthood. For a general sense of how this happens, picture the carnival trickster's balloon sculptures. Imagine he has blown up three balloons, large, medium and small, one inside the other, all tied off at the base. The base of this configuration would represent the brain stem and the connections downward into the spine.

The smallest balloon is often referred to as the "reptilian brain," because it is the part of our brain that we share with all vertebrates. It contains the most basic control centers which organize and manage bodily functions like heart rate, breathing, temperature control, and basic reflexes. It is the part of our brain which controls our autonomic nervous system, which would keep us alive even if we were in a coma.

We consider animals whose brains lack the larger two layers to be lower on the evolutionary scale, beginners in the brain department. It is noteworthy, however, that the brain of a fetus begins to develop just as the reptile's did, with the lowest centers maturing first.

The second layer, around and above the reptilian brain, is sometimes called the mammalian brain, which we share with all other mammals. It contains the emotional centers, called the limbic system. These emotional center make it possible for us to feel love, anger, sadness, to bond to others of our species, and to care for our young rather than slithering away. We see this bonding behavior in other mammals and identify with it.

The third and outer layer, the cerebral cortex, contains areas which permit the development of judgment, rational thought, language, and abstract reasoning. This area increases in size dramatically as the child grows to adulthood, eventually reaching a size and weight which is more than three times the size of the infant brain.

The central layer in our adult brains contains complex connections to the other two "brains," creating a web by which memory and emotion can be connected upward to our reasoning, logic and abstract thinking, and downward to our primitive reptilian functioning. All are necessary to our well-being. Without our reptilian brain we would not be capable of instantaneous fight or flight responses which protect us in life-or-death moments. On the other hand, without strong connections to our reasoning powers, emotion would take the form of unmitigated raw fear, lust and violence. We see this radical lack of upward connections in the person who responds to being cut off in traffic by leaping out of his car and killing someone. It is not the traffic, or any kind of "stress" for that matter, which is to blame for this individual's lack of control. Rather, it is the lack of previously established neurological channels connecting the emotion, anger, to higher levels of judgment which involve abstract moral concepts and the power of reason.

At birth, the infant's brain has reached the state in which the reptilian areas are mostly well established, the limbic areas are present but largely undifferentiated, and most of the enormous potential of the cerebral cortex is yet to develop. In the mammalian (limbic) brain, billions of neurons stand ready to be patterned, brought into alignment to form neuronal pathways, or channels, as the infant experiences life and their own response to it.

Childhood Conditioning Lays the Tracks

Picture the newborn in its crib. A person comes by, smiling and cooing to the child. The baby will look deeply into their eyes, experiencing the sight of a human face, the smiling eyes and mouth, and the pleasant sound. A pathway in the baby's limbic brain begins to form, registering the pleasurable sensations the baby feels, the sight of the smiling face, and the recognition of the person, who becomes associated with pleasure. A pathway for positive human interaction and bonding begins. The baby has the chance to be curious, to reach out for more, and eventually, as the child's cerebral cortex grows, to remember these interactions in peaceful moments, savoring the giggles which are now embedded in the baby's nervous system. Connections are made upward and outward, into the beginnings of the reasoning brain and downward into the baby's body. The child begins to form rudimentary notions about itself and human life which involve feelings of safety, comfort, goodness and fun.

Now imagine a different scenario: the baby hears the sounds of people fighting, voices raised. A pathway begins. The mother enters the room, fresh from a violent argument with her husband. She glares at the baby, upset and resentful at having to change a soiled diaper. The baby, already in an aroused fearful state, registers fear at the sight of her mother's glaring eyes and angry "vibe." The mother handles the baby roughly, all the while exuding frustration and anger. (The baby does not know, of course, that the anger is primarily felt toward someone else.) A beginning channel forms with fear as its primary feeling tone, combined with the recognition of the caregiving mother with her angry eyes. The more often these kinds of experiences are repeated, the stronger and deeper the neurological connections become.

The fear response in the baby initiates a cascade of "fight or flight" hormones on directions from the reptilian brain. They flood the body, touching off a series of reactions in the autonomic nervous system. As adrenaline rushes into the bloodstream, cortisol levels rise, the infant's heart rate increases, breathing speeds up, digestion stops, the bronchial passageways expand to allow more air into the lungs, and blood flow drains away from the brain and into the extremities. The baby in the crib is not able to either fight or flee, but is flooded with the intense physiological response nevertheless. The baby can only lie there feeling overwhelmed and upset. Naturally, it begins to cry. This sort of unfriendly and chaotic environment will lead to further rounds of fear-inducing interactions as the overwhelmed mother attempts to impatiently silence the infant. In a state of frustration and anger, she is incapable of providing the soothing which would comfort the child. The infant's brain channels which associate emotion with human interaction form patterns downward, directly from emotion to fight-or-flight. Thus begins the negative feeling tone which will become the foundation for later feelings of mistrust and self-doubt.

We can see how this scenario, if it were experienced frequently, would create brain patterning which would lead to difficulties later in life. Picture someone who commits a crime of passion, or responds to an employer's criticism with rage. This person, in whom the limbic/reptilian brain patterns predominate, would leap to attack someone who offends or threatens them. They have relatively fewer neurological connections to higher brain functions than they have to reptilian responses.

Other important capabilities are compromised in this reptilian-dominated configuration. The ability to foresee consequences and to recognize the possible impact of this present moment on one's future are also sacrificed. These higher levels of awareness also require that we have formed strong connections from the cerebral cortex to our heart and soul. The connection to our soul requires that we bypass the reptilian centers. It is that bodysoul connection which allows us the awareness that life goes on, that things pass. Our inner being, our true identity, will go on through this life and beyond.

There are secondary physical effects to the adrenaline-pumping fight or flight response as well. Once the sympathetic nervous system has done its job of alerting all the important energy-diverting systems, the body is in a state to effectively respond to physical danger. If the fear continues indefinitely, as with anxiety attacks, the body systems will reach overload, where the stress of staying in a three-alarm state becomes dangerous. The over-stressed body will eventually slam into a parasympathetic response. Bronchial passageways constrict, stomach acid begins to flow again, blood flows away from the extremities back to the brain, and eventually heart rate and breathing return to normal. These push-pull physical reactions suggest possible complications from overuse of the finely balanced sympathetic/parasympathetic response, such as asthma, ulcers, high blood pressure, forgetfulness, colitis, and weakened immunity, to name a few. In addition, heightened cortisol production has recently been cited as a factor in weight gain.

Modifying our emotional responses requires restoring the fight or flight response to its intended use. It is meant to be a lifesaving energy boost to protect us against real and imminent physical danger, like a tiger in the forest, or a mugger approaching on a dark street. Otherwise, it is a programmed response which simply ruins your life and your health.

Your Pre-Installed Software

The brain passageways I have referred to as "channels" were laid down in our brains, with philosophy and feelings and attitudes interwoven before we had any knowledge of how to understand them or know whether they were true or not. This occurs because the limbic areas of the brain take in information in a multifaceted way. Emotion, images, thoughts and sensations all become melded before they are stored in memory. Thus, memories are not simply factual. They are a rich combination of sensory recordings and emotional responses, combined with whatever bodysoul wisdom we had available to us at the moment. Added to the mix are intellectual interpretations and prejudices we have learned along the way.

Memories are stored in interwoven layers, each experience recorded in association to those that came before. In this way, the earliest brain channels become reinforced or weakened, depending upon their relevance to later events. They operate in our consciousness like a posthypnotic suggestion, as if a hypnotist had made suggestions while we were in a deep trance state and left them there. They remain there, the DNA of our identity and our world view, coloring everything we think and do. It is now our work as adults to rework and revise those feelings and attitudes.

However, these were not rational ideas to begin with. Most of what we store in our first years is a result of other people's attitudes and beliefs, and the way they look at us and the way they treat us. This is what makes them so difficult to change. Because they are not rational, they are not subject to logical modification, or simple argument. We can make changes by approaching it more directly, literally reworking our brain channels through action, the way an athlete "grooves in" increasingly advanced skills through practice. In this way, we can create new connections, reshaping the way we use our brain and our vision. In the process of that reworking, we change the way we experience ourselves and the world, gradually modifying and replacing earlier channels with expanded pathways which allow greater access to higher levels of functioning.

The Vibe You Took in With The Milk

The following exercise will allow you to identify some of the major themes you will probably recognize as problem areas in your own life—those brain channels you will want to change.

Beginning with the acknowledgement that babies are observant, sensitive and able to pick up the mood of people around them, imagine yourself as a 3-month old infant at feeding time. Put yourself back there, being held by your mother, or the caretaker who most often fed you. You are alert, hungry and ready to absorb what comes to you. You can sense your mother's emotional state, although you have no words. Her "vibe" is by now familiar to you. You know her smell, and the smell of warm milk as you drink from the bottle or the breast. Like a tuning fork, you vibrate in synchrony with the electrical energy which emanates from her. Are you relaxed and cozy in her arms, or do you feel uncomfortable, anxious or afraid?

You may be able to remember what her eyes looked like when she gazed at you. Was it lingering and warm, impatient and glancing, cold and distant? If your early memories escape you, and your associations are to her disposition as you knew her later, it probably does not matter a great deal. People tend to remain relatively consistent in their basic orientation toward life over time.

Now, put the meaning of the electrical energy you are sensing into words. What did you absorb with the milk? What philosophy of life was written in your mother's "vibe," what ideas about herself and her place in the world? What was her attitude toward you? Was it different from her attitude toward your father, siblings and others? What was her attitude about her place in the Universe, and her relationship to spirituality? Finally, where in your brain did you register the feelings you absorbed there?

Make a note for yourself about what you took in there, and what was missing. It will give you a clearer picture of what you need to address in your work as you go through the book.

The following chapter will begin to describe the process by which we can identify the brain patterns we need to change, by concentrating on the way we see the world—literally, how we use our eyes

NEAT FREAK

How can you live this way? She said
As she opened my closet door.
No one will want you, to live with you, ever
Your whole life is on the floor.

The Board of Health would condemn this place
If they ever caught a trace
Of that cat box, my nose is insulted
The fur everywhere's a disgrace.

The sink is overflowing
The kitchen's at sixes and sevens,
If cleanliness is Godliness,
Then you'll never make it to Heaven.

But then I suppose it's a good thing
You work as hard as you do.
You'll be able to care for yourself
And us, if we ever need you to.

If I were you, I'd hire a maid
Since you're such a shaker and mover,
Then you wouldn't always have to feel
Ashamed to invite us over.

MACHO

I may not be young as I once was
But I can still wow the fans.
I'll trash you at tennis, or golf or the hoops,
And you'll learn that you can't
Beat the Man.

Me and my team,
We'll defeat you, you'll see, kid,
We'll wipe the floor with ya, Son
We'll turn up the heat,
Keep the pressure on
And you'll wish
Youd'a never been born.

Well, you know we're the best team
And you just got lucky.
Our best guy came down with the flu
If it hadn't been raining,
You know we'da won it.
We're totally better than you.

That umpire was crooked
He sucked, man, admit it,
You won on that crazy freak bounce.
But we don't begrudge you,
You needed the win
Like I said, it's the spirit that counts.

CHAPTER SEVEN

FEELING LIKE A CHILD

We all know the feeling. Your day is going well, you feel good about yourself, when suddenly someone—a stranger, your boss, a loved one—says something disparaging, critical or mocking. At least, it seems that way to you. You feel a stab, as if you've been hit in your solar plexus. The blood rushes to your face, and you are completely unhinged. Raging inside, you struggle to maintain your composure, but all you want to do is lash out, strike back. If you could strike this foe dead in their tracks in this moment, you would do it. Waves of humiliation wash over you, as you absorb the unflattering comment. You condemn yourself for having responded so emotionally, even as you struggle to find a retort which might restore your dignity in the eyes of others, and yes, even in the eyes of this assailant. You are now in the throes of a full-fledged fight-or-flight response, in danger of acting out the emotional and physical havoc it can produce.

If after several seconds have passed and you have neither punched the person in the nose nor shouted a "F—you!" you may have time to regain your composure before you do something to ruin your life. Meeting aggression with aggression rarely serves to do anything but inflame the situation. Since you didn't start it, escalating the conflict would not work in your own best interests. It could, however, strengthen your adversary's position, since you could then be accused of equally bad behavior. Unfortunately, thinking rationally is probably not your strong suit when you are experiencing a fight or flight reaction. Your intelligence would benefit greatly if you could avoid generating this body-altering adrenaline rush in the first place.

We live in a society where adrenaline-pumping aids surround us. The majority of movies, video games, sports events and TV programming are specifically designed to activate our fight-or-flight reactions. In fact, the more adrenaline the event inspires in its audience, the more accolades it earns. With every passing year, the bar is raised, not to reward artistic excellence, but to provide ever more heart-pounding thrill for the over-stimulated, insensate audience. In order to extract oneself from this addictive sensation overload, we must first learn to reject the cheap thrills being fed to us for someone else's commercial gain in favor of the rich rewards of genuine intimacy. A fulfilling human life cannot be shaped around artificial emotion.

So, be ready to fend off the ever-present seductions of artificial emotion-generating media, with its call to respond with panic or rage, and get ready to address its destructive effects on your actual, everyday life. Now let's address the humiliating incident above in a new light, without resorting to a fight or flight response.

If you can learn to freeze, take a breath, and reach downward to anchor yourself in your present-day bodysoul, you will give yourself the option to respond with calm assurance rather than panic or rage.

Imagine a recent incident in your own life. With reflection, you may be able to precisely identify how old you felt at the moment the insult hit. (It feels like a poke or a stab in your gut.) How tall did you feel? What physical strength were you aware of at the time? What perspective were you taking toward the person who offended you? Were you imagining yourself small and helpless in the face of an overwhelming adversary? Did you attribute greater power or importance to this person than they deserved? These are the earmarks of what we will call a Child Position, to distinguish it from the experience of being an actual child.

What you have just experienced is the living, breathing example of the feelings and thoughts our protagonist illustrated in Chapter 4, "How A Sit Down Strike Becomes a Way of Life."

People have often said to me that in their worst moments, they feel just like a child. We do have that ability, to time-travel, reproducing the feelings and thoughts and ideas, just as if we were back there, six years old again, or 3 or 12. When we do this, it is not just any child's experience we are reenacting. It's as if we become the child we were, back there at home with our parents, reliving the pain and anguish we felt then. The experience can be so vivid that we literally feel small; our arms and legs feel short and weak. Worst of all, our brain becomes paralyzed, or we revert to simplistic self-referential bouts of fear and paranoia. What is going on here?

Neurologically speaking, what we are experiencing is the firing of neurons along the lower brain channels from limbic to reptilian, from emotion to fight or flight, with little reference to the higher, later formed brain processes.

When someone is functioning in this predominantly lower brain configuration, it can be observed in their eyes, and in their facial expression. We are all familiar with the "deer in the headlights" look that signifies a stunned, fearful, childlike stance. Our emotional state can be read in our eyes, literally in the way we focus. The particular way we focus is in turn determined by our internal settings—those brain channels we have described earlier which were created over a lifetime of experiences. Thus, no two people will see the world in exactly the same way. By looking into a person's eyes, it is possible to observe their present emotional state. Gazing deeply into the person's eyes, behind the surface presentation of mood and facial expression, it is possible to grasp the meanings inherent in the backdrop of long-held feelings and attitudes we might call their world-view.

Stress Is In the Eye of the Beholder

The developmental stresses of infancy and childhood affect not only our feeling states, but our visual circuitry as well. Imagine the optic nerve as it develops and grows. In the corpus collosum, the central information superhighway, the optic nerves crisscross to provide processing on each side of the brain for information originating from both eyes. This means that the left brain processes half the visual field of the right eye, and half the visual field of the left eye, and the same on the right. This produces an elegant fail-safe protection for our capacity to see the whole field of vision even if some brain injury or eye problems should prevent optimal processing. In most of us, the system is complete and functioning nicely, providing a Technicolor 3-D experience from early infancy onward. Throughout the years of development, the optic nerve lengthens to accommodate the brain's growth. However, for many of us, our "feel" of the center of operations is still forward, as if our brain were still small.

This sketch gives an approximate picture of the relationship between the child and adult brain.

Notice the distance from the front of the brain, where the infant's eyes would be, to the child center. It is a relatively shorter distance, approximately one-half that of the adult's.

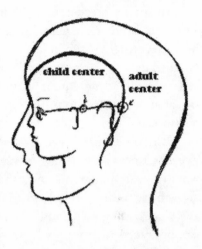

Let's consider the "deer in the headlights" look in terms of these brain pictures. The fear we observe in the person's eyes resembles the eyes of a child, dilated with terror, as if the adult were recreating the brain configuration of a child, with the brain center close behind the eyes. This stance creates a feeling of being up too close, as if one were being bombarded, and everything is larger than life. This is the anxious state that infants and children feel all too often. When adults feel it, it is like a neurological flashback, a reliving of the total experience of being a small and vulnerable child, emotionally, physically, and mentally.

Visual Pathways Record the Tracks of our Tears

Note: The following discussion about visual focus and its relationship to psychological states has not yet been documented scientifically as far as I know. It is the result of my own 35 years of training and practice. What I describe is what I see. I welcome the opportunity to record these phenomena using MRI or other brain scans, but have not yet had the opportunity to systematically do so.

Vision is one of the first senses to fully develop. An infant at twelve weeks has nearly adult capabilities visually, but little of the experience or brain development to understand what she sees. However, life requires that we somehow absorb and record our experience as we go, and vision plays a major part in the recording of those experiences. Think of how many expressions we have that refer to both vision and a psychological state: "I see;" "That's clear;" getting something into perspective; having a vision (plan); being a seer (a wise person); being blind to the truth, and so on.

An infant presented with disturbing events is put in a difficult situation. Many children witness things they would rather not see or hear; nevertheless, the brain lays down memory traces of emotionally charged experiences deep in the nervous system. Imagine the cringing sense of dread an infant would feel repeatedly, looking into cold, threatening eyes of an unresponsive parent. It could make a child not want to see.

Remember the classic technique children use, putting both hands over their eyes and saying "Nanananana" to block out what they don't want to hear? If parents and others do not heed the child's attempt to show he is feeling overwhelmed or distressed, what is the child to do?

We are intimately connected, body and mind. Diseases of all kinds can be traced to emotional stress. We are able to influence our blood pressure, our digestion, our immune systems, and perhaps even the development of Alzheimer's disease with what we do with our minds. Even vision can be compromised by the need to avoid emotional trauma in childhood.

When the stress becomes too overwhelming, the child may learn to monkey with his vision, for his own protection. As part of their instinctive need to survive, some children very cleverly learn to unfocus one eye (usually the right one), or turn one eye outward slightly. This lessens the visual impact when unpleasant emotional content is perceived. Others may learn to use one eye at a time, alternately. This reduces the three-dimensionality of their vision at the necessary times—it becomes difficult to "see the whole picture," literally. The options are many, when it comes to seeing less clearly.

Children have reasons other than family abuse to find ways to not see what is in front of them. The child is presented with befuddling challenges. Most of the cultures on the planet require massive dishonesty in the simplest of social interactions. (Think of the comic possibilities in "Do these jeans make me look fat?" or the late George Carlin's brilliant riffs on our contorted social dealings, or the antics of the crew on Seinfeld.) An innocent child could not help but be overwhelmed by the expectation that he be able to double-think every interaction in order to be liked and accepted. A child is not intellectually equipped to deal with the complexities and sensitivities of the adults they encounter.

As language begins to develop, children naturally say what they see, in a very direct and uncensored way. They have not yet developed the "seven-second delay" that adults have, to edit or monitor what they say for the benefit of their audience. This charming quality leads to situations which adults may find terribly embarrassing, since we have completely bought into the idea that lying is "polite" and therefore necessary. For instance, when he was three, my son sweetly asked our neighbor, "Why are you so fat?" His question came out of curiosity, nothing more. He really wanted to know. Had we not been stuck on the elevator with 6 floors to go, I might have spared him the sudden flash of outrage and indignation she unleashed on him. I was able to later reassure him that it wasn't his fault, but the lesson may have lingered for him, as it did for me. I would handle it differently now, some 45 years later. Rather than sheepishly escaping, I would protect the child rather than the touchy adult. I would hold her accountable for her aggressive actions toward a child, by saying something like, "Why are you so angry when a little child asks a simple question? He didn't mean any harm. Stop frightening him." I cannot have a do-over at this point, but perhaps my experience will resonate with other young parents.

Such upsetting social events are likely to leave a residue of fear in the young child, especially if it confirms what they have already experienced at home. A young child who encounters the accusing attack of a parent saying, "What are you looking at?" will learn to look away. Humiliating criticism for expressing the obvious, like "Daddy's old" will teach him to pretend he doesn't see. Eventually, the child will become less observant as well as less expressive. Incidents like these put the child in an impossible bind: "If I see it, it might come out of my mouth, so I mustn't see it." Children will learn to fear their own vision and the thoughts that follow, especially in an environment where the adults around them have much to hide.

The stop-seeing-stop-thinking command operates below consciousness, like an automated stop-loss order in a trader's stock portfolio. (You can put the order in place, and your investment will be sold automatically whenever its price reaches the specified level, without any further intervention on your part.) When your emotional radar detects a rise in disapproval or anxiety in the other person—the hint that your potential well-being might be in jeopardy—your stop-loss kicks in.

Once we have put these not-seeing-too-clearly patterns in place, we carry them with us into adulthood, long after the survival need to be unclear has passed. By then, it feels as if it is just who we are. This leaves us seriously compromised in our day-to-day functioning, since many of our "spontaneous" reactions are anything but that. We have been programmed by our own experience to respond with fear and caution. We are left with the lingering shadow of long-ago pain which imposes itself, unbidden, into our daily functioning. These unbidden shadows produce a similar effect in all of us: They increase our fear, and reduce our ability to be creative and to love freely.

It is logical that these "stop-loss" blockages would register as physical blockages in our visual equipment, just as emotional memories are stored in the muscles and nerves of our body. Here is an example of the analogous physical blockage, as it was experienced by Laura.

Having suffered for some time with vague body-aches and feelings of malaise, Laura scheduled a deep massage session in hopes of finding some relief, especially for the nagging ache in her left upper arm. With concentrated work, the tension in her arm muscles began to ease. Suddenly she was flooded with memories of her father, a doctor, sternly commanding her to stand still while he abruptly and unceremoniously jammed a hypodermic needle into her upper arm. This was his manner of administering her periodic immunization shots. As the sobs poured forth in the massage room, she realized how betrayed and confused she had felt when her father, generally the more reliable parent, inflicted pain on her without apology or explanation. The entire experience: emotion, meaning, sensation, memory, all were stored in the tissues and nerves of her arm.

The traumatic incidents we see and feel in childhood are stored in an analogous way in the nerve channels of our optic system, and can be released in a similar way. Like massage, we can work out the blockages by soothing and easing the nerve passages through breathing and relaxation practices directed specifically toward the optical channels. The next, and most crucial step, is to literally move the point of focus from the forward child position to the center of our adult brain. Without that important work, you may feel better, but you will still see with the eyes of a child.

The Legacy of Amos Gunsberg

The basic understandings I use in practice were originally developed during the 1950's and 60's by Amos M. Gunsberg, M.A. The original assumption behind Gunsberg's work was this: Since vision is such an important and early brain function and such an important part of our processing of life experience, every trauma which initiates or strengthens a disintegrative or dysfunctional response (neurosis, psychosis, depression, etc.) will be registered in the neural pathways of the visual system. Fortunately, recent research has begun to bear out this general approach, although studies have yet to be conducted to identify specifically visual disruptions, as far as I know.

In his recent book, *The Neuroscience of Psychotherapy*, Louis Cozolino confirms,

> "If everything we experience is represented within neural networks, then psychopathology of all kinds—from the mildest neurotic symptom to the most severe psychosis—must be represented within and among neural networks . . . Children victimized by psychological, physical, and sexual abuse have a greater probability of demonstrating electro-physiological abnormalities in executive regions of the brain vital to neural network integration (Ito et al., 193; Teicher et al., 1997). These studies reflect the central relationship between neural network integration and mental health." (P. 25).

Gunsberg saw the crippling effects of these "electro-physiological abnormalities," (which I prefer to call "glitches") in the characteristic way people tend to process information in their visual circuitry. He worked out a system of exercises which, when combined with coaching-style feedback, directly address the fixed focus which results from living life as if it were still childhood in one's optical circuitry. The next step, learning to focus in the center of one's brain and to stay there as a way of life, allows a dramatic shift to optimal, reality-based vision. The genius in Gunsberg's work was this—the ability to see the problem and offer a solution, by helping the person to literally change their center of operations.

He saw that there was an optimal brain configuration which allows adults to function most effectively, with the brain as a tool of the self, a clearing house where moment-by-moment experience flows into the brain centers through all the sensory systems. To see our present reality clearly, we must allow those channels to flow uninterrupted, and to gather the information in the center of our brain, where we then place meaning on what we see, hear, touch, smell and taste. In the ideal free-flowing arrangement, information will be processed moment-by-moment, unhampered by "electrophysiolgical abnormalities." In practice, this means the observer will be free from antiquated, fear-based interference along the sensory channels. This does not mean we will feel no emotion, but it does mean that the emotions we feel will accurately match the current events.

In the 30 years I spent as his student and apprentice, I practiced Gunsberg's techniques myself, and learned to teach others. These are the basic concepts and methods I have carried on in my own work. I have also learned along the way that this balanced position of operating as the captain of your ship, quietly gathering and processing information just above and behind the center of your brain, also opens you to spiritual connections and to a sense of communion with the natural world. There, in the conduit where reality meets feeling, is a portal to beyond—the connection to our Greater Soul, and access to an expanded awareness that reaches beyond present-day reality. For now, we will concentrate on the practical applications for healing trauma-based visual blocks.

Markers Along the Pathways

It is possible to observe patterns in the way people register infant and childhood pain along visual pathways. Trauma experienced in infancy appears to be registered close behind the eyes, with the accompanying feelings of inchoate despair and confusion. The infant felt but did not understand the pain it experienced at the hands of primary caregivers, brothers and sisters and other close family members. Later trauma creates blockages further back along the optic nerve, as if the lengthening growth of the nerve has determined the location of the fault-line.

Here are a few incidents which were told to me by clients:

A young woman suffers from suffocating fear. Her shadowy memory of the following event has been confirmed by her mother's vague nod. As a 9-month old infant her 4-year-old sister tried to smother her with a pillow. We can imagine the baby in its crib, suffocating, flooded with terror and confusion, overwhelmed by a full-out adrenaline rush, without the option to either fight or flee. As she told the story, her characteristic wide-eyed, childlike gaze became even more baby-like, as if she were experiencing the event as an uncomprehending infant.

As a toddler, a man was pushed down the stairs by his sister. Here, the experience was registered along with a greater sense of knowing the attacker, understanding the danger, and creating a relationship channel in which fear and hatred became the underlying tone. This type of trauma would be registered slightly farther back, with the more differentiated meaning accompanying it, but still with an overwhelming feeling of helplessness and fear. This young man's characteristic gaze was also childlike, but carried with it an emotional tone of bitterness and resentment.

In both cases, the child was truly an unsuspecting victim without any resources to either fight back or escape. It appears to me that later incidents with increasingly differentiated meaning tones are registered further back along the optic nerve line, progressively closer to the center of the brain. As the weight of repeated trauma becomes too much for the child, he seems to become "stuck" at a less than optimal focus point along the optic nerve.

Usually, that sticking point is forward of center, as described above. "Helpers" and "doers" especially are inclined to use a forward position, as they reach out with their eyes to connect with others. This contributes to the off-balance, overwhelmed feelings which often lead to burnout and exhaustion. Some people may focus one eye forward and the other one too far back. Occasionally a person may go too far back with both eyes, creating a faraway and detached feeling, a state of intellectual functioning without feeling.

Fortunately, we can address these childhood-induced brain "glitches" directly by working to open the visual channels, literally pulling our point of focus back, into the center of our adult brain.

I will describe the basic method for identifying and smoothing out the blockages from childhood. The following chapter expands on exercises to do in the process of moving to a centered adult operating position.

Working It Out

Describing the give-and-take of a therapy session is something like trying to capture the action of a tennis match in words. However, I will attempt here to highlight the main points, to give readers a general picture of how the work is done.

Let's pretend we're in an individual session. We sit facing each other directly, looking into each other's eyes. (You might try looking at your eyes in a hand mirror.) Let's begin with the following exercise:

Picture your eyes, working like a film camera. The camera's lens is like the lens of your eye. It brings the picture in, sending it back into the camera (your brain) where it is recorded on the film. Thus, we do not see with our eyes; we see with our brain. The image travels along the optic nerve into the brain where we place meaning on what we see, record, cross-reference and store it.

Now, breathe so you feel yourself breathing, taking the oxygen in, feeling the tingling sensation along the passageways as you breathe. Continue to breathe comfortably and fully. Feel yourself in the center of your brain, pulling the oxygen in to you. Bring it in through your eyes, along the optic nerve and into the center where you experience "I." You are there, safe and sound, inside yourself. Like the pilot in the cockpit, you have instant access to all your senses, memory, reflexes and library of knowledge.

Choose something neutral at eye level to look at. Now, pull back, back, until you feel yourself putting more distance between you and the thing you are looking at. Feel yourself moving back, the way a TV camera moves back on a dolly, allowing a greater field of vision. There, in the center of your brain, you will find a new delight—your "funny bone." (It's not in your elbow. It's in the center of your brain.)

Continue practicing the breathing and pulling back until you feel your center of gravity and the channel of your inner being align, north to south, earth to sky, with you as the channel through which light energy flows. You, in your truest innermost eternal consciousness, are an integral part of the flow of life which goes beyond our usual understanding of time and space. We are an integral part a Universe we cannot imagine with our finite brains. What we do matters, and the energy we put out when we interact with others is an important part of our contribution to that Universe. We do reap what we sow, and what we sow is the sum of all the interactions of our individual and collective lifetimes.

Continue your practice, every day if possible, using this and other exercises in the book until you "drop in" to what some people have called "The Zone." We always see the same response: smiling, laughter, occasionally irrepressible giggles. Here in the center of your brain, everything takes on a slightly amusing cast.

Once there, you reach the astonishing truth: It is impossible to be here, alive and free, and be depressed or anxious. Thoughtful, if necessary, but depressed, never. Here, breathing is fun. Seeing is fun. Feeling is fun. Life is worth living.

"Sometimes when you have scrutinized a face long and persistently, you seem to discover a second face hidden behind the one you see. This is generally an unmistakable sign that this soul harbors an emigrant who has withdrawn from the world in order to watch over secret treasure, and the path for the investigator is indicated by the fact that one face lies beneath the other, as it were, from which he understands that he must attempt to penetrate within if he wishes to discover anything. The face, which ordinarily is the mirror of the soul, here takes on, though it be but for an instant, an ambiguity that resists artistic production. An exceptional eye is needed to see it . . . to follow this infallible index of secret grief."

—Either/Or—Soren Kierkegaard

CHAPTER EIGHT

LEARNING TO BE BLIND

It is our birthright to become the person we were meant to be, living with the highest levels of intelligence, physicality and vision we can reach in this lifetime. Unfortunately, most of us leave childhood in a compromised state, not having developed our greatest potentials. Most of us are operating in a child position most of the time, so acclimated to the feel of it that we barely notice our own developmental retardation, although we find it extremely annoying in others.

The pathway back to wholeness can be a difficult one for those of us who were torn from ourselves at an early age. It takes determination and courage to overcome the dread which resurfaces when we reclaim ourselves. The compromises we made may have literally saved our lives at the time, but they no longer serve us. Instead of living freely, we dedicate our lives to preserving old compensations.

When we became old enough to really "see" what the adults around us were doing, and what it meant for us—usually somewhere between six and ten years old—we no longer wanted to add up the evidence and come to the obvious conclusion: They are crazy and I am doomed! or some variation on that. Instead, we learned to look without seeing, and think without looking.

Now, we are working our way back to a more natural setting—the optimal, centered configuration which is normal for our species, although it may not be the most common one. Our equipment is marvelously designed for seeing and processing reality. We would not have survived as a species if this were not so. A number of recent studies have demonstrated inaccuracy in people's ability to remember and report past events. This has cast doubt on our capacity as humans to record or remember accurately. However, those studies could also demonstrate that our thinking can be skewed by previously grooved-in channels, placing an "unconscious" interpretive slant on what we see. Neurologists call the tried-and-true well-worn channels "attractors." We are literally inclined by neurology to use what we already have.

Here, the goal is to allow the prejudicial emotion-laden attractor channels and optical nerve "glitches" to dissolve, in favor of laser-sharp Telepathic Vision. You will notice that as you increase your visual acuity, your *perspective* will change. Colors become brighter, physical features take on depth and meaning you had not perceived previously, and anxiety melts away. You will begin to see yourself as an integral part of the Universe around you. Trees, rocks, birds and flowers will begin to speak to you in their quietly musical energy-voices. They speak of shared experience, gifts of communion, of love, and of the Spirit which created us all.

This telepathic vision state is very different from the Child Position we have described earlier. Neurologically, it includes the free flow of energy along all the nerve pathways of the body and the brain. The center of the brain becomes the clearing house of incoming information, processing sensory information and emotional responses without static or interference. This does not make us robot-like or less than human. It simply allows our powerful adult human capabilities to operate, full speed ahead. Whatever you try to do in this more creative, resourceful state will be accomplished more effectively. Your efforts will be more focused, your powers of concentration more potent, and your attitude will turn from cautious to "let's go."

It is not an accident that we use the word "perspective" to mean a psychological state which implies objectivity or wisdom, and a visual capacity which recognizes multi—dimensionality, going far beyond the capacity of our five senses. (There are probably five or more we have hardly begun to develop.) Expanded perceptual abilities are available to us as part of the practice of telepathic vision.

I once worked separately with two people who, through a mutual friend, had both been referred to me. They each had worn glasses for many years, and they also happened to use the same ophthalmologist. Several months into their work with me, after they had consistently practiced a full range of the focusing exercises, they each went to their eye doctor to change their prescriptions. They both seemed to be seeing less clearly with their glasses. In the first case, the doctor expressed amazement at seeing an adult patient's eyesight improve so dramatically. The following week, he found it remarkable that his second patient had improved in an equally positive way, but still he found it hard to believe that "psychotherapy" could have any effect on someone's eyesight. Unfortunately, the prejudices encouraged by his medical training (and probably his restricted focus) overrode his curiosity.

It is not our goal here to develop a fixed or all-purpose gaze. Those were the characteristics of the survival-at-the-risk-of-all-else single setting we were forced to adopt in childhood. Laser-sharp concentrated focus would work well for a quarterback or a diamond cutter or a brain surgeon in the operating room, but it would not serve well in the presence of a glorious sunset, or while writing a symphony. The requirements of those activities call for a more open, receptive state, involving greater right brain activity. These are normal orientations in the way we use our complex equipment, just as a photographer can adjust a camera's f-stop, shutter speed and focusing mechanisms to suit varying needs.

In the following section we will identify some of the characteristic ways in which we interfere with our functioning. Next are some exercises to achieve a freer flow.

Losing Sight

Let's look again at the familiar off-center focus—the "deer in the headlights" look. Here, the person (or the deer) is fixed in a fear-induced state, all systems paralyzed. In a deer, it is a normal response to being faced with a speeding object which does not match any familiar phenomenon in the natural world. In a person, it is usually a more habitual style in which there is a block along the optic passageway, close behind the eyes. It suggests a childlike configuration. It often appears this way. Imagine the limpid, innocent baby-eyes of Marilyn Monroe at her most convincingly vulnerable best. Many people find this "look" charming; it tends to elicit the unconscious response of nurturing we would feel toward a small child. Unfortunately, the charm can be short-lived, when others discover the "baby" is frequently as irresponsible and self-absorbed as an actual three-year old.

Paris Hilton made news by giving us an insider's view of what this stance feels like, confessing that she feels she is not very smart, because she is often very forgetful. The sad possibility is that she is probably intelligent, but learned this setting early on to adapt to a difficult and overwhelming environment. Perhaps she has kept it beyond its original usefulness in childhood.

However, humans are resourceful and clever. We can learn to employ a habitual setting to our own advantage. This then becomes a prime reason for keeping an off-center setting. It can be disarming to others. Because they are not seeing clearly themselves, they tend to be taken in by the soft, childlike gaze of the female kitten, or the innocent boy-child, and forget to notice that this person in front of them is not a child but a full-grown adult, with adult capabilities and intelligence.

There is another common setting we often see in people whose families tend to be aggressive and overpowering. It is the "back off" stance. Here the person uses their eyes primarily to send a threatening message rather than seeing. The message takes the form of a warning, sent with every glance, that others must not get too close or take advantage. This is the visual version of "the best defense is a good offense." Because they are sending rather than receiving, their eyes have the quality of being opaque and unfathomable. This stance would certainly make the person feel safer, but it interferes with the ability to bring in information. In reality, it would have the opposite effect, leaving them vulnerable to the very things they are trying to fend off.

A third common technique is to simply take one eye out of the action. This is often, but not always, the right eye. It generally appears that the dominant left-eye arrangement supports a predominantly intellectual, detail-oriented stance. In most people, the right eye is more intimately connected with abstract reasoning, spatial relations, creative thinking, and direct processing of emotional experience.

Using one eye at a time allows the person to separate intuition from intellectual concepts, abstract thinking from logic. It permits them to look right at something without "seeing" the underlying meaning, and to feel strong emotional states without firm grounding in present-day reality. This creates a habitual sense that "the right hand doesn't know what the left is doing." They live in a constant state where they may find themselves saying, "My heart wants one thing, but my head says the opposite." It is by definition an unsettling state, one which would only be established in the face of horrifying contradictions. It would be perpetuated out of fear of *actually seeing*, once and for all, what those contradictions were. (Daddy is not my boyfriend. Mommy wishes I would disappear.)

In some cases, the child who simply stops using one eye might be diagnosed with "lazy eye" syndrome, but often it goes unnoticed. The following exercises will help to bring eyes and brain into synchrony.

Exercises for Clearing the Channels

Keep in mind that our goal is to accomplish two things:

1) Clear the visual channels to provide optimal focusing and processing, and
2) Rework neurological channels in the brain which carry emotionally charged information to its action-conclusion. This requires redirecting our responses away from the more primitive downward channel (the fight or flight response). Instead, we move to the balanced central clearinghouse position where we have access to creativity, higher level reasoning and spiritual connection as a basis for action.

To accomplish these changes, it is important to remember that old pathways were laid down over years, and through many repetitions. We cannot expect to rework them completely with one try, or one weekend. The work we do here is designed to lay down new pathways. It will be your part of the work to "groove" them in, through practice, until the new channels take on greater familiarity than the old ones did.

We now know through recent brain scan research that new skills go through a common development in the brain. First, your cerebral cortex engages the task. For instance: I serve this tennis ball by standing just so, holding my racket this way, aiming the ball carefully while calculating how high to throw it, how fast to bring the racket around, and so on. As the skill becomes familiar through many repetitions, the brain eventually moves the knowledge to a lower and more permanent place. Then, all at once, you know how to do it in a different, more familiar way. As they say, it's like riding a bicycle—you never forget.

Here, we are dealing not only with a new skill, but also with undoing old ones. The good news from the brain scan studies is that our brain is malleable. When the new skill takes predominance, the old channels literally melt away, as the previously dedicated neurons gravitate to provide more "fire power" to the new channels. However, along the way you may be faced with the neurological version of resistance. Attractor channels stand ready, luring you back to old patterns. You will need to "put your foot down" in your brain. Refuse to use the old channels. Hold out for something better. Be resolute, and your brain will follow.

As you read the following exercise, practice it as you go. Take as much time with each section as you need. Once you have learned it well, do it every time you brush your teeth, walk out your front door, climb a stairway, take an elevator, or go into a bathroom. It is meant to be done often, until it becomes your familiar setting—the one you think of as *you*.

Begin with breathing. Breathe into the center of your brain, feeling the tingling and awakening all through your brain. Send the oxygen downward into your heart and then to your whole body. Create a sense of plenty—plenty of space in your brain, plenty of oxygen to nourish and sustain every cell in your body. Do it until you feel your body and brain humming.

Keeping your eyes open, focus on a neutral object at eye level. Let go of your eyeballs. Allow them to rest comfortably, while you move your point of activity back, into the center of your brain where you have instantaneous access to all your functions: reflexes, memory, creativity, senses. You are safe, breathing deeply, surrounded by your own intelligence. As you look at the object across the room from you, be aware that as you move your point of focus back along your optic nerve, you will feel you are literally moving back, creating more breathing room between you and the object you are looking at.

As you continue, feel the oxygen easing and soothing your whole brain. Allow your brain to ease, starting at your forehead. Smooth and relax your face muscles, easing the area between and above your eyes, where your third eye is waiting to open to the truths of the Universe. There in the center of our prefrontal cortex, we can channel the wisdom of our ancestors and connect with our Greater Soul, which carries with it the accumulated wisdom of our eternal existence, and which evolves and grows as a result of our present experience here on Planet Earth. We are the sum of our body, brain, heart, our bodysoul and our Greater Soul. Our bodysoul, the one who experiences this lifetime in this body, operates like a Walkie-Talkie radio to our Greater Soul if we are open to it. So, open your channels, peel your ears, and pay attention. Your Greater Soul is dying to have a conversation with you.

Let go of your brain, letting it rest comfortably on the base of your skull. Your brain will take care of you. Your heart will continue beating, the blood circulating, the food digesting, and so forth. Should you wish to vary your breathing, or calm your heart rate, you only need to provide the directions to set your "computer" in action. The same with your eyes. You only need to aim them. Your equipment will do the rest, bringing in the pictures, developing them, taking the information back into your brain where you cross-reference, classify and store the information. Once you do that, the information is yours, a part of your unique storehouse of information.

Examine in detail the physical object you are looking at. Notice that you do not take in the object itself. You are creating a replica, for your own use. The object remains where it was, outside you. You are acknowledging the comforting truth: "I'm in here. Everything else is out there." The goal is to achieve a levelheaded, straight-ahead, calmly appraising gaze, without judgment or opinion. The object you look at does not care whether you like it or not. It is what it is.

For people who suspect they may have created a lazy eye habit, and for anyone who wants to ensure accurate five-dimensional focusing, here is an additional exercise. Cover one eye, do the breathing and centering exercises as you did above for five minutes or more. Then open that eye gently and notice any differences in the combined effect. Repeat the exercise with each eye, gradually bringing both eyes into synchrony. It may take some consistent practice to bring both eyes to equal strength. Like any physical exercise, the muscles will need to adapt.

As we work to feel our way along those pathways, cooling and healing the blockages, we can see the progressively stronger convictions which accompany "sore spots" along the optic nerve: philosophy of life and identity conclusions which linger, literally lodged in our neurology, profoundly influencing the way we "see" life and our part in it. In this way, we see/feel/think conclusions like "I'll never be enough," or "I'm defective," or "Life is a hopeless struggle," based entirely on the way we have been treated, and even more importantly, the way other people looked at us.

As you learn to move your point of focus to an optimal configuration, these convictions are gradually revealed, and can be resolved in the therapy process. In this way, we move back and forth from practicing new ways of functioning to resolving the old reasons for not seeing clearly. This is necessary because although many people are able to readjust to a more adult, optimal setting initially, it can be difficult to maintain. The tendency is to revert to the old tried and true arrangement regardless of how dysfunctional it might be. However, practice and determination can result in a new neurological setting, and with it, a new way of seeing the world, literally and figuratively.

I have produced a companion CD to assist you in practicing these exercises. With it, you can create the optimal calm state in your brain which will help you to feel more centered, solid and stable, preparing you for higher levels of clarity and accuracy. At the same time, you will experience yourself becoming friendlier, more loving, more understanding, and less tolerant of destructive behavior. Yes, I said less tolerant. The clearer you become, the less likely you are to agree with, or even be interested in another person's melodrama. However, having developed a friendlier basic stance, you will find the shenanigans of others more amusing and less irritating than previously. Forgiveness comes more easily, and you will find you no longer need to take everything quite so personally.

It is crucial that you follow through with these practices. Action is the tool which solidifies and grooves in your new settings. Go out and do something to express your friendliness. Spend a day in the forest without uttering a word. Indulge in helping others to accomplish their goals, whatever they may be. Revel in the sense of community and belonging that comes with reaching out. Even if you're not feeling it yet, do it anyway. Act as if you really like helping others, and the change will follow.

Contagious Consciousness

In doing this work as a route to deeper spiritual experience, I have come to appreciate that without a firm grounding in our physical bodies, at peace with our material existence, we will not find abundance, and we cannot soar.

Spiritual growth, we are often told, requires faith, but many religions presume that faith means placing your trust and unquestioning loyalty in the hands of another person—the leader of the church, or the head of a religion. Here, I use the word spirituality to mean faith that there is meaning in the Universe, even though it is mysterious and beyond our understanding. Faith that there is a Higher Power behind these mysterious workings, and faith that the Universal flow moves toward love and creativity. We are all a part of that flow, growing and evolving together toward a kind of unity that most of us can only dimly sense.

Quantum physicists suggest that we do communicate with the world around us in mysterious ways, through the transmission of our thoughts and feelings, and that we in turn are affected by the human consciousness around us. Experiments in consciousness have revealed powerful interactions between people and plants, people and animals, machines and animals, and planetary effects of mass consciousness.[8] The world of science is changing to encompass the mysterious forces which have been invisible to us, except through intuition and faith. As far as I know, the exact medium of transmission of psychic information has yet to be explicitly identified and named. For our purposes, I will refer to it by the colloquial term for nonverbal electromagnetic transmission: "vibes."

We are a part of the electromagnetic field, as unaware of it as a fish moving through water. Nevertheless, we are profoundly affected by the quality of human consciousness around us. The effect on children is so powerful that many of us come out of childhood with the feeling that we are merged with our parents, connected by an umbilical cord or energy field which envelops and overwhelms us,

---

[8] To explore these concepts, I refer readers to the work of the International Consciousness Research Labs (ICRL), The International Organization for Noetic Studies (IONS), which was established by astronaut Edgar Mitchell; studies by Rupert Sheldrake; the work of Cleve Backster, which has been described in *The Secret Life of Plants*; Gary Zukov's *The Dancing Wu Li Masters*, and Machaelle Small Wright's *Co-Creative Science*. Follow the trail from these sources to a wealth of information from dedicated researchers who make fundamental connections between science and spirituality.

In this configuration, like the Hurt Child in the first poem, we can feel imprisoned, overwhelmed by the suffocating feeling that we are not in charge of ourselves. We feel we are somehow the sum of the experiences we had as children, rather than an individual in command of our own thoughts and feelings. People often say things like "I hear my mother's voice coming out of my mouth—and I swore to myself I would never be like her!"

What We're Up Against

From birth to about two years old, we are completely immersed in the culture that is our own family. During those years, we absorb and digest the emotional atmosphere, value systems and attitudes that are the outward expression of our parents' thinking. This occurs long before we have the language to agree or object to the ideas they express with every look, every shrug, every smile or eye blink or frown. It also occurs before we have the conscious experience of an "I."

Between two and six, we develop the language to express what we have learned, those lessons which were laid down in the tracks which in turn became the earliest foundation for our view of the world and our place in it. Listen to any group of three—or four-year-olds playing house. You will hear a vivid rendition of their parents' attitudes toward work, neatness, food, fun, the power hierarchy in the family and more. From 6 to 18 or 20 we then learn the more complex language of relationships with which we can rationalize, explain, defend or argue against the thinking we now assume to be just *what is*. Our thinking—our attitudes and beliefs—are the inevitable outgrowth of our earliest experience.

In your mind, you are your parents. In your heart and in your soulbody, you are your self.

Absorbing the mother's electromagnetic energy and therefore her *thinking*, came with the milk, and with endless hours of close contact throughout a long childhood. A similar process occurs with other family members. The work we are doing here will not change that fact—it was what it was—but will allow a reversal of the original process, in which your own electromagnetic state of being was swamped and overtaken by another's. In clearing the channels, you restore your self and your own ability to perceive and adapt to reality—you become your own CEO. A computer analogy works well here. It is as if we are removing the old software program from our operating system, storing it as an old file, inactive but available in memory. Our own newly-updated operating system, driven by our own heart, soul, and life energy, becomes the primary one. This operating system, unique to our own equipment and life experience, can be updated as we evolve and learn, unlike the old adopted one which was set and unchanging. Like any belief system we might take on whole, parent-inspired attitudes are immutable because they were never a part of our fluid experience-driven intelligence. As with an antiquated computer system, updating can be a great relief.

The adult state feels like a very different brain configuration from the child one, using the highest levels of prefrontal cortex (the "third eye" area of the brain). In this state, which people often experience in meditation, the connections from brain to heart to soul to Spirit and back again flow directly. This subdues and bypasses the anxious brain chatter which can start an adrenaline freak out. It is the state we are working toward in all our waking hours as well. Here, unlike childhood, our adult free will requires us to make our own choices, moment by moment, and the choices we make matter. This is not "being responsible" as we generally define it. It is a deeper internal sense of our own place in the greater whole, and what will fulfill us. However small our speck of life may be in the Universal scheme of things, we matter, and so does everyone else. Our actions have an impact on others, and theirs on many others.

At ease, in the center of your brain, anchored in your heart, you can look at other people—even the ones you had decided were your enemies—from a relatively dispassionate point of view, with a certain amount of compassion for the fact that they too have probably traveled a difficult path, and may be struggling with the same kinds of emotional injuries as you are.

The process of "seeing" is a largely intuitive, heart and soul-centered way of looking at another person, without judgment or analysis. It requires the seer to assume a neutral, observing stance, without ego—or self-involvement. We look deeply, not to use the information in any way, (unless we are specifically asked to do so) but simply to be with the other person in a moment of acceptance, recognition, and acknowledgement of shared human experience.

SPARKLE PLENTY

I am a live wire, always on,
Radiating sparks.
The center of all eyes,
The short and the tall guys,
They all flock to hear me,
They love to be near me,
They all want to draw on my power.

So witty
So charming
They say I'm disarming,
And always the maven of fun.
So let them admire me,
Wine, dine and desire me,
I just love to flirt with them, Hon'.

I love dressing up in my heels and my mini
The clubs call my cell to invite me.
So pour the Chablis and come dance with me
We'll just have to ignore all the clamor.
Paparazzi, you know, I'm their favorite show
I'm enthralled with myself
And the glamour.

GLUTTON

I savor the flavor of well-marbled fat
A fine red to go with it, Ah, heavenly that,
A courtesan fine with which to dine,
I smack my lips at the sight of her hips.

I'm a connoisseur of the female arts,
And after the meal we'll have one of their ports,
And some chocolates to go with the strawberry tarts.
I'm a pleasure-giver, a whipped cream survivor,
Now let's see how you tittle my diddly diver.

Ah, the pleasures abound when I'm out on the town,
The friends gather near when I buy rounds of beer.
Oops that's my last hundred, let's call it a day,
Come home with me Sweets, for a roll in the hay.

I'm a hedonist true, and I'll do right by you,
Ha, ha, what a lark . . . take my keys—it's too dark,
We're a little bit tipsy, it must be the drinks,
Jus' help me to bed, dear, we'll catch a few winks,
Then I'll take you to breffas' and buy you that dress
That you saw in the window, now jus' lemme rest.

Yes, slip off my watch if it catches your hair,
You're a schweetheart, dear girl, put my coat on the chair.
There's a robe on the door an' the baffroom's jus there
I'll wait for you here till you come back
Now . . . . . where???

CHAPTER NINE

WHAT YOU SEE IS NOT WHAT YOU GET

As you begin to observe and modify your own visual settings, you will become more aware of the record of life experiences you can see in the eyes of others. Be daring. As an adult, you will no longer be admonished for looking, or devastated by the truth of what you see. First, a small warning. Be prepared to observe a preponderance of people who show deep levels of fear, sadness, or thinly veiled rage: the recorded history of trauma, pain and disappointment they "wear" in their nervous systems, mostly from childhood struggles. If you are willing, when you look into the mirror, you will see it in yourself.

There are at least three levels of functioning we can observe in the way a person uses their visual equipment. They are:

1) The surface presentation (the face they want you to see);
2) The person's conscious attitudes and feelings about their presentation and the effect it is having on you, and
3) Where they're coming from (their fundamental sense of their place in the world, including their spiritual connections).

When you are operating optimally, looking from the center of your own brain into the center of the other person's brain, you will begin to see these subtle variations. Experience and knowing what to look for will increase your skill. Having nothing to hide also helps.

The Mask

The Mask is the surface presentation, including the facial expression, which the person wants you to see. Let's use the example of a hypothetical person we will call Abbie. Abbie is smiling, saying something friendly. However, if you look into her eyes you will see a different emotional tone. Her eyes are unfocused, blank, as if she is preoccupied with some inner concern. She is not ignoring you; this is her usual "setting." The discrepancy between her facial expression and her visual setting tells us that Abbie is uncomfortable showing her authentic self to the world. This does not necessarily mean Abbie is a liar or a bad person, although she might be less than honest if she feels threatened. It does mean that she has learned by experience to be afraid of people, and to hide her true feelings behind a false self. Abbie's preferred mask is one of friendliness ("See, I'm harmless"), but it could be one of worry ("Look, I care.") or even a snarl ("Back off, Buster, I'm dangerous.").

Contrary to popular belief, a person's true character does not necessarily show on their faces, at least not when they're aware of being observed. We are not as simple as that. What reliably shows on a person's face is the mask they have consciously practiced since childhood. This was illustrated for me in an unexpected moment with my 2 ½ year old grandson. I walked into the bathroom to help with teeth-brushing to find him, barely tall enough on his little stool to see the mirror, practicing "making faces." The effect was something between an evil glare and a grimace. In as nonchalant a tone as I could muster, I asked what he was doing. He said, "Mean face." Fortunately, this was a passing fancy. He has grown into a pleasant, flexible expression with which he faces the world.

Presumably, we have plenty of chances throughout childhood to decide what will become our favored mask. The events of life, the level of stress it brings, and the family's preference for particular types of masks—or none at all—will determine our final choice.

Unless you catch a person completely unaware, in a rare and truly unguarded moment, what you see is what they want you to see. To determine what lies behind the mask we must look into the person's eyes.

The Person Behind the Curtain

Like the Wizard of Oz, we are aware of our presentation and the effect it has on others. A mask is a deliberate deception. Also like the Wizard, it might have begun as a way of helping the world to feel less afraid, less incompetent, less threatened by them. For a child, the world is defined by parents, and many parents cannot be objective enough about their children to resist comparing themselves at the same age. This cannot result in anything good. We are each different, with different abilities and advantages or disadvantages. Nevertheless, many parents cannot help but constantly compare themselves to their children, feeling envy for the Twenty-first Century luxuries that make life easier for their children than it was for them. A child senses this jealousy, and the inadequate feelings it reveals. No child wants to shine at the cost of making a parent feel inadequate. Children use their telepathic skills to "sniff the breeze," monitoring parents moods and adapting to their needs. At the same time, the child uses her limited reasoning powers to figure out what will work to appease or comfort the parent, as well as what might (hopefully) work to get the nurturing and care the child needs for herself.

Many of us learn to be a "self" through this arduous process of reasoning, calculating, and gauging what will work in our particular environment, rather than exploring and practicing our unique abilities and talents, then expressing them spontaneously. In our American culture where climbing the economic ladder is indiscriminately prescribed as "success," individual exploration has been left mostly to chance. We have been asked instead to shape ourselves to fit into the demands of the hierarchical structures which awaited us:

Find a job, especially one that will provide large amounts of money and "security," then fit yourself into it, or prepare from early childhood to take over the family business.

Join a church, and adopt all the dogma and explanations it teaches, whether it makes sense to you or not, so that you may be seen as acceptably "religious."

Give up your dancing (music, painting, etc.) to produce and care for children, because your parents need grandchildren to play with and progeny to carry on the family name.

136

These are some of the conditions which effectively demand a chasm in our being, a divide deep and invisible enough for us to go on living without being overwhelmed by regrets or resentment when we give up our dreams.

In his book, *The Neuroscience of Psychotherapy*, Louis Cozolino has described this process as left-brain reasoning faculties taking precedence and control over right-brain processes. This does not allow expression of authentic feeling, intuition and the acknowledgment of one's own needs. Further, it creates an unconscious division within the neurological channels of the brain, which are then layered over with conscious justifications and rationalizations.

In lay terms, as we practice the not-seeing/not-knowing strategies which are required of us in childhood, we create the structures in our brains to accommodate these needs. One experience at a time, we lay down the tracks for keeping it secret from ourselves that we have just pretended we don't know something. Thus, we perform the psychological gymnastics which requires forgetting, and then forgetting that we have forgotten.

Volumes have been written in the field of psychology about the troublesome division between true and false self. I believe this is what we are speaking of here. The first two forward layers—the Mask, and The-Man-Behind-the-Mask make up the false self and the conscious effort to present it to the world. The third layer—where we're coming from—is the true self. As it was described in the last chapter, this would be the bodysoul/Greater Soul which the child feels to be his true identity in hiding. It is an effortful adaptation on the child's part to meet the demands of a critical family and culture. It is probably so common as to be the norm in our society. We create the barrier and the conscious justification layered over it to suppress and hide from ourselves and the world what is truly, authentically closest to our hearts. Cozolino and I, among many others, are describing a strategy which probably would be unnecessary in an environment where the child's deepest feelings, needs and aspirations were simply acknowledged and taken in stride by the adults around him.

Self-hatred is the natural accompaniment to pretending to be different from who you actually are. The self-hatred we practice is hatred of what is deeply authentic and creative in ourselves. This hatred has been passed down through generations of parents, in the context of centuries of cultures which mostly denied the existence of either bodysoul or Greater Soul. Given the indomitable human spirit, there are examples of enlightened spiritual leaders in every generation, but our history books are replete with tragic stories of how original thinkers have been met with scorn, resentment and even death for their real contributions to the human endeavor. With this psychological and cultural background, it is little wonder we find ourselves divided against our true nature, and showing it in our behavior toward to world at large.

Thus, the conflict between the child's true self and his world becomes the reason for creating the mask in the first place. Here we will concentrate on the effect of this division on the way we use our eyes, and on what we can observe in others in this regard.

Let's use our example of Abbie to illustrate just one possible example of the difference between the presentation (mask) one shows to the world and the way she truly feels about the world. First, a little biography. Abbie's early life was fraught with strange and dangerous events, which she remembers dimly and without any accompanying feeling. This alone tells us how difficult it must have been, for her to have come out of it in a completely numb state. As she has been able to piece the story together, she now believes her father must have been involved with foreign mobsters in the drug and prostitution business. Incidents of shootings, strange car rides and whispered conversations were familiar. When she was about six, her father suddenly disappeared, and the family was left destitute, in the hands of a drug-addicted and exceedingly irresponsible mother. She was told he was dead, but later found out her father had been taken into a witness protection program. Sexual abuse and possibly child pornography were just a part of what followed for Abbie. A serious illness provided Abbie with one of the high points of her childhood—a hospitalization in which she was ably cared for by kind and sympathetic nurses. Abbie left home at 16, managed to support herself and finish high school, and she later went on to college, married, and started a career. By cultural standards, she was very successful. Unfortunately, she was unable to feel much of anything, and this had begun to seriously affect her relationships.

Abbie's smile is not an expression of something she is feeling. It is the deliberate mask of friendliness she presents to the world. She smiles with her mouth, but not with her eyes. Abbie does not look deeply and confidently into your eyes, welcoming connection. She remains separate and aloof in spite of her smile. If the smile were consistent with an inner state of friendliness, you would see her inner twinkle, sparkling in her eyes. It would be accompanied by warm emanations in your direction, the outward expression of an inner sense of harmony. This is not the case. Her gaze is blank, lifeless and cold. Whoever Abbie really is, she is not visible to anyone. Not only is she blocking others from access to "the window to her soul." She is also blocking information from coming in. It is as if she has a filter in place which stops all but the most basic visual information. This tells us that she is living in a world of her own making, based on what she habitually thinks or imagines rather than what is happening around her. Because of this characteristic stance, Abbie is likely to be "blind" to new ideas or changing conditions in the environment. She relies instead on a familiar "Woman behind the Mask" system of beliefs and reactions which was laid down in childhood, and which has become her default position. She can tell you what this conscious belief system is, and how she applies it. Abbie believes she is utterly consistent in shaping her behavior to fit her belief system, and she is proud of it. She is not aware that her belief system and her mask have little to do with who she is or how she feels. However, the blockage itself tells us that this system was put in place out of fear, even terror. She carries the pain and fear of childhood as electrical patterning in the neurological bodysoul, hidden from view, and mostly hidden even from herself

For Abbie, little has changed since she was a child. Since the block was put in place to hide her feelings—those deepest of intimate bodysoul needs and desires—it has allowed Abbie to go through life without feeling anything directly. Given that this strategy probably saved her life as a child, she would be likely to deny or downplay the ways in which her automatic responses lead her to grave errors of judgment.

Since Abbie's visual configuration is a rigid departure from the optimal state which allows for a free-flow of information, we can imagine the difficulty she has in maintaining it. Short of severe brain damage, one's original potential for clear vision remains dormant, even if it is not fully in use. Therefore, Abbie is vulnerable to being "shaken" from her self-imposed blindness and the mask it covers up. Should this happen in your presence, you might be astonished to witness a moment of intense feeling emanating from Abbie's true self, repressed and suffocated all these years. In stunning contrast to her docile mask, you might see a flash of hot rage, or wanton sexuality, or unseemly greed. Pent-up needs and passions remain under the surface, festering unexpressed. You might think this impossibly uncharacteristic, given the mild-mannered person you are familiar with. If you had paid attention to the clues, you would not be surprised. Her presentation dramatically belies the "look" in her eyes.

Anyone who felt extreme fear in childhood on more than rare occasions probably lived in an environment which provided other serious challenges as well. They are likely to be feeling unsatisfied and hungry to have their most basic needs met. Our Abbie, given the opaque quality of her gaze, presents a living paradox. She wants to exhibit a friendly demeanor, which she learned would get a positive response from the world, but she does not trust or believe that nurturance will be forthcoming. Because of her mistrust, she would be inclined to forego or even reject it when it is offered, maintaining her behind-the-scenes belief that other people are dangerous and untrustworthy, while she is friendly and deserving. While this was true in her childhood, it is no longer the whole story. Abbie grew up, gained in strength and influence, and can now do far more damage to herself and others than she could at age 6, when she first shut down. In doing so, she cut herself off from her own heart-centered internal sources of emotional information which would provide an accurate reading of her present-day emotional environment.

Our internal sources (our know-it-in-our bones inner compass) allow us to develop conscious knowledge about ever-changing reality. Abbie does not have accurate information about the present. She has beliefs. Because she is completely out of touch with her innermost feelings, she must rely on her intellect for all decision making. This is like trying to operate in a vacuum. There is no up or down, no grounding, and no connection to her own heart, body, and intuition (her gut feelings). There are only ideas, words, and justifications. Her feelings, when she has any at all, are a reflection of past events, revisited. This arrangement leaves Abbie vulnerable to aligning herself with anyone whose belief system (their intellectualized moral principles and philosophy of life, based on what their childhood felt like) is similar to her own. If the person or organization espousing these ideas has also captured the feelings of longing, rage and fear Abbie felt, she is likely to align herself with them to feel the sense of belonging she never had in childhood. This is the route people often are following when they end up in a gang or a cult.

Abbie is one of the many unhappy people who is searching for some combination of satisfaction and justification for what she thinks she feels. She is a likely candidate for membership in a highly structured organization which can provide an external substitute for her disconnected internal guidance system, something that can make her feel safe and sure. There are any number of religious and political groups which play into the need for confirmation, justification, and cover. Fundamentalist religious groups who endorse hate and supremacy are in direct contradiction to the teachings of the prophets and leaders they say they follow, like Jesus or Mohammed. These original teachers, and other prophets through the ages, based their primary teachings on ideas of love, acceptance, inclusiveness and compassion, not divisiveness and hatred. Abbie, like millions of others, is missing her Truth-o-meter. She is guided by words and ideas which resonate to the hidden feelings of rage, resentment and fear emanating from her true self—stunted, suffocated and concealed behind the mask of friendliness she works so hard to maintain. If she finds such a philosophical "home," she will likely try to convert others, since she is confident that she is right in her beliefs.

When a person tells you about themselves and their belief systems, take it seriously, but put it in the context of what you see and feel when you look into that person's eyes.

The Fabricated Self

For those of us who are compromised in childhood, it is a matter of survival when we separate from ourselves, create a false mask, then identify with it as if it were who we are. This is the process described in Chapter Four which leads to the psychological Sit-Down Strike. It progressively deepens the abyss between our true selves (our bodysoul) and the mask we present to the world. As the years go by, we become increasingly attached to the precious creation which is our fabricated "self," until it becomes a source of pride and ego. We learned to turn against our true natures early. We then continue to operate in the world as if revealing true feelings would lead to our demise. We have more than enough reasons to want to keep the arrangement in place, except for one thing. It feels awful. Deep in our heart of hearts, we know we are not being authentic. The innocent spontaneity, passion and curiosity of infancy have given way to depression that lingers like a low-grade infection, leaving us exhausted, pessimistic and lonely, always skirting the borders of despair. The loneliness we feel is the longing to be connected with our own heart and soul, and with something beyond our selves.

Where We're Coming From: The True Self

Any discussion of true selves presents an inherent difficulty. A human being who has built a false self system is equipped with a true self in hiding. This automatically implies a certain amount of disappointment, missed opportunities, stifled needs, resentment and frustration. This is the grumpy, dissatisfied bodysoul we are afraid to show the world after a lifetime of hiding. We fear that, should we drop our mask, we will then live out the rest of our lives as the outwardly unpleasant version of all the negative feelings we have left unexpressed. Of course, then no one will want us around. Fortunately, this is not the case. Psychological fresh air and sunlight begin to heal the beleaguered bodysoul. Once we develop the habit of being truthful about our feelings, we become more skillful in our expressions, and far more aware of others' feelings. The people around you who preferred falseness will fade away, and other more vibrant and welcoming friends will come forward. Of course this transition is not necessarily a smooth one, but I have never seen it bring the lonely wasteland of rejection most people anticipate.

We have very few models of people who have developed their true selves without the scaffolding of false masks and roadblocks around it. Let's look at what a true self might look like when the person has not been forced to dissemble or hide. Let's start with what we can see. We'll call them the True family. Steve and Ellen, the parents, are good-humored and tolerant. Close friends know them as generous, kind and ready to help whenever needed. They have an easy affection for each other and their children. They express their warm feelings for one another with small gestures, smiles, and friendly jokes. There are few squabbles or disagreements among family members, but when there are, they are settled with kindness and a full hearing in the forum of the family group. Grandparents, aunts and uncles are an important part of the family's life. Weddings, anniversaries, and holidays are celebrated together with great hilarity and fun, while continuing the respected traditions of the past.

The parents are hardworking and competent at their work, but are uninterested in cutthroat competition or any project which would bring honor or fame only to them as individuals. Their preference is to include others, and to share in the pleasure of cooperative work and play. Steve is a musician, and Ellen has a talent for bringing out the best in people, and has worked as a nurse and midwife. They admire and respect one another, and support each other's endeavors as a matter of course.

The True children are known at school and in the neighborhood as well-rounded, curious, and very respectful of others. They are talented in the arts as well as mathematics and science. They enjoy their friends as much as they enjoy spending time with the family, but they do not belong to any clique or exclusive group. The family works together to accomplish day-to-day chores and household responsibilities. The children are expected to contribute to the well-being of the family in every way they can, according to their age and abilities. They tend to spend their free time involved in community projects and charitable work. The entire True family is known for their spontaneous generosity and their willingness to help others. It is their way of life.

If you think that these are impossible people, I refer you to Inge Bolin's intimate descriptions of the Chillihuani people of the high Andes. The people she met there during long visits to their village tend to fit the description of the Trues, above. Her depictions of the gentle childrearing practices in the remote villages above 18,000 feet stand in stark contrast to the methods we are familiar with. From the time they can walk and talk, children are incorporated into the working life of the family, appreciated and praised for their age-appropriate competence at every level. By seven or eight, children have the vital job of herding the family animals. They take them to the high pastures to feed during the day, and bring them back in the evening. Their bravery is appreciated and respected by their elders, so the children show no reluctance to do their difficult tasks willingly.

By adolescence (which is not seen as a separate age group), they are fully involved in the functioning of the social life of the village, and are given many important responsibilities. Among these is helping to arrange and oversee the festivals and celebrations which are so important to village life. When these children make the long trek to attend school down the mountain, they generally excel in subjects like mathematics and science. Since the children are generously but appropriately praised and accepted by the adults, there is little need for negative commands or punishments. They simply do what is needed, as their parents do. Self-esteem is not an issue, because children know they are valuable and worthy.

These indigenous people have been overlooked because of the remoteness of their villages. They lack of material wealth by which we tend to exclusively measure success. Nevertheless, these descendants of the Incas have preserved their remarkable way of life, probably for thousands of years, without the aid of modern technologies of any kind. They are an enduring example of excellent child-rearing techniques which result in well-integrated, cheerfully cooperative children and adolescents who demonstrate remarkable skill, creativity and bravery in their execution of important family work and community service. Here, the focus is on good work joyfully performed, combined with a strong spiritual foundation of respect for all life. Unconditional acceptance of children and each other has produced whole communities of generous, cooperative people. They seem to have no need for deception or artifice. Apparently, it is possible to create a culture in which True is the norm.

To be a True, we Westerners need to modify our internal relationship with ourselves and our communities. We must retrain ourselves to consider the greater good, not simply what benefits us individually. Those impulses toward caring for others remain deep in our hearts and souls, dormant but not gone. Rather than put our intellect in charge of all actions and decisions, we must put heart first, body second, and mind as the distant third. In this arrangement, brain is only the tool by which we accomplish what our hearts inspire us to do (how to order the materials to build the school, or where to get the brushes and paint for creating your painting).

This is a radical shift from thinking about thinking, thinking about acting, and thinking about feeling which most of us have settled into as a way of life. We have even convinced ourselves that thinking is action. Ironically, this leaves us paralyzed, trapped behind our masks, thinking about how to maintain our effortful deceit, calculating and controlling our every move, and analyzing our every thought.

Seeing the Mask in Others

In observing others, we are looking for the story behind the story. You will need to use your powers of intuition along with assessing the individual's visual focusing. Experience will help you to identify where along the optic passageway the individual seems to be "stuck." The farther back toward the center, the more adept the individual will be in their intellectual explanations and interpersonal manipulations. The key is in "taking the temperature" of the person you are looking into, without being swept up into old relationship patterns from your own childhood. We can read the quality of emotional warmth or coldness better if we take into account not just the "vibe" the person puts out, but the simultaneous signals which show openness or not in the person's visual workings.

Some time ago, I met a man who was reputedly known for his great personal warmth and helpfulness; however I found the encounter chilling. Deep inside his eyes was a fixed focus which seemed to be cold and rigidly unchanging, regardless of the emotional tone or activities going on around him. He remained blandly smiling, the perfectly approving guru, regardless of the context, as if absolute friendliness alone were the mark of spiritual enlightenment. I refer to this presentation as deceptive because it is simply impossible, and patently inappropriate for any human being to be constantly friendly and smiling, no matter who crosses their path, or what happens in their presence. Sometimes, after all, it is appropriate to "throw the money changers out of the temple." He probably congratulates himself for being kind and magnanimous, but his friendliness is an eerie mask.

We cannot know the details of what is behind a mask, but we can know that the motivations behind it are based in self—and ego-protection, rather than genuine kindness or compassion. Like Abbie, he is disconnected from his heart, living in his overworked left brain. A mask which is fixed and unchanging in this way is a product of the "Man Behind the Mask:" calculated, artfully arranged, and disconnected from authentic feeling responses to the present.

Louis Cozolino describes it this way:

> "Our hidden layers present to us a picture of the world with an agenda based on what worked in the past . . . They highlight some aspects of experience while diminishing others, direct us to orient to certain aspects of the environment, and completely block awareness of others. By definition, the hidden layers are never directly seen. They are like black holes, known only by the effects of their gravity on other celestial bodies." (p. 161-162)

These hidden layers are the neurological connections which were laid down in the first years of life, based primarily on the quality of interaction with our parents, eye to eye, heart to heart, brain to brain. They in turn passed on their own unconscious feelings and attitudes about connection, trust, and life itself. Most of us do not question our basic wiring, since it has been so long with us, but we could. We can use the power of our hearts and our conscious mind to uncover the secrets we have been hiding, even from ourselves. Some of those secrets will be about other people and what *they* are hiding.

A True Self Unbound

If the child is especially lucky, he may experience a family member or a kindly mentor who will encourage his need to grow and expand, especially in the areas of art, music, and original thought. Many of us have experienced the thrill of creating something beautiful, something wonderful which flows directly from our hearts, in the form of a gift presented to the world in sound, movement, poetry or art. The exhilaration and fulfillment in that act of creation resonates in our innermost being, and our soul shouts, "Yes!" Then, as the moment of ecstatic fulfillment passes, we become aware of the response from others. Was it applause—a resonating "Yes!" from the world? Or was it a bland "Nice, but you'll never make a living at it." Worse yet, "What are you, some kind of nerd?" Or perhaps, "Why don't you just give that up and get a real job?"

In our current American culture, the creative, right-brain activities which develop our strengths in abstract thought and original thinking are considered "extracurricular," as if building a uniquely creative self were a luxury. We can do better. We need to understand the difference between training a drone and developing an original, creative leader. What is more important, we must find it in ourselves to be generous enough to stop applying the cruel and inhumane methods we were taught. We must turn to our hearts for relief. With a compassionate heart, take your poor aching self under your wing, like a small child who remains there in your heart. Breathe Light, and heal.

Chapter Ten

CLAIMING YOUR BODY, PUTTING DOWN ROOTS

We are fundamentally psychosomatic beings. We experience psychological pain the same way we experience physical pain—in our bodies. We have direct nerve connections from our emotional brain centers to our hearts—and to every organ and cell in our bodies. A disappointment in love leaves us feeling "brokenhearted," "sick at heart," or "with a heavy heart." Our appetites are affected, our digestive systems falter, sleep patterns are disrupted, and our immune systems are compromised when we suffer a severe emotional blow.

In childhood, we feel our emotional states in our bodies without the full understanding that these physical symptoms are an accurate response to the environment. Few children are lucky enough to have parents who confirm this by acknowledging, "Yes, Son, your stomach aches because your friend Johnny is moving away and you miss him," or "Yes, dear, your head hurts because you're angry," or. "Of course you feel like crying when your brother makes fun of you. He was wrong." Instead, many parents respond in one of two ways:

1) They run for the medicine cabinet, or
2) They tell the child that they shouldn't feel the way they do, with some kind of admonishment like "Stop acting like a baby," or "You're just looking for attention."

Either way, the child feels sick and defective. The logical response for a child in this predicament is to blame his body.

Young children think of their bodies as "Me." They are not yet able to conceive of a fully developed self-identity—seeing themselves as a conscious entity separate from others, with their own volition, thoughts and motives. Until about age 15, children tend to refer to themselves as if their physical bodies were the totality of who they are. This is why physical appearance and physical abilities are so important in the middle years of childhood and beyond. Children whose attributes are outside the current cultural norm, say, severely overweight or clumsy at games, suffer feeling inferior, unacceptable, even if they are not viciously teased. Just being different is difficult enough for children. In the best of circumstances they require reassurance and kind affirmation of their value if they are to make the adaptations necessary to cope with life in their culture.

When the child is burdened with the additional pain of feeling unaccepted by his family, the dilemma becomes unbearable. For instance, it is especially difficult for children who may be overweight because they are trying to find solace in food. Emotional wounds create the hunger, but soothing the pain with overeating creates a secondary problem which then becomes the focus of the child's inner war. This, like other self-destructive compensations, serves to provide a "reason" for the child to feel self-hatred, rather than hating the family who caused their original unhappiness.

There is an evolutionary benefit to this transfer of anger to one's self, of course. It does buy time during which the child can focus all manner of resentment and ill will inward, thereby sparing the older generation and the child's community the uncontrolled rage which would be so dangerous otherwise. The child bears the burden, spending months or years in sullen withdrawal or insolent rebellion until she eventually develops the intellectual capacity to judge that it would not be practical to murder her parents. This transition usually occurs about the time children become old enough to be truly dangerous. Meanwhile, the burden of guilt accrues in her own consciousness; she knows she should not be so ungrateful, so unlikable, so impossibly disrespectful, but she can't help it.

Boys in our Western cultures have the additional burden of surging testosterone, fueling the aggressive inclination to lash out when frustration mounts. With few productive outlets for adolescent energy other than competitive sports, and little opportunity to play a constructive role in the work of the family and community, our children are left to fall back on entertainment and constant interaction with technology rather than people. Few children are lucky enough to have intimate connections with trusted adults who can introduce them to the real experience of being working members of society. Instead, children have become a separate social class from their parents. Even poor parents have children who are overfed, overindulged and idle for long hours every day. The result is a volatile mix which leaves large numbers of young people disconnected, discontented and "spoiled."

To a parent who has just spent ten or twelve hours in a stressful job, this idle state might seem like paradise, but the child himself probably feels frustrated, bored, worthless and ungrateful. The children are ripe for gang membership, criminality, teen promiscuity and other "antisocial" behavior as a way of experiencing some sort of initiative or self-expression. These conditions of alienation and loneliness so many of us experience in childhood are inherent in the cultural conditions we unwittingly perpetuate. (See Chapter 16 for more detailed discussion of educational and childrearing practices which contribute to these ills.)

So many good people who are now adults struggling to recover their sanity might have become as terminally antisocial as their more deviant peers, had the conditions been ever so slightly different. Had a kindly neighbor, an interested teacher or a concerned aunt not offered a hand at some crucial point, any number of us might have been driven to the point of "flipping out." Instead, most of us learn to turn our rage inward, and for the most part, keep it focused there.

The obesity epidemic among our young people simply tells us that our children are hungry for real satisfactions and are not getting them. Food is the most available, socially acceptable addiction. Obviously, not all children who are overweight have been abused. Many have "only" suffered the neglect and lack of human contact resulting from spending long days in front of a TV set or computer, or in large groups of their peers without close and loving adult companionship. These children feel empty, dissatisfied, and rudderless. They often become obsessively preoccupied with appearances, making them even more vulnerable to feeling inadequate because they can never have enough belongings, or look good enough to feel whole.

Again, our culture provides abundant distractions. When we are old enough to have the means and procure the substances, addictions offer an option for combining momentary forgetfulness with prolonged self-denigration. Many will graduate to alcohol or drugs or sex when the opportunities arise; the dynamics are the same in each case. All the familiar addictions carry with them a common underlying dynamic—a feeling of disregard, contempt or hatred for the body's basic needs and inherent value.

The Mind/Body War

Whether the path leads through childhood neglect and abuse or urban-variety idleness and boredom, we are raising huge numbers of people who hate their bodies, and have little respect for physicality unless it relates to either sex or food. We begin our school and work lives in a state of war with our own bodies, wearing our self-hatred in a never-ending struggle which may last a lifetime. Our bodies become the focus of blame: the defect in me must be in here somewhere, in the Me I have known since childhood.

At the same time our bodies are becoming Enemy Number One, our minds are being praised, prodded, aggrandized and glorified as the Answer. As we will see in later chapters, education is directed toward training a brain (with little regard for the body it lives in) to fit into a culture where left-brain analysis, opinion, computation and attention to detail are generally seen as the highest level of achievement. Thus begins the dichotomy in which people are being truthful when they say, "My brain says one thing, but my heart says another."

In popular usage, we generally think of "mind" as the collection of thoughts, ideas, and opinions that float through our brain, the thinking faculty we refer to as "I." This ability is often cited as the dubious proof of what separates and elevates us above other creatures—our capacity to think about our own thinking. For our purposes here, I will define this thinking "I" as the human faculty which combines what we have learned and experienced, including our conditioning and emotional experience, with our sense of self (our bodysoul).

Although there are still some who would like to argue that they are capable of pure, rational thought, unaffected in any way by emotion, the field of emotional intelligence and the massive accumulation of brain scan research have fortunately put this argument to rest. It is generally accepted that there is no such thing as "pure" thought separate from emotional experience. Now, it is time to address the second corollary issue: There is no such thing as brain without body, in spite of the way it might feel when you are suffering the results of the inner war between "I" (our thoughts and opinions) and "Me" (the physical body we have been at war with since childhood).

We need to be in harmony with our bodysoul, and by extension with our Greater Soul, as well as our thoughts if we are to find peace of mind in this life. To do this we must take a tolerant view of the complex feelings we carry from childhood, and encourage a more sympathetic attitude toward ourselves. Notice how the "me" (the physical self) you disapprove of as an adult originated with the "me" you unfairly learned to dislike as a child. Only when you are able to love and admire the child you were, can you expect to heal the adult you are now.

Exercises to Heal the Mind/Body Split

Begin with this simple exercise. Make a picture of the child you were. Choose a young age if you can. Place him or her outside yourself, just across the room. Look at that child the way a loving aunt or uncle would, beaming friendly sunshine and acceptance toward the child. Suspend any judgmental or disapproving attitudes you might have previously held toward this child, and allow yourself to be curious. Notice what the child is feeling and thinking. Watch as you would watch a movie, being aware that you are not that child. You are here, in the present, breathing your own air, thinking your own thoughts, as free of the people who disappointed you in childhood as you wish to be. Compared to that child's life, your adult existence is easy. You eat whatever you want, sleep when you want, work at a job you choose, live where you wish, and pick your own friends. This is nothing like the prison that was childhood. As a child, you could not leave. You had no real choices about the important things in your life. Now you do.

First, make certain you are not blaming that child for the predicament he or she was in then, or the one you are in now. The child was not to blame. Children respond as they must to an impossible situation. Do not criticize the child for the feelings he or she displays. Above all, do not condemn the child for being "weak." All children are weak, by definition, and all children are affected by their parents' needs. It is an unfortunate prejudice we tend to hold against ourselves, that we "should have fought back." It is rarely the smartest thing a child might do to risk death or desertion by challenging an unpredictable parent. On the other hand, rebellion might in fact be the child's best strategy, if his mother felt she needed a ticket to sainthood, or his father required a convenient outlet for his violent rages. Perhaps one parent was using the child to humiliate or belittle the other parent. Perhaps peer influences demanded insolence rather than respect. Do not imagine that if you did not fight back it was a character flaw or weakness. Small children might occasionally risk their lives for the sake of a principle; but that is generally the province of adults. So, let your small self off the hook, regardless of what happened back then.

Breathe deeply and comfortably, feeling your present day size: your accurate height, weight, the span of your arms, the size of your hands, the distance from the center of your brain to the soles of your feet. Don't worry about whether you think you're too fat or too thin or too out of shape; those things you can change if you decide to. Instead, simply enjoy being present. Breathe nourishment into every cell, confirming your ownership of this precious present-day body in which you live now. It has carried you all this way, from the small child you see just across the room to the place you are now, at this point on your path, still evolving, still growing.

Now, tell the child the truth. Explain what was going on in the world at the time, what was happening with the parents, why they behaved as they did, and why the child was feeling bad. Reassure the child that it was not fair, and that all children suffer when things aren't fair. When you're a child, you don't know there are other children who are unhappy too. It seems as though everyone else is okay, and you're the only one who's so miserable. It wasn't you. It was just a difficult environment. It would have been difficult for any child.

Let the child feel the relief of knowing: "It's not your fault."

Now you are in the position of being a champion for that child, who is the mirror of your sorely neglected bodysoul which needed to grow and flourish. You can now stand up for what is right for children, and let your child self be a participant in the integrity and character you are developing. As a gesture of respect for your Greater Soul and the bodysoul which is your present day representative here on Earth, ask what he/she wants for you. Have you become the adult you wanted to be? Have you exceeded expectations, or are there still things your

Greater Soul would like for you to accomplish? Remember, everyone benefits from your spiritual growth. You get to take it with you, back to the Greater Soul who awaits your return. Take the time to ponder the long path that has taken you from that young age to the present, with all the unexpected events and the knowledge you have accrued along the way. Picture that timeline stretching into your future, and include your Greater Soul's hopes and dreams in your plans for that future.

Breathe into the center of your brain, and send the oxygen downward, into your bones—into the marrow of your bones. Send the oxygen through every cell, reclaiming and rejoicing in your own territory, your own body. Put down your roots, solid and strong, anchoring yourself in the steady sense of knowing you are here, you are alive, and you are You.

Thank the child/bodysoul for making it possible for you to be here. It was the child's sturdiness and resilience which carried you through, making it possible for you to live through childhood as effectively as you did. You are here now, alive, breathing, and able to go on. Now you make your own choices, thanks to that child, who was perfect just as he or she was. You too are perfect just as you are, and you're learning.

What we do is not the same
As what we say we do.
Or if we did, we won't do it again,
And we didn't really mean to.

If we really knew, and acknowledged we knew,
It would be harder to do it the next time.
Instead we deny between me and I
That we did what we did; we say it's a lie.

Or we did it because, but we don't really know
(or let ourselves know) the because.
Because if we really admitted the cause
Then we'd have to know we did it.

And we don't want to know, not ever, not really,
It's just too hard to be real.
Our ego's at stake; our own high opinion
Of me and the way that I feel.

What we do is not always the same
As we tell ourselves we did.
We may tell ourselves it's the opposite, really,
Innocent, friendly, and blameless.
When in fact it appears,
Through the crocodile tears,
We were angry, mean, and shameless.

We may tell ourselves it is our idea,
We thought it up in our own head.
If it's bad for us, it probably isn't
'Cause that would be truly mad
And we're not insane—not really, not truly,
We just can't admit we've been had.

But who's directing the drama?
And what are we acting then?
If we're honest we'd say at the end of the day
We're producing our parents' play.
In our hearts and souls where the truth be told
We know that the case files are cold.

They were grown before we were born

And they've already sown their seeds,
So why do they need to get into our heads
To prevent us fulfilling our needs?

Do you think it's true that they did it too?
That they gave up their lives
And their will and their minds
To do what their own parents do?

So why not break the chain, my friend
And write your own unique story?
It's only one life, and you have this chance
To go out with your own blaze of glory.

CHAPTER ELEVEN

THE FORKED PATH

"... If one is whole, one will be filled with light, but if one is divided, one will be filled with darkness."
—Gospel of St. Thomas

You will find that once you have made peace with the child/ bodysoul you are, and you have taken him or her under your wing, it will be easier to breathe into the center of your brain, soothing and clearing the optic pathways. You can now nurture and reassure the child that everything turned out alright in spite of the traumas of childhood. Moving back to the center of your brain feels right once you fully acknowledge you are no longer that child.

Compared with children, we are over-qualified for life as adults in the Western world, when you consider our physical strength, our enormous brain power (including intuition), our relatively abundant individual freedoms, and our access to skill training and intellectual resources. We have every ability we could need to create a life filled with richness, excitement and love. People everywhere are awakening to the truth that we have become distracted from real happiness by the single-minded pursuit of material wealth. Once we have enough to live reasonably comfortably—enough food and reliable shelter, and a few necessities like access to the people we love—the rest is irrelevant to our "happiness quotient." The over-the-top joyful life comes when we develop our spiritual connection to our Earth, our fellow creatures, and our Higher Power, however we may define it.

The exercises presented here are intended to help you achieve that spiritual connection, by clearing the neurological pathways which were blocked or constricted by childhood experience. It is the brush with destructiveness and evil which leaves us distracted, unbalanced and sick at heart. Of course, this applies to adulthood as well. You may notice that in clearing away the obstructions, you feel a renewed zeal, an energized commitment to pursuing a path of light and love. This is a wonderful development. I have just one small warning about the use of these precious new energies.

Anyone who has suffered trauma in childhood is presented with a forked path: the choice which leads to destructiveness and darkness, or the path toward creation, light and community. The greater the exposure to darkness (as abuse of power, either psychological or physical) the greater the attraction to the path of destructiveness. Those of us who were inundated with ill will, jealousy and other forms of negativity in childhood become so disoriented that we may be fooled into thinking we have chosen the path of Light when we are supporting or nourishing Ego and darkness.

For instance, let's take the issue of forgiveness. We are taught that to forgive is divine, and that we should love our enemies. This is the hardest of all spiritual teachings for most of us, not only because it requires giving up old anger, but also because it is can be dangerous to our well-being if we take some of the lessons too literally. It is not true that forgiveness requires re-establishing a relationship with someone who abused you. (More about forgiveness in Chapter 30.) This version of the misunderstood concept of forgiveness is a siren song for those who tend to forget that they are valuable too, in their own right, and worthy of protection from harm. This is our first responsibility: to cherish and preserve our own bodysoul and mind so that we can help others as we are called to do so.

Many people refer to the suffering Jesus went through as a reason for continuing the things in their own lives which cause them suffering. Jesus did not give us the example of his death on the cross so that we would needlessly mimic his crucifixion. We have the revealing example of his moral struggle beforehand—his reluctance and anguish, and his decision to offer himself when his arrest seemed inevitable. It would be illogical that all of us be asked to sacrifice in the same way, yet some people feel the irresistible urge to offer themselves up on a cross of their own making. In doing so, they are sacrificing themselves by reconnecting with those who have abused them in childhood and beyond, to no end other than finding themselves re-injured, while the perpetrators continue their abusive ways. It cannot be that those who have suffered at the hands of abusive caretakers should be then condemned to a life of repeated abuse in the name of goodness. We must look more deeply into ourselves and our own intentions.

Many a formerly abused adult may find themselves mysteriously attracted to evildoers of every stripe, even to the extent of becoming romantically involved in spite of their best judgment which tells them to beware. They will usually couch their interest in altruistic terms: they want to help the abuser to lead a better life, to see the light. The results, however, usually belie their intentions. The abuser rarely changes, and the "helper" eventually becomes increasingly disillusioned and bitter, feeling wasted, heartbroken and unappreciated.

The attraction to Darkness is a universally troublesome issue for people, especially as we regain our creative energies by releasing old blockages. It is probably the most common stumbling block, the Achilles' heel of people who wish to dedicate their lives to the goodness they longed for in childhood.

Perhaps we need a clearer definition of what forgiveness and genuine goodness require of us in daily life. Here are some of the observations I have made in thirty years of practice with people who continue to suffer at the hands of abusers even in adulthood. The wounds are mostly self-inflicted, in a roundabout way. Here are the usual conditions:

1) The person we will call the Helper, intent on being generous and giving, usually chooses someone whose mode of operating is similar to their parents', or they may continue the struggle with the parents themselves. Thus, the Helper, intent on proving the power of their own goodness, ignores previous lessons, and chooses to pour their heart energy into someone who is cruel, has a penchant for inflicting pain, and is relentlessly unapologetic. Such a person would generally not be a good candidate for conversion by any normal means, but nevertheless they become the Helper's primary "target."

2) The Abuser has shown no genuine need or intention to change by reaching out to the many sources available in the culture. Sitting in a pew on Sundays, or attending a self-help

seminar or reading a book doesn't count as real change. Those of us who have done it know that change requires sustained self-motivated effort. No one has ever changed for someone else.

3) The Helper pursues the goal of getting the other person to love them and to change with nearly messianic dedication, contrary to logic or reason.

4) The Helper's cries of pain usually include the protest: "I would never do such a thing to another person."

In this miserable scenario the "Helper" is not helping anyone. Perhaps he or she continues to give what she believes the other person needs, or what she feels she wants to give, but she is not serving anyone well. It is a good way to build up a self-satisfying image of goodness, helpfulness and generosity, but that is ego-building, not helping others. Insisting that another person has to change, and you know just what it is they need to change, is supremely controlling and arrogant. (It does help to call it by its most unattractive name, doesn't it? It makes it so much less charming, and less tempting to continue doing it.) More about the problematic giver versus taker issues in Chapter 19, "The Goodness and Mercy Trap."

What Being of Service to Others Really Is

If you want to reach for something greater than yourself, then helping others is a way to do that, but it shouldn't hurt. You have already suffered a lot. Your precious energy should not be wasted. If you are like the "Helper" described above, and the other person feels tormented or annoyed by your help, then it is not help. You are inflicting your own values and needs on them. In the end, this will not be fulfilling to you or to them, even if the whole world agrees with your complaints about of their bad behavior. If you are scrupulously honest with yourself, you will see that you are reenacting the same sort of dark, oppressive, and controlling childhood demands you suffered at the hands of powerful others. They probably also claimed they were doing it "for your own good."

How do we determine whether we are doing something genuinely good and selfless, or we are enthralled by our childhood-induced need to control and manipulate others? The rule of thumb is this: Give the other person what they specifically request, in the form which they request it, without judgment, and without any expectation of reward or recognition.

Let us look at this issue from another angle. In the above scenario, the Helper lacks respect for one God-given principle: the other person's free will. Just as you have the free will to pull yourself out of the destructive and/or violent childhood vortex you were born into, so does anyone else have the right to pursue destructiveness. They are entitled to wallow in it, dedicate their lives to it, and so learn from the consequences of it. Interfering with that process is standing in the way of their learning, and possibly of their own soul development. This mysterious process of soul evolution is beyond our knowing. Once we can accept this, it makes backing away easier. We have no right to interfere, to play out our own ego needs for love and self-justification by insisting on pushing our view of goodness on another person.

We do have the right to express our inherent goodness by giving someone a hand when they ask for it, but repeating the offer over and over after they have shown no effort to "improve" themselves is not helpful to them or to you.

Perhaps this is one of the lessons Jesus, Buddha and other prophets were trying to teach us: Sometimes you just have to resign yourself to the fact that you can't change your enemies (or your friends) by the force of your own personality. Sometimes you just have to trust that they will learn the lessons on their own. The best you can do is to be an example.

The possibility of making our mark, proving our value by changing someone else (or changing the world) is a seductive idea. It emanates from the child brain configuration, when being liked and admired by our parents was a matter of life or death. If they don't like us, they might not feed us or protect us. In that stance, our overriding concern is: "What do they think of me?" Our goal is to shift back into a neutral, appraising stance "How do I feel about them?" This is not unfriendly or judgmental. It is simply the accurate use of our intuitive faculties. Making choices based on our intuition and our heart's desire is our natural, optimally functioning adult state.

Choosing Light

With the picture of your own path stretching out ahead of you, and you moving along it, calmly observe the events and people you come across. See yourself evolving, learning, and rejoicing. As you celebrate your adult intelligence and strength, breathe deeply into the center of your brain and continue with the exercise of putting down your roots in your own bodysoul and into the Earth.

As you feel the pathways in your brain awakening and new channels being formed, do not be alarmed if you feel a momentary headache or dizziness. This is a good sign that you are disconnecting old concepts and prejudices in favor of a new system which embraces equality, creativity, and unquestioning worth—yours and that of every living thing on the planet. Imagine yourself basking in the light of Spirit, showered with the feeling of unconditional love which pours down over your head, into your brain, and throughout your system. Put your hand on the back of your head as you absorb the healing Light. Feel the depth of your brain, and position yourself just above and behind the center, as captain of your own body-ship.

As you breathe in the Light, acknowledge the precious connection you have with your present-day self, and with the body you have been given to experience this journey. Safe and at ease, surrounded by Light, envelope yourself in the loving heart-energy you emanate. It ripples around you like a protective cloak and emanates outward to warm and reassure others. You are safe. Inside your own heart, you go on. In this configuration, you do not "give of yourself." You can give of your energy, your time, your affection, even your money, but you cannot give of yourself, because no one else can use it. They have their own. Respect and cherish that separateness, the basis of each person's free will. At the same time, allow the awareness of our absolute interconnectedness. Each of us—every creature and plant and rock—is a part of the greater whole. Living your life in celebration of Oneness allows you to never feel alone, because you never are.

PART IV.

DANGEROUS LIAISONS

ON LIVING INSTEAD OF ADDICTION

It isn't the alcohol in the end
That will ruin you, it's the lying.
Drugs bring relief when you're hurting again,
Like they say, "He's feeling no pain."

But you've been taught to barter your friends
For a nickel bag of escape,
And escape you must, for there's nothing left
When you've sold your soul down the river.
You follow your craving
And caring be damned
It's the heart that goes first
Not the liver.

You don't want to die because you've not lived
You don't want to live for the dread.
Without your heart, without your soul
You must feel alone
And dead.

But why would I help you, you say,
What's my game?
For me it's a matter of thanks
For I was in your place,
And someone helped me,
To breathe, to stand tall and be free
And these days I joyfully claim the right,
To be whole and to live in the Light

But what do you do, and where do you start
When you've been so removed
From your own human heart?
When you've made it your way
To lie, cheat and betray?
When you turned your back
On your sisters and brothers,
And found yourself
Preying on others?.

You've told yourself you can't stand to care
You deceive and deny your true feelings,
You mustn't soften, you mustn't share
You mustn't dare to be human.

But what about past sins, and weakness, and evil?
Insist that you own it, and grieve,
Or take my hand, and borrow my strength,
While you build up your own
And breathe.

Now wake yourself up, and shake off these lies
You can join in the fun and good cheer.
The human race is running—time flies
But you're still in the game
If you're here.

And what's so bad about living and loving
And finding a way to show it?
You'll never regret the glorious truth:
"I am one of God's souls
And I know it."

CHAPTER TWELVE

THE MOTHER OF ALL ADDICTIONS

Recovery from being the child of a Dark One takes determination. Emotional maneuvers we practiced to protect us from pain become a part of our world view. For instance, a tendency to run away to lick your wounds in private, which might have provided a lifesaving respite in childhood, becomes the basis of a life-style of hiding. All the while, you may consider yourself to be the most available, generous and sociable sort of person, which you may be, except when you're not.

The outward style may vary, but the tendency to fear closeness is a common theme. We justify and explain our own behavior to ourselves as if it were perfectly normal and necessary. Even when it leads to dangerous and self-destructive behaviors like drug or alcohol addiction, we cling to the addiction (the adult version of licking wounds) as if life depended on it. Lost inside our fear, we do not see that the adult addiction is a reenactment of the desperate measures we used as children to save our own sanity by not feeling the pain.

Often, the fear of closeness is submerged beneath even more painful feelings of worthlessness. Victims of predatory parenting frequently describe feeling empty, overwhelmed with self-doubt and despair. This combines with a frazzled, raw-nerve feeling which builds to such intensity that the person cannot stand it. They turn to alcohol or drugs to try to sooth their jangled nerves, or they involve themselves in a high-intensity life filled with long work hours and high stress, or all of the above. Their relationships are filled with conflict and struggle, because they look to their loved ones to soothe their pain, and they can't find it there. They are driven to distraction and sleeplessness by the physical symptoms which return whenever the work is done or the drug wears off.

Voices from the Brink

Anyone who has tried to free themselves from an addiction can recognize the feelings described here. It is a painful, confusing state to feel you are being controlled by a substance or another person. If we fully accept that the addictive behavior is an attempt to soothe the raw, jangled nerves of a person who has suffered profoundly, we will find healing techniques to provide the human nourishment they need so badly. For the addict, intellectual understanding is not enough, and it is not just a matter of will power.

This is a question I have pondered for many years: "What does an addictive relationship really have in common with a drug or alcohol habit?" I have observed that addictions are often exactly like a relationship with an Abuser. They promise comfort and love but end in betrayal, destroying the individual's self-esteem, fostering feelings of self-loathing and shame.

My first inkling about the question came in 1978, while I was working in a minimum-security jail. I interviewed a pathetically sad young woman who had been jailed for heroin use. She was homeless, without family, job or hope. When I asked about her drug use, she said, "Heroin was the nicest thing I ever met. It made me feel normal, like other people feel when they're happy, only I needed heroin to feel it." Soon afterward, I met with a young man whose arms and legs were riddled with the knotted scars of innumerable heroin injections. He told me his mother had introduced him to heroin when he was 15. It was the only thing she had to offer him, because she didn't know how to be a mother. She felt better when she used it, so she gave it to him. He could not imagine how he would be able to give it up, since it made him feel like he was close to her, and it was all he had. To these two sad young people, heroin was relationship and love, however self-destructive that supposed love might be.

When one has an Abusive parent, the element of self-hatred is inevitable. Depending on whether the Abusive parent is the mother or father, there are some differences in the effect it has on children. For many generations we have lived in a culture where the mother has had primary responsibility for the childcare in the family. Until the 70's it was because women stayed home. Today it is because so many divorced or single parents are women. Either way, it is especially damaging when the Abuser is the mother, because the child associates her presence with basic nourishment and care, and because her impact is so pervasive from birth. Since Abusers are frequently very controlling, the Abusive mother might garner even more influence over her children by excluding others, preventing contact with those who might otherwise offer some respite from her oppression. When the father is an Abuser, the child may still receive some genuine warmth from more caring family members, simply because his absences allow it.

In my experience, it is common for an Abusive woman to marry a man who feels inadequate or weak—someone she can manipulate and control. When the roles are reversed, a male Abuser will often marry a woman he can lord it over and control. This imbalance leaves children confused, frustrated, and aware that there is something terribly wrong with the way they feel, and the way their family works. These are the people who frequently find their way to therapy, seeking an explanation for their anxiety, depression, and especially numerous forms of addiction. In these cases, the addiction is generally the pain killer which worked best to subdue the objections of a suffering bodysoul.

The following is a composite narrative drawn from the writings and descriptions of several friends and clients, speaking from their child point of view. Of course, socioeconomic differences and childcare arrangements vary, but the impact on the child is profound in every case. This is the way childhood felt to them, and perhaps to those of you who were raised by a predatory mother:

> "I look into her eyes, yearning for her to look back at me, to see me in here. Her face turns toward me, and I see her eyes, vacant and dead, except for the glint of something dark. It feels as if she is disgusted, filled with hatred and disapproval toward me. She wants to punish me for something, or devour me. I don't know what I have done to make her feel that way. I have never seen her eyes soften with approval or affection. Always she condemns me, hunts me down to point out my mistakes or my faults, then she pushes me away. It hurts me so much I want to

scream with the pain of it. My heart feels like it is being torn apart, but I cannot cry in front of her or she will sneer at me, or punish me more, or leave me. I don't know what to do. I can't make her love me, and I can't make her stop. I have done something she disapproves of, or not done something she wanted. What was it? I feel guilty, filled with shame.

"Why can't I make her love me? What is wrong with me? Other children have mothers who smile and hug them, and I see the children laugh and kiss their mothers. They want to kiss their mothers. I only kiss my mother if she asks me to. When she hugs me, I feel cold, chilled to the bone. I think I am just not able to love anybody.

"Sometimes I feel sick, like I want to throw up or faint. When she is angry, I feel terrified, and when she looks at me, I see the flash of hatred in her eyes, and I feel the energy flow from her into me, like a lightning bolt that sets all my nerves on edge. I am a raw nerve. I feel like a drop of water hitting a hot skillet, and I fear I will disintegrate, lose myself in the fear and the fire. I tried to run away, but she mocked me. She knew I had nowhere to go, because I can't find another mother. No one would want me.

"But sometimes I escape, and I run into the woods and press my face in the grass, or smell the fresh air, and I feel better. Or my good uncle comes to visit, and he makes jokes, and he looks at me with twinkling eyes, like his eyes are laughing and asking me to laugh too. Then the ache goes away, and I don't feel afraid as long as he is there, because my mother acts friendly, and she brags about all of us, like she made us, and she did our homework and got good grades and made the team, and she's proud of what she did. She acts that way when friends come over, too, so nobody knows that she really hates me.

"She gets mad at my brother too, but then she tells him how he's going to be a doctor or a lawyer and make her proud. Not me. She says my room is so messy, I'll never amount to anything, and no one will ever want to have me around. I sometimes lock myself in my room so no one will know I'm crying.

"I have nightmares a lot, like I am being chased by a monster or a lion, and sometimes I get so scared I can't even move. When I can't sleep, I go into her room, but she just says to go back to bed, "It's only a dream," like I'm being silly. Then I feel so alone and empty, I wish I were dead.

"When she gets dressed up and goes out with my father, she looks really pretty, and she smiles and says nice things to people, like how wonderful and smart they are, and how much she admires them. They think she is so nice. They tell me how lucky I am to have such a wonderful mother. They don't know what it's like."

Sandra M. put it graphically. She had complained that it took her decades after leaving her mother's house to learn how to sleep. She felt like "the prey that cannot sleep as long as the predator is around, but predators sleep soundly because they have nothing to fear. I had to teach my brain to even think about sleeping. I got so exhausted that I was cranky and nasty, and then I would fight back and stick up for myself. It was as if I was so tired I didn't care if I would be killed. But I started to learn to speak up, and fortunately my husband does not interfere with my wanting to be independent and outspoken. Along the way, I began to be able to tell myself it was time to sleep, and I finally started to be able to do it."

Eventually, having acknowledged that sleeping pills and alcohol interfered with her ability to sleep through the night, Sandra has found some peace in her stable life as a mother and wife. The distance of years, and a life of spiritual study and self-examination have brought some resolution. The sleeplessness and anxiety she had felt all her life were a result of conditioning—the constant fear of the predator in her life—which she had carried with her from childhood.

Fortunately, Sandra's hard work, growing insight, and a deeply spiritual philosophy helped her to avoid becoming further involved in adult relationships which would replicate her childhood psychological abuse. Many others do not fare so well, but become embroiled in a lifelong struggle with one Abuser after another.

There is a rather different developmental thrust when it is the father who is the seducer and manipulator. To a child, the father is a particular kind of cultural icon—he represents the external values and measures of success in the culture. A male Abuser may find ways to gain success and prestige in the world of politics, sports, or business, thereby gaining unwarranted respect from his family. (We have seen this in companies like Enron and World-Com, which were run as if they were the private candy stores of a few dedicated Abusers). The Abusive father is likely to take on mythical proportions in the child's mind, at least for a time. It is difficult for a child not to be enamored by what appears to be special strength-of superhuman proportions-when the father weaves his charm. The child may see the father overpowering his wife, confusing and defeating her with his manipulations and betrayals. She may appear weak, emotional, and overly sensitive compared to the hard-edged arrogance of a skilled Abuser. In this conflict-filled environment, the child may lose respect for the mother. Although she is the source of human warmth, it is presented in a messy package of tears, frustration and (to the child) inexplicable anger toward the godlike person who seems to charm the whole world.

Children of Abusers are driven by a sense of desperation and longing which acts like a magnet, pulling them toward the same kinds of people who hurt them in childhood. This is the "blood from a stone" attraction which takes on the intensity and compulsive quality of an addiction. To understand this, we must first eliminate the common explanation: that they genuinely want to do it over, better, to find the love and acceptance they missed out on in childhood. This is not true. Even the most desperate of lovers glimpses the futility of it before the relationship becomes serious. Like Maria, they sense danger, but go ahead anyway. If they really wanted acceptance, they would pursue someone who is accepting and genuinely capable of love. It is unlikely the victim was utterly without evidence that the person she is involved with might be dangerous or unreliable. Often, she knows by the person's reputation precisely how ruthless or insensitive he has been in the past. She may even have been warned by her friends. Still she refuses to entertain the idea that it might be turned on her.

Some have described the attraction as compelling and mindless, going against all reason and intelligence. Many clients describe it this way: an attraction they know consciously to be perilous or at least pointless, but their feelings lead them deeper into danger. This separation of thought and feeling has often been shrugged off as an example of the "mind-body" separation. However, this is a neurological impossibility, since we are fundamentally psychosomatic. Rather, this is as an example of an attraction which was entrained into our neurological system by long months and years of being "under the spell" of an emotionally barren parent. We know that early contact with an Abuser lays down channels in our brain which prepare us to anticipate emotionally empty interactions. This leaves us endlessly hungry and unsatisfied, longing for more, and longing to use the strategies which worked for us in childhood.

Attractor channels laid down in early childhood influence our attitudes and expectations about relationships, and about life itself. Once these channels are established, they are more likely to be used, and continuously strengthened by further use. Thus, an attractor channel which leaves the child emotionally bereft, but for which there is no ready alternative, would create a feedback loop in which the attraction leads to less and less satisfaction, and more and more use. Then, like the laboratory pigeon pecking frantically to get cocaine or the rat running itself to death for the reward that rarely comes, the person becomes a desperate and frustrated creature, acting on his early programming. That early programming is a system of conditioned responses which can only lead to greater isolation and dissatisfaction.

Anyone who has tried to free themselves from an addiction can recognize the feelings described here. It is a painful, confusing state to feel you are being controlled by something outside yourself. No one would choose to feel that kind of helplessness and defeat, if he were to admit it was really his own doing.

Acceptable Addictions

Perhaps there are other, equally compelling reasons for "fatal attractions" which make them difficult to leave behind. This is true even when we recognize the fruitlessness of it, and even when we may consciously acknowledge a strong distaste or disapproval for the other person's dishonesty or unethical behavior. This is the difficult part for most people to own up to: that they are secretly in awe of the Abuser's inclination to destroy and walk away. Chapter One,

"Shock and Awe" describes the child's tendency to look up to and admire parents, no matter what, and to see whatever parents do as "love." This is the training which can lead an intelligent, exuberant child to turn away from nourishing relationships, life-giving healthy foods, community activities, creative and honorable work, to pursue instead a life filled with stress, conflict, and frustration. This expands the possibility for addictive behavior to nearly everything in life which can be consumed.

In a consumer-driven society, the possibilities are endless for a person whose attention has become focused, as we saw earlier, on fight-or-flight feelings and abusive relationships. Because we have to make sense of what we are feeling, we tend to associate the fear response, and the accompanying loneliness of closing down the heart, to tangential issues in our environment. Stress and frustration feel like something is lacking: We feel the need for more money, more material possessions to stave off worries. This leads to hoarding, workaholism, and extreme greed, the socially acceptable forms of addiction.

The Me Generation of the 80's was famous for the increase in programs, products and activities to promote self-help, self-improvement, self-analysis, self-promotion, self-knowledge, self-respect, self-reliance, and self-esteem. However, it was only the beginning of what was to become an overwhelmingly self-obsessed culture.

We have had many examples in recent years of what's wrong with our culture, and how money and fame can't buy love. Along came Anna Nicole Smith, who was willing to prostitute herself for wealth, with tragic consequences. Next came Britney Spears, who by all our culture's standards did everything right. She worked hard even as a child. She made enormous amounts of money and garnered worldwide fame. Millions of fans loved her. She could not have tried harder to reach the Dream. She was taught, as we all are, that if enough people love you, you will be happy. It isn't true. She was duped. She was so thoroughly groomed to be attractive, lovable and sexy that she never learned to give love. Faced with raising children, she found it nearly impossible to stay with them and love them, because it was not what she was trained for. Then came Paris Hilton, who is a caricature of an "achiever." She is famous for posing, and we only find her posing interesting because she is enormously rich. She did not even earn the money herself, but never mind, it still counts. Posing, or "stylin,'" as some teens call it, is the ultimate child's plea: "Look at me, look at me!" In what seems to be the most decadent plunge into petulance, superficiality and material indulgence yet, we now have the incessant embarrassment of reality shows featuring "Real Housewives of Somewhere USA" to convince the world that Americans truly are insane. We can only hope the producers of these shows really intended tongue-in-cheek satire.

Among bad-acting female celebrities, Lindsay Lohan has taken the prize for outrageously irresponsible behavior, periodically resurfacing to capture coverage in the media, while Tiger Woods and Donald Trump have proven that both excess and arrogance have no bounds.

Materialism, the financial addiction, has become so common in the American culture that we hardly blink when informed that Corporation X had just paid its CEO 100 million dollars for a year's work. This, while he out-sourced 25 percent of the company's jobs to Asia. His salary comes to 2 million dollars a week! $400,000 a day! $45,000 an hour! All right, let's say he works horrendously long hours. It's still about $30,000 an hour. What were we thinking? These proportions reflect our idea of the worth of a person's labors.

We have not left slavery behind, when a worker's year is equal to his master's hour. We have simply moved the scale upward. Our slaves are paid in money, and they are free to move about to other low-paying jobs, but the masters still take more than their fair share. Even many poor people do not find this obscene. They may be envious, but would gladly accept such obscenity should it be offered to them. Polls have revealed that 65 percent of Americans expected to be in the top five percent of wealth at some point in their lives. Who could blame anyone for wanting to take part in the omnipresent displays of wealth all around us? Sleek and powerful cars, fashionable clothes, gourmet food, tantalizing new technologies, luxury housing and the credit to make it all yours. Who was not worn down by the sheer weight of it?

Think of the irony of a recent television ad campaign which promises priceless moments in your life made possible by using a credit card!

The demise of the housing bubble has alternately been blamed on dishonest lenders who peddled "sub-prime" loans, investment sharks who packaged and sold the questionable loans, and most commonly, the greedy homeowners who selfishly took on more debt than they could repay. This chain of greed and corruption did not begin or end with the homeowners who wanted to live in the style to which everyone else seemed to have become accustomed. The addiction to money is an epidemic from which no one has been immune.

As a society, we are so immersed in our feelings of self-imposed stress and dissatisfaction that we tend to believe it is just the way life is. It is actually a symptom of deep and early emotional starvation, topped off by years of living in a culture of unhappiness and craven greed. In an effort to scratch the incessant itch of fear, self-hatred and hunger, we medicate ourselves with goods and gadgets, sex, drugs and alcohol, pseudo-mansions and fancy cars, but the itch remains. We cannot be soothed by physical/material means because it is not a physical need. It is a sickness of the heart and spirit, propelled forward in time by endless repetitive firings in the attractor channels of our brains and the urgings of advertisers. To heal these sicknesses of the heart and spirit, we must look elsewhere—away from the enticements and sedatives offered by the legions of commercial enterprises which vie for our attention and our money. The age-old truth is that there is a place in our hearts that can only be fulfilled by connection and service to others, and faith in a Higher Power.

The more shadows we dispel, the more we are able to acknowledge there is a warp in our psychological make-up. It is not our doing, or anyone's "fault." It originates in the destructive family and cultural influences on us. Once we identify the origins of this malaise, it becomes easier to find healing techniques to restore us to sanity and inner peace.

In the Wake of Prosperity

Most children would rather be "cool" and in charge than suffering. Can we blame them? Unfortunately, to be "cool," many of those sensitive individuals require drugs (legal or not) to subdue their troublesome emotions.

The young people who have come to my office recently discuss their anxieties and their difficulty "fitting in" with their peers. They describe drinking to excess as a common pastime. Young women express alarm about the safety of their friends who drink to the point of passing out in strange apartments, throwing up in public, losing their wallets, and remembering nothing of what they did the night before. Men who refuse to take part in these debacles describe themselves as a small minority who are mocked as "puritanical" and dismissed by their carousing friends. I mention this not to prove that young people are "going to the dogs." It should give us pause, however, to wonder where we might have gone wrong as a culture. These young people clearly have not found meaning in their lives, or a way to relate to each other comfortably and directly without the aid of chemical substances.

Stella Chess, in her longitudinal New York Study, which followed 113 children from early infancy to adulthood,[9] emphasized the contribution of innate temperament in the development of the person. The broad conclusions of the study were that individual children can generally be classified as easy, difficult, or "slow to warm up." After many decades of concentrating on studies which seek to identify generalized genetic or environmental causes to explain maladaptive behavior, perhaps it is time for us to resume this line of inquiry, to reconsider how individuals respond to their surroundings, how profoundly sensitive some of us are, and how valuable that human capacity really is. Some people are indeed slower to warm up, or have difficulty adapting, and may be left in the dust by their more competitive peers through no fault of their own.

I would like to offer the possible explanation that those among us who have had thorny struggles adapting to our cultural environment are like the canary in the mines. (Before modern air monitoring technology, coal miners would take a canary in its cage down into the mines with them. If the canary stopped singing, they knew they were in danger and had to get out immediately.) Perhaps the unruly, confused and self-destructive addicts among us are the ones who are most sensitive by temperament, the ones who have been driven crazy by the toxic conditions they have encountered in every facet of their lives, from childhood onward. In my experience, they are often unsung poets and failed visionaries. This is not a romantic aggrandizement or an apology for bad behavior. Everyone needs to be held responsible for destructive behavior, especially when it affects others, but perhaps our tendency to see addiction as a lack of will masks the true identity

---

[9]　See Chess, Stella, et al, *Your Child is a Person,* and numerous articles about the study.

of these individuals who present us with a wake-up call. There is something profoundly toxic in our way of life.

The focus on physical and/or material (hedonistic) pleasures and painkillers keeps us preoccupied with our bodies, and with using our brains for the endless indulgence of calculating and conniving our way toward satisfying our cravings. Earning, buying, snorting and competing, we reduce our attention to a version of humanity which is body and brain without heart or soul. In so doing, we end up feeling neither happy nor safe, with a worried mind and a broken body.

Vibrational Levels

Imagine the feeling of being around someone who is under the influence of drugs or depression. Their energy field is heavy, leaden, dead. Our language is full of references to the kind of energy we exude, depending on our mood. A light mood, like a bright light or a high note on the musical scale, is experienced as a higher vibrational level. Hatred, a black mood, deep despair, all are felt as low, dark energy with a lower vibrational quality. Laughter and love, which emanate directly from the heart, feel uplifting, while depression, an emotional response to a dark mindset, is a downer. Light/dark, up/down, high/low; we all know what these words mean in human feeling terms. We describe them to each other, assuming a familiarity of experience, but what is it we're describing?

The vibrational differences we are sensing are a result of the kind of energy a person generates in each of the levels of being: heart, soul, body and brain. A dark, heavy arrangement places the brain/body in the primary position, with little attention to the soul or heart. In action, this means that someone who is experiencing addictive emptiness and longing would be focused only on her own body, what sensations her emotions produce in her body, and what she thinks about it. It is a completely self-absorbed, self-centered arrangement. The most corrosive, soul-stunting attitude of all is feeling sorry for oneself. The lightest configuration would be heart/soul dominant, with the body/mind in service of heart/soul intentions. This is a configuration which centers on others rather than Ego. There is little thought about self, one's own needs, or even one's own emotions. The focus is outward, with body and brain as the handy tools of action, when the action is based in connection, compassion, love, kindness, generosity—the higher, lighter feelings. Perhaps this is what we mean by "enlightenment."

Picture yourself walking through your life. What energy do you leave in your wake? Do you emanate waves of negativity, depression and Darkness, spreading ripples of despair and hopelessness as your moment-to-moment offering to the world? Are you an anxiety-monger who ignites fear and dread in others? Are you a rage-a-holic who provides the spark for other people's emotional tinder? Are you the arrogant judgment which increases self-loathing in others? Or are you bringing Light and an atmosphere of acceptance which inspires others toward positive and loving action?

The higher vibrational responses which become possible when we move away from the fight-or-flight response take place in the connections between the prefrontal cortex of the brain (which includes the area known as the "third eye") and the heart, and from portals in the center of our brain to the Source of All Things beyond our present Earth plane. Recovery and freedom can be achieved through understanding our beginnings, practicing meditative exercises, doing enlivening physical exercise rather than deadening addictions, and heartfelt, soul-satisfying connections with others.

The twelve-step Alcoholics Anonymous programs address addiction largely by encouraging spiritual growth. By inspiring a connection to a Higher Power as well as intimate relationships with others, this approach provides a direct antidote to the emotional and spiritual starvation most alcoholics experience as a part of their addiction. The AA approach purposefully directs members' attention away from their own bodies and self-obsessed minds toward service to others. Perhaps those who have not yet succeeded using this approach were held back by attractor channels which dragged them back into feelings of self-hatred and despair. Healing takes time and sustained effort.

You can abandon the pathways in your limbic brain which were laid down in childhood without your permission. Armed with the knowledge that you will need to "reconstruct" your pathways to process friendly human contact, you can begin to change. With determination and daily practice, you will begin to overcome the addictive attractions in your life, whether they are a direct attraction to a destructive person, or the addictions to mood-altering drugs or alcohol, cigarettes, food, sex or shopping which you use to subdue your frazzled nerves. Chapter 26, "How Can I Get Over it?" offers some practical steps to assist in your recovery, but first let's take a deeper look at a related forms of human emotional distress: lovesickness

THE RAT

I am a rat, the master of low life
I love to cut and slash.
My upper lip is curled in contempt,
My playground is garbage and trash.

In underground caverns, drug houses and taverns
I stalk the young and the fair.
With promise of pleasure, of surfait and treasure,
I lure them into to my lair.

The arrogant takers, the movers and shakers
Find company here at the bottom.
I dine on self-centeredness, greed and self-pity,
They think they're in charge, but I've got'em.

My teeth itch with hunger, I savor their flesh,
It's my pleasure to cheat and destroy.
Morality, decency—they are my prey
Darkness is my joy.

THE LAMB

I am a lamb, a little lamb
All mindless innocence,
I just sit here and bleat, I nap and I eat
Without guile, suspicion or pretense.

All the predators come,
I'm alone and forsaken,
All hungry and panting, they taunt me.
My blood makes them drool,
They're so wondrously cruel,
I can see in their eyes that they want me.

I am a lamb, sacrificial lamb;
It's my destiny to be beaten.
I suffer their glances,
Their hungry advances,
I will give of myself to be eaten.

Chapter Thirteen

KILLING MARIA

The following story, like the game of Clue, is a murder mystery. Your challenge is to determine who is the real perpetrator in the attempted murder of Maria. There are several suspects, and a plot line which covers half a century. In the end, you will see the twist which uncloaks the true murderer, when the unlikely motive is revealed.

My neighbor, Maria, wanted to know what an "Abuser" was. I began a tentative definition by saying, "Someone who is lacking in basic human qualities like caring and empathy, who causes great pain and anguish in all their relationships . . ."

"Like . . . atrocities?" she said. I nodded.

"Oh my God," she said. "I was raised by Abusers! My parents were Abusers. My grandparents were Abusers! I suffered so much pain . . . so much pain. It is still hard for me to have relationships with humans because of them. All my life I've suffered. I've had to work so hard to recover, but some things have helped. I've been in therapy, I love nature, and I love my dog, my wonderful dog. (Here she looked at her handsome dog lovingly, and he returned the gaze.) But there's this man, someone I had a relationship with for 13 years! I'm addicted to him. I left him, but I couldn't stay away. I knew it wouldn't work, but I kept going back, and I still love him. I'm sure he must be an Abuser, but what can I do—I've never known any other kind . . . He is just like my mother."

"You should tell my story," she went on, "if it helps other people . . . I'll tell you my story, and you can use it to help people understand."

Maria's story is especially interesting because it illustrates so vividly the Shock and Awe Principle (the tendency we have as adults to be

184

attracted to the very qualities which caused us suffering in childhood). It is a double-whammy for anyone who has been raised by an Abuser, especially when she is your mother.

"Addictions!" she said. "You have to explain this addiction thing. How having an Abuser for a mother leads you to addiction. I am your book!"

Here is Maria's story as she told it to me:

> "My picture of my mother is this. She is sitting in a big armchair with her legs crossed, with her back turned to me, smoking a cigarette, acting as if I'm not there. (She demonstrates, with her nose in the air, affecting the exaggerated pose of a 40's movie queen.) I'm next to her on the arm of the chair, trying to get her attention, trying to get a hold of her, and she won't look at me, she's acting as if I'm invisible.
>
> "She was so beautiful . . . I used to think, 'Why can't I get her to love me? It must be my fault.
>
> "They were just so awful to me. I felt as if I was being amputated from myself. My grandfather was a raging alcoholic, and my father was an alcoholic. He was physically abusive, and he sexually abused me. My mother divorced him, but then she married another man who was also an alcoholic, and he was just as abusive. It was all just so horrible. I was so traumatized; it's hard for me to talk about it.
>
> "It's easier for me to talk about the people I was involved with later. Here's one example that tells you what they were like. The man I was with, the one I've been so in love with, was named Paulo, and he had two friends, Jose and Anna who had both emigrated from Colombia. First Anna came, then Jose, and they got married, and then Jose got Paulo to come. Jose was married to Anna, but he spent all his time with Paolo."

I asked whether she thought Paolo might have been in a homosexual relationship with Jose, and whether that might explain his coldness toward her, Maria emphatically denied this. She said it was impossible because of Paolo's enthusiastic participation in the sexual relationship with her. She had never experienced anything as exciting with anyone else. After offering some very convincing details, she went on,

> "They had a really strange way of talking about things. Their ideas were so bizarre, I didn't really believe them. I thought it was some kind of joke. Here's just a part of it: They thought everybody was bad, but especially the Jews. The Jews were to blame for all their suffering, for Communism. It wasn't just Jews. They hated everybody . . . the Italians in Brooklyn, fat people, government, everybody except them, the little group of the three of them. One time Paulo said he was a Neo-Nazi Fascist. When I didn't understand why they felt that way, Paulo would just say, 'Ask Jose. He'll explain it to you.' It was as if they had a little cult, and Jose was the leader, and Paolo wanted to be like him. They were supposed to be best friends, but here's what happened that was so shocking.
>
> "I knew the Colombian contractor that Jose and Paulo worked for, and he told me this. When Paulo first came, and Jose got him a job with this contractor, he told the contractor that he should only pay Paulo half of what he paid him, because Paulo was new here, and it would seem like a lot of money to him. This was supposed to be his best friend!

I confirmed that this lack of loyalty is one of the characteristic attributes of Abusers. They are really incapable of genuine friendship. Even in a sexual relationship, they may seem to express warmth, but they are just taking part in a physical experience, like an athletic event. It has nothing to do with love, no matter how fabulous the physical experience might seem.

> "Oh, that's right! When I first met David, the man I am with now, my dog had just died, and I was feeling so bad, I really needed a hug. He gave me this wonderful hug; I can still remember it. It was so warm and wonderful, not

at all sexual. Paulo didn't hug. He didn't know how to hug, or to give a massage, or any of those things.

"I was so addicted. It was like a drug. How am I going to get over that?"

I told her I thought that calling it what it is—being attracted to Darkness—makes it less attractive. The way she was being treated felt so bad because it was abusive. Trusting her own inner guide works like protective radar. She needs to remember her first reactions to a person. Most Abusers give themselves away early on. Pay attention and do not deny what you see and feel.

"Yes, the end was always there, even in the beginning. The first time I saw Paulo, I thought he was so beautiful, but I felt . . . scared. He had just recently come to this country, and he was glowing. He had long flowing hair, and a beard, and he was like a beautiful, fabulous Conquistador. I said to myself that I could never have him; he's not available. I tried to explain to myself why I felt scared. I thought, 'He's probably married'."

She had sensed something immediately. Like most of us, her "radar" was working perfectly. He was unavailable, and she was scared. Those feelings were perfectly accurate premonitions of what was to come. A conquistador is "one who conquers." She was picking up something important, and she was drawn to it.

"Paulo was making pottery with folk art designs on them, and I was playing around with Guatemalan folk art designs. I made a design where I used traditional folk art symbols to form his name, and I used it on a present I gave him. A little while later he showed me a collage he had made to sell, and he had signed it with the design I made. He didn't even ask me. Can you believe that?"

I said that yes, I could believe it. This is typical Abusive behavior. Since they are usually not very creative themselves, they steal other people's ideas. It's not armed robbery or breaking and entering, but it's still robbery. Intellectual property rights mean nothing to them.

"Right! And no creativity! He just got a book and copied things and put them on his crafts. The stuff he makes is really nothing. He's supposed to be an artist! He just looks like one! He plays the role.

I asked Maria what she thought was the worst thing about her relationship with Paulo. Her answer revealed that she was focusing on Paulo's bad behavior, rather than her own attraction to it.

"I think this was probably the worst thing Paulo ever did to me. One day near my home I was attacked at gunpoint. I tried to get away, but one of the men grabbed me and had his gun to my head, so I gave him my purse.

"Just then a car was coming down the street, so I ran and started screaming and banging on the windows, but it turned out to be the getaway car, and the two muggers got into the back seat of the car. I was devastated. Another woman just down the street had been killed by the same guys two weeks before.

"After the attack, I went home and called Paulo because I was so upset. He came, but he was furious with me because I had messed up his plans to help me. He yelled at me, accusing me of being selfish, and saying the attack was all my fault. He was saying things like, "Look what you've done to me." Then he picked up the phone and called Anna. I'll never forget him standing there in the hallway, talking in a really calm voice to her about a sofa bed, and never even mentioning the attack! It was as if he was beating me up with his words. I had known him for three years at that point, and I stayed around for ten more years.

"He did do some good things for me. I was in Colorado, and I had found a summer place I really loved. I agreed to buy it, and then I had to go back to Brooklyn to arrange for the money. I had to be back in Colorado to close the deal on the house in a week, and I asked Paulo to drive with me. So we went, but then he tried to talk me out of buying it. He didn't want anything good for me.

"We were driving back, and he was physically violent with me. It was night, and I was driving and he was just raving and beating on my head.

"Another time he got violent, he hurt my wrist, and I knew, I knew right there he could just kill me. He killed me emotionally and mentally, but I just knew I had to back off and pretend to be light and smiling, to save myself." He was violent with me a few times, but you know, I kind of blocked that out because it doesn't go with the relationship somehow.

"I can see now that it was when he didn't have power over me; he knew how to shut me down. He couldn't stand it when I was happy and smiling."

Here, Maria illustrates a move that is typical of victims under the spell of a Dark One. She saw that he was violent, but rather than leave to save herself, she took it upon herself to placate him, as if her submissive behavior would somehow change his tendency to be violent. She never did say what good things he had done for her, except for accompanying her on the long drive during which he beat her up.

"When I'm out in nature, I'm very expressive. I was singing, and I said, "There's a holy spirit in the sky", and he got so angry, he was telling me I was crazy, and why couldn't I be normal. When I was feeling good, he would just tear me down."

I pointed out how consistent his timing was, hitting her on the head after she had bought the house she loved, and ridiculing her when she was ecstatic on a beautiful day. Both times she was feeling happy and full of life. Of course, he was trying to get her back in line because the house represented an opportunity for her to be far away from him, and to escape his hold on her. Piling on after she had been attacked was like kicking her when she was down. He needed her to be weak and unsure of herself. People who are exuberant and happy are harder to manipulate. These were strategies to keep her under his control, deliberately timed to keep her in check.

When I mentioned that Abusers are generally killjoys, she continued:

> "One New Year's Eve I got dressed up, and I was dancing and having such a wonderful time. He mocked me and made fun of my dancing. I was so hurt that I did something I sometimes did when he hurt me so much. I would just go numb. I would go into a state where I wouldn't even talk. I would just be gone . . . not feeling anything . . . like an out-of-body experience."

I explained to Maria that this kind of dissociation is something all of us are capable of. It is the kind of separation that allows people to live through terrible physical pain. It is not the kind of drastic compensation a child should have to use just to survive life with their parents, but when you are raised with an Abusive mother, the terror of looking into her cold and empty eyes can drive a child to separate from herself. Then it becomes a lifelong way of dealing with emotional pain. The worst part about using this kind of "protection" is that it allows you to stay in the abusive relationship.

> "I was just so enamored with all that love. I felt like I loved him so much. I thought he felt the same for me. I have to be grateful for him, because I got in touch with so much love."

Here is a mistake victims often make when they draw an Abuser to them. The capacity to love was in her. She was learning to love, to reach out, to feel deep human feelings. It was not caused by him. She had been attributing her ability to love to him, when it was the depth of her own soul that was being revealed. She had a choice to proceed one of two ways: She could choose to defeat those tender feelings by offering them to an Abuser, or she could free herself to love someone who would return her love.

"Yes, it's why I knew I was ready to find someone like David. It's as if I was preparing all my life for this relationship, this love I feel for him. I told you how he hugged me when my dog King died. It's so different; we're learning how to be with each other. I needed someone like him, who would be overboard generous and kind. It's so different."

She picked up the thread and wove another story, this time illustrating the Abuser's tendency toward shallowness and superficiality.

"Paulo had all these weird preferences—things he thought were of great importance. He was always finding fault with things. Nothing was ever right. I had bought some blankets. I just loved them, and he said, "Well, they'd be all right if it weren't for that black stitching on the edge." There was always something wrong with everything!"

What was it that finally made her decide to leave?

"I had had a big problem with my landlord. I had to be out of my house in five days, and I had no place to go. Paolo lived in a big house that had belonged to an old woman. He wasn't paying rent. Then she died, and he stayed there by himself for years.

"So he had this big house all to himself. As a last resort, I asked him if I could stay there, and he said the dog couldn't come, and I wasn't allowed to use the phone, and all these other conditions, so I just said, 'That's it. Enough of this.' The next day, I found a place, and that's where I met David and everything changed.

"It was right about that time, just before I found my new place, when I also saw my mother, and I really saw her. My sister was there at the dinner table saying all kinds of crazy stuff about when she was a heroin addict, and my mother was just sitting there with her hand over her mouth, saying nothing! The whole thing was crazy.

"So that's when I decided I wasn't going to tell her or Paulo where I was. I have this wonderful man in my life now, and we're working things out, so I don't want to do something like getting involved with Paulo again, but I still love him! What am I going to do to get over it?"

What Maria was calling love was actually an attraction to the abuse itself. In the evolution of coming through childhood as the target of Abusers, she became an Abuser herself, with the same target, her suffering bodysoul. Like the slight of hand of a practiced magician, Maria found an Abuser to do the dirty work of humiliating her true self, all the while pretending not to see that the source of abuse was hidden under her own cloak. It was she who kept going back to the man who caused her pain. Instead of acknowledging that she was in charge of the abuse, she continued to identify herself as a victim. Ironically, she was both victim and Abuser in her own game of "Kill Maria."

If Maria is to be free of her attraction to abuse she will have to recognize the siren song for what it is: a call to murder, the murder of your own precious bodysoul, your true self in hiding. Constantly attacking your bodysoul destroys the connection to your compassionate heart, to your Greater Soul, and to a Higher Power. In the process, you become like them, a Head without a Heart, a virulent Abuser behind the cloak of victimhood.

THE SNAKE'S REWARD

If only you'll love me
I'll give you my heart.
I've been lonely, forsaken,
A being apart.
Just tell me you love me
I'll do what you like
You have given me purpose,
A new lease on life.
Don't leave me, desert me,
I need you, my love.
I'll wrap myself 'round you,
Thank God that I've found you,
Come sit here beside me
And listen to me.
I'll make you lasagna,
Dark chocolate and brie,
We'll sip dry champagne,
And soon we'll be three.
Our dreams will come true
If you're feeling it too
Oh how thrilling to meet you
My name's Mary Lou.

Chapter Fourteen

CHILDREN OF DARKNESS

No one sets out to have a painful, heartbreaking relationship. We always hope, in the flush of a new love or a new friendship, that it will be a satisfying experience. We tell ourselves and our friends that this one is going to be different. Smart people who have managed successful careers, business dealings and other personal endeavors, may find themselves completely undone by a relationship that turned out to be anything but what they thought they were getting into. We hear the familiar refrain over and over, "How could she do this to me?"

We have seen in past chapters how people can be made vulnerable by early, difficult relationships which predispose them toward abusive liaisons in the name of love. It is fairly easy to see how other people get themselves into destructive relationships. We can see it coming when a friend announces her engagement to a "bad boy" whom she expects will reform. What can you say to her that might help her to avoid the inevitable? How can you do the same for yourself? If you had a way of reliably identifying an Abuser by their behavior would it make a difference? Would you forgo the temptation to embrace the Abuser who will become an accomplice to the killing of your own weakened bodysoul?

The Abusive Personality as Archetype

The people I am calling the Children of the Dark or Abusive Personality Types have been variously described in the annals of psychiatry and psychology as sociopaths, psychopaths, anti-social personality types and extreme narcissists.

We are very reluctant to admit that such characters live among us, in every country, town, perhaps even in most extended families. It is more comfortable to believe they are foreign, alien, not related in any way to *us*.

Martha Stout, in *The Sociopath Next Door*, suggested they were about five percent of the population. I believe the number is underestimated by at least half, since the population of women heart-breakers are not counted in the same category with embezzlers and con men. Was Bonnie really less destructive than Clyde?

Devastating encounters with Children of Darkness are so common that you only need to ask a gathering of friends and acquaintances. You will be regaled with such tales of heart-break, betrayal and double-dealing that everyone will be left saying, "How could they do that?"

I believe the Dark Ones can be viewed as an archetype. We all recognize a villain or villainess, con man or siren as real-life individuals as well as dramatic literary figures.

As Carl Jung explained it, "(I)t is impossible to give an arbitrary (or universal) interpretation of any archetype. It must be explained in the manner indicated by the whole life-situation of the particular individual to whom it relates . . . . Archetypes come to life only when one patiently tries to discover why and in what fashion they are meaningful to a living individual."[10]

Archetypes are universal. They are characters or concepts which appear across cultures and across time. Jung gives the examples of the wise man, the great mother and the myth of the hero. The hero myth varies from culture to culture, but recurring themes describe the hero performing courageous acts for the good of others. In Greek and Native American mythology, the hero myths also serve to warn of the human failing of hubris. Hubris is the tendency to overreach which leads to abuse of power—the shadow side of heroic action. The Abuser is this shadow side. He is the anti-hero who conquers for personal gain rather than the greater good. His or her motive is to control rather than rescue, subdue rather than uplift. These characters are fascinating to us because they often possess the personal power

---

[10] Jung, Carl G., Man and His Symbols, chapter 1, Approaching the Unconscious, p. 96.

and attractiveness of the hero or heroine, but they use it to Dark and destructive ends.

The following is a description of what an Abuser might act like, what he or she looks like in action, and what it feels like to be in an encounter with one. I have capitalized the term Abusive Personality Type to distinguish them from others who are not as extreme or consistent in their abusive behavior.

In contrast, I have also presented a classification of character traits and virtues which are the opposite of an Abusive Personality Type. In the American culture, we have a great tolerance for Dark (Abusive) values in our everyday lives. This is partly what makes it so difficult to differentiate what is good from what is truly destructive in our acquaintances and in ourselves. However, a highly evolved human would never operate in the world the way an Abuser does. It is still possible to find human beings in whom integrity, honesty and good will are the bedrock of their beings. These are the honorable human qualities against which we will be measuring Children of Darkness.

Truthfulness is the essence of good character. You can use these descriptions to look honestly into your own actions toward yourself and others. You can free yourself of the residual attraction to Darkness which you may have carried with you from childhood. Unearth the killer you may be harboring behind a veil of innocence.

The Dark Ones in Literature and Film

There has long been a fascination with psychopathic murderers. Many Americans are familiar with vivid depictions like Anthony Hopkins' portrayal of the vicious killer in "Silence of the Lambs," or Tony Perkins' classic Hitchcock villain in "Psycho." These horror films leave us with the impression that a psychopath is in a distinctly different class from the rest of humanity. I will offer examples of how the psychopathic murderer and the everyday Abuser in our midst are more alike than they are different, and are more like us than we care to acknowledge. The main difference between the violent psychopath and the everyday Abuser is in the use of physical means to reach their ends (the psychopath) versus emotional, financial or social means (the sociopaths). I would group them both under the heading of Abuser, but have concentrated here on the less well-understood sociopathic-style

Abuser. The goal is to avoid the drastic consequences of an encounter with any of these Dark Ones rather than identify them after the fact.

We can all recognize the obviously evil characters who represent Darkness: Dracula, Darth Vader, or The Joker from Batman. Most of us do not meet folks sporting fangs or a black cloak. The destructive individuals we meet in daily life are more like *Mommy Dearest*, the story of the beautiful and talented Joan Crawford. The cruelty of her character was revealed by her long-suffering daughter, to the shock of those who thought they knew her. This glamorous and respected woman harbored intentions that were as dark as any psychopath's, but her tactics were not fatal. Children's stories often feature Abusers like Snow White's evil stepmother. She was beautiful and powerful, but she was viciously jealous of the young Snow White's beauty. We could think of these people as the psychopath without the chainsaw. They may not commit murder outright, but a close relationship will always lead to harm and sometimes to severe losses.

Robert Lewis Stevenson, in his classic story, *Dr. Jekyll and Mr. Hyde*, has given us a picture of a man's descent into Abusive behavior. Dr. Jekyll is inexorably attracted by the lure of unearthly power over his own human inner workings. Little by little he engages in experiments with his physical and emotional state which take him further into the experience of unbridled appetite, until he is irreparably changed into a vicious, inhuman creature that cares only about satisfying his own lust for ego—and physical satisfaction, regardless of the cost to himself or others. This evolution is graphically described: Hyde gradually gains in strength and stature, while Dr. Jekyll, the previously upstanding citizen with but a taste for "playing on the dark side" becomes the incarnation of destructiveness, as he dedicates himself to his dark research.

Stevenson uses the device of an experimental drug as the lure into evil, and the final trap from which Jekyll cannot extract himself, but the story is psychologically accurate for anyone who dabbles in Darkness. The more we invest in our dabbling, the more we strengthen our destructive stance; the more we experience that stance as power, the more inclined we are to continue. Stevenson's Jekyll was not a victim of an innocent mistake, but a dedicated participant in his own downfall, caught up in the idea that he could outwit God and Nature while indulging in destructive activities without paying the consequences.

So it is with our own identities. The stance we value, nurture, defend, and literally live and breathe is the one we will learn to call "I." Ironically, when we are taught inhuman values during childhood, it is the normal *human* adaptation to learn to behave in *inhuman* ways. These tendencies incline us toward a desire for invulnerability, which makes us and many of the people around us "Wannabes"—people who wish they were as untouchable as the coldest Abuser. Especially to a suffering child or teenager, the possibility of a life without the painful burden of feelings like love and sensitivity to others might seem appealing. Many of us carry this myth of fearful self-protection in the back of our minds, convincing ourselves it is only fear which leads us to deny our tender feelings. Thus, our understanding is confounded by the confluence of denial about our own tendencies, and our own awe of the cold, unfeeling stance which we may have secretly seen as ultimate power.

We will assume that if you are still reading, and if you are open to change, you are not an Abuser. However, most of us have felt the attraction to the unfeeling attitudes the Abusers represent. Therefore, most of us could be classified at one time or another as Wannabes. Thus we have the three categories: sensitive and caring humans, waffling Wannabes, and outright cold-blooded Abusers. For our purposes, we will try to tease out the differences, with the understanding that an Abuser—the darkest of the Dark Ones—are like a separate species. They tend to be completely unapologetic about the damage they do, and uninterested in changing. They seem to be unchangeable, at least by our limited present-day techniques.

This is not an exercise to separate US from THEM. To some degree, we are them. As you learn to identify your own attraction to Darkness, and accept it as a part of your own make-up, you will find you are able to begin to consciously shift your allegiance toward Light and openness. Developing a set of guidelines to identify what Abusers do versus what decent, evolved people do is as much about evaluating ourselves as it is about protecting ourselves from others.

We are looking for a set of behavioral guidelines which will help us delineate between the decent humans and "Wannabes" in one camp, and the Abusers in the other. To clarify these differences, we must have two things: first, a clear description of what a "full-blooded" highly functioning human looks like, and second, a contrasting description of the motives and behaviors which identify the Abuser.

Our project is made more difficult by the fact that some humans will mimic Abusers some of the time, but Abusers mimic human virtues all the time. They may not appear selfish or callous at first glance. If they are skillful at it, they may go undetected for some time. Most Abusers make it their life's work to "pass" among unsuspecting humans to do their dirty work more effectively. They can frequently be found in the most altruistic positions, in the helping professions, in politics, charitable activities, teaching, and especially under the cloak of religious piety. All these activities make a good "cover" for their sole purpose in life: to gain power over others and to destroy human values.

A further difficulty is presented by the fact that there are probably two rather different styles of Abusers: those who appear introverted, and those who are extroverts. To understand what underlies their surface presentation, it is important to look beyond these overt personality styles, which may have been determined by temperament or the family values and traditions they were raised with. We are familiar with the extroverted political leaders like Saddam Hussein, Stalin and the like, because they have garnered publicity and subjugated large numbers of people. However, the reclusive accountant who embezzles his church's tornado relief funds, leaving his neighbors stunned and devastated, is probably cut from the same cold-blooded psychological cloth.

We are most familiar with the Abuser of relatively high intelligence and attractive looks. Although both these qualities might increase an Abuser's ability to be conniving and manipulative, they are not a prerequisite. There are Abusive Personality Types at every social and financial strata of society.

In popular parlance, the tendency to think of any behavioral aberration as "crazy" has led to the popular belief that people who do remarkably destructive things must be mentally ill. Most Abusive Types are not "out of control" or irrational in the familiar sense, like someone who does not bathe, or mumbles to themselves incoherently. The Children of Darkness we are referring to cannot necessarily be distinguished by their bizarre or odd appearance or behavior, and they are fully aware of their actions. They tend to look normal and fit into their surroundings unless it serves their purposes to act irrationally so that they can "plead insanity" for their crimes. Therefore, we do not think of them as mentally ill.

If there is a neurological or physical condition which would describe an Abuser it would be "heartless." Of course, it is impossible for a person to live without a heart. The physical arrangement which results in an Abusive Personality may one day be found to involve undeveloped or missing connections between the emotional centers of the heart, the limbic (emotional) and prefrontal (judgment) centers of the brain and the yet "undocumented" bodysoul. In the meantime, we will rely on behavioral descriptions to identify the Children of the Dark.

The most difficult obstacle to overcome in our efforts to identify the truly Dark Ones among us is our natural reluctance to acknowledge that a person might be as destructive and malevolent as she seems. Sometimes, when it comes to deciding whether to approach or avoid a person who might be dangerous, we are tempted by the Shock and Awe Principle to ignore our best instincts. Instead of taking definitive action when we should, we tend to apologize for bad behavior by categorizing it as ordinary bad manners, or ignorance ("She really doesn't know how hurtful she is.") Thus we override the intuition which would normally lead us to heed the old proverb, "If it walks like a duck, quacks like a duck, and looks like a duck, then it probably is a duck."

Identifying What Good Is

At the other end of the comparison spectrum, we have a culturally muddy view of what being highly evolved actually looks like. Until recently, the medical model of psychiatry with its emphasis on disease created the impression that mental health would be the absence of mental diseases. Fortunately, our discussion is now forwarded by a serendipitous development in the field of psychology. Positive Psychology, led by Martin Seligman, stresses the development of good character as defined by universally understood virtues.

The following is a brief summary of the classification which is used by Peterson and Seligman in their volume, *Character Strengths and Virtues*. They have provided an excellent base for comparison by making it easier to classify an Abuser by identifying the character strengths they are missing completely. There are also several character traits which show up in an Abuser in subtly different forms from those which we admire in humans of good character.

Peterson and Seligman's classification enumerates six fairly distinct character strengths are generally admired across cultures. Under each character strength, they have provided descriptive terms (those qualities they call virtues) to give us a picture of what a person of high character would look like in action. The six main categories are listed below. In parentheses are the more specific virtues which they grouped under these general headings:

Wisdom and knowledge

Cognitive strengths that entail gaining and using knowledge (creativity or originality, curiosity, open-mindedness, love of learning, and perspective or wisdom).

Courage

Emotional strengths that involve use of will to accomplish goals in the face of opposition, both external or internal (bravery, persistence, integrity or authenticity, and vitality or vigor).

Humanity

Interpersonal strengths that involve tending and befriending others (love, kindness or nurturance, and social intelligence: being aware of the motives and feelings of other people and oneself).

In this category I would like to add the terms *empathy* and *conscience* for the special purpose of our discussion of Abusers.

Justice

Civic strengths that underlie healthy community life (citizenship, fairness, leadership).

Temperance

Strengths that protect against excess (forgiveness and mercy, humility or modesty, prudence, and self-regulation or self-control).

Transcendence

Strengths that forge connections to the larger universe and provide meaning (appreciation of beauty and excellence, gratitude, hope or optimism, humor, spirituality).

Peterson and Seligman have included a selection method which helps us in our analysis. One of the criteria they used for choosing what a virtue is, is the ability to identify its "Nonfelicitous Opposite." These Nonfelicitous Opposites are like the shadow characteristics of the hero, the expression of destructive intentions. Especially in the area of Humanity and Justice, this discussion can help us in our search for the traits which clearly identify Abusers.

It is inspiring to consider these timeless, universal character virtues, and to think of the people in our own lives who have managed to live in such a way as to embody them. If we strive for integrity, these are the qualities we strive to develop in ourselves. By defining what our portrait of an Abusive Personality is (what not to be), we are also clarifying what we demand of ourselves as a highly evolved, more virtuous person—one who can be measured by our treatment of others.

For Your Own Good: Identifying an Abuser

Peterson and Seligman's descriptive terms provide a handy starting point for our portrait of an Abuser. I have not strictly followed their organization, but have used it as a backdrop to illustrate the differences between virtues and vices, virtuous human behavior and Abusive behavior. Many of the categories overlap. There is no absolute demarcation between traits; I intended them to be descriptive. The differences I focused on here are between Light and Dark, virtuous vs. Abusive.

Humanity

The qualities which we think of as virtues in the Humanity category include love, kindness, nurturance, generosity, and sensitivity to others—the qualities we might think of as "heart" or generosity of spirit. The Abuser, on the other hand, displays the "vices" of selfishness, stinginess, mean-spiritedness, spitefulness, lack of insight, and insensitivity toward others.

I will define the terms "conscience" and "empathy" which I have added to the list. According to the American Heritage Dictionary (2000), conscience is "the awareness of a moral or ethical aspect to one's conduct, together with the urge to prefer right over wrong."

Empathy is defined as "identification with and understanding of another's situation, feelings and motives."

The inner sense of right and wrong which humans generally experience as inborn is what makes us flush and sweat if we attempt to lie. A well-developed adult conscience produces a world-view which simply would not allow us to perform heinous acts because they would feel completely anathema to us. An individual with a highly developed conscience would consistently demonstrate behavior and attitudes which personify this tendency toward integrity and honesty. An Abuser, on the other hand, might be fully aware of the immoral or unethical aspects of their conduct, but feel no urge at all to prefer what others might consider the right thing to do. Thus, we have the first Abusive character trait:

1. *An Abuser has no conscience as we know it.*

Because we cannot measure the virtue of good conscience except through observing a person's actions, Abusers take advantage of this fact by controlling what others know about them. They may move frequently, change social circles, or otherwise manage what people find out about them. They tend to be good at public relations when it comes to their own identities. In this way, they avoid detection, by keeping a cloak of mystery about their own history of dishonest actions toward others.

The effort to *appear* honorable has nothing to do with sensitivity toward others, the way most of us would care about what people think of us. On the contrary, an Abuser cares only about protecting his own "good reputation" in order to perpetrate further deceits. Abusers' ill treatment of others is restrained only by the fear of getting caught or being exposed, not for any love or concern toward others. They would, and often do, rob their own grandmothers. Their behavior suggests that no inner compass guides them or provides brakes on their transgressions against others.

An Abuser experiences no kinship, no sense of being one of a larger community to which she feels a sense of bonding or loyalty, hence no feeling of "us." If an Abuser does join a "club" it would be for self-protection or mutually profitable criminal activities. Her lack of genuine connection to others allows her to lie, cheat and steal without remorse.

An Abuser would think nothing of borrowing your favorite sweater and not returning it, over your adamant objections, or "forgetting" to pay her share of the rent. If you question her on it, she will act insulted and make it look as if you are being unreasonable or stingy. Here, it is not so much the small act itself which is the tip-off. The warning signs are in the unswerving sense of entitlement, and the repetitive inclination to use other people and their belongings.

On the other hand, should you show kindness or generosity to an Abuser, it will be interpreted as weakness, an opportunity for her to take advantage of you unless the Abuser detects that the kindness is backed up by strength. In that case, she will feel aversion, not knowing what to expect. Abusers will avoid people they cannot manipulate, since they only want to play if they can win.

We admire honesty and integrity, and we look for these qualities in our dealings with others. Highly functioning humans would do the honorable thing because they prefer it, whether anyone is looking or not. An Abuser would see no point in this. From their psychological vantage point, only a "sucker" would give up the opportunity to gain the upper hand. The Golden Rule is nothing more than a silly nursery rhyme to an Abuser.

2. They have no real empathy for others (emotional intelligence).

An Abuser does not feel what you feel. He may learn to identify, name, and copy human emotions, even to the extent of spending hours in the mirror practicing to get the right expression to go with the emotion he is trying to portray. These are admirable acting skills, but it does not mean he knows what the emotions of love, loyalty or even genuine sadness feel like. When it comes to the range of feelings we associate with emotional depth, they are severely deficient. For instance, in the presence of another person's pain, the Abuser would feel complete indifference or even amusement. He would not bother to show concern or sympathy unless it would benefit him in some way. In the previous story, Paolo displayed this insensitivity when he refused to acknowledge Maria's distress at having been attacked at gunpoint. He did not even pretend to care, or to understand how painful this experience had been for her. Rather, he saw her distraught emotional state as a bother, something which interfered with his more important concerns about picking up a sofa bed. This utter lack of understanding or sense of proportion about emotional issues is typical of an Abuser's thinking. They are utterly lacking in emotional intelligence.

The experience of empathy is based on an intimate exchange of information. It feels like a transfer of energy, as when a person receives and understands the "vibe" of another. We often experience this as we look into another's eyes. The eyes of an Abuser are cold and empty, except when they are trying to appear otherwise. With an Abusive Type, the exchange of electrical energy is lacking. The Abuser may send a message to seduce or threaten their target, but there is no reciprocal energy flow. Communication with a Abuser is one way: from them to you. Folk tales describing "the evil eye" are no doubt referring to the piercing glare my brother Tom called "the rat look."

The Abusive mother uses her gaze toward her children to intimidate them, rather than affirm a sense of closeness or bonding. There is no heartfelt moral teaching and no emotional connection between an Abuser and a child. Her lack of empathy does not allow her to know or care what the child feels. Only her needs are expressed in a "relationship" between her and her child. Children are just pawns to be manipulated and used, as she uses the adults around her.

An Abusive mother will have nothing of what is often referred to as an innate mother instinct. One young man told the story of his grief upon learning that his father had committed suicide. Stunned and bereft, he went to his mother's home, where she gave him the reason for his father's suicide: "We were arguing about you."

3. They have a very limited emotional range.

Human feelings run the full gamut from joy and spontaneous exuberance to sadness, passion, anger and fear. The Abuser, on the other hand, experience only a narrow range, on the continuum from annoyance to irritation to hostile rage. Moral anguish, passionate loyalty, and enduring love are unknown to an Abuser. They will stick with a relationship as long as it is comfortable, convenient or profitable to do so. They are morally lazy and will sell out if something better comes along.

They feel rage if a lover or friend leaves them. Their vindictiveness may last a lifetime, but they are not heartbroken. Vulnerable partners may mistake this possessiveness and jealousy as love, but at its base it is a sense of proprietary ownership rather than genuine affection.

The "positive" emotions one might see from an Abuser may take the form of fake friendliness or a slyly triumphant grin (or sneer) when they feel they have added another notch to their belt of human undoing. Satisfaction for an Abuser is always melded with triumph. Deception, or beating out a competitor, or crushing another person's will are victories.

The Triumphant-Abuser expression can be seen on the faces of terrorist organizers who have plotted the most heinous of crimes. As one trainer of suicide bombers proudly said, "We have the advantage over the Israelis because they love life. We love death." Here, an interesting comparison can be made with the bombers themselves. Those passionate idealists who give their lives for their cause by strapping on explosives and blowing themselves up are probably not Abusers themselves. However desperate and destructive their tactics, the ones who live through it say they genuinely believed they were giving their lives for an honorable cause. An Abuser would neither volunteer to die nor willingly sacrifice anything for a cause. It is a good bet that the schemers who dreamed up the tactic of using *other people* as walking bombs may be Abusers.

In recent years, Americans have witnessed the most horrific abuses coming out of the conflict in Iraq, in which videotaped jailers at Abu Ghraib and elsewhere smile, strut with pride at their cruel handiwork, and take trophy photos. We do not know if these soldiers were genuine Abusive Personalities or Wannabes. Wannabes can be manipulated into performing inhuman acts. However, we can be fairly certain that the hand of an Abuser was behind the planning and approval of such sadistic acts of humiliation and degradation. A Wannabe may try to outdo or impress his Abusive leader. Whether Wannabe or Abuser, both celebrate their grim victories similarly, with cynical and smug triumph at a feat of destruction. Such is the face of Darkness.

4. *They are incapable of authentic kindness or generosity.*

Genuine "tending and befriending others" comes straight from the heart. Since they feel no loyalty or connection to others, there is no inclination to act out of kindness or generosity. They are unable to nurture others. For instance, my mother's willingness to pay for my brother's house came only from her wish to control and dominate him. It did not come from an impulse to provide him with comfort or security.

Abusers may make a public display of giving gifts or doing favors. It is important to note that they would never do these things anonymously. Acting like a good person is simply a means to an end: a public relations campaign to appear generous, trustworthy, or kind. It may even be a very large part of an Abuser's activities, but their main concern is what's in it for them. For instance, my mother belonged to many charitable organizations, especially those which benefited orphans and people with handicaps or mental illness. Although she actually spent little time working for these causes, she peppered her conversations with references to her charitable associations. These activities provided a network of connections in the community as well as a number of social events each year where she could be admired and photographed. The test of whether a person is genuine in their giving is whether they continue to be generous when no one is looking.

Abusers are notoriously insensitive in their dealings with other people's emotional difficulties, especially when the issue concerns them. They will remain resolutely unapologetic, regardless of their crime. If you object to abusive treatment from them, they will say, "You're a troublemaker. Why can't you just get along?" Instead of discussing your complaint, or considering some kind of compromise, he attacks. Whatever the problem, it is never his or her fault. Blame is always someone else's. Abusers do not accept responsibility.

As a ploy to appear conciliatory, the Abuser might admit to a mutual misunderstanding, especially if there are witnesses. As a strategy for achieving conflict resolution, an Abusive Type will hold to the principle: "The best defense is a good denial." (or "The best defense is a vicious offense")

All this can be devastating for a child with an Abusive parent. Any expression of unhappiness or dissatisfaction from the child will be met with accusations that the child is being selfish, greedy, or faking it for attention. The child, suffering real pain for legitimate reasons, is torn from her underpinnings, or as Maria described it, "amputated" from her own feelings. Regardless of the issue, the person lodging the objection will be blamed, accused, slandered, insulted, and made to feel guilty and inferior for even bringing it up. This strategy is used in every area of life by Wannabes and Abusers who wish to get the upper hand and keep it. A recent example in the U.S. political arena was the attack on anyone who questioned the authority of those in charge by labeling all dissenters as "traitors," in spite of the time-honored democratic tradition of loyal opposition.

Because of the Abuser's lack of social intelligence (the ability to understand and respond to the needs and feelings of others), a relationship will be fraught with accusations and missed communications. Along with his lack of empathy, he will also frequently misunderstand others' motives because of his self-referential view of the world, assuming unfriendliness or personal attack where there is none. He expects to be attacked because that is what he would do. What frequently looks like paranoia is really more about projecting his own attitudes onto others.

Temperance

The qualities which are grouped by Seligman above under the category of Temperance are so out of fashion in Twenty-first Century American culture that they may seem old-fashioned and quaint. In a society where the fruits of greed put people at the top of the social ladder, women's evening dresses are designed to remind you of fancy underwear, and pornographic images flood the airwaves, temperance has been associated with prudishness and attacks on First Amendment personal freedoms. In our enthusiasm for freedom of all sorts, we have unfortunately lost sight of the benefits of living in an environment which is modulated by adherence to higher standards of personal responsibility, prudence, humility and modesty, forgiveness and mercy, and reasonable self-regulation. As the pendulum has swung away from temperance, we have moved instead toward more extreme forms of shameless self-promotion, unwarranted pride, greed, grandiosity, recklessness, and hardheartedness. One identifiable quality which stretches across all the realms of personal, social and political life is the omnipresent expression of arrogance.

5. *Abusers are arrogant.*

Of all the expressions of intemperance, arrogance most vividly demonstrates the pervasiveness of Dark values in our self-indulgent society.

Arrogance is one of the qualities which makes the Abuser so attractive to others. Their lack of humility is so utterly complete that to unwitting observers it may look like resolve and self-assurance. Their absolutely unswerving sureness can be captivating. A practiced Abuser can emanate such a powerfully confident vibe that others are bowled over by it. Self-reflective people, accustomed to struggling with feelings of self-doubt and guilt, might easily be fooled into thinking they have met a truly remarkable human being, at least at first.

The Abuser feels utterly superior and apart from other people. On the surface, this does look like self-confidence. In their assumption of superiority, they often see themselves as powerful leaders. When humans, in their desire to have a strong leader, agree with the Abuser's self-assumed greatness and rally around what they believe to be a leader of heroic attributes, the Abuser may rise to a position of great power. Regular humans fall into a trap when they assess the Abuser's arrogance, by assuming he thinks the same way they do. While it is well known that arrogance in a less self-assured person is often a cover for feelings of inferiority, this is not the case for an Abuser, who really believes he is better than the rest of us.

Arrogance can be seen behind numerous historical examples of individuals whose wild ambitions transcended any reason or logic. For instance, Moammar Ghadafi in Libya refused to give up power even as the entire world sympathized with the protesters who risked their lives to defy his brutal rule. His is a modern day lesson in blind arrogance and greed. It will probably take years to uncover the extent of despotism and corruption which has starved the people of the Middle East in the name of "law and order."

Hitler has been known as the most obvious example of an Abuser, although he may have been too passionate in his beliefs, and too hot-blooded in his rage to be considered a true Abuser.[11] If his ranting tirades are eventually shown to be a calculated rabble-rousing

---

[11]   Personal communication, Glenn McGuire, 2008, New York City.

strategy—a good acting job—then he would qualify for APT status. Either way, he was very effective at bringing out the basest, most Abusive leanings in others. Hitler believed he could conquer the entire world by manipulating his followers to do his bidding, and by running roughshod over anyone who stood in his way. He flattered his followers into thinking of themselves as superhuman. This was especially appealing to those Germans who had been raised in the cruel and excessively strict tradition of childrearing practiced during the early part of the century.[12] These were practices which tend to leave children either seething with rage, or passively admiring of cruelty. Having been humiliated and degraded themselves, it must have seemed a seductive option, to turn the tables on the whole world: Gain power and riches, while wiping out anyone who annoys you, especially if they challenge your idea of your own greatness.

Because of the self-centered superiority of Abusers and their Wannabe associates, there is one thing they really cannot stand. That is an encounter with anyone who is independent of them, unbowed and enjoying it. They will try to crush any form of celebration which does not celebrate them personally, because they feel the need to be in control of everything and anything around them in order to confirm their sense of superiority.

As we have seen in earlier chapters, a childhood which leaves a person feeling unworthy and injured is a recipe for vulnerability to Abuser's values. As long as children are abused or neglected, we risk fostering the growth and popularity of vicious dictators and their Abuser-Wannabe followers, because we all want to feel a sense of personal power, one way or another.

Justice

Seligman and Peterson's category of Justice offers a revealing basis for comparison with the Abuser's dictatorial methods of leadership. The virtues of citizenship, fairness, and democratic leadership are anathema to an Abuser. Rather, Abusers tends to be egotistical, selfish, prejudiced, disloyal, and suspicious of others. Their self-centeredness tends to make them the kind of poor leader who brings disaster on their followers.

---

[12] Alice Miller discusses these issues in her writings, especially *For Your Own Good.*

6.   An Abuser is not interested in good citizenship or teamwork.

Abusers do not understand why humans help each other or stand up for themselves based on human principles. They are baffled at why anyone would stand up for someone else. This tendency to demand justice for one another is a threat to an Abuser's free reign, but he is at a loss to truly understand why people do it. Although they may use the right words to pretend they understand, they truly cannot comprehend concepts such as cooperation, friendship, and community. They know what these things look like when others do them, but they have no emotional meaning for an Abuser. They sense this difference, and feel extremely uncomfortable at being reminded of their deficit. In order to feel superior to others, they cannot acknowledge they are missing anything of value. Hence, they fear close contact, especially with Heart-centered humans who openly show their love of life, their sense of fair play and their enjoyment of others. These are the competent humans who are most likely to stand up to them, to reveal their weaknesses, and to expose them as unjust and uncaring.

To maintain control, Abusers may become so hell-bent on achieving their goals that they become careless and cocky. They assume they have the power to manipulate and trick others; some even think of it as magic. They also presume that most people are stupid. Ironically, this is a fundamentally stupid position to take, since it means they are constantly underestimating their enemies, the humans. They are especially unhinged by our tendency to forge voluntary alliances and to rush to the aid of our friends because we care about their safety and well-being, even when there is no profit in it for us. An Abuser would never do this without the promise of a payoff. Cooperation, to an abuser, takes the form of "ganging up" or buying favors.

Stories are epidemic in recent years of star-quality athletes being arrested for rape, gun violence, reckless driving, and drug taking. Fans are shocked, as if athletic ability should naturally be accompanied by good character and concern for the team's good name. If we want athletes who are good role models for our children, we will have to do a better job of screening out the bad actors earlier in the process, rather than betting everything on winning at any cost, without regard for the morale of their teammates and fans. The lawless athletes who showed such physical promise have taken on the Abuser's attitude that they are entitled to the "spoils" of victory.

Here is an example that helps to illustrate the difference between virtuous humans and Abusers in action. Imagine a man is driving along near a river. He hears screams and sees a mother on the river bank waving frantically. In the water, a child is struggling, fighting against the current. The man speeds to the river bank, jumps into the river and pulls the drowning child to safety. When the community gathers and the TV reporters proclaim him a hero, the man says simply, "I'm not a hero. I just did what seemed right." Now picture the Abuser driving along the river. Seeing the desperate scene, the first thought would be, "Hell, that water's cold, and there's no one else around. I'd ruin my good suit, and what would it get me to risk my neck. Let the lady save her own kid." Unless it was likely to bring personal advantage, the Abuser would keep on driving.

7. They feel they are above the law.

We hold life to be precious, ours and that of others as well. We value justice, equality, and evenhanded fairness in our system of laws. An Abuser, on the other hand, wants only to gain advantage over others, by any means available. In their own eyes, they are above the law. Yet, they will be the first to complain, point out others' transgressions, and pursue legalistic attacks on their enemies. From the Abuser's point of view, the law is there to assist in persecuting others. Often, they are very adept at "throwing the first stone," but even here, their inability to understand the spirit of the law is sometimes revealed. In holding someone accountable, they will often hold strictly to the details of the law, while showing they really don't "get it." Here's an example: An Abuser hears about a robbery in which the convenience store owner is shot by the robber, using the owner's own gun, which turns out to be unregistered. The robber flees with $15. The Abuser's commentary: "Jeez, the guy was really stupid. All that for 15 dollars! They should charge the store owner for having an illegal gun! It was his own fault he got shot anyway."

Breaking the law is preferable to upholding it, if getting away with the crime is a good bet. An Abuser building a skyscraper would prefer to put extra sand in the cement if the inspectors weren't looking. The safety of others would never be a concern. Paying taxes is an unbearable annoyance, since the Abuser would not willingly contribute to anything for the public good, but they will always be the first to complain about the quality of service. They consider law-abiding citizens to be sheep. For instance, an Abuser would never make the effort to return a lost wallet, unless a reward was forthcoming. She would take the position: "Finders keepers."

They are vindictive. If reported for an illegal or immoral deed, the Abuser will use any weapon within his power to avoid exposure and punishment. The first line of defense would be to discredit the victim using slander, loud public protests of innocence, and nuisance lawsuits. Since his idea of justice is completely self-referential, he cares not a whit whose life may be ruined in his own attempts to avoid punishment.

8. *Abusers are financial opportunists with no sense of responsibility to the rest of the world.*

Stealing is a primary method of acquiring whatever the Abuser wants. "Borrowing" valuable belongings and not returning them is a favorite ploy. He would think nothing of driving your car and bringing it back with the tank empty, or using your good name to garner special favors from others without your knowledge. In more educated Abusers, stealing takes the form of plagiarism, intellectual property infringement, and copying ideas from others who are more creative and imaginative than they are, as Maria discovered in Paolo's penchant for borrowing others designs. He saw nothing wrong with this.

During the Twentieth Century, corporate and governmental institutions created a worldwide business model based on greed and deniability which has changed the entire financial and social structure of the Western world. Vast sums of investor and taxpayer money has been siphoned upward, disappearing into the overflowing coffers of powerful bankers, military contractors, oil producers and hedge fund traders, to name a few. Wannabes fell all over themselves to pass accommodating laws, and to feed at the trough, while the vast majority of American people and others around the globe, drunk with greed themselves, threw caution to the wind and emulated the Abusers.

A recent Ponzi scheme in the U.S. is possibly the greatest privately-accomplished scam to date. Bernard Madoff bilked thousands of people of nearly 50 billion dollars. He was a respected official of high rank in the financial community, who traded on his reputation to deceive his victims. Even though his published balance sheet made no sense, and his returns seemed "too good to be true," people gave him their savings. In the aftermath of the scandal, one can only be amazed at the complete stupidity of Madoff's actions, and the questionable naiveté of his victims, many of whom were supposedly sophisticated and powerful investors. The way he duped his victims is telling. He constructed his scheme on the model of an exclusive private club: by invitation only. In so doing, he became the Jim Jones of the financial world. Like a cult leader, he played on his clients' emotional needs at the same time he offered them social status, wealth and prestige. Little by little, he gained absolute financial power over many of his victims, who entrusted everything they had to him. He was already an exceedingly wealthy and powerful man with contacts in the highest levels of society. He could only have done it for the thrill of conquest.

Cheating, betrayal and double-dealing are coin of the realm for an Abuser, but they will not be obvious or blatant about it. Successful deception requires an element of surprise. A skilled Abuser may alternate long periods of feigned friendliness and reliability with one sudden and unexpected act of betrayal. In the case of Madoff, the "sudden" revelation of wrongdoing could only have been delayed by cooperation from like-minded high-level financial officials and other co-conspirators who were benefiting from his or their own similar grand schemes. Greed is a characteristically Abusive vice which has been raised to the status of respectability in the Western world. It has been systematically institutionalized, and has spread to financial markets worldwide. The ripple effect of this infection is likely to resonate for years to come, as history reveals the previously unfathomable depths of soulless corruption.

The ability to blithely maintain a falsely friendly face while picking pockets is not a new phenomenon. Only the massive scope of the dishonesty is new. The Abuser's ability to maintain a false presentation requires no special dedication or persistence for him. It is as natural as breathing, since there is no heart connection to an authentic conscience-bound self from which alarm bells of guilt might sound. It is this guiltless, pseudo-confident quality which confuses others, lulling them into believing the Abuser is really "one of us." (Someone you might want to have a beer with.)

An Abuser with money can be counted on to use his wealth to seduce and manipulate others. In a marriage, he will insist on controlling the purse strings, and will encourage financial dependency in others in order to control them. A will is a weapon in the hands of an Abuser.

More subtle examples are often brushed off as simple bad manners or thoughtlessness. Over time, they can reveal a dark intention. Examples include taking advantage of others' generosity by never offering to pay for meal when eating out with a group, or collecting undeserved disability payments from the government.

9. *They fear exposure.*

A con artist can only succeed at his game as long as his victim believes in his good will. For this reason, he cares very much what other people think of him, because being liked is essential to "getting over." To achieve this, Abusers will study what humans like, what their weak spots are, and will develop a repertoire of behaviors that are appealing. Depending on the Abuser's upbringing, they will usually develop a blood lust for the type of destruction which was most highly valued in their own family, and their focus will be on developing the skills to achieve it, while avoiding detection. Their idea of conquest may be financial, intellectual, sexual, emotional, or any combination of these entertainments.

Just as high-functioning humans use their energy to be creative, constructive and cooperative, Abusers will use theirs to undermine, undo, and compete in the hopes of destroying or utterly controlling others. Should the person or persons under her control show an inclination to escape or tell the world, the Abuser will begin her attempt at controlling the rebellion by employing flattery and threats. If this does not work, in family situations she will use the common strategy of "making an example" by sadistically punishing the erstwhile escapee.

Cult leaders like Jim Jones, who arranged for 900 of his followers to swallow poisoned Kool Aid, had maintained his hold on his followers by isolating them from contact with the outside world where they might have found comfort or support for their doubts. These tactics work especially well on children, and on adults who feel insecure and needy. The threat of abandonment, rejection, withdrawal of love, financial support or membership in the Abuser's inner circle are all powerful emotional weapons.

Courage

The Positive Psychology category of Courage can be used to compare traits which go beyond the inclination to act bravely under fire. Other less obvious qualities include day-to-day traits like integrity, determination, and inner strength—those characteristics we are referring to when we say a person has "true grit," or "mettle." These qualities may be imitated by Abusers, but the similarity is less than skin deep.

10. They are liars.

Dishonesty springs from a lack of courage to live life fully, to experience intimacy and deep emotion. The Abusers' aversion to "straight shooting" is most easily detected in day to day life by their inclination to lie. This is one of the most pervasive tendencies which separates them from more scrupulous humans. Many Abusers are highly skilled liars.

Con artists rely on this capability to dupe their victims. The victims will often report afterwards that they are amazed to find out they were tricked, because the con artist seemed so nice and friendly. In other words, he showed no signs of nervousness, discomfort, or hints of guilt. These are the telltale symptoms we use as humans to detect whether someone is lying or not.

Most humans find it difficult to lie, and have a physiological reaction which involves an elevated stress response, including sweating, increased heart rate, and other symptoms which are commonly known as the galvanic skin response. Although we are trained from birth not to tell the truth if it concerns something people consider "impolite," we must work at it to learn how to lie. In other words, humans generally do not find it easy or enjoyable to lie. Abusers see no reason to tell the truth. They often presume that everyone lies. Lying is preferable to honesty, since it provides a chance to get the upper hand or to play cloak-and-dagger games. It gives them a thrill. Lying by omission is especially useful.

Beware of the person who lies to you, especially if you love and trust them. Since Abusers make their points by tricking and deceiving others, it is natural for them to lie as an integral tool in their weaponry of deceit.

11. They are cowards.

Abusers may seem to show admirable traits like bravery, vitality and authenticity. Displays of bravado and absolute conviction make them seem right and superior. This gives them a fake veneer of power and righteousness.

In the short term, an Abuser may seem to have nerves of steel. However, the similarity with genuinely courageous people is purely superficial. The Abuser may place himself in danger without flinching, like a "hit man" in a movie, but he has probably calculated the probabilities at hand. He believes the danger is minimal and the risk is worth taking. Their "brave" acts are not done for the benefit of others; they are only signs of reckless indifference to life. They expect fame and/or gain in the end.

The Dark Ones among us may exhibit a flamboyant enthusiasm for taking on enemies, but they are much more likely to encourage others toward dangerous action (like warfare) than to fight themselves. They are quick with brave talk, but they don't enlist out of patriotism. If they do go to war, it is to indulge their prejudices and their blood-lust.

Because of the obsession with power, they tend to be attracted to sophisticated weaponry, displays of physical strength, and the prospect of starting and watching "a good fight." George C. Scott captured these qualities brilliantly in his role as General "Buck" Turgidson, in the classic 1964 Stanley Kubrick film, *Dr. Strangelove*. Although Gen. Turgidson appeared to be clearly insane at times, (and I have said Abusers are not generally "crazy") we might stretch our definitions for this instance because of the hilarious comedic effect it offered, and because the General was clearly intended as a film character, not a psychological profile. Nevertheless, his enthusiastic lack of insight or social conscience creates an ingenious caricature of the Abusive character's mind.

12. They may be sexually vital and attractive, but they are predictably fickle.

The Abuser does have the normal measure of physical vitality and energy. We must not assume this is accompanied by a normal measure of anything else we hold dear, like sportsmanship, or integrity.

Here is one of the most confusing elements about a relationship with a Dark One. Especially in youth, they may show remarkable facility in athletics, and their animal magnetism draws many an unsuspecting person into their field of attraction. Once taken in, the appeal of a sexual relationship with an Abuser can be nearly irresistible. They may show real relish and skill in the physical act of lovemaking, but for the Abusive One, sex is an athletic event, physically pleasurable, but devoid of any emotional connection. This is why they often prefer multiple or secret partners. Some prefer no partner if the emotional entanglements are too bothersome.

Some Abusive Personalities are especially attracted to sexual conquests. Their tastes may be remarkably wide-ranging, and their tactics can be truly shocking to the people around them. Like Don Juan of literary fame, the Abuser is not attracted by the individual qualities of the woman he pursues. Any woman in the vicinity is fair game, by virtue of her capacity as a sexual vessel. Infidelity is an especially attractive game for an Abuser, unless it interferes with gaining or keeping power over others, or if it takes too much effort. Of course, not all unfaithful partners are Abusers, but Abusers are very likely to be unfaithful.

How does an Abuser respond to a partner's infidelity? With seething resentment, blame, hatred, and vicious attacks. Remember, they want to be admired and adored, treated as the Center of the Universe. They expect respect and loyalty to them, but feel no need to reciprocate. They will capitalize on their partner's feelings of guilt by using shame, threats and violence. To an Abuser, seeing fear in a victim's eyes feels as good as being loved.

Abusers who do not have the skills to qualify them as sophisticated Don Juan types may still succeed in keeping an emotional stranglehold on their partners. Through a combination of alternating seduction and emotional abuse, the Abuser erodes the other's deepest sense of self, leaving them feeling stupid, unattractive, and utterly dependent, unable to break free of their Abuser. We see this pattern with battered women, who will return to the batterer even though he may be an incompetent loser, less attractive or competent in every way than she is. Nevertheless, she has become convinced she cannot live without him, because of her own lack of self-worth.

An Abuser with good looks will play this card to the maximum. You would never hear an Abuser complaining about being loved only for his looks. To him, good looks are his most valuable possession: the medium by which he lures and seduces his victims, whether it involves a business venture or a sexual romp.

13. In spite of their animal attractiveness, Abusers lack passion or persistence. They are lazy.

An Abuser's dedication to his craft or his conquest does not spring from the sort of passionate emotional thrust that humans feel when they pursue something or someone they love. When we experience the inner drive toward a goal, it is generally with a strongly positive valence that we rise to meet our challenges. With an Abuser, the drive is based in a cold, calculating single-mindedness, in which the goal is to devour, possess, or destroy the object of their attention. They are not interested in building, nourishing, or forwarding another person's well-being or success. Just the opposite. It is a cannibalistic hunger which drives them, and it is the destruction of the essence of the human spirit which satisfies them, temporarily. Their hunger is like a constant itch that needs to be scratched rather than a burning passion.

It is this lack of passion which makes Abusers appear lazy—or perhaps "laid back" by comparison with their peers. In school, they would rather cheat than study. At work, they rely on their facile charm to talk their way into or out of any situation, and to carry them to success. Abusers learn early how to cut corners and to use their wiles to get other people to do their work for them.

Wisdom and Knowledge

The category of Wisdom and Knowledge, as it is presented by Peterson and Seligman, provides an interesting glimpse into the intellectual functioning of an Abuser. Rather than curiosity, creativity and open-mindedness, the Abusive Personality's thinking process tends to be closed-minded, incurious, dogmatic, unimaginative and lacking in perspective.

14. Abusers lack creativity, imagination and curiosity.

"Creativity" includes the ability to think in novel and productive ways, and to express new ideas effectively. Abusers may gain some success by copying others' work, but rarely initiate discoveries or produce anything imaginative or new. Like Maria's friend Paulo, they might be adept at rearranging other people's ideas to produce some fairly creative-looking commercial products, but their "art" bears marks of egotism and self-aggrandizement. They are not able to be great masters or original thinkers.

Most Abusers are also oddly lacking in curiosity. Because they have no respect for truth, they are not interested in the world around them, except in so far as they need information to impress others or increase their power. They do need other people's creative ideas to pass off as their own, but they rarely pursue knowledge for its own sake, or admire others for their accomplishments. They are often jealous of the fruits of others' labor, but reluctant to earn anything themselves. Thus many Abusers are underachievers. They are morally and intellectually lazy. In some instances, the pursuit of political or sexual power may appear passionate on the surface. Creepy stalkers and political megalomaniacs share a narrow energetic focus. It precludes other interests and makes them especially dangerous. This is not authentic passion as most of us understand that emotion. Rather, it is the drive to inflate their own egos.

15. Abusers are remarkably inflexible, dogmatic and judgmental. They have little respect for scientific fact, or for the opinion of others.

Abusers often demonstrate a shallow, superficial sense of intellectual priorities and preferences which may seem extremely odd. Maria gave the example of Paulo's fascistic hatred of various ethnic groups. Racism, sexism, and hatred of all kinds are the Abuser's extreme expression of this tendency. It seems to emanate from the marrow of their bones. It took a full-blooded Abuser to come up with the idea of "ethnic cleansing."

These dangerous prejudices might be mistakenly interpreted as joking or mere exaggeration. Witness the modern-day popularity of ranting "right-wing" talk-show hosts whose raw hate-mongering and judgmental opinions are considered entertainment, legitimate political discourse or even news. The Abusers' lobby in Congress has become a powerful force for "social conservatism." Abusers and their Wannabe associates can be found emphatically promoting the following sorts of ideas, which Heart-centered humans would find absurd: gay people threaten the institution of marriage; dark skin indicates inferior intelligence or laziness; poverty or hurricanes or floods are a punishment from God for immorality; trees and endangered species are superfluous; women are inferior and weak-minded, and freedom of choice for women threatens the foundations of civilization. The tendency to think in terms of absolutes, such as frequent use of the words "all, always, and never" indicates this type of unthinking, negative assessment of the world. It is based on prejudice and ill-will rather than analysis.

16. The Abuser has a Code of Ethics.

These descriptions may suggest that Abusers oppose laws and ethics, but this is not always the case. Some have a strict code of ethics, such as the rigorous code that has maintained the cohesion of the Mafia for many generations. Maria made a crucial mistake when she disregarded Paulo's stated philosophy. It sounded so utterly ridiculous to her that she assumed it was a joke. However, his behavior was consistent with his acknowledged "Neo-Nazi Fascist" creed. He really did hate everybody.

The Abusive Personality code of ethics may vary somewhat depending on geography or cultural background, but such codes have been with us through the ages. The Abusers' "moral code," like the behavior it justifies, has little in common with the Boy Scouts' Promise or the Hippocratic Oath, but it does support a conscious system of beliefs which underlies their arrogant and selfish behavior. The basics go something like this: "I'm out for Number One. Losers get distracted when they wallow in their weak emotions. It's stupid. I'm better off because I don't get involved with those sappy feelings. I have my friends and associates, and we take care of each other. They back me, and they never rat, or they won't be around to talk about it. They know they better not cross me. Nobody gets away with disrespecting me, no matter who they are. You can't trust strangers. You never know who's out to get you."

Abusers would never let loyalty or friendship block their own ends. They define absence of care as superior strength, a badge of courage and invulnerability. They also believe it gives them the edge in making "rational" decisions, while their lack of emotional intelligence makes them fundamentally stupid in every area of human life that really matters. Because of the inherent belief in their own superiority, Abusers feel entitled to crush anyone who is different from them, by whatever means necessary. They do not apologize.

Beneath the considerable charm of many Abusers is a disguised, cold contempt for humanity and life itself. The Abuser's core philosophy of life boils down to this: "It's a dog-eat-dog world out there. Watch your back. Everybody's out to get what they can, so get yours first."

In direct contrast, enlightened and humble people have encouraged human virtues through written and oral teachings which have been passed down through the ages. Examples include the Ten Commandments, the Hindu Bhagavad-Gita, the Five Precepts of Buddhism, the Islamic Code of Ethics, the Twelve Steps of AA, the U.N. charter, various professional codes of ethics, marriage vows and other pledges. These are traditional affirmations of the positive character traits and virtues discussed here.

17. An argument with an Abuser is a tear-your-hair-out Alice in Wonderland mind-scrambler.

An argument with an Abuser is a mind-numbing dead end street. You cannot present a logical argument based in facts and expect to have any impact. They have complete disregard for any reality other than their own. They do not care about anyone else's opinions or feelings. Since "truth" is any opinion he holds at the moment, there are no limits to what he or she will say to make a point, using whatever tactics appear to have the greatest impact. An Abuser is only interested in "facts" which suit her purposes.

Let's say you are debating the feasibility of building a new coal burning plant on the shores of the pristine lake in a protected wilderness area. You present your argument against the project, saying, "Here I have the evidence from twenty scientific studies, warning against what you are trying to do." She may say, "You can't be sure of that; statistics always lie," or "Science isn't everything," or simply, "You're attacking me." Yet, when she wants to present a case, she will use volumes of statistics and so-called facts, real or imagined, presented in the most dramatic and emotionally manipulative way. An Abusive schemer uses a debate as an opportunity to seduce or strike fear into the heart of her opponent, whichever is likely to produce the effect she wants. (The smoking gun may become a mushroom cloud!) Facts are irrelevant. Unfortunately, good and well-meaning people will be drawn into debates about the merits and disadvantages of torture, for instance, or defiling precious wilderness areas, or denying health care to poor children. These are options which would simply be unthinkable in a culture with a higher level of social intelligence than our own. Polite newscasters and political pundits consistently miss the point, in their efforts to show their knowledge and expertise. Arguing the fine points of whether it is a good idea to rape and pillage, and under what conditions, could only occur after the Abusers have defined the territory, silenced all the ethical people, and put everyone else to sleep.

In a personal relationship, the Abuser will stop at nothing to win an argument, even if it leaves you devastated. Name-calling, insults and character assassination are favorite ploys. You will be reminded of how everybody dislikes and distrusts you, and how everybody agrees with her. Whatever your weak spot, the Abusive One will find it and attack, pushing your hot buttons until you wear down or break. Styles vary. One Abuser might prefer playful, mock-humor humiliation. Another might practice head-on belittling, scorn and sarcasm, or threats of abandonment or physical violence. Others develop skillful hit-and-run public putdowns like "I remember when you were thin," or "Darling, you look so tired. You must be working too hard," or "You just aren't college material," or "You're so shy. No wonder nobody likes you." No insult is too extreme or off limits if it achieves the purpose of diminishing your self-confidence. Abusers like their victims off-balance and weak.

There are no win-win outcomes for a Dark One; any compromise or concession is seen as a loss. In their eyes, their own needs and feelings are reality, and they will be insulted if you don't agree. Only when they are utterly overpowered, and all their previously mentioned strategies have failed will they back down or consider negotiations. In defeat, they are vindictive cowards.

Transcendence

Transcendence is a virtue we associate with an appreciation of worlds beyond our selves. This includes a deep appreciation for art and beauty, a profound connection with the Earth and all its creatures, an attitude of gratitude for life itself, or a belief in a power or powers greater than oneself.

First, let's define the difference between spirituality and religiosity. Because of their overlapping meanings in common usage, they are often confused. In its broadest definition, spirituality implies a belief that life has meaning and an abiding faith in the power of intelligent forces in the Universe which reach far beyond our Earth-bound existence. A person need not belong to any particular religious organization or subscribe to any formally documented dogma or creed to live a spiritual life. On the other hand, a religious person is one who subscribes to an established set of ideas and beliefs as they are taught within the formal organization of a particular religious group, and who identifies with those teachings as his or her commitment to a moral code. While it is possible to be spiritual without being religious, all the major religions require a belief in some version of God-power as a basic tenet, thereby encouraging (but not guaranteeing) a spiritual approach to life.

The Abuser departs completely from the practice of transcendent human virtues. They have no need to believe in a God because they think they are God.

18. They have no capacity for genuine spirituality. They feel no connection to anything greater than themselves.

Genuine spirituality or a sense of higher purpose would be beyond imagining or caring for an Abuser, although they can say the words, convincingly. The ministry or the priesthood is a perfect subterfuge for an Abuser. The robes themselves imply the character traits of spirituality, kindness and generosity. Since respect is granted by tradition, the Abuser needs only to keep up pretenses to maintain his cover. This is something imposters of all kinds have learned to use to their advantage. There is a widespread human tendency to believe that "the uniform makes the man." Our inclination is to accept that those who hold formal power deserve our respect, even if we have no real knowledge about the person. This system works well in the hands of people who feel genuine concern for their followers. It can be a terrible trap in the hands of an Abuser, as we have seen with many Catholic priests and Fundamentalist preachers.

A favorite ploy in U.S. politics in recent years has been fake religiosity and the use of moral-sounding labels to curry favor with the public. This, in spite of the Constitutional requirement of separation of Church and State. This cynical maneuver is hypocritical at best, since educated people are fully aware that if a person truly intends to uphold the laws of the land, there is no need to advertise their personal religious beliefs. The Constitution and system of laws in the United States provide ample guidelines for a society based in ethical and moral values. The use of religion as a bragging point is designed to elicit associations to goodness and purity. It helps to disguise the fact that the Abuser's self-assumed mantle of entitlement frees him from any involvement with spirituality, gratitude, forgiveness, mercy or humility. Abusers are the antithesis of a person on a spiritual path: They strive to serve only their own ego needs. They are completely self-centered in their attitudes and pursuits.

Decent people have an admirable tendency to want to make amends with their friends and relatives, especially as they get older. The possibility of a life ending moves us to express our love, and to give and receive forgiveness. Abusers, on the other hand, frequently indulge in deathbed vindictiveness. One client told me this story: She went to see her mother in the hospital, knowing the mother had only a short time to live. She wanted to make a gesture of reconciliation, and hoped to receive reassurance before her mother died. The daughter opened the subject by telling her mother that she loved her, but had always sensed that her mother had not felt the same way about her. The mother replied, "I never wanted you."

19. They are Killjoys.

The startling tendency to suddenly attack in a moment of joy or celebration is based in the inability to truly celebrate anything. A jealousy for all beautiful things, unless they can be possessed completely, precludes any sense of wonder or shared happiness. In a close relationship, this tendency can be shocking, sudden, and devastating. It is all the more unexpected when the Abuser's partner may be basking in the glow of a thrilling sexual experience or a moment of fun where the Abuser has been charming.

Maria described Paulo's attacks on her when she was feeling most beautiful. From her point of view, they came out of the blue, unprovoked. She did not know it was her beauty and vitality which was the provocation.

Freedom is the enemy to their power. The Dark Ones hate seeing a person feeling good about herself, or about relationships with others. They see this as a threat, and respond with jealousy. They know their power over another person may be threatened by success in the world, so they will curtail freedom and stifle joy in their partners and in their children to maintain that power. In our earlier example, Maria's sister had become an abject slave to her mother's whims after years of failed attempts at living on her own.

It is our natural inclination to expect approval from those around us when we do something successfully. This is what makes the Abuser's disapproval so stunning, and so incomprehensible. Anyone with doubts about their own worth will feel the rug being pulled out from under them, but will assume that they must have done something wrong, or they must be misinterpreting the attack. It is unthinkable that someone we love would attack and try to undermine us simply because we are smart or successful or beautiful.

An incident in my own life provides a good example. Upon successfully completing a cross-country trip with two adults, five children and a dog packed into the car, I arrived tired but triumphant at my mother's house. She greeted me in her driveway, giving me an arrogant once-over glance. Sneering disgustedly, she said, "You look like you've been pulled through a knothole."

There is a simple measure which reveals the Abuser's intentions. If you, the target of the attack feel suddenly and profoundly hurt, disappointed and confused, you can be fairly certain you have just been the victim of a "shark attack": an Abuser has hit her mark.

This utter inability to revel in someone else's good fortune is one of the characteristic earmarks of an Abusive Personality. This is not simple thoughtlessness or grumpiness, or a fleeting bad mood. It is the symptom of the underlying character trait of malevolence. It is one of those indications which lead us to say to a friend: "Run, do not walk, to the nearest exit."

20. They have no respect for the environment or the health of the planet, and no respect for other species.

The Abusers' lack of sensitivity to environmental issues is profound. They really don't get it. Abusers are unable to imagine the interconnectedness of all living things. They don't care if their actions cause pollution, death, or the complete destruction of the planet and all the creatures on it, because they have no more love for other living things than they have for people. Since nothing living is precious to them, nothing is worth preserving. This is the attitude which psychologists address when they cite cruelty to animals at a young age as a diagnostic indicator for psychopathology. Killing stray cats for fun, or torturing dogs, or blowing up frogs with firecrackers exemplify a disregard for life which goes far beyond the realm of normal mischief.

Their obliviousness rises out of a lack of real comprehension of the laws of cause and effect. The concept of Karma, popularly referred to as "what goes around comes around," or "you reap what you sow" is incomprehensible to an Abuser. They have little concern about serious consequences when they destroy the people and other living things in their path. Not only do they lack what some might call the fear of God; they cannot even imagine any cosmic or universal law which might apply to them, to which they might be held accountable. Asked to imagine Judgment Day, a Child of Darkness would only chuckle and picture other people being deliciously punished, while he revels triumphant in the idea that he can manipulate God, if need be.

Avoiding Self-Helpitis

For those readers who may be feeling guilty about unfriendly actions you might have taken over your lifetime, I want to reassure you that it takes more than one incident, or one or two of the above characteristics to qualify for Abusive Personality status, but those actions are important in your own assessment of yourself, indicators of secret attraction to Darkness. The fact that you are questioning yourself and your own actions suggests you have a conscience and a capacity for regret, and therefore growth, so be ruthless in your pursuit of the truth about your own inclinations toward Darkness.

Many of us have been encouraged to behave in "macho" or "tough" and inhumane ways by our cultures of origin or by our immediate families. These tendencies are pervasive in our society and many others, providing "cover" for your own inhuman behavior, should you choose to use it. It is a challenge each of us must deal with when we leave childhood, where we have had ideas "instilled" in our formative brains before we had the experience or reasoning powers to question them. Understanding is not enough. It is our responsibility as thinking adults to review the teachings which were handed down to us, to question, assess, and identify where Darkness is revealed in our own behavior. This process goes far beyond seeing your own victimization as a child, or identifying the insanity in your family. Seeing the destructiveness in our elders is only the beginning in the process of deciding for ourselves whether we wish to choose a different path, even if it means standing up against their Abusive behavior, and our own.

There may be other distinguishing characteristics which will be found to make identifying an Abuser easier. This is not a definitive list. As Carl Jung suggested in his description of archetypes, every incident, every relationship is different. The proof is in the living encounter. I hope this classification will be useful as a starting point in helping people to understand what they are dealing with when they take on a close encounter with a Child of Darkness.

The Abusers I describe here are a broken and soul-empty lot who can only find satisfaction by consuming others. They have lost the struggle to remain whole and are jealous of those who have succeeded. Once they have lost the struggle to be human, with the inherently human capacity to be drawn toward and nourished by Light, they can only live by Darkness. That darkness is for us an unfathomable emptiness. The person—or rather the walking, talking specter of a person—is no longer nourished by companionship or love; he or she is incapable of feeling that kind of warmth. What is left once a person has lost the struggle to be fully human is a Head without a Heart. They can still walk and talk like the rest of us, but their existence is an expression of self-referential thoughts, prejudices, opinions, beliefs and the feelings that spring from those thoughts without the softening influence of Heart feelings like compassion, empathy or love. In other words, they are the most extreme example of a Head Person.

The infallible indicator of Darkness is an attitude of unrepentance. This is something the courts have long known and applied in their decisions. If a person shows no remorse, and even "cops an attitude" about what they have done, you can be sure they will do it again.

Seeing their brokenness for what it is, you may rightfully feel compassion, but be warned: Feel it from a distance. If you come too close, you will be burned, and if you refuse to acknowledge the abusiveness for what it is, you will be volunteering for Darkness as well.

RAPE STAR

I strut and I swagger; the lights make me glisten
Their Mommies and Daddies forbid them to listen
I dance and I prance, I writhe and I lick
I strut and I thrust and I grab at my dick.
They think I'm a hero, a macho boy wonder
The music is hot and the drums are like thunder.
I curse and I rail, it's a big f—in' show
I call them all Baby and Momma and 'Ho.
The tweenies are best 'cause they're new to this dance
They're forbidden to come so just give them the chance
The young ones, the sweet things, they roll over first
They mob the back stage and they tear off their shirts.
They just can't resist me, they love me, I'm King
Talk dirty and grope them, and show them my thing.
It's the butt pat, the crotch grab, I'm hot, Man, the best,
I'm the Man, I'm the Body, I'm golden,
I'm sex.

KITTEN

Soft and cozy,
Silky and sweet
Purring my dulcet song.
I'll nuzzle your face
I'll nibble your feet,
We'll howl at the moon all night long.

My big eyes enfold you,
I'll stroke you and hold you,
Diversion, desire and delight
Are my trade; I'm a Lady of the Night.

Sensations of love more intense than you dreamed of
Will take you away from your dull life.
No one will know that I've pleasured you so,
Leave your worries and troubles and strife.
With nibbles and licks, let me show you my tricks,
Things you'd never do with your wife.

This priceless thrill, it's the simplest thing.
Drink this wine and your body will sing.
You know the secret to unlock it –
Remember to bring a nice diamond ring,
And your little gold card in your pocket.

I'm the sexiest kitten extraordinare,
Come recline in my lovely lair
I'd never bite or scratch, no not that.
My tiny claws are precociously formed
But it pains me to have to use them.
I am a kitten—be feline forewarned
Be good or you'll bring out
The Cat.

Chapter Fifteen

WHY BE A WANNABE?

"The existence of free will always implies the possibility of
creating evil, as well as good."
— Dan S. Ward, PhD — *Reincarnation is Making a Comeback*

The second "diagnostic" category which I have used for
people who act like Abusers some of the time, and who
espouse Abusive values, is "Wannabe," because they
wannabe more like Abusers. Wannabes have their reasons, as follows.

An Abuser-Wannabe is a person who thinks that Abusive Types
have all the fun, and all the power. Their philosophy of life is based on
the following reasoning:

1). Darkness (evil) is power
2). Abusive Types use Darkness to their advantage.
3). Abusers know how to control others.
4). Abusers get what they want.
5). Abusers are never suckers or wimps.
6). I want power and control.
7). Therefore, I wanna be an Abuser.

The logic is flawless, but the original premise that evil is power needs
to be challenged. Notice there is no mention here of being human, or
loving, or creative. These qualities have simply been lumped together
under the category of "no power." Who would want no power? In this
value system, all tender or loving human feelings have been defined by
default as the opposite of power: weakness.

I have made the distinction between Abusive Types and Wannabes because, while their attitudes and behavior may frequently seem identical, there is a real difference in their intentions and motivation. Unlike Abusers, Wannabes are not indifferent to human values and human feelings. Rather, they are at war with them. They may hold the same contempt for the "softness" of being a caring and sensitive human being, but because of their more intact human "wiring," they are sometimes unable to be as coolly indifferent as they would like to be. They are not completely free of feelings of guilt or empathy. As such, they envy the Abuser's ability to maintain cold-blooded indifference at times when the Wannabe would feel emotional stress. This sometimes leads the Wannabe to extreme acts of cruelty or viciousness, as a means of turning their backs on what they see as their own weakness. The Wannabe sees the Abuser as having the edge in the project of gaining power over other people.

Because of their common philosophies of life, Wannabes are often found in the company of the Children of Darkness. They lean consistently toward the Abuser's camp, although they may remain covert in their admiration, like the wife or husband who pretends ignorance of their spouse's criminality. They frequently take the roles of groupies, admirers, devotees and advisors whose support increases the power and credibility of the Abuser. Caught in the web of seduction and drunk with the taste of reflected power, these besotted apologists lend credence and humanity to an otherwise inhuman project. Without them, the Abuser would be easily exposed. They provide "cover" by reinterpreting the Abuser's actions, reworking what would otherwise be baldly revealed as atrocities.

The Wannabe at Home

In a family overseen by Abusers and their Wannabes, these cover-up tactics are devastating for the victim. Take the example of a young woman I will call Emily. Emily's father had become progressively more sexual in his advances toward her as she approached puberty. Innuendo turned to furtive touches and eventually to midnight attacks. Emily, alerted by a school program on sexual predators, told her teacher. With the help of enlightened school authorities and a dedicated attorney, Emily's father was eventually convicted and jailed. During the trial ordeal, Emily's mother and one sister publicly confirmed that Emily's version of the story was undoubtedly true. However, after the father's conviction, Emily was shunned by the family, blamed for the decline of their financial and social fortunes. The mother, and even the sister who was being groomed for similar use by the father, accused Emily of putting her own selfish feelings before the family's welfare. Her brother, whose rage toward Emily did not abate in the 20 years following the trial, accused her of arrogance, selfishness, and of using their father's weakness to take advantage of him, thereby destroying him emotionally. It was the family's play on Emily's human decency which caused her the most pain: "He loved you; he just didn't know how to show it. You betrayed him."

Emily, who as a brave young girl of 13 had stood up for truth against all odds, found herself, at 32, filled with self-recrimination and guilt. Although she had left home as soon as she was able, a recent visit to attend the funeral of a favorite aunt had left Emily devastated, struggling against a deep depression. Although she understood intellectually that what her father did was wrong, she could not forgive herself for what she saw as her part in destroying the family. With closer questioning, it was revealed that the family was very much intact and bonded around their animosity for Emily. The father, who had long since been released from prison for good behavior, was welcomed back into the protective circle of the family. The family was solidly united in their self-righteous conviction that Emily, with her "selfish" feelings, was to blame for everything. Emily suffered doubt and regret about her actions, and sought help for the agony of having been shunned by those she had loved as a child.

Fortunately, Emily was able to regain her balance with support for her accurate view of reality, and by again tapping into the considerable human strengths which had gotten her through childhood. Emily's story is a positive one, because she eventually transcended her abusers. However, blaming the victim and protecting the perpetrator are all too common. Thousands of sexual abuse victims were tormented by priests who were then protected rather than prosecuted for their crimes. Victims' public testimonies of debilitating confusion, self-doubt and shame reveal that secret abuse often leaves insurmountable emotional scars. Generally, their stories vary from Emily's in one important regard. At the time of their abuse, no one showed disapproval or brought the perpetrator to justice. Instead, these victims suffered alone, unrecognized and unsupported until their childhoods were long gone, lost to an emotional vortex of shame, self-blame and fear.

These victims were doubly injured, first by their sexual abuser, then by the circling wagons of the Wannabes who protected and covered for the criminal actions of the Abusers. Here, the abuse of power was pervasive because it went unchecked by any person or institution which might have challenged the priests' power. Many parents, if they were told at all, flatly refused to believe that their priest could have done such a thing, thereby automatically putting the priest's power above the word of their own child. As we now know, if any accusations were made, the priests in question were often simply reassigned to positions of power over different children, and if the accusations persisted, the priests were reassigned again in a round robin of continuing child abuse.

The conspiracy was sometimes repaid in kind, as I was told by Betsy. In her case, it was a priest who perpetrated the cover-up. Betsy, at 10 years old, was desperate to stop the lascivious neighbor who seemed to have her parents' permission to take Betsy and her sister anywhere he wished, for long periods of time. These visits included movies during which Betsy was fondled in the darkened theatre. When it became obvious to Betsy that her younger sister would be next, and her mother scoffed at her accusations, she went to the priest to seek help. Instead of intervening, the priest dismissed her, saying, "Don't you ever say such a thing about an adult again!" The insult was even harder to overcome because Betsy attended the neighborhood Catholic school where the nuns were extremely authoritarian and punitive. She had nowhere to turn.

Betsy, a fundamentally decent and loving person, came to therapy because she was plagued much of her life by difficult relationships. These were people who preferred to see her submissive, rather than expressing the exuberance and determination which bubbled just under the surface. The positive trajectory of her life was slowed as she struggled to overcome the influences of her Abusive mother who had knowingly turned her over to the neighborhood pedophile. With hard work and deepening insight, Betsy's capacity for empathy emerged in her later years when she became a gifted social worker and advocate for children.

Surrounded by people in power who had misused her, for a time Betsy became a willing accomplice in her own oppression. Having lost track of her innate strengths, she tolerated abusive experiences which reenacted previous pain. This familiar pattern is repeated in households across the country, and probably around the world: A person who has been overpowered by destructive caretakers eventually relives their abuses with the help of an ever-widening circle of friends, lovers and even their own children, who carry on the manipulation and oppression which are the essence of the Abusive Personality orientation.

Ultimately, anyone who has adopted the Abuser's philosophy of life is dangerous, because their orientation is toward Darkness.

CONFESSIONS OF A SOUL KILLER

I don't want to exist
Because then they will kill me.
So I will "kill" myself.
I'll wake up a zombie
That way I can fool them.
Who cares if you just kill yourself?

I will kill myself,
Then at least *I* am doing it.
Under *my* control.
It's not *happening* to me
It's not happening to *me*
Because I'm the one playing the role.

Someone else here is suffering
That one—not me.
While I feel unlimited power.
He's just a wimp
A sniveling simp
But I am the man of the hour.

If I kill myself,
I'm expressing myself.
It must be my self, you see,
It's the thrill of the kill
I'm doing it, aren't I?
No one else is making me.

I have to do this
It's what they wanted
Then I'll be beatified fully.
They will be sorry
When I'm blood and gore
And there's no one left to bully.

They didn't know
When they tried to kill me
That I'd be sufficiently brave.
I'm better at it
Than they ever were.
I will laugh all the way to my grave.

Chapter Sixteen

TO BE OR NOT TO BE

I have chosen the stories of two real people, whose names and circumstances have been changed, to make the Abuser versus Wannabe classifications real in everyday terms. The first is an unusually self-revealing discussion with a man in his late 30's in his last group therapy session. He had been in therapy for a number of years with me leading up to this final week. The second is about a colleague and friend of mine who had taught college classes while I was studying psychology, and who traveled in the same social and professional circles I did over a period of about 10 years. We had many friends and acquaintances in common, including a woman who rented space in my house, a peer group of psychologists and social workers who met to discuss our work, and his third wife. The way these two men dealt with close relationships offers many similarities, and some revealing contrasts. Ultimately, I believe those contrasts illustrate the difference between a Wannabe and an Abuser.

Joe's Group Session

It was our usual policy to tape sessions for later review, should anyone want it. Members were so used to the presence of the tape recorder that they no longer noticed it. The quotes from Joe and other group members, with all identifying information removed, are taken directly from the tape-recorded transcript. This particular session was a very unusual occurrence. Joe was in the throes of openly struggling to resolve his own version of "to be or not to be"—a human with human feelings, sensibilities and emotions, or a cold and unfeeling Child of Darkness. The quotes offer an especially revealing glimpse of what it

238

feels like to be inside the mind of a cold, unfeeling Abuser, and why he prefers it that way. The group members' complaints also recapitulate the familiar refrains which are so often heard from the Abuser's loved ones, such as "Why do you behave the way you do, and what on earth were you thinking, and why don't you change, and why would anyone want to be so cruel?" Joe offers clear answers to these questions, in moments of heart-wrenching honesty.

Joe had been a member of the group for several years while he was getting a social work degree and using the group experience as part of his training. Although he had professed to want to work with people as a psychotherapist, his own therapy experience had led to little more than cosmetic changes. No amount of encouragement or exploration had cracked the hard shell of emotional defenses Joe kept in place. His job experience so far included limited work with hospitalized geriatric patients in a very structured program where he was closely supervised, and where he had had little opportunity to be emotionally challenged. Until this time, life had not presented Joe with a compelling enough reason to drop his guard, but this week he was confronted with an incident concerning his wife's cancer treatment which seemed to have shaken his reserve.

During this rare opportunity to hear Joe's inner thoughts, I encouraged him to freely express his Abuser tendencies in the hopes that he might hear the dead-end quality of his philosophy, and reconsider his choice. Barring that, at least the others would witness it, and see it for what it was: an empty, self-congratulatory stance based on self-delusion and superiority. Maintaining it left him impervious to their kindness and concern.

When Joe revealed his true feelings toward life and love that evening, there was an intense, cliffhanging atmosphere which cannot be revealed by the written words alone. It was as if we were all fighting for Joe's soul, and his right to be human. This work of self-discovery often is truly a struggle between the warring inner forces of Darkness and Light.

You will notice that throughout the discussion we used the term "stance" to describe Joe's heart-less orientation. This definition he had of himself was a position he was taking, rather than an irredeemable description of his inner being. I always work on the assumption that if there is any fundamental change to be made, it will come out of the acknowledgment that we each choose how we live our lives, and therefore we can modify it.

Joe's Dilemma

Joe had always maintained a superficial, joking air of camaraderie. However, his jokes were seldom genuinely funny; rather, they revealed a cynical, sarcastic view of life. On this one occasion, Joe dropped his jocular presentation to report moment by moment how he was feeling and what he was thinking.

Joe had previously told the group about incidents in childhood in which his father had beaten him unmercifully, until he learned to go numb, feel nothing, and even laugh at his father as he was being beaten. During those earlier group sessions he had been shown compassion and support in his efforts to come back to life, to recover from the state of suspended animation he had been forced to take on as a child. The group on this evening was reduced in size by the unusual absence of all but two other members, both of whom Joe had known for some time. The following excerpts focus mostly on direct quotes from Joe. Throughout, the others made comparative observations about themselves and supportive suggestions which are not included here.

As the group began, Joe described how he "did not bother" to ask his wife the result of a crucial oncologist's report when she returned home from her appointment. He said, "I attacked Emily again. I pushed it over the line. She was really angry." When he was asked what was going through his mind, that he would ignore something so important, he said, "I don't remember a point where I said, 'I'm going to get her.' I set her up, caught her off guard, so it hurts that much more." Here, Joe has confessed. He had intended to hurt her.

The others were agitated, upset by what he had done, and by his obviously self-congratulatory demeanor. They questioned him directly about what he was trying to accomplish by this, and if he was deliberately trying to push her away. In a completely unemotional tone, Joe said, "I guess that's what I set out to accomplish. Keep myself alone and separate and alien, to deny myself human contact. If I admit I need human contact, then I'm admitting I'm human. I feel unlovable, because that belongs to others. I avoid closeness and intimacy, and I'm above needing and wanting."

Asked why he wants to be so detached, he said, "Well, I can win, or I feel like I win. I go for the feeling of power. I don't have to acknowledge I need other people. I get to be the only one who's completely separate."

Frustrated by the fact that Joe seemed completely out of reach, Ellie anxiously tried to offer Joe a different perspective, by reminding him of how he was reenacting feelings from his childhood, when he interrupted her, saying, "Naah. It's all about me. It's just all about me. This crap about missing her when she goes away is just a load of shit. Designed by me to make it look like I really do care!" After a long pause, he added, "But if I truly didn't have a conscience I wouldn't have showed up tonight."

As I gently talked to Joe about his cold stance, I mentioned that he was expressing a classic Abusive Personality stance; he was showing all of us that he is the sort of person we need to protect ourselves against. As I said this, he began to cry. Asked about the source of the tears, he said, "I don't know. Maybe it's for what I am, what I thought I have to be."

As Joe began to compose himself, I asked if he could imagine a life in which he genuinely cares about himself and others. I was sending him as much warmth as I could, to encourage his more open emotional state. I asked, "Can you imagine foregoing the blood lust in favor of belonging, being one of us?"

His response showed that he had again closed his heart and returned to a cold, calculating attitude. He said, "In this stance, no. Right now I have no connection to caring about Emily at all. I'll tell you how I feel. Void of emotion, especially caring. No connection to anyone here, and really alone."

Caroline added, accurately, "And really, really angry. What does this anger have to do with having a conscience? You seem to have a sense of pride."

"That's the only thing I allow myself to keep. It has nothing to do with conscience. The rage is all-consuming. I give in to it, I feed on it. I don't say this to scare anybody, but I want to kill!"

Ellie, looking very frightened, said, "We're not afraid!"

I decided to defuse the high tension by trying to nudge him off his high horse. I said, playfully, "Yes, Joe wanted us to be afraid."

Joe responded vehemently, "Every ounce of energy goes into that! Everything is based on that! It's powerful! I get . . . the thrill of the kill!" Although the words were alarming, Joe sounded more like a frustrated child than an adult.

At this point, Ellie's anxiety got the best of her, and she asked me, "It doesn't matter what happened to them in childhood, right?" Joe answered the question, "It's not an excuse at this point." Ellie said, "Even if it's really horrible?" I concurred with Joe. "It's not an excuse for trying to damage other people."

Joe continued this way for some time, explaining to the others with occasional expressions of regret, what it was like to feel like an Abuser, or a committed Wannabe. He also continued to intersperse the discussion with periods of clearly acting the part. He talked about his process in therapy, and his relationship with the other group members, acknowledging, "I have to admit a lot of things. I have an opportunity to move ahead. As a kid, I said, 'I'll get out of this.' Now I have an opportunity, and who's stopping me? I've been such a jerk." He went on to describe his feelings toward Caroline, who elicited mixed responses from him over the years, but who "has a great smile, and she likes me." As he talked, he became more and more vague and detached. Ellie broke in to remind him that he admired Caroline's wholeness, and that's what he wanted too.

Joe's reaction was telling. He said, "From this stance that feels like an insult." Then, struck by the meaning of what he had just said, he looked around him as if waking from a sleep, and said, "This is stupid!"

I encouraged Joe to keep breathing, to feel his connections to his body in the present, and to be aware that he makes his own choices now. When I said, "You breathe your own air now," he began to cry again, deep, sorrowful sobs.

He cried out the pain, "I wanted them to care so badly. But they didn't give a shit." He continued to cry hard for several minutes as the group sat quietly, passing the Kleenex and waiting respectfully. Eventually, he dried his eyes, laughing, and said, "I feel good. I wish I had that on video." As the group ended and the others warmly congratulated him on his good work, Ellie said, "He let it go!" Joe responded, "He feels a life-filled flush." This odd use of the third person to describe his own feelings was prophetic. His final comments were said in a faraway monotone voice: "I've got a lot of living to do and a lot of enjoying to do . . ."

Joe's attraction to Light was already waning.

Group Dynamics

It is revealing to see the way the others in the group responded to Joe's confessions. His mean and controlling behavior toward his wife angered the two women, but Ellie tried to explain his behavior on the basis of repeating childhood experience. Even if true, this does not exonerate him for cruel behavior.

In their attempt to transmit a sense of hope and caring, they did what caring humans often do. They expressed their feelings of empathy and hope against all odds, trying to breathe life into a recalcitrant being who feels empty and apart. Regular people find it difficult to believe that someone like Joe really might not want to change, for you, for me, for anyone they know, and certainly not for themselves. Not only is that idea hard to accept, but like the group members, we constantly read human feelings into what they say, rather than taking their admissions at face value. Throughout the session, as the other members staunchly offered support and encouragement, they frequently reinterpreted his statements to allow for some possibility of human feeling, (especially Ellie) even when Joe had told them otherwise. Of course this is natural, since human feeling is what we know, but this tendency to "anthropomorphize" the Abuser blinds us to the true meaning of what they experience. Theirs is an orientation so completely different from deep human feeling that we must, for the moment, suspend what we think we know and feel, and listen closely to what they are actually saying. We must not assume they feel what we feel. Perhaps we must not even assume that what we think we feel is actually as different from Joe as we would like to believe.

It has been many years since this group took place. I have learned a great deal more about the neurological connections between heart and brain, body and soul. I would now work much more directly with Joe to practice breathing and focusing exercises to establish heart connections. Perhaps hypnosis would have helped Joe to bridge the fear and make spiritual connections to his ongoing sense of life and purpose. I cannot guess whether the outcome would have been different, but certainly the deepest issues would have surfaced in much the way they did here. Ultimately, the dilemma would still have been the same as it is in every human life: to choose warmth, companionship and love, or arrogance, disdain and distance from everything real.

In our follow-up work together, I had hoped to encourage Joe to hang on to the "life-filled flush" he felt so briefly, but Joe did not return to the group. He came to his scheduled individual session complaining that he felt he was not getting anywhere in therapy, that he had been made to feel foolish, and that he saw no value in continuing. Reminded of the group's obvious concern and the important glimpse of his own humanity, he became increasingly angry. Apparently, it was my reference to his "humanity" he could not tolerate. He had chosen to return to his old position in which he felt no anxiety, no pain, no love, no caring, and no joy. He had some moments of real feeling and decided his cold, unfeeling stance was better. In making this choice, he relinquished the support and affection of the group and gave up on his childhood dream of a better life. Nevertheless, it was more important to him to maintain his old stance toward the world than to risk feeling so much.

There were several moments in the group when Joe said something which sounded like a real feeling or a moral assessment of his own behavior. This would have been a sign of genuine humanity. However, his statements had an oddly distant feel. For instance, at one point he observed that his uncaring attitude was not "classified as being human." Joe understood that other people would not approve of his behavior. This does not necessarily mean he disapproved of it himself, or that he wanted to change it.

It was the only time Joe had cried in his work in therapy. In doing so, he allowed the group to know what the issues were for him in a startlingly honest way. Why did Joe reveal so much if he didn't intend to change? Perhaps for a moment he was considering joining the human world. Perhaps he was bragging, or testing us to see if we would fear him. The small group pulled together, trying to understand and to help him to move toward genuine human feeling. For a brief time, he seemed to be swayed by the invitation.

I had continued to work with Joe for several years because I had hoped he might come through, with enough encouragement and kindness. He had followed the rules of decent behavior toward me and members of his therapy group. However, he had always maintained an emotional distance I did not experience with other clients.

Was Joe a dyed-in-the-wool Abuser or a wavering Wannabe? It was difficult to tell in the one group meeting where he seemed to soften momentarily. There was one vivid moment when he seemed to wake up. He had heard himself say that the idea of wanting wholeness for himself felt like an insult. He seemed to awaken briefly, when he said, "This is stupid." That hint of awareness, and the brief moments of seeing he had been offered the opportunity to change and it was up to him to take it, all suggest that Joe still possessed a small thread of connection to his human heart.

By the time Joe returned several days after the group, he had completely redefined what happened there. For the first time in our work together, he lashed out at me. Rather than acknowledge the intimacy and support he had experienced, he insisted he had been "made to feel foolish." Nothing would convince him otherwise. He seemed to feel no regret, no loss at giving up on the work. I felt it. It was as if I was witnessing a suicide.

I never saw Joe again, but I have not forgotten the sadness of seeing a person turn his back on kindness and hope. In his own poignant words, "If I admit I need human contact, then I'm admitting I'm human." Perhaps somewhere down the line, life has persuaded him to reconsider his choice.

An Abuser Speaks From the Grave

As I was beginning my psychology studies, I encountered a man named John who was a philosophy professor in the college I was attending. I have included his story here because he was an example of someone who was clearly an Abuser. At no point in the time that I knew him or in later years, which were described to me in detail by someone who was very close to him, did he ever seem to change, or even entertain the idea of changing.

John had been awarded full scholarships because of his family's poverty. His ability to process astonishing amounts of written material had made his university studies fairly easy, but in spite of his high intelligence, he lost his job as a college teacher because of his inability to publish anything. Although he seemed to like teaching, what he relished most was the adoration of his students and the opportunity to show off his acting skills in the classroom. All his lectures were carefully scripted to include jokes and practiced comments. Like Joe, outside of his practiced performance, John was very friendly in a superficial and rather bland way, with a lack of spontaneity that bordered on deadpan.

When his teaching contract was not renewed, John decided to switch careers to become a psychotherapist. He went on to study social work, because he could attend the university where he taught and finish the program quickly.

It was understood in our circle that anyone who intended to practice as a psychotherapist needed to be fully aware of their own past emotional issues. Most of us were involved in ongoing psychotherapy, and tended to discuss our pasts freely. Presumably because of financial difficulties, John spent far less time than the rest of us in therapy, but he did talk about his childhood experiences. In his case, it was more a form of storytelling than self-revelation. It seemed unusual to me that even though he told of the most horrific trauma in early childhood, he showed little emotion. In my naïveté at the time, I attributed his calm demeanor to the possibility that he had remarkably evolved past the apparent trauma. As a struggling student, I was also unduly impressed by his appealing professorial demeanor, as many others seemed to be. John was happy to fill the role of gentle guru for his students and friends. Here are some of the facts of his childhood as I heard him tell it:

John was an only child, raised by a single working mother who frequently left him alone in their apartment, even as an infant, for long hours. He vividly remembered the sensation of terror and loneliness he felt in his crib, longing for her to return. His father, a merchant seaman, was all but absent in his childhood years. When his mother was at home, her treatment of him was frequently demanding, cloying and childlike. Her combination of neglect and anxious emotionality left him bereft and lonely. As her fortunes improved after a remarriage, she was more present in his life, but John was unable to feel close to her, or to genuinely return her affection. He never forgave her for the early abandonment.

John's story was heart-rending, and his telling of it elicited warmth and support from colleagues and friends. It was the 70's, and we were high on the human potential movement which promised to bring happiness to all people, with the application of enough kindness and unconditional love. I too offered support and friendship, in the years before I came to fully understand just what this brand of intellectual facility and charming demeanor disguised.

One incident which was relayed among our circle of friends was John's attempt at house-sitting for a mutual friend who did not want to leave his extensive collection of houseplants unattended during a vacation. By the time the friend returned, the plants were nearly dead, the cupboards were bare, and John seemed oblivious of the fact that he had taken on any responsibility for his friend. He seemed to have interpreted the whole affair as an opportunity for him to enjoy his friend's house, and to entertain a number of girlfriends in comfort.

Like other communities where an Abuser has made his mark, many of the people he had taken advantage of eventually began to talk to each other, and wonder how they could have been duped into believing he was a caring, sensitive guru. Unfortunately, this was only after much damage had been done.

Unethical Practices

It soon became clear that John was inclined to cut corners where ethics were concerned. His first act as an unemployed philosopher, before he had even begun training as a social worker, was to have business cards printed showing his PhD, with the title of psychotherapist under it. This was intended to mislead people into thinking his degree was applicable to the practice of psychotherapy, which it clearly was not. John seemed to feel that his past experience as a teacher of philosophy, and the fact that many of his friends were licensed therapists, gave him special allowance to begin working as a therapist himself He did not feel it necessary to complete the bothersome training and credentialing process. He held the startling conviction that even without training he was a superior therapist.

Around this time, John invited me to attend a professional training group, which he described as dynamic, enlightening, and run by a charismatic Gestalt therapist. Having found a group which would accept him at face value, John became a flattering follower. As I later learned, he traded his salesmanship for many hours of free therapy and training, and garnered legitimacy by association in the process.

The group method was psychodrama, with some elements of Primal Therapy, as it was practiced by Arthur Janov, author of the popular book, *The Primal Scream*. I was dubious, but very curious. I attended one unsettling session.

I was introduced to the psychologist who was running the group. He struck me as an extremely nervous, intense little man. His eyes had a beady look because of deep, dark circles around them. Once the group began, he became expansive and enveloping, orchestrating and controlling the high-pitched emotionality of the group. As the session progressed, people spent a great deal of time on the floor, alone in writhing psychodrama reenactments of childhood pain, or together in piles, hugging and weeping in cathartic release. As each person took their turn in the center of the group, it felt far more like a theatrical spectacle than a therapy session. I learned in passing that this was a group for both clients and therapists. As part of the process, clients were given the role of therapist and invited to "heal" their own therapist! I was horrified by the blurring of boundaries and the artificial emotionality which was enthusiastically applauded by the leader. I found the whole display unnerving. These down-and-dirty techniques were touted to be the new and better form of Gestalt therapy, but the whole session felt like a mass orgy.

My friendship with John cooled as a result of my disillusionment with his unethical behavior. I knew I probably would not see much of him in the future. I decided to invite him to my house, ostensibly to recover several books he had borrowed. Actually, I wanted to ask him something I had wondered about for some time. Over tea, I asked him, "When did you give up on life—on being one of us?"

He answered without hesitation: "Two."

Many years later, I learned from his estranged third wife that he had indeed established a thriving psychotherapy practice, and he had finished his social work degree. He had also apparently had sex with at least one former patient. This is considered unethical behavior for a licensed social worker (or psychologist, or psychiatrist, as well).

John's wife also informed me that he had always been emotionally unavailable. He was mostly absent from their two children's lives, and he had never really been there for his two children by a former marriage. One revealing incident occurred when his first wife attempted suicide, and John left his 12-year-old daughter to handle the situation alone.

John's practice and his failed marriage ended when he died in his 50's of bladder cancer, which he had neglected until it was too late for treatment.

Although John lived and worked in the house they had bought together, and he supported the family financially, their relationship deteriorated to a standstill after a few years. The financial needs and responsibilities of raising two children kept her in the relationship for fifteen years. When he died in 2005, she opened the channels with his children, former wives and friends to help her put together a picture of his lifelong pattern of manipulation and self-centeredness. Like most of the people who were involved with him, she wanted to understand her inability to connect with him on an emotional level, although she ultimately suspected it had not been because of her. I confirmed for her what she already knew, and told her I would be using John as an example of sociopathic behavior in a book I was planning.

As I was about to send this manuscript to her for approval, I received a call from her, asking if I was still working on my book. She had found a storage file full of John's journals and wondered if I would like to see them. I went to visit her, with enormous curiosity and wonder at the prospect of reading journals written 35 years ago by a man I hadn't seen for about 25 years. It was surreal, the prospect of reading the handwritten pages—thousands of them—telling the innermost thoughts and musings of the man who had become for me a model of the Abuser.

At first it felt strange, reading a dead man's most intimate thoughts, even with the permission of his wife. What I found there was simultaneously astonishing, moving, and predictable. There were letters addressed to me, to his wives, his friends and lovers and his family members, but mostly the pages were analysis and reflections on his own inner thoughts.

The timing was prophetic. It must have been a message from Spirit, handed to me at just this moment, like a gift from the grave. I immersed myself in the stacks of lined yellow pages written in his small, cramped handwriting with its dagger-like r's and t's.

I will tell you my feelings as I read on and on, for several days, absorbing the deepest meaning of what these writings could teach me.

In His Own Words

As the years played out on the pages, with all the entries carefully dated through 1976, 1977 and 1978, I saw the pattern of his musings repeated over and over. They went like this:

> "I saw Suzanne today in my therapy group. She is ending her relationship with Dan and is feeling conflicted about her choices. She is inclined to question her own decisions because of the way her mother always doubted her. She was interested in my observations about her need for support to achieve the freedom she has always longed for. I felt her warmth and openness after our exchange. I am very attracted to her way of looking deeply at the people around her. She has freckles and blue eyes. I wonder if Suzie and I would find the companionship we both know we need. I will meet with her to explore her feelings about this."
>
> . . . and two days later,

> "I am deeply in love with Adrienne. It has taken me a long time to allow myself to feel these feelings, but I am now willing to explore deeply with her, to see if she is becoming the right person for me to build a life with. She has been reluctant to trust me because of her abandonment issues (father's leaving at 12) but she seems to be changing, to be more open and available to me. I want to know where this will lead.

> "I am working hard on my tendency to manipulate others in order to win people over. I must ask myself whether anything I did could have caused her to distance herself, but I feel she has been sleeping with someone else. Her children were away today, and when I called her at noon she sounded sleepy. Was she just leaving her bed with someone from work? She sounded distant, elusive. She has hinted that she doesn't think it will work out with us."
>
> . . . and later the same day,

"Joy called. I have missed her, have been waiting for her call so that we could plan our weekend together. I am deeply attracted to her. I love the way she plays with words, the way we laugh together. I enjoy her intelligence. She is not heavy and serious, distracted by her work the way Adrienne is. I will spend the days with her, immerse myself in her, confirm for myself whether this is the woman I will find deep satisfaction with, the possibility of building a life together."

. . . and just one week later,

"Adrienne is busy. She hardly acknowledged me when she picked me up at the airport. She is far too preoccupied and self-absorbed for us to create a loving, caring partnership. I must concentrate on my own thoughts, try to understand why I led myself to believe that Joy might make a meaningful place in her life for me. She did not ask me to stay longer when I told her I was leaving. She didn't seem to care. I must address the tendency in myself to want to convince people that I am trustworthy. I must be trustworthy. I will explore the connection between how my mother behaved toward me (manipulative) and the tendency I have to want people to pay attention only to me. I must look more at how my father's abandonment created the need for reassurance from others."

. . . . and only one day later,

"I am hopeful, ready to start over. I finally understand how I must be open and willing to join Adrienne in her life as well as expecting her to join me in mine. I realize now how much I love her, in spite of her limitations. She is lovely. I love the way she smells, the way she feels. We made love, and it felt right, complete."

. . . . and a mere three days later,

"Suzanne has agreed to come to my apartment for dinner tonight. We will drink wine together and laugh. She is so much lighter in her attitude than Joy or Adrienne. The children were with Georgette after their mother's suicide attempt. I was telling Adrienne about Georgette, and she said, "Shouldn't you be with them?" I was furious. She is so judgmental and demanding in her tone. She is incapable of feeling empathy for me because of her mother's viciousness. When she disagrees with something, she attacks, and the condescending tone she uses is designed to humiliate me into doing what she believes is right."

. . . and a few hours later,

"I must examine why it makes me so angry when Adrienne reminds me of my responsibility to my children. In my therapy group David confronted me about my glib response when he challenged me about why I dismissed his question about my being truly committed to the things I say are important to me. George doesn't intervene when they go on and on. Last week David interrupted me when I was giving my history and said, *"Yes, but how do you live your life?"* I think George saw how he was trying to compete with me, but his intervention didn't stop David from continuing his attack on me.

. . . as a result of the group member's penetrating question:

"I have talked to Adam about the possibility of forming a peer group with the three of us. I will talk with Ron about it. I believe a men's group would be far more helpful than the therapy group, especially with David. I don't feel they are really on the same level with me. They all seem so self-absorbed and indecisive that they are really not able to focus on me or be present with me. They are unable to see my world through my eyes. Suzanne is more accessible. She does not interrupt or make judgmental comments about my way of thinking things through. I am looking forward to our dinner, to making love to her softly, to seeing her open herself to me. I am willing to explore the possibility that we could build a life together, a partnership in which we each accept the other as we are, laughing and playing together. I will see how she feels about it . . . .

"I must spend some time thinking about the existentialism paper, comparing the structure of the divided self and how it relates to problems with achieving Piaget's concept of de-centering. I'm excited about sharing the ideas with Adam and getting his take on the perspective. I must address the tenure issue while there is still time, or maybe I can just quit and start a new career that will be more suited to who I really am. Do I really enjoy teaching or do I just enjoy being in front of the class, hearing the respect in their voices when I get them to think in new ways. Are they really new ways, or am I building up my ego?"

. . . and by the very next day,

"I really see now. I see what I can do differently. I am thinking about asking Adrienne to marry me and start our lives together. I am ready for a new level of experience. Suzanne is too immature to offer me the challenge I need because of her obsession with following through in George's group. She denies it, but I think she is entertaining the idea of sleeping with David. I see now . . . ."

. . . and finally,

"To love a woman . . . I gave my heart away. Where did I put it? Who did I give it to? To whomever will play my kind of "loving" game. My heart is sugar-coated—to lull you and appear vulnerable—an act now which was once a reality. I felt vulnerable. She lulled me and then dumped me. Now I take revenge again and again. I am dangerous to women. Seductive and hurtful. Once I have her I will always dump her like she did to me." . . .

Here, I stopped reading to get my bearings. The feelings were flowing through me in waves. First, the but-for-the-grace-of-God feeling. We were not all that different in the beginning, when I was a graduate student and he was a guru-professor. Graduate school had encouraged all of us to be almost as much in our heads as he was. Fortunately, the rest of us moved on to more heart-centered lives.

Next came the sad realization that his life and this intimate blow-by-blow description of it is an object lesson for all of us. He knew how to rationalize, analyze, dissect and ponder, but he didn't really feel anything deeply except his blood-lust, the revenge against the mother who abandoned him. He blamed others for his emptiness and dissatisfaction. He could even see some of his own manipulations and deceptions, but he rationalized about it until he felt completely innocent. He always blamed his childhood (and others' childhoods) for deceitful adult behavior. Convenient, and so close to the way most of us were trained to do therapy! A cautionary tale, for sure.

After a few hundred pages, I had the sickish, empty feeling I remember from many years ago when I was leaving the movie theater after seeing "La Dolce Vita." What was that all about? Debauchery, arrogance, self-deception, conceit, endless, useless self-congratulations. The same. Fellini called him Marcello. We called him John.

Finally, I felt compassion for his emptiness, and absolute wonder at the thousands of hours he must have spent writing these pages. Notes in the margins showed he had reread them in 1989, and he had saved them through many moves. Many of them were addressed to me, as if he somehow sensed I would be able to use them one day? It did seem that way. I'm not sure yet of all the ways I will be able to learn from this, but I quote from them now for others to learn from as well.

He was all in his head. All intellectualizations without any reference to heart feelings. Separated from his bodysoul, he was dead. I had never felt sorry for him before, because he betrayed every friendship, used everyone who came into his life, but now I see it differently. I am feeling what forgiveness means. No anger, judgment or even disapproval, just compassion. It makes no sense to be angry or to hate someone like this. In spite of his glibness and articulateness, he was broken. He couldn't use the love or the help he was given because it would have meant he would have to feel, and he was too afraid. He had to reject the people who loved him most because he would have had to return their love, and he couldn't, or he wouldn't. It was tragic. His superior intelligence and even his relentless efforts to understand left him completely lost. He was so sure, so positive he was right, and so utterly insecure.

John went from one obsessive fantasy to another, to the neglect of his children and the productivity which would have preserved his teaching job. Focusing longingly and hopefully on nearly every woman who crossed his path, he convinced himself it was love he was feeling, when it seemed to be only lust—the compulsive need to experience sensual pleasure—the only way he had of feeling alive.

He could not have been a more vivid example of the case of the Head person who took the fork in the road that led him into Darkness—endless, hopeless darkness. Perhaps his life will not have been completely in vain if people learn from his example not to make the mistake he made, putting all his trust and effort into trying to make his brain lead his life.

Adding It Up

Discovering who may be a dyed-in-the-wool Abuser and who is a waffling Wannabe becomes clearer with cumulative evidence. However, if you are using these guidelines to determine whether or not to marry the guy, or to hire her as your personal assistant, I would add this caveat: If you really have to think long and hard to guess whether a person matches all of these measures or just several, they are probably going to be trouble either way.

Even under the best of circumstances, with many years of help, and assuming they come willingly, it is very hard for an Abusive-leaning person to make the change. I have very rarely seen these people succeed admirably, through determination and will on their own part, after years of hard work. More often, they reach a crossroads, as Joe did, then they go back, all the way back to what they feel as a refuge from pain and fear, a coldly indifferent stance, devoid of human feeling. I always mourn their loss.

THE SNAKE
by Oscar Brown, Jr.

On her way to work one morning
Down the path longside the lake
A tender hearted woman
Saw a poor half frozen snake
His pretty colored skin
Had been all frosted with the dew
'Poor thing,' she cried,' I'll take you in
And I'll take care of you.'

"Take me in, tender woman,
"Take me in for heaven's sake
"Take me in, tender woman,"
    Sighed the snake.

She clutched him to her bosom
"You're so beautiful," she cried
"But if I hadn't brought you in,
By now you might have died."
She stroked his pretty skin again
And kissed and held him tight.
Instead of saying "thanks"
The snake gave her a vicious bite.

"Take me in, tender woman
"Take me in, for heaven's sake
"Take me in tender woman,"
    Sighed the snake.

"I saved you" cried the woman
"and you've bitten me, but why?
"You know your bite iis poisonous
"And now I'm going to die!"

"Aw, shut up, silly woman,"
Said the snake with a grin
"You knew damn well I was a snake
"Before you took me in!"

"Take me in, tender woman
"Take me in, for goodness sake
"Take me in, tender woman,"
    Sighed the snake

CHAPTER SEVENTEEN

LESSONS WE LEARN IN A REALLY BAD RELATIONSHIP

"Music, to create harmony, must investigate discord."
—Plutarch

Why are they here among us, these people who seem to be a different sort of destructive being? They are often talented, captivating, and they seem to have great potential, until you look closely at their moral decisions. In a recent session with a vibrant young woman, the litany of complaints was all too familiar.

This was her story: "I had a boyfriend that I was totally in love with. I introduced him to my friends, my family helped him get an apartment, and he even stayed with us for a while. I was so in love with him, I thought it would last forever. But last week we had an argument, and he left for California without me—we were going to go together—and now I'm devastated. How could he do such a thing? I would never do that to another person. I loved him so much, I thought he loved me."

After he left, she discovered he had been "talking to" five other girls, with varying degrees of personal involvement, and his job sounded like he was some kind of bookie. "I was thinking, maybe I should go to California and beg him to take me back. That's when I called you."

She kept saying, "I loved him so much, I thought he loved me. He said he loved me. How could he do this to me? I would never do such a thing to someone else."

I thought about how remarkable it was that so many people had said exactly the same words to me over the years. It had become a diagnostic sign for me. I could almost always guess that this person had been the victim of an Abuser's heartlessness when I heard these words, along with seeing the devastation of an otherwise seemingly well-grounded person. These victims did have a common characteristic: they appeared to give their love in an openhearted, generous way, assuming it would be reciprocated. These people did not say they wanted to change the person they loved. Although the young man Lisa loved had apparently used her and everyone around her for his own convenience, she did not see the relationship as abusive. From her point of view, the breakup had been sudden and unexpected.

Many who have made these complaints to me were young people experiencing their first serious relationship. Until the blow of betrayal and deceit hit home, they were not suspicious or guarded in their dealings with others, and even afterward, they maintained a belief in the basic goodness of others. Unfortunately, they made no distinctions about the true meaning behind the selfish actions of their loved one. There often was another theme in common. These seemingly open-hearted people rarely appreciated their own qualities fully. They carried a persistent shadow of self-doubt which clouded their ability to accept their own value. This made them more vulnerable to falling for the promises the Abuser offered.

I listened again to the familiar refrain, "I would never do such a thing to another person." Perhaps they really were telling the truth about their own bodysoul integrity, but didn't appreciate the meaning behind what they were saying. This experience of being betrayed and mistreated brought out their strongest convictions about decent treatment, and about one's responsibility to others. They were absolutely adamant about the fact that they could not, would not under any circumstances, behave the way they had been treated. Of course, this raises the question of the double standard they hold concerning the way *they* should be treated. How could they continue to love someone who would do things they would never do?

Our basic values about how other people should be treated become an integral part of our being during the long years of childhood. Because those standards have become a part of our being, like breathing, we take them for granted, *as they apply to others*. As children, we simply expect others to be the same as we are. Along the way to adulthood, we come across many who prefer dishonesty and deceit. We may appreciate the difference in ourselves when we develop a strong inner-directed inclination toward honesty and kindness toward others. However, most of us are raised in a religious and cultural atmosphere which makes a glaring exception for how you should treat your *self*.

Our Golden Rule says "Do unto others as you would have them do unto you." It does not say "Do unto others as you would do unto yourself," or "Do unto yourself as you would have others do unto you." Many religious teachings take the opposite approach. You are encouraged to flay and punish yourself, be vindictive and unforgiving of your own mistakes, as if self-abuse were the path to righteousness. It is, if you use the modern version of righteousness to mean a bossy know-it-all attitude. Following these teachings leaves you out in the cold, disconnected from your loving bodysoul, suffering the despair of the long-suffering victim. Once again, you are the accomplice to your own misery.

In a culture which promotes self-abuse and artifice, a young person who might otherwise have learned to love and protect herself may develop attitudes which better match her peers. Eventually, for the sake of acceptance, she may begin to make allowances for others who don't live up to the same standards she once held, and in the process she is unconsciously drawn into the grey world of compromise and concession. Like Lisa, anyone who falls in love with a Dark One or Wannabe will find themselves at a moral crossroads. She must choose one of two paths:

1) She will decide to live by principle, acknowledging one must never do something like that, and apply it to everyone, or
2) She makes a compromise: She would never do something like that, but it's okay if he does.

The second choice requires that she turn toward Darkness, embracing a path which will inevitably lead to some kind of pain and destruction.

Here, our traditional childhood training can cause great confusion. Because it encourages rule-bound behavior, it does not leave room for the young person to listen to his or her heart, where the obvious answers lie. Many are led astray by applying a popular concept of unconditional forgiveness. They ask me, "But aren't I supposed to forgive, even if she did something that hurt me?" Here, I believe they are asking about the "turn the other cheek" teachings of Jesus. I probably do not understand all the implications behind this cryptic lesson, but I do feel fairly certain that Jesus would not encourage someone to pursue a self-destructive relationship. Standing your ground when you are attacked, or showing an attitude of kindness to your enemies does not mean sacrificing yourself by jumping headlong into a power struggle with a Dark One.

Following vaguely understood religious precepts and cultural habits interfered with the higher level of integrity many of these people might have been inclined toward. They say they would refuse to be deceitful because it feels abhorrent to them. It makes them sick. However, they do not fall out of love when *they* are treated badly because they treat themselves badly. This application of the double-standard Golden Rule leaves them facing directly into Darkness, calling it love.

A devastating heartbreak often causes victims to regret an open heart, and the accompanying instinctive tendency toward fairness and generosity.

They are then presented with a second emotional crossroads:

1) They could use this experience to confirm the bitter disappointment they felt, by concluding that they were stupid to give their hearts so freely, and by learning to be more like their Abusers—cold, calculating and uncaring, or

2) They could use it as an opportunity to acknowledge that they were indeed capable of great love, and reaffirm the connection to their bodysoul, the source of integrity and love for their own personhood.

In a relationship with an Abusive Personality, the Abuser gives 0% of the love. Their loving partner gives 100%. This demonstrates how able the partner is to offer unconditional love, continuing to provide the total amount of love in the relationship, regardless of the lack of loving energy in return. This is a relationship between a Head Person (the Abuser) and someone who will either give it up and return to their true identity as a Heart Person, or become over time like the Abuser themselves, by accepting the unloving treatment.

Even a truly loving person can be tricked for a time in a relationship with a clever Abuser. At first, it is possible for a person to be providing all the love in a relationship and not realize this is what is happening. It is because we feel so fulfilled by loving another. In the act of offering unconditional love, a mysterious secret of the heart is revealed. When we love—that is, when we act on our loving feelings toward another, it feels wonderful. We bask in the pleasure of feeling our hearts open, loving feelings flowing toward the one we love. In the process, our body responds by producing pleasure hormones similar to the "natural high" endorphins produced by sustained exercise. I believe this is what we mean by being "in love." We are generating love, and it feels great. Of course, in the best of relationships, both partners are doing this, and they learn how to be loving toward each other in a reciprocal, creative way which can last a lifetime and beyond.

In a relationship with an Abuser, you are providing all the love, and s/he is basking in it, the way a snake basks in the sunshine on a rock. Until the disastrous finale when you discover you are expendable, you may be lulled into the erroneous belief that you are being loved in return—not because she has shown herself to be loving, but because you feel so gratified by the act of loving her.

The idea that it is a strength to express your love freely and without conditions contradicts what our culture teaches about love and relationships. As conventional wisdom would have it, you are supposed to hold out, play it cool, be hard to get until you find someone to love you, cherish you, meet your needs. This is not love. It is a manipulative power struggle.

Be the Love You Want

The version of love most of us are searching for has been packaged and sold to us in the form of commercial advertising. The message is designed to convince us that by expending great effort to look fashionable and own expensive objects we will attract love. However, we need to hold ourselves responsible for our own participation in this propaganda-fest which inspires nothing but greed and self-indulgence. Under the guise of self-help, we are told to pay more attention to ourselves and our own needs. Even writers who discuss spirituality often do not make the connection that the opposite of self-indulgence is service to others. It is the missing ingredient in our frantic lives, and the activity which will restore balance and provide fulfillment.

Being of service to others comes from the same place as being loving. It originates in our hearts in harmony with our bodysoul, and it produces the same warm glow of satisfaction. Like a good romantic relationship, it often requires creativity as well as love to make it work well. Volunteering to mentor a child who is struggling, or making chicken soup for a sick friend, or picking up a few groceries for your neighbor may not be as intense as being in love, but it does produce a rush of well-being in yourself and in others. It creates a flow of positive energy outward, moving from you to them, from you and them to the world. This is the soul-nourishing combination of Light-filled creativity and love.

Perhaps you or someone you know has experienced something like Lisa's heartbreak, when the man she adored blithely went off with another woman, after pledging his undying love. However painful the disillusionment when it comes, you have experienced a life-affirming experience in the meantime. You have proven yourself to be a lover of the first rank—a person who is capable of offering love, even in the face of getting nothing—0—in return. However problematic your choice of love object, the result is the same. You have shown yourself to be capable of unconditional love.

The great religious teachings through the ages have carried similar messages concerning the ability to love unconditionally. At their base, most traditions agree that the ability to feel and express unconditional love is a primary goal of spiritual development.

Victims who seek help for their broken hearts come to therapy because they feel the need to make sense of why they became victims, and how they can avoid such pain in the future. Our culture offers little in the way of training or solace for someone who has been so injured. Advice tends to range from encouraging vindictiveness ("Slash his tires!") to cliché reassurances ("Time heals . . ."). What we need most after such a disappointment is a way to regain our dignity, and to restore our faith.

We can accomplish both those important goals by stepping back from the present situation to consider the life lessons which are imparted by this kind of blow. A relationship with a Child of Darkness does indeed teach you how deeply you are capable of loving, and how deeply your integrity is ingrained in your being. You can use the experience of betrayal and heartbreak to confirm for yourself once and for all: "I will never do something like that to another person." Now add the addendum to the Golden Rule, "and I will never accept it for myself again." Possibly, a relationship with a Dark One is the quickest route to learning those profound lessons so completely, and in a short enough length of time to prepare you for something better in your later life.

Getting it Right.

A mistake is something we do once. If it is something we do over and over, the same way, then it is not a mistake.

Fortunately, we have our connections to a Higher Power and our own intelligence which allow us to remember, reconsider, and do it differently the next time. What is more important, by forging strong connections with our bodysoul, we have great inner strength to rely upon.

We have all done things we truly regret, like welcoming a Dark One into our lives in some capacity. Perhaps choosing them meant that you turned your back on someone who was kind and decent. These choices can create important turning points in your life. You made the choice you did because of your feelings at the time, and because you were not aware of important truths about the person you were dealing with, and the life-preserving need to uphold your own self-respect. Now, with greater experience, you are armed with information about the kinds of people who will inevitably cause you pain if you embark on a relationship with them. You are also armed with information concerning how to identify destructive people, whether they be Abusers or their admiring Wannabes. It is possible to make different decisions than you once did because you are learning and evolving. That is a human strength. We cannot change the past, but we can try to do things better in the future. We can apologize when we hurt someone, and we can try to make it up to them. We can do the same for ourselves.

If you have suffered a heartbreaking relationship, you will need to forgive yourself, and reassure yourself that you don't ever have to do *that* again. Not doing it again is the true apology to yourself, and it frees you to go on, wiser, stronger, and with an open heart and the positive expectation that next time, you will treat yourself better.

PART V.

THE LOVE WARS: TAKING CHILDHOOD
INTO RELATIONSHIPS

I love him, regardless.
You love who?
HIM.
What do you love about him?
Well, he's funny. He makes me laugh.
Yes, but you say he's mean.
Do you give any weight to that?
Oh, I saw my mother yesterday.
Are they similar in any way?
I want to talk about sex.
And with the abuse, is it worth it?
Oh, but the feeling is so, so good.
I know he can love me; I wish he would.
And what do you do with the rest, in your head?
I like being next to him, when we're in bed.
And what do you do with the rest, in your head?
Well, I don't notice the rest just then,
I sort of look away, I guess.
You ignore what you don't want to see,
And look at the small part that meets your needs?
What do you mean, "Meets MY needs?"
I love HIM. I want to help HIM.
Oh?
Of course. My motives are pure.
So you make up things to pretend you're so sure
That you're doing something real.
You're living a dream life, and what a raw deal,
You leave your poor self to suffer and cry
And then you wonder why?

I don't know what you're talking about.
I wish you would help me to figure out
Why I always get screwed by men.

Chapter Eighteen

LOVESICKNESS

Romantic love. We have Shakespeare's Romeo and Juliet, Tristan and Isolde of Wagnerian opera fame, Dante and Beatrice, who appear in Dante's *Divine Comedy*, and Maria and Tony of *West Side Story*, the musical modern-day *Romeo and Juliet*, to name just a few. There seem to be famous stories about unrequited love, lost love, love gone wrong, love gone suicidal in most cultures, for most eras. In Japanese folklore, there are stories of two lovers killing themselves with the same sword rather than be parted, and in Korean tradition, there is the idea "sang sa byong"—to die for love—generally understood to be the tragic demise of a young man whose love is taken from him because of social class or family arrangements. The lovesickness we speak of here may be caused by the betrayal of a loved one, or it could come about like the tragedies of old, through circumstances beyond the control of the lovers themselves, like family, cultural or social constraints, great distance, or moral duty.

Lovesickness is a symptom. It is not a diagnostic category, nor an identifiable physical condition. This does not make it any less real for the person suffering from it. While most of us do not literally die from lovesickness, it does take a toll. The aftermath of a heartbreak can leave the individual angry, depressed, and worst of all, cynical about love. As a learning experience, it offers an important turning point in the development of a person's character, and a possible crossroads in their life path. How we deal with love's disappointments will determine whether we heal and go on wiser and stronger, or close our hearts, shutting out the possibility of future pain, and with it, the possibility of great love, richness and adventure.

There are millions of suffering individuals whose lives have been turned upside down by the experience of falling in love so hard that when the relationship doesn't work out, they feel sick at heart. The feeling can linger for months, or in some cases even years.

Our lovesick and sex-obsessed culture has a lot to do with creating the expectation that love is the answer, the antidote to all our ills. If we can just get someone to love us enough, then we will be happy. Love is understood as a sensation—something you feel, rather than something you do. Songs and movies all promise exciting, fulfilling love relationships which seem to develop instantly and last as long as the partners stay beautiful, witty, and "hot." Popular songs since the 40's have described love in terms like we-two-are-one, you are my better half, and you complete me. This is a recipe for disappointment. No other person can complete you if you are not a fully functioning adult to begin with. A partner can bring fun, interesting activities, companionship and the opportunity for give-and-take (one word), but the most successful long-lasting relationships are those in which the partners share an abiding respect and admiration for one another. In the atmosphere of shared concerns, love grows.

The disappointment one feels when a loved one leaves can be painful, but the worst pain comes from feelings of humiliation, and the gnawing reminders of what might have been. These regrets, frustrations and resentments about what should have been, what could have been, are the root of the most obsessive and lasting feelings of lovesickness. The lover who longs for the missing partner may think he is being generous in his feelings. After all, we are taught that loving another is a good and giving thing to do. However, the lovesick-unto-death lover is expressing a feeling that is all about ego fulfillment. The obsession is really about "Does he love me as much as I love him?" or "What does she think of me?" and "What do I think of what she thinks of me?" In other words, it's all about me.

There is a direct link between self-centeredness and misery. Happiness comes from being of service to others, not from being loved. Genuine love is doing something in the service of another person, and is the route to fulfillment. There can be a confusion here as well, since we are so used to thinking in self-fulfillment terms. Giving the other person something you want, or something you want them to have is not love, or giving. It is imposing your will on the other person. This is where obsessive "love" (the self-generated sentiment) bleeds into lovesickness, with the ego-centered demand: "I gave to you, now you need to give to me!" Spurred on by our sentiment-besotted culture, we forge full speed ahead into misery and frustration, and wonder why it feels so awful.

As technology has replaced human interaction, and earning has replaced living, we have become more vulnerable to feelings of loneliness and lovesickness, because we spend so much of our time communicating with electronic devices instead of people. Texting is not communication, because there is no human contact in the transaction. However there is an even more pervasive problem—one which touches every person in our Western culture, and probably most other cultures as well. It is a deep underlying cause, a current of feeling so deep and abiding that it affects nearly all of us. It is spiritual hunger.

Lovesickness Springs from Spiritual Hunger

This spiritual hunger has nothing to do with religion, or the adherence to any particular religious dogma. Neither does it have to do with the gesture of going to a church or temple or mosque. It has to do with belonging. We all need to experience ourselves as a part of a greater whole, something beyond ourselves which gives our lives meaning. It takes the pressure off needing to totally belong to your-one-and-only love. Otherwise, the primary person you become involved with has to literally carry the weight of the Universe on their shoulders.

You do not have to believe there is a big man with a beard in the sky looking down on us, meting out punishments and rewards. As John Lamb Lash comments in his book, *Not in His Image*, this is the "off-planet landlord" interpretation of God. At the same time, many religions also teach us that "God" or "Spirit," is in everything, everywhere. Whatever your understanding of the workings of the Universe and the forces behind it, it is reassuring and hopeful to know that each of us is an important small part in the fabric of life, and that life is just that—an interwoven, interconnected web in which each of us has meaning, and each has an impact on the greater whole.

The physicists are hard at work on this issue of interconnectedness, to discover what properties and interactions occur in the "dark matter" between the particles and molecules which appear solid to us. Evidently, they are just an infinitesimal part of the actual dynamic energetic interactions which go on everywhere around and inside us. To grasp the new ideas coming to us from every area of research and exploration, we must open our minds and open our hearts, with the understanding that much of what we learn will require expanding the limits of our learning. We must be open to revising much of what we thought was settled "knowledge."

This Too Shall Pass

Let's start with the idea that life goes on beyond the grave. Many of the world's religions and about two-thirds of the world's people take these ideas for granted. It is worth looking at whether there is any scientific proof for these ideas, because of the implication it holds: This is not all there is. Life, in some form, goes on. Therefore, this love, this relationship, this moment in time is not all there is. Most of us are familiar with the concept "eternal soul," but have little in the way of concrete evidence for what that might mean, although we might have a sense that there is more to us than just this body we live in presently. The age-old concept of "mind" or soul, as separate from the actual brain, implies this. Let's look at any evidence we might have to suggest that there is more to life and to love than this present, frequently frustrating, difficult and seemingly meaningless struggle we call life.

Raymond Moody, in *Life After Life*, notes that when the people who experienced near-death experiences came back to tell what they had seen, many of them reported that two things came through to them about what is really important in life. It was learning to love other people and knowledge. Since his book came out in the 70's, thousands of people have survived near-death experiences, which have become so common as to have earned the acronym, NDE. The experiences these people describe are astonishing in their simplicity and similarity. Most people report that they found themselves hovering over their bodies, watching the proceedings, often in an operating room.

One woman observed that the doctor's favorite silver pen rolled under a piece of equipment. Later, when he came to visit her, she mentioned it. He was astonished. She could not possibly know about that—she was dead when it happened! Most of Moody's subjects also describe going through a tunnel, or traveling toward "the Light," a tremendously bright, welcoming light, where they are greeted by previously unfamiliar people they refer to as guides or helpers, and friends or relatives who have passed away before them. All seem to feel so welcomed, so filled with an inexplicable sense of unconditional love that they are overcome with it; as a result they are reluctant to return to their earthly existence.

This does suggest that this life is not all there is, and therefore not our only chance to experience love. Others experiencing an NDE were asked by someone who seemed to be in a position of authority how they felt they had done in this life, and whether they thought they had learned what they had come for. This seems to be as close to "Judgment Day" as it gets: a self-critique, along with viewing and re-experiencing one's actions toward others in a profoundly meaningful way. We seem to be far more self-critical than those beings in the spirit world. If this is a reflection of how God is, then it's someone or something which emanates unconditional love. This is the best argument I know of against being judgmental and self-hating, and against being obsessed with a single person as the source of love in your life.

After an NDE, some people report having been told they must go back because their work is not finished; others go back because someone at their bedside is calling to them. Most agree that the things they saw and felt were life-changing, causing them to reevaluate their lives, and to revise their values, away from materialistic ego-driven striving and selfish love-seeking toward becoming more helpful and loving toward others. Are these remarkably similar experiences just a brain glitch, neurons firing arbitrarily, or an electrical storm in the brain, as the skeptics suggest? Anyone with an appreciation for the complexity and individual neuronal patterning each person establishes during life would find this explanation less logical, less rational than to simply accept that something is going on here that allows us a glimpse into our soul future and past.

If we can open our minds and hearts to the experience of belonging—to the planet, to the human project and its halting evolution toward unconditional love, we can raise ourselves out of the ego-centered longing for the love of another, whether it be your mother or your lover. Take heart in the knowledge that love is not something we need to earn, or achieve, or be worthy of. Above all, it is not something we can *get* from another person. It is something we can practice. When we do that, the lovesickness and emptiness subsides, and is replaced by a feeling of wonder.

The more we give, the better we feel, and the more generosity and good feeling comes our way. These benefits are not the reason to do it—that would be reverting to egotism. This is simpler than one might expect. You do not have to volunteer for life in the Peace Corps or give away everything you have, including the shirt off your back. There is a simple rule: Find a need and fill it. It must be an expressed need. Something the other person wants or needs. Provide it for them, without judgment or question. Start small. Drive your neighbor to a doctor's appointment. Baby sit for an hour for a harried mother so she can do something on her own. Sit down on a bench next to an old person, and let them talk. You will find yourself feeling less needy (because you're not thinking about yourself) and more open to the sense of hope and heart-centered belonging. This is the beginning of what we refer to as a spiritual path. Lovesickness will subside into the misty past.

CHAPTER NINETEEN

THE GOODNESS AND MERCY TRAP

Even without the trauma of having been raised by an Abusive parent, good and decent humans are vulnerable to the tendency to want to forgive hastily, and to hope that their own good influence, encouragement and good will is capable of changing someone, as long as they are still walking around and breathing. The reasoning goes something like this: "I am a good person. I would never do something cruel. I make every effort to be helpful, encouraging and patient. I try to please others and make them happy." When this doesn't work with a Dark One, it is tempting to take the next step, to try to cajole, convince, wheedle, manipulate or strong-arm the Abuser into changing.

I am here to warn those people that it is not only delusional to think you could change a Child of Darkness, but it goes against a long human history to the contrary. Ruthless people who have not been "saved" by any influences in the past and see nothing wrong with the way they are, are not likely to change once they are beyond childhood. This does not mean you should cultivate an attitude of meanness and ruthlessness yourself to deal with such people, but it does mean it is sensible to be prepared to protect yourself or simply walk away.

One recent victim uttered the heartfelt conviction which dooms him and his fellow sufferers to endless bouts of hopeless struggle: "But there is good in everyone. You just have to make the effort to bring it out. I know Lila has it in her. I would take her back in a minute if I see any sign of her changing. I still love her."

This idea that there is good in everyone may be true, but it is not up to you to bring it out. That is soul business, not our business. We know there are truly dangerous people, like Jeffrey Dahmer who from

274

his jail cell warned his captors that they must never let him out, because he would kill again. He acknowledged openly that he enjoyed killing people. Whether there might be good in someone, underneath or in spite of their bad behavior, is not for us to judge, or to "bring out" in someone else. What matters is whether the person in question is willing to act in a way that is kind or friendly, right now, of their own volition.

We cannot make someone else happy if she is determined to be grumpy or depressed; neither can we make someone else be good. The impulse must come from within the person herself. If we wish to inspire others to behave honorably or lovingly or honestly, we can set the example by behaving that way ourselves. We provide a model for others to follow. There is absolutely nothing more we ought to do to influence another person in the direction of what we think of as goodness, because our own definition of what goodness is has probably been corrupted or influenced by what we were taught and how we were treated.

There is a second issue at stake here. What is it in the make-up of the "Fixer" that compels him or her to keep trying to change another person? You will notice similarities to the Helper in an earlier chapter who tries to bribe, cajole and seduce the recalcitrant lover into giving them the love they need. The Fixer is a bossy take-charge activist who will enlist help from others, and whose zeal is intended to override any objections from the unwilling Fixee.

The Fixer's Project

First, we must ask ourselves the question, "Why would one want to try to change an Abuser, when it is fairly obvious that it is an impossible task?" Second, "Why would one want to try to change anyone other than themselves?"

Let's use the most powerfully unattractive description of what is really behind being the "Fixer." Trying to change another person is taking a position of superiority and arrogance: "I see what is wrong with you, and how you should change. That makes me the powerful expert in charge of morality and good conduct. I judge you and proclaim you an inadequate failure. I know what you need to learn, and how you should improve yourself." In other words, this makes me a (judgmental) God. Truly acknowledging that this could be the motivation behind "well-meaning" actions leads to a painful realization. In taking on the project of being a Fixer, we also take on the mentality and operating methods of the Children of Darkness. The tendency to use others to feed a sense of superiority and power is the essence of Abusiveness and Darkness.

You may be screaming objections in your head, "No! I would never do that. I was only trying to help! I could see that his life would be better, he would be happier, if he would just change the way he acts (. . . treats people, handles money, dresses, approaches work, wears his hair, etc"). All these things might be true, of course, but if you really object to so many of the things your loved one does, why are you together? Of course, it's because you love him/her. But love means acceptance, compassion, forgiveness, affection, not judgment, criticism, and intolerance. If you cannot feel these things for the person you are dealing with, perhaps the relationship for you is based in issues of power and the pain you have brought with you from childhood. Someone to fight with is not the same as someone to love.

We are at a disadvantage when we set out to form lasting relationships in adulthood. The traditional notion is that marriage is a commitment, as in prison, and that adulthood is filled with burden and sacrifice. We have few models of couples who are comfortable, accepting and happy with each other. For many of us, establishing a partnership, having children, making and keeping friendships is a matter of flying blind. Even if our parents managed to stay together and remain civil to each other, it is likely their relationship was based on traditional patterns and expectations which have changed dramatically during the past generation. We may have to learn to leave behind much of what we have been trained for, rewarded for, and taught was the best way to be.

Given that most of us experience numerous difficulties in childhood, if only because of the harsh and disrespectful way children are treated, we can assume a fairly large number of Earth's people have been psychologically injured. Poverty, physical punishment, neglect due to a parent's alcoholism or drug use, being teased or discriminated against because of physical, ethnic, or personal differences—all leave lasting scars in our psyches and warp our perceptions. These injuries make us vulnerable to what seems like power, as we have seen in Chapter One.

It also leaves us wanting to be powerful ourselves. If you are one who wants to be powerfully good, to make the world a better place, then you are also vulnerable to the Goodness and Mercy trap. What may have seemed to you to be the opposite of the dark machinations of an Abuser is actually the opposite side of the same coin.

If you are still reading, take a deep breath, and let's explore how people get seduced into thinking they are doing a good deed when they try to be the "intervention" in another person's life, and why those relationships are so hard to leave.

Know What You're Dealing With

We all know of cases where a person has been twisted by life's experiences into a bitter, hostile being without mercy or kindness. In the Twentieth Century, we learned to examine the past for formative influences which led to present behavior. Although it was a step toward better understanding human nature, it also encouraged an overly-indulgent attitude toward destructive behavior. The result has been an attitude of excusing responsible for the things people do and say when they are hurtful to others, on the basis that it was their parents' fault. As we will see in "How to Raise and Abuser," this is the perfect formula for encouraging Abusive behavior.

The cumulative weight of psychological and cultural influences has probably left us with a far greater number of Wannabes and Abusers than we have previously been willing to admit. The evidence is being presented almost weekly in the U.S. media of horrific selfishness and abuse of power in our political, religious and financial institutions, and one might easily experience an uneasy suspicion that the revelations have barely begun.

There has long been the natural reluctance to extend the concept "sociopath," or Abusive Personality Type, to those around us who are not murderers, criminals, or con men with oily hair and a trench coat. If we include the entire population of people who have behaved, on a smaller scale, like Bernie Madoff, Kenneth Lay and Jeffrey Skilling of Enron Corporation and Bernard Ebbers of WorldCom, all of whom have gone to prison for fraud involving accounting schemes, we may find numbers in the thousands. Add in every person who has sexually molested or severely beaten a child or someone physically weaker than themselves, and the numbers increase logarithmically.

The diagnostic categories above have generally excluded women, because of the nature of our patriarchal system in which men have higher profile positions in society than women, and because women are less likely to be involved in violent crimes. This does not mean women are less hurtful. Women have for at least 5,000 years been the primary perpetrators of what we think of as crimes of the heart. We do not have a criminal category for people who break others' hearts, but we would if we were truly the greatest country in the world. Therefore, in the interest of gender equality and equal representation, I will classify all the physical, emotional, financial and social forms of betrayal as crimes of the heart, because they all wound others and promote Darkness.

Self-Defense Is Not Aggression

The people who insist there is good in everyone seem to be the ones who most often end up in destructive and painful relationships. (This is similar to the person who says they never trust anyone. They seem to be the ones who are always being cheated.) These unwavering convictions hamper their ability to defend themselves when it is appropriate to do so, because they are not discriminating; they are not adding up the tally of past offenses to come to the obvious conclusion that this person they are dealing with is not a good bet.

Many of the people who become victims of Abusers or Wannabes have suffered in their own childhoods and sincerely do not want to become like the people who abused them. They have made a vow to be the opposite of the Abusers in their actions and thoughts. Since children tend to think in black and white, they are likely to come to very simplistic conclusions. To a child, anyone who hits or yells or says mean things is bad (abuser), and to be the opposite is to never hit or yell or say mean things. There is no room here for cause and effect considerations, and no clearly defined concept of self-defense. In the effort to be fair and good in their own actions, they disregard the fact that when the other person starts the trouble, they have a right to defend themselves, or leave.

These victims often make the complaint, "But if I fight back, I'm being aggressive just like them, and I don't want to be like them." I have heard this statement so frequently, I think it bears some analysis. This complaint contains several assumptions, including:

1) The only way to defend oneself is to "fight back;"
2) Self-defense is aggression, and
3) If the victim of aggression defends themselves they become identical to the original aggressor.

Many victims of childhood abuse are truly unaware of the clear moral difference between attacking someone without cause and defending yourself when you have been attacked. They have forgotten that our system of laws is generally designed to protect someone who acts in his own self-defense. This is understandable, since the same system did not protect them as children, when they were clearly innocent and unable to seek justice.

Children whose emotional or physical safety has been compromised by living in the presence of cruelty do not develop the natural abhorrence for aggression. The fight-or-flight response has been diminished to allow them to go on living in the only environment available, regardless of the discomfort it causes. They have thereby dismantled their own self-defense systems, making it possible to rationalize and compromise their own safety and their own integrity. This is the working model of someone who has suppressed their bodysoul protection, the internal armor which guards against emotional as well as physical danger.

Here it is helpful to look at the way these conditions were described by Erich Fromm, who drew a distinction between "benign aggression," a defense against attack, and "malignant aggression," sadistically torturing or killing for the thrill of it.

Erich Fromm was a social psychologist who produced an impressive body of work, beginning in 1941 with his book *Escape From Freedom*. Other groundbreaking books followed, including *The Sane Society* and *The Art of Loving*. He is generally considered one of the great advocates for Humanism; his political views were referred to as Socialist Humanism. In his book, *The Anatomy of Human Destructiveness*, Fromm makes an important distinction which helps to illuminate the question of where aggression comes from, and how to define it. He criticized the tendency of the times, encouraged by animal researcher Konrad Lorenz, to lump all aggressive acts into the same category, whether they are examples of an animal defending its territory from attack, or a human sadistically killing and torturing for the thrill of it. Fromm also objected to Freud's use of the term "instinct," and later "Thanatos" (death instinct) to explain aggression, which implied that all destructiveness was somehow instinctual. Fromm suggests the following two entirely different categories, which are very useful when we are trying to decide whether a person is an Abusive Personality or not, and whether an action is self-defense or not:

> "The first, which he shares with all animals, is . . . defensive, benign aggression . . . in service of the survival of the individual and the species, is biologically adaptive, and ceases when the threat has ceased to exist. The other type, "malignant aggression", i.e., cruelty and destructiveness, is specific to the human species and virtually absent in most mammals; it is not phylogenetically programmed and not biologically adaptive; it has no purpose, and its satisfaction is lustful." (p. 25)

Fromm's distinctions are useful here. The "malignant aggression" he describes as cruelty and destructiveness are synonymous with an Abuser's aggressiveness. He also noted that legitimately defending one's "vital interests" is not a case of malignant aggression. These concepts apply to social issues as well as individual relationships. Unfortunately, this concept of defending vital interests has been perverted by our own government to include attempts to control, subjugate, torture, diminish or destroy another person, another country, or our own planet. It is a classic Abuser's sleight of hand to merge these definitions in order to suppress resistance to an Abusive attack.

Fromm's sections carry titles like "Vengeful Destructiveness, "Ecstatic Destructiveness", and "The Worship of Destructiveness," all of which describe the kind of behavior we are addressing here. He also made the point that this sort of sadistic and cruel behavior was "character-rooted" rather than instinctual or a response to physiological human needs. This is crucial to understanding why Abusive Personality Types don't change, and why you should avoid them. If they have grown to adulthood behaving heartlessly, it has become a character trait, and therefore is probably the way they will continue.

Although Fromm's arguments were tailored to the prominent issues of the day in the early 70's, his concepts illustrate the essence of the truths carried forward here. He emphasized the inhuman qualities of the subjects he analyzed, like Hitler, Stalin and Himmler, and searched for concepts to characterize them. However, in his effort to separate his subjects into psychoanalytic categories like anal, sadistic and necrophiliac, he stopped short of the more profound conclusion that emerged from his analysis. These characters had one glaringly obvious trait in common: they were all inhumanly cold, vicious and life-destroying opportunists whose goal it was to gain power over others and destroy human life and human values. Thus, they all belonged to a single category, which I have called Abusive Personality Types.

Ultimately, differences in style or personality are irrelevant. In the glaring lack of the character trait we call humanity—the one that makes all the difference—they were identical, as the Children of Darkness probably have been since the beginning of time.

Go Ahead, Defend Yourself

As for the worry that taking the defense will make you just like them, this fear is ungrounded. Regular humans, no matter how angry they might become because of abuse or betrayal, do not automatically turn into cold-blooded Abusive Personalities in the process of learning self-defense. In practice, it has the opposite effect. Learning to defend yourself effectively on a day to day basis frees you from having to constantly think about how you are going to protect yourself. The more secure you become in holding out for decent treatment in your life, and the less anguish you experience because of interactions with those who would abuse you, the more generous and comfortable you can be with others who deserve your trust and good will.

Generally, objections about not wanting to be aggressive are expressed by people who are involved in a relationship they do not want to leave. By eliminating that choice, they have automatically deprived themselves of half of the normal fight or flight response to danger—the one which would allow them to respond without the need for any aggression at all.

There are options other than fighting or fleeing. You can show an Abuser you mean business by simply refusing to provide the special favors and advantages she demands until she shows respect and consideration toward you on a consistent basis. However, this is exactly the problem. Showing an Abuser you mean business will predictably lead to a vicious confrontation. In other words, it will lead to further aggression, no matter how reasonably you present your case. This is probably the evidence the victim does not want to see: that they are powerless to ask for something they need or want, because an Abuser, by definition, doesn't care what they want. Standing up to him in any way will reveal how belligerent he really is, and the lover does not want to see that it's hopeless.

This has been a serious problem in political negotiations in the U.S. in recent years. Negotiators have been willing to make unfair and unwieldy compromises out of fear that, should they stand their ground, it would be revealed just how hopeless the process had become, how utterly irrational and unyielding the opponents actually are. Sincere lawmakers must fear the consequences for our way of life should the world discover that there is a large percentage of politicians who truly do not care what happens to the country, as long as they retain their power. Ultimately, the result is probably what the negotiators, like the lovers described above, fear most. When you refuse to go along with a Child of Darkness, they will destroy what you hold dear and eliminate you, one way or another. A relationship with an Abuser will always end up as a hostage situation, sooner or later.

In your own life, be prepared to say "Good riddance" and celebrate your freedom. Run out of the burning building and never look back. You will have learned one of life's great lessons—that loving an evildoer is promoting malevolence, even if it is only directed toward yourself. You are a person too.

The futility of trying to successfully negotiate with Abusers was especially apparent with Bill, who had suffered physical attacks and verbal humiliation on a nearly daily basis, beginning around age two. Any effort to please his father by helping around the house would be met with a verbal assault: "That's another job don't apply for." He was frequently forced to spend excruciatingly long hours alone in his room without books, toys or friends. His mother alternated between cloying adoration, with comments like "You are my life," and sexual titillation.

She paraded in front of the young boy in her underwear, asking him, "Do you think I'm pretty?" Nevertheless, he blamed himself for being a coward, unlovable and worthless, the cause of their hatred.

Bill smoldered with resentment toward both his parents. He was especially disgusted with his mother, whom he saw as the cold, calculating architect of much of his suffering. Rather than confront them, he turned his anger into self-hatred. As an adult, he had not made any serious attempts to defend himself, other than reducing the frequency of his visits. This then became another subject of their complaints against him: He was neglecting them. This was a classic "blaming the victim" move, a typical Abuser's technique.

Bill was getting fed up with their ongoing vicious treatment of him, and at age 32 he determined that it was time for him to make a stand. On a visit to his parents' house, he firmly but calmly objected to their disrespectful behavior toward him, and insisted they must change their ways if they wanted him to visit them. His mother was hysterically irate that he challenged them, his *parents*. She lunged at him with fists flying, right there in the kitchen. As she pummeled him with all her might, he restrained her, then pushed her down onto the kitchen floor. She was not injured. As he reported, he didn't stomp her into the ground or step on her face—which he felt would have been warranted—but he did defend himself appropriately, given her 30 years of abuse. He felt certain she would see him as someone to be reckoned with in the future, and he was right.

This marked the beginning for Bill of a new kind of self-respect. He began to see himself as someone who was worthy of decent treatment, and that it was simply self-defense when he responded to someone who had clearly and repeatedly attacked him first. By defending himself in the present, Bill began to restore the dignity he had lost when he was humiliated and degraded as a helpless child. In the process, his injured bodysoul began to heal, and his native ability to defend himself was restored.

Someone who is resistant even to the idea of self-defense might ask, "What about passive resistance?" Unfortunately, this strategy often fails when you're dealing with a heartless Abuser. Since they have no scruples, they interpret any reasonableness as an invitation to assume greater power over the pacifist, whom they see as a puny weakling, inviting attack. The point has been well made that Gandhi succeeded in his sit-down resistance against the British because they were a people who, in spite of their imperialistic tendencies, still had scruples. Gandhi made the British look bad in their own eyes, and they responded eventually by backing off. The same could be said for Martin Luther King and the white American majority. Had he been dealing with an entirely Abusive population, or a predominantly Abusive leadership, his passive resistance would have been taken as a welcome opportunity to slaughter the troublemakers. This was the dynamic in much of the South during the Civil Rights marches of the 50's and 60's, when thugs in police uniforms attacked peaceful protesters.

When dealing with Children of Darkness, the honorable and otherwise effective strategies of passive resistance will not be effective unless there are others who will step in to impose external constraints on the perpetrators. Even then, we can expect only cosmetic changes. As we have noted, a dyed-in-the-wool Abuser, or even a Wannabe, does not change his stripes as a result of short-lived external pressure. An Abuser will only go underground and put on a good show, until the next time, but it is better than allowing them free reign. If the forces of Light—those who stand for fairness and justice—maintain their strength, their conviction and a united front, over time the Abusers will die out or give up. It takes daring and a conscious commitment to holding out for what is right, without adopting their Abusive tactics, to defeat the forces of Darkness.

Bill's case is an interesting illustration of the failure of passive resistance. His parents did not see his absence as a sign that they might be doing something to cause it; they attacked him for neglecting them. Furthermore, he had no choice but to defend himself when he was attacked, but he did it with restraint. He did not "fight back" with his mother; he simply stopped her attack. His use of self-defense was restricted to applying only the amount of force needed to prevent himself from being injured, not to inflict injury. This is not aggression. Finally, his actions did not make him more like his parents. He came away with greater good humor, and confidence that he need not be as Dark as they were to protect himself and to maintain his own dignity.

Perhaps you are not convinced that the object of your affection is truly hopeless. Perhaps you still feel that expressing your complaints clearly and forcefully will bring results. You might feel inclined to bring in a panel of experts, friends, relatives and neighbors to second your outrage and pressure your loved one into changing. This would only be instigating a group manipulation to try to pressure him. Do you really want to be the point person for a pack of reformers whose focus is the person you say you love? Ask yourself: "What sort of sainthood am I aiming for, exactly?"

SADIST

Now you've done it; you're to blame
You're lazy and willful; it's always the same;
I'd swear that you do it on purpose.
I'll wash out your mouth and box your ears
If you don't stop those girlie-girl tears.

I've just tried to teach you,
To shape you, to reach you,
You think you're so smart you can boss me.
I'll give you something to cry about
And then you'll be sorry you crossed me.

What's that look? I'll defeat you!
You force me to beat you, you slackard, you devil,
And don't you dare give me that face.
You'd spare me the trouble, the anguish,
The bother
If you'd once learn to stay in your place.

THE NURSE

You're the light of my life, it's the giving I love,
And the world's a cruel place, you know.
You're weaker, I'm better, be safe, lean on me,
For you, I'd walk miles through the snow.

I know you want my help, poor angel,
I know you can't do it without me.
You suffer and struggle; I'm right here beside you
With solace and wisdom, you'll see.

What's that bruise on your face, my baby love?
Is it something to do with that girl?
Did somebody hurt you, my sweetheart, my darling?
You're just not equipped for this world.

Send you off to reform school? A slander, an outrage
They've just made an awful mistake.
You're just so amazing, so smart and so charming,
I know that you did it for my sake.

I've just tried to help you—you've never been strong
Such a sensitive child, Mother's never been wrong.
I never stop and I never tire,
To protect you from danger, I try
How lucky for you that I do this so well
If I didn't you surely would die.

CHAPTER TWENTY

HOW TO RAISE AN ABUSER

We can go a long way toward understanding where an Abusive Personality Type comes from by looking at cultural influences, family childrearing practices, and the way an infant's brain develops. For it is in the beginning of a person's life that we can mitigate the formation of an Abuser-in-the-making.

Children are experts at detecting feelings. In their newly formed pure state, they are more emotionally intelligent than most adults. They are also more closely connected to their bodysouls, and therefore more connected to the wisdom of the ages. A sensitive adult can learn a great deal by asking a young child how they feel and what they think about the events in their lives. By showing the child respect, you will begin a new kind of relationship based in mutual appreciation. The child comes by this naturally. You will have to work at it to recover the kind of curiosity and wonder a child feels naturally. This is not because the child is naïve. It is because you have lost touch with your bodysoul and thought you were smarter than the child because of it. If we can learn to look to our children for their sensitivity and wisdom, we will gain perspective on what really matters in life and what causes pain. In the process, we will change our entire culture to one which nurtures kindness rather than toughness, Heart People rather than Head People.

There are experts who believe a Child of Darkness is a different species—a creation of some aberrant genetic process alone. Robert Hare, the author of the book, *Without Conscience*, is probably the most famous expert on criminal psychopaths—especially those who have perpetrated unthinkably gruesome murders. He has concluded that this tendency must be genetic, or inborn, mainly because their actions seem otherwise inexplicable. Certainly his subjects meet the definition of other-than-human, having the quality of another species. (Like Hare, I would call the violent Abusers "psychopaths," as distinguished from the sociopathic Abusers whose crimes are mostly interpersonal.)

While there may be some people who are born with their capacity to relate to other humans missing or damaged, it is not necessary to assume this when we try to explain why some among us are Abusive Personality Types. Throughout childhood, attractor channels for relationship must be created day by day, month by month during the critical first two years of life for any child to learn to be a cooperative, adaptable human being. The emotional environment plays an enormous part in the organic formation of a personality.

The relationship Abusers in our midst who do untold damage among friends, lovers and children do so without threatening them with weapons, and their preferred tactic to gain power over their victims is not physical abuse. They may however resort to physical means when psychological manipulation fails, especially with children and physically weaker spouses. The difference between an Abuser and a regular person is not defined by an overt preference toward aggression or physical violence; it is the tendency to turn every relationship into a power struggle. Theirs is a game of unmitigated cruelty, manipulation, and psychological mind-games. Tactics which go right to the heart of the victim are their everyday means of gaining influence over others.

Let's begin with a story which illustrates the influence of a culture and family on the development of a child who is being groomed to be an Abuser. *The Sagas of Icelanders* offers a uniquely detailed glimpse into day-to-day life 1000 years ago. It is a collection of medieval tales, told by an anonymous storyteller in a straightforward, unadorned style. The stories describe the comings and goings, work and play, family relationships, battles and struggles of the early settlers of Iceland, most of whom came from Norway and retained close ties to the families and ways of life there.

I have chosen this saga to illustrate the kinds of family interactions which lead to Abusive or psychopathic behavior. Its unusually detailed telling of family interactions and attitudes toward children makes it a valuable resource for understanding a Western culture far older than our own.

The sagas are vivid in their depiction of innumerable interpersonal conflicts and the ways they were resolved, capturing the sense of give-and-take, strict adherence to cultural traditions and a sense of fair play, side-by-side with a taste for ferocious battles and lawless plundering of neighboring countries. Viking raiding forays were expected to be bloody battles, with the goal of bringing home as much booty as possible. In battle, excessive violence and bravery were considered the same. At home, farming families generally lived peacefully, spread sparsely across the Icelandic landscape, governed by a democratic system of judicial and legislative groups. There was no king or executive leader.

The following is a synopsis of one of the sagas. This story takes place around 1000 A.D.

The Skallagrim Family

Skallagrim was a wealthy and successful farmer and landowner, an early Icelandic settler who refused allegiance to the Norwegian king. He was an adventurer and warrior, a poet, an industrious ironsmith. He was also a hot-tempered man, given to sudden fits of violence. Egil was his second son, an extremely fast-developing child, very large for his age. He also showed a precocious ability to make up and recite poems by the age of three. He was impetuous and quick-tempered, and everyone was aware that they had to teach their sons to give in to him. He accomplished his first murder at age seven. Here is the story of that fateful event.

Thord, Grani's son (Thord Granason) was a neighbor and a promising young man, and was very fond of Egil Skallagrimsson. (Skallagrim's son).

A ball game had been arranged early in winter on the plains by the River Hvita, and crowds of people came to it from all over the district. Many of Skallagrim's men attended, although Skallagrim himself stayed at home. Thord Granason was their leader. Seven-year-old Egil asked Thord if he could go to the game with him. Thord agreed, and seated Egil behind him on his horse, and they rode together to the games. When they reached the playing fields, the adult players were divided up into teams. A number of small boys were there as well, and they formed teams to play their own games.

Egil was paired against a boy called Grim, the son of Hegg. Grim was ten or eleven years old, and strong for his age. When they started playing the game, Egil proved to be weaker than Grim, who showed off his strength as much as he could. Egil lost his temper, wielded the bat and struck Grim, who seized him and dashed him to the ground roughly, warning him that he would suffer for it if he did not learn how to behave. When Egil got back on his feet he left the game, and the boys jeered at him.

Egil went to Thord Granason and told him what had happened. Thord said, "I'll go with you and we'll take our revenge." Thord handed Egil an axe he had been holding, a common type of weapon in those days, and they walked over to where the boys were playing their game. Grim had caught the ball and was running with the other boys chasing him. Egil ran up to Grim and drove the axe into his head, right through to the brain. Then Egil and Thord walked away to their people. The dead boy's people seized their weapons. Oleif Hjalt, a friend of Skallagrim, rushed in with his men. Theirs was a much larger group, and at that the two sides parted temporarily, but as a result, a quarrel developed between Oleif, who was acting as Egil's champion, and Hegg, the dead boy's father. They fought a battle later that day, where seven men were killed. Hegg received a fatal wound and his brother Kvig died in the battle.

When Egil returned home, Skallagrim seemed indifferent to his son's actions, but Bera, his mother, said he had the makings of a true Viking when he would be old enough to be put in command of warships. Then Egil spoke this verse:

> "My mother said
> I would be bought
> A boat with fine oars,
> Set off with Vikings,
> Stand up on the prow,
> Command the precious craft,
> Then enter port,
> Kill a man and another."

This is the recipe for training a murderer. Thord, the young man whom Egil looked up to as a role model, might have counseled Egil to cool off, to remember that he was only seven and therefore not expected to be as strong as the bigger boys. This could have helped in socializing Egil to accept his own limitations. Instead, he handed Egil the axe. It is a vivid example of adults behaving as accomplices to a child's crime. Never did anyone reprimand Egil, or attempt to intercede to calm the situation or make amends to the dead boy's family. Thus, Egil's rash behavior caused the death of eight people in a single day, at least three of them from a nearby family, and yet no censure or punishment of any kind was pronounced.

Apparently Skallagrim was not concerned about the impact his son's behavior would have on the community, or what it said about his son's developing character. The mother, however, was unabashedly approving. Her mention that his behavior was fitting for a Viking on a warship made no distinction about its being unacceptable at local social events. With her enthusiastic approval, Egil's path was laid.

Egil went on to a life filled with blood and conquest. He was respected for his abilities as a warrior, but mistrusted in social situations. He repeated this type of revenge killing several times, but always managed to escape or be pardoned because of extenuating circumstances. (The other man shouldn't have cheated him, etc.) Could Egil's tendency toward murder be attributed to his genetic makeup? His father was prone to violence, but he was not a "loose cannon" in the community the way Egil was, so his tendencies cannot be attributed to nature alone. In his case, we must look to the "nurture" in his childhood to explain his actions. Egil did grow up in a culture which was relatively permissive in their attitudes toward murder, but the other children were not behaving as he did, and they did not appreciate his bullying attitude, so in this case, we cannot assume the cause of his violent behavior was "peer pressure" or the culture at large. The responsibility can be laid directly at his parents' feet.

Egil's family groomed him to be a killer. At seven, a child is not a free agent. Had he been discouraged from attacking the boy at any point, the outcome might have been very different. The message was clear: Become a Viking warrior who kills people, and your mother will be very proud. No need to look further for genetic influences here. Although we may be able to identify a gene that predisposes a person to physical violence, it is a stretch to imagine a gene or genes for approving of someone else's committing a murder, and since today's

Norwegians and Icelanders have changed their ways very quickly, in evolutionary terms, and are no longer marauding Vikings, we might safely presume Egil's behavior was learned.

How far have we come, really, in the last thousand years? Children are not allowed to get away with murdering their classmates, at least not after the fact, but vicious bullying is an epidemic, and we have done very little in the way of prevention. Children are playing violent video games in which murder and mutilation are common fare; movies and music promote violence and depersonalized sex. Studies reveal that children watch approximately 28 hours of television a week, more time than they spend in school. The typical American child will view more than 200,000 acts of violence, including more than 16,000 murders before age 18.[13] As media moguls will tell us, most of those children don't become murderers, therefore it's all right, relax. True. They don't become murderers, but what about their human sensibilities, their ability to feel empathy for another person? What about their humanity?

Egil was a violent killer, but the unpremeditated nature of his reported crimes suggest that he might have been a Tenth Century Wannabe rather than a cold-blooded psychopath. Since he was given to violence, we cannot strictly compare him to our social Abusers. However, we could suppose that if you can train a child to be a murderer by age seven, you could just as easily train him to be a manipulative liar. Nothing presented here precludes the possibility that another child, in a very different family, might also turn out to be an Abuser, or tend toward Abusive Personality Type behavior as a result of neurological damage or a predisposition toward "soulless" behavior. There may be more than one way to become an Abuser, but just because there are some who might be "genetically predisposed" does not excuse the insensitive treatment of children which goes on every day, in every town, without intervention from others who could make a difference. Some Abusers are made, not born. Those are the cases for which we as a society are responsible, and which would be preventable in a kinder, gentler culture.

---

[13]   Eugene V. Beresin, M.D., "The impact of Media Violence on Children and Adolescents. Opportunities for Clinical Interventions," American Academy of Child and Adolescent Psychiatry, online resources.

Are today's parents all that different from Egil's? I have personally witnessed several unsettling incidents in a principal's office, after a child was removed from class for disruptive behavior. On one particularly memorable afternoon, a boy who had yelled, "Go f—yourself" at the teacher was taken to the office to wait for his mother. When she arrived, she flew into a rage, accusing the principal of incompetence, favoritism, and failing to teach the children anything. She blamed everyone but her son for his bad behavior. The son sulked in his chair, with an arrogant smirk on his face. Any hope the school might have had of socializing this child to fit in or learn anything receded from view. Not only that, but he could henceforth be counted on to disrupt classes, create havoc in the hallways, and terrorize the playground.

Unfortunately, this was not an isolated occurrence. The principal of this mostly middle-class school told me that every week he receives threatening phone calls from parents concerning a child's failing grades, "unwarranted" detentions and suspensions, and "unfair treatment." These were not requests for help or questions about the actions. They were belligerent refusals to cooperate with the school's attempt to maintain discipline, if it meant disciplining their child. Just as Egil's parents were training him to be a murderer, these parents are training their children to be Abusers, by convincing them that they are above the rules, and they are not required to treat people decently. These lessons are not lost on the other children, either. They frequently follow suit because they want to be "cool" too, and they have seen that the punishment is slight or nonexistent. I am not advocating stiffer punishments here. By the time it comes to that, it is already late in the game.

The children described here have been taught "family values." Unfortunately, their families value Abusive behavior. We must be willing, as a culture, to admit that we are largely allowing our children to be raised by Abusers—our unruly neighbors, toy and clothing corporations, music and video producers, prison-for-profit owners, and the media criminals who create an endless stream of lucrative cultural pollution and poison our young people with it. As parents, we are too busy and preoccupied with the trivial details of life to concentrate even for an hour a day on our children's inner being and their ability to expand their sensibilities as they grow, rather than shrinking to fit the demands of a competitive and belittling culture.

How are we to counteract the wave of Abusive Personality influences in our culture? I have seen families who were at their wits' end, trying to understand why one or more of their children were behaving badly in school, refusing to help out at home, and generally behaving disrespectfully toward everyone around them. These were concerned parents, usually both of them working, who were outraged at their own child's laziness, disregard for other people's feelings or belongings, and "lack of ambition." I often hear, "If I had ever behaved that way, my parents would have killed me."

Punishment Never Works

Frequently, families are caught in a destructive feedback loop: The worse the child does in school, and the more defiant he becomes, the more punishments they try to devise to bring him into line. Depriving the child of TV, video games and nights out creates an atmosphere in the home of sullen warfare.

Punishment never works. It may subdue the child temporarily, but it simultaneously sparks the child's fight or flight response and its attending Ego strategies. He is placed in a position where he must defend himself from attack (the child feels the punishment as an attack, and rightfully so). Since he is fully aware of his disadvantage in the family power structure, the child is forced to go underground, thrown back on his own imagination to devise methods of revenge, or possibilities for winning his freedom. Since compassionate conversation is precluded by the parents' power play, the child must learn to lie, connive and manipulate to restore his pride. This sets up a pattern for the child where Ego and pride are in the ascendance, and Heart feelings are stifled, crushed under the weight of feeling a parent's vengeance. (Punishment is after all, the parent's righteous-sounding excuse for revenge.)

The child sulks, acts resentful, and complains about how all the other kids have new cars, 4-wheelers, better computers and cell phones, fewer chores, and bigger allowances. What they really mean is that other children have more of what they need from their parents—emotional support and respect, and patient guidance. The child may not be able to put this into words, but he feels the emptiness of being left adrift with nothing to go by but the cruel imposition of rules about what he is *not* allowed to do. What is *not allowed* covers the entire universe of possibilities outside what his parents order him to do. In this family, the number one rule is that he must obey. This leaves a creative, energetic child with the option of stifling his inspiration and his originality in favor of slavery. There isn't a human alive who would volunteer for that choice. Why would we expect our children to accept it willingly?

Eventually, the child must develop ways to subdue his inclination to defy them, since he has learned that his own rebellious actions bring on the painful specter of a parent filled with rage and vengeance. By puberty, as the child's drive toward individuation reaches new levels, the impossible dilemma becomes clearer to the child: he must find a way to not feel. First, he will try to turn off his heart, becoming numb to the lingering pain of being at odds with the parents he has loved. Since other people in his life may stir feelings of friendship and love, he must find other ways to subdue his passionate feelings. This is where friends with drugs and video games may seem to be the only way out for the child who feels trapped.

The desperately controlling parents suspect the child has been smoking marijuana, and they attempt to stop it by imposing another round of punishment and threats. A younger sibling is showing signs of behaving disruptively. The parents are beside themselves with frustration and worry.

Behind this painful scene, there often is a backdrop which exacerbates the family's problems. Both parents may be either emotionally unavailable or they are working long hours, and their time at home is limited. They are constantly under stress to try to keep up with the day-to-day demands of their work, combined with the cleaning, laundry, errands, cooking, homework, and sports activities. Even with both parents on the go every evening and weekend, they are always rushed and feeling the pressure. The children have long hours of after-school activities or day care at the end of their school day. When they are not being surly, they appear exhausted and dazed. They spend most of their time with their peers, either unsupervised, or in large groups with one or two adults. Their conversations with each other are constant—cell phones, instant messages, text messages, but they rarely share their feelings with adults. Even with friends, the content of their talk is superficial, indirect, and stylized. A large percentage of them feel that school is a drag and a bother. They have little thought about what they will do after high school, except perhaps college, which they assume will be an exact extension of what they are currently doing.

What went wrong? How did the family become a house full of strangers? How did these children become so shallow? Are they really as Dark as they seem? Are we in danger of being surrounded by young people who are empty, selfish, poorly educated, and destructive? Are you a parent who is in danger of finding that you have nothing in common with your own children, and you are beginning to feel horrified with their behavior? Read on.

Parental Patterns Set the Wheels in Motion

I have observed a pattern in families where children are showing Abusive attitudes. I have seen it so frequently that I now think of it as the family formula for creating an Abuser, or an enthusiastically dedicated Wannabe.

There are two elements which are frequently present in the family background. One is a harsh and overly critical parent whose heavy-handed approach to the child undermines the child's self-confidence and self-esteem. This parent figure, frequently but not always the father, I call The Critic. The other element is a second parental figure (sometimes a grandparent) who consistently objects to the criticism of the child. Trying to counteract what she feels to be hurtful, she criticizes The Critic for his harshness and sides with the child. This parent we will call The Apologist. In "making it up" to the child, she is inclined to downplay the child's bad behavior, even when it may be turned against her. She frequently indulges the child's increasingly unreasonable demands. This pattern of alternating criticism and indulgence usually begins when the child is very young. It escalates as she gets older. This may be the pattern of parenting with all the children in the family, but it is often focused on one child who is seen as the troublesome one. Occasionally, a single parent may play both roles alternately, or two parents may take turns being Critic or Apologist. The effect is the same. It destroys the child's connection to his true self—the bodysoul which would have been his guide to right and wrong.

There is no beginning or end in this ongoing scenario. Punishment and indulgence follow so closely on one another it is difficult to determine which came first. In the ongoing battle over the child's battered psyche, the child is defined alternately as the perpetrator of endless misdeeds and as a helpless victim. The child soon learns to combine these supposed attributes to his or her own advantage. She demands special favors, presents and privileges, and uses threats and tantrums if she is not given what she wants immediately. The Apologist, feeling guilty and unwilling to be seen as the abusive one (or, in the worst cases, trying to show up the Critic as abusive) succumbs to the child's tactics and gives in to her demands, thereby encouraging further destructive behavior. The child eventually internalizes the idea, "I am special. The world owes me."

Taking a page from each parent's book, the child eventually learns to bully family members and others the way the Critic bullies him.[14] He then justifies his own behavior by pleading victim status and insisting he is entitled to compensation for the abuse he has suffered. These strategies then become the basis for a scam the child learns to use at every opportunity. Neither parent really wants to admit they have trained a con artist who is playing them both. Instead, they cling to their original descriptions of a disobedient, unruly child/innocent victim. Meanwhile, the stakes get higher as the child gets older. The family goes from fighting about unfinished homework projects and messy rooms to who is going to pay for the car he wrecked.

No matter how serious or how trivial the offense, the family continues to play out the same power struggle, over and over. The Critic insists the kid just needs to be treated more strictly, and she will "learn her lesson" while The Apologist insists she will learn to behave better if she is treated more gently. Ironically, in early childhood The Apologist seems to be more fair and reasonable, but as the child perfects her lying and cheating skills, it becomes obvious the Apologist is blind to the child's bad behavior. No matter how much evidence may be presented against her child, she clings to the idea that the child is just confused, or hurting, misled by others, or going through a stage. It becomes clear she is unwilling to uphold even the minimum standards of reasonable behavior with this child, whom she sees as

---

14   We are not talking about an infant here. Young children are not capable of this kind of intellectual gymnastics. Infants are not demanding or manipulative. They simply have needs.

exceptional. In this way, the indulgent Apologist is not so unlike Egil's doting Mother, who smiled on her son after he put an axe through his playmate's head.

The male child learns he is above the law, a prince who is entitled to special dispensation at all times. The female child is a princess, to whom all things should be given without her having to make the least effort to earn them. She too thinks she is above the law, and is just as dangerous as her male counterpart. Girls are less prone to violence, and may not attract the attention of the police as often. Their transgressions are more often of a personal nature. Deceit, shop-lifting, sexual infidelity, promiscuity, and personal betrayals are the crimes of favor among teenage female Abusers. They are irresponsible in all their dealings.

These children, meanwhile, have learned to take pride in the techniques they have perfected at home for "getting over." They have long ago adopted The Critic's attribution of them as loser, troublemaker, monster, leech, as well as the Apologist's description that they "can't help it," and therefore shouldn't be held responsible. This identity fits right in with the sleazy behavior they learn to adopt. They learned early on that they could lie, and The Apologist would cover up for them. As they enter teen years, and have access to a wider range of "educational" influences, they will study Abusers' techniques the way other children learn to carve figure-eights or program computers.

Violence and lawlessness are serious problems with this group. Their pandemic promiscuity creates a serious social problem because out-of-wedlock pregnancies are rampant in this group, and a teenage Abuser is among the worst of all possible mothers. For this reason alone, it behooves us as a culture to make available effective birth control methods to prevent these irresponsible individuals from reproducing themselves. Extensive social programs are not necessary. Few Abusive teenagers would choose to put themselves in the position of having to nurture a child if an easy alternative were available.

Whatever religious or moral preferences we may uphold for ourselves, it is simply masochistic for a society to pretend that any program suggesting abstinence or "Just Say No" could have any affect on this population of self-indulgent ne'er do wells whose main preoccupations are sex, drugs, junk food, shoplifting and video games. We are inviting a population explosion among the most destructive elements of our society, and providing no supervision or help for the infant who will probably spend its crucial formative years without a father, and with a mother who is worse than unfit to raise a child. Notice that I have not said here that all single mothers or even all teenagers are bad mothers. I have simply made the claim that all Abusers are bad mothers, and a teenage mother is likely to have even fewer compensatory supports for the infant than an adult, who might be more likely to be associated with a spouse or other adult who could mitigate the Abuser's preference for crushing the child's spirit.

The patterns I have described here are common in our culture. As children, we have not been taught how to recognize, protect and preserve our own bodysoul. We are therefore completely unprepared to teach a child how to be true to an inner guide which connects them to the Universe and provides them inner strength and innate wisdom. To do so would create humans we do not recognize, who surpass us in every way. Are we willing to accomplish that, or would we prefer the criminal behavior we recognize and feel more equipped to handle?

Here, I have presented examples of overt teaching—the philosophy of life which parents transmit to their children through thousands of comments, gestures, lectures, and day-to-day object lessons. As we have seen in several earlier chapters, there are also deeper and earlier experiences to be considered.

Allan N. Schore, in his book, *Affect Dysregulation and Disorders of the Self*, gathers numerous recent studies in brain research. Combining his work with the history of studies in "attachment theory," he illuminates how an infant's brain develops, and how that development is affected by the emotional tone of the child's day-to-day experience. Attachment theory has developed out of the work of John Bowlby, who emphasized the importance of the infant's early attachment to the mother. The work has been carried forward by the exponential growth of research made possible by film and video analysis of mother and child interactions beginning in the earliest days of life.

We now know that there is a critical period during the first two years of life when the infant's developing brain will be adversely affected by a traumatic or neglectful environment. The neuropsychobiological findings (the brain pictures we see reproduced frequently in our magazines and newspapers) can now be used to illustrate the understandings from previous developmental psychology studies—"that the maturation of the infant's brain is experience-dependent, and that these experiences are embedded in the attachment relationship" (Shore, 1994, 2000c; Siegel, 1999).

As we saw in discussions about the triune brain, the infant's interactions with the mother and other caregivers directly affect the infant's ability to form positive emotional attachments in later life, and they do so by promoting or preventing the formation of neurological channels in the brain. These neurological connections, or lack of them, will determine whether the infant will have the later capacity to regulate emotion effectively, and whether it will be capable of close and enduring emotional relationships.

Above I have described the "family values" version of creating an Abuser. The cases of Egil and the child of the Critic and Apologist family are probably scenarios for developing deep-rooted Wannabe characteristics, rather than cold-blooded Abuser. The earliest years in these cases may have been fairly nurturing for the child. The indulgent and attentive Apologist might provide much of what an infant needs for the child's first two years. It is the development of an individual personality and the thrust toward expressing one's will at around two years old which begins the serious battle over the child's identity. Either way, without intervention, the resulting citizen will behave selfishly, and will be predictably unreliable and destructive toward others.

I have illustrated these developmental scenarios to offer a context for understanding how they got that way, and why it is such a hopeless cause to try to change someone who has taken on this stance as their life purpose. These tendencies run deep, all the way back to the earliest foundations of a newly forming personality. The ongoing influence of a parent who approves or indulges these behaviors means that the Abuser or Wannabe sees nothing at all wrong with their attitude, and would resist changing on these grounds alone. Ultimately, it is this conviction about their own rightness which makes the Abuser so dangerous, and so impervious to change.

Unfortunately, it is often that very attitude of rightness which we find compelling and attractive. Helpers and reformers are attracted to the challenge of trying to have an impact—to try to "get through" to the adult Abuser, whether to spare society, or to prove their own powers. Lovers, friends and followers are attracted by the air of self-confidence which they may lack themselves. Either way, an Abusive Personality is dangerous, and should be regarded as such. Tearful confessions, protestations of innocence, and promises of change should be taken with an eye for the context, the person's history, and a carefully measured assessment of any hint of remnants of the "rightness" attitude: a tip-off that you are being conned.

Perhaps you recognize the story of your favorite Dark One's childhood in these descriptions. If so, expect to be treated as if it is your job to love them and to indulge their every whim, because their definition of being loved is synonymous with being pampered and indulged. You will feel no genuine warmth.

Until we are willing to completely reverse our attitudes toward children, we will encourage the Abusive values we live with now. We can begin with the premise that sensitivity is a weakness. It is not. It is a wondrous strength which puts us in touch with truths beyond our present knowing. Allow our children access to their bodysoul sensitivities and they will lead us to unimagined discoveries. They will also have a capacity for love and service to others which transcends anything we have accomplished. Enlightened children can truly save us from ourselves. Let them grow.

CHAPTER TWENTY-ONE

PLAYING ON THE DARK SIDE

IGNIS FATUUS
By Aline Kilmer, The Poor King's Daughter

"Your fires are false, they tell me. So?
I knew it long and long ago.
"But I choose false ones for my play,
They are the safer any day;
"And if I burn my hands a bit
Why, who will ever know of it?"
All this I said when I was proud,
Under my breath, almost aloud.
Then I plunged boldly in and played,
By my own fires I am betrayed.

C ontrary to popular belief, psychotherapy clients, at least most of those I have met, do not come with the purpose of laying blame on others for their own shortcomings or failures. Just the opposite. They often insist they are to blame for everything, including their own bad childhoods, their ensuing destructive relationships, and their current pain. It is an ironic twist in the power game when the victim tries to feel more worthy and more powerful by assuming they are the focus of all bad things. ("Wouldn't you know it? It always rains just when *I* plan a picnic; the traffic jam always happens just when *I* am in a hurry; the bad people always find *me* to take advantage of," etc.) Ironically, there is a feeling of security in believing you are the cause of everything. At least you are not helpless, and being the focus of all things, whether bad or good, does carry with it a certain sense of importance. Laying claim to being a magnet for all bad things makes you the center of the universe! This turnabout, if only in your own mind, is an attempt to compensate for the insults of childhood, when you were utterly helpless. This means you have developed a Dark identity. You attract Darkness, therefore you are Darkness. Your picture of who you really are in your innermost self is of someone who is a secret but undeclared Child of Darkness.

This makes you the perfect target for the proud Children of Darkness, who practically salivate with pleasure when they come across such willing participation in the most entertaining cloak-and-dagger game in town. Perhaps this is what happened to the Poor King's Daughter when she took it a step further. She convinced herself she could out-manipulate the manipulator, and be the Player who feels pride but no pain.

Anyone who has been raised by an Abuser or a dedicated Wannabe will come away from childhood feeling depleted, overwhelmed, empty, like a *nothing*. The natural response to this constant belittlement is to fight back, inside our own minds, where the secret story of our innermost self is being told. *"No! I am not powerless. I am not unlovable! I am not nothing! I can change things. I will prove it by making you love me! (You who are incapable of love) . . . And I will not give up until I have redeemed myself by earning your love. (You who are a Child of Darkness.)* "This is the story told in Chapter Four, "How The Sit-Down Strike Becomes a Way of Life."

It is this deep need, to prove ourselves powerful and therefore worthy, which fuels the drive to doggedly pursue the project of reforming a Dark One, rather than seeing the Darkness in yourself. In the throes of fending off attacks on your bodysoul, you have learned denial: denial that you were affected by the Darkness of your attackers, denial that you became like them. But there is something worse. As you let go of your own precious bodysoul and plugged yourself in to the "power" of your tormentors, you also let go of the deep, spiritual truth that you are a Child of God. You do not have to prove your worth or earn it. You do not have to redeem yourself. You only need to take hold, restore your deep connection to your true self, and with it your sense of love and gratitude for having been born. Your important work is to free yourself from the Darkness you carried with you from childhood and to be an example for others that the love and the hope you wish to find in the world resides in your own human heart.

Without the connection to your own bodysoul, the source of genuine self-worth, you are left with the gnawing need to prove to yourself you are not-like-them. In this state, it is most tempting to find a cause and attack it with great fervor. For the Fixer, it takes on the semblance of a campaign. She who professes to love the Abuser goes to great lengths, even extreme financial sacrifices and emotional hardship, to convince the Fixee to forgo the Dark attractions which have attracted the Fixer herself.

The Stockholm Syndrome

The Stockholm Syndrome refers to a psychological dynamic in which captives in a hostage situation fall in love with their captors. Long-term hostages have reported feeling awe and affection toward the captors who bring them food, and who refrain from killing them. The most famous incident in recent history was that of Patty Hearst, who became entangled in a controversial legal battle over her participation in an armed robbery. She was convicted because of her seemingly voluntary cooperation with the violent gang who had abducted her. She served nearly two years in jail, but was eventually pardoned when authorities acknowledged she had been brainwashed by her captors. She was helped to overcome the destructive effects of her captors through treatment rather than punishment.

Although the Stockholm Syndrome is thought to refer to hostage situations, it is the same as the dynamic we have been describing in families. Since it is well documented that this "fatal attraction" affects adults who are captives, it follows that children would be even more vulnerable to the tendency, given the length of their "captivity," and their inability to comprehend the situation.

By entering into a relationship with a Dark One, the victim is playing the game they learned in childhood: the cat-and-mouse strategies they were forced to hone while trying to survive in a destructive "hostage" environment. Long years of dealing with a stronger, bigger, smarter parent who also happens to be unloving puts the child in the position of admiring and loving a person who is fundamentally malevolent. She has been physically close, literally breathing the same air as the rejecting parent., craving closeness and warmth. The child from infancy on has no choice but to intimately connect with the one whose malevolence causes them suffering, but who brings them nourishment and some protection at the same time. The ambivalence a child feels in these circumstances is heart-wrenching.

The painful ambivalence and mistrust a child carries away from this kind of relationship can show up later as fear of commitment, especially in opportunities for healthy relationships,. Thus, the abused child grows up with a double-whammy, psychologically speaking. Not only are they intensely attracted to destructive relationships; they are repelled by the very people who could offer them real comfort and affection. A healthy and strong, loving person would expect to be treated with respect and trust because of their nature. The "hostage" has been trained to experience conflict, struggle and duplicity in close relationships. Next to that, a calm and loving union is frequently described by the adult hostage/victim as "boring."

The reason a calm and loving relationship might seem boring is because it lacks one crucial element: the power struggle.

On the face of it, there appears to be a gross imbalance in these relationships. One partner, the "hostage," seems weak and vulnerable. The other, the "captor," feels entitled to be given to, without regard for the cost to his partner. Their unspoken agreement is that the captor is the stronger one. Herein lies the real "fatal attraction." Closeness with the "captor"—especially physical closeness—allows the adult "hostage" the opportunity to live out, or relive, a blissful merger with the one who represents ultimate power. This blissful-merger feeling is especially heightened when it is based in the feelings of intimacy and closeness of a sexual relationship. The paradox here is that the "hostage" is actually taking a sense of power and secret triumph from the encounter. Therefore she is not giving anything at all. The "captor," whom we have previously characterized as the Abuser, is giving their "victim" the opportunity to join in the exercise of cold-blooded power. Does this then make the Abuser the "giver?"

Given the endless variety of roles humans are capable of playing, there are endless permutations a couple or a family might indulge in. A seductive Dark One knows how to appear to be a "giver"—magnanimous and openhanded. Generosity is the lead-in for the Abuser whose behind-the-scenes attitude is, "You'd be nothing without me."

The ultimate irony is that the attitude which attracts us to the Dark One in the first place becomes our downfall. The quality of invulnerability which we mistakenly associate with strength and power is based in nothing but cold, calculating malevolence.

As adults, pursuing the unreachable, we are caught in a feedback loop of our own making: The very thing we find irresistibly attractive is the same quality which frustrates us: the Abuser's indifference and sense of entitlement. It is the refusal to see our own denial and complicity, and our own attraction to exercising power over others which repeats the pain of childhood. That "ultimate power" is the power to take over and own you, body and soul. In this way the victim becomes the besotted coconspirator in his own destruction.

How Could S/He Do That to Me?

There are two imbedded questions here. One is "Why me?" The other is "What is wrong with him/her?"

The victim of an Abuser, especially when he has adopted the role of a Fixer, insists that he cannot understand what possessed his loved one to behave in such heartless ways, even though she may be behaving in much the same way his mother did. He insists it is so incomprehensible to him that he may dismiss it, finally, leaving the question unanswered. Because he denies any knowledge of the frame of mind which would permit such cruelties, it just doesn't compute. This is a serious blind spot in people who are inclined to be good and decent, but who have been raised so close to Abusers that the question "How could he/she?" echoes in their minds day after day, throughout childhood and into adulthood. They become used to asking, but it has been unsolved so long that they no longer even expect an answer. Perhaps this is because they prefer to maintain the illusion of their own innocence (as adults) rather than acknowledge the part they have played in the abuse. The adult who has repeatedly been an Abuser's mark has become accomplice rather than victim.

Accomplices have numerous convoluted ways to avoid leaving the destructive relationship. Often, they claim saintly patience and forgiveness as explanations. I have heard grown clients explain their loyalty to hideously abusive parents with statements like "It will kill them. I don't want to be responsible for destroying them." Here is the secret tradeoff referred to above: "I may seem like the victim, but I actually hold great power."

Here we have the simple answer to the question of why they did it to you. It is because they can. The accomplice's insistence that their favorite Abuser will not do horrific things to them is certainly naïve, but it goes far beyond naïveté. Behind the insistence that "s/he won't do it to me" is a pet delusion: "I am more powerful than they are. I have the power to make them obey me, even though other people have not been able to accomplish this. (I will succeed in making a silk purse out of this sow's ear!)" This is not love. It is a power struggle which pits one "lover's" addiction against the other: Darkness against Darkness, the mutual death of two bodysouls.

Once your participation in the deadly game has been declared, the question "How could they?" is moot. It is who they are and you are their accomplice. Why would you expect them not to do it to you? Abusers destroy because they enjoy seeing others taken down, in one way or another. This is the character-rooted malignant aggression Eric Fromm referred to. Their methods may not be physical murder, but their cruelty and indifference to human feeling is so predictable that it is foolhardy for anyone close to them to imagine they will not eventually be victimized.

Gavin de Becker has written a very helpful book called *The Gift of Fear*, which is a must-read for anyone who is in an abusive relationship, or believes they might be. De Becker shows how predictable violence is. He teaches women to listen to their instincts when fear and suspicion sound the alarm, and to act unhesitatingly on those feelings. Chapter 10, "Intimate Enemies," reminds us that the Abuser's partner has the experience to predict violence, based on past behavior. She has seen the rages and violence and has lived in a state of fear, although she has stifled the self-defense warning signs in order to stay with the Abuser for reasons of her own. Violence, like other acts of betrayal, rarely occurs without warning. In most cases of domestic violence, the victim senses the danger and could have saved herself before the disaster.

As de Becker teaches, the instinct toward self-preservation is still there in adults, regardless of upbringing, so it is not a hopeless challenge to change your response to threats from others, even loved ones. It is a matter of relearning, beginning with the heart-centered feeling that you are deserving of decent treatment, no matter what, and that abuse is not love.

PART VI.

ABUSIVE INSTITUTIONS

GOING CRAZY

They told me I was crazy,
That what I saw wasn't real.
So I put a veil in front of my senses.
They told me how I should feel.

Then I wouldn't know and I wouldn't say
What they said I was crazy for seeing.
So I won't feel crazy, at least they won't hound me
If I can get used to agreeing.

I put a veil in front of my eyes
So I wouldn't feel crazy around them.
Because if I didn't, I'd keep on perceiving.
My common sense would astound them.

I had to believe, so I wouldn't feel crazy
They yelled at me every day.
Instead of seeing, I believed,
And now I don't get in their way.

And then they'd keep saying, over and over,
You freak, you're an alien's turd.
With your fancy ideas, you just don't belong here.
You must have been left on the curb.

But I couldn't not know, when I was young,
What I saw when it wasn't veiled,
I knew it once when I wasn't crazy
Before my senses failed.

All that made it harder 'cause inside I knew
That I knew and I saw what was hidden,
I saw they had secrets, and more than a few,
But then again, maybe I didn't.

If I didn't see, then they couldn't see me,
And I could hide the facts,
    like what I saw, and what they did,
    and the truth of their dishonest acts
    that they are what they are, and not what they say
    that they're arrogant, ignorant, lazy,
If I didn't see anything, life got better.
Does that mean I really am crazy?

CHAPTER TWENTY-TWO

HOW SCHOOLS, POLITICS, SCIENCE, RELIGION AND DESCARTES LED US ASTRAY

"We have it in our power to begin the world over again."
—Thomas Paine

The family with its beliefs and values is like a tributary that flows into the larger river of cultural traditions, each family adding its influence to the larger community. In an ideal society, the family and all its members would enthusiastically embrace childrearing practices which foster a kind, mutually nourishing environment. This philosophy of life would then be mirrored in the schools and other social institutions. In the best of all possible worlds, the government and its representative institutions would support and protect these humanitarian values, exerting social pressure by example to encourage decent behavior, even without legal intervention.

In such a harmonious society, the value system of the culture would actively reinforce the best and most creative inclinations of its members. Unfortunately, we have not achieved anything resembling that state. Our "popular culture" has run amok, to the point where rap singers are murdering each other in turf wars, and the more indecently our political representatives behave, the more famous they become. These characters have become role models for television-watching children. Meanwhile, our Congress wrangles over basic governmental responsibilities, leaving the traditional "safety net" which once minimally protected the poorest and oldest among us is in shambles, and our international reputation dishonored. Meanwhile, the only funding which can be agreed upon goes to more police and military expenditures which have generated colossal debt.

These massive programs make insecure and paranoid leaders more comfortable, but they leave a society with nothing to show for its bloated expenses but an empty treasury and a worried citizenry, fearing for their future. Bridges collapse, credit ratings fall, and still the voices of greed and entitlement ring out: "No! We will not help our fellow citizens. We need more for ourselves!"

Democracy has its limitations. Sometimes fear, stirred up by a passionate-sounding spokesperson, can inspire the mob to sanction atrocities. In the current era, majority rule is often overridden by the loudest and most angry voice if it is transmitted over the airways often enough. The insecurities of the majority are being exploited by a cadre of powerful and selfish leaders whose characteristics fit the category of Heads-without Hearts.

In a ruthless play for power and profit, the Dark Ones have been in ascendance in American politics and finance for several generations. Young people no longer experience the security of knowing their elders are capable of good will, cooperation and intelligent guidance. We have reached the forked path in our political lives. Should the resistance to government help for the weakest among us continue, we will soon be forced to choose whether we will care for our elderly neighbors and poor relatives ourselves, or whether we will leave them to die.

Education for the Nineteenth Century

Public schools used to be valued as the resource which could make the difference between a life of struggle and one of security and accomplishment. Today they are seen by a large number of children as a bother and an impediment to their freedom. As one retiring teacher said, "The only question they ever ask is, 'Is this on the test?'" As a result, schools are focused on the barren demands of arbitrary test scores. Teachers spend their time keeping law and order in the classroom, and trying to persuade students to fill a chair for enough days a year to be able to keep the flow of funding going.

Gore Vidal has said that he never met a 6-year-old that wasn't interesting, and never met a 16-year-old that was. In between lie 10 years of classroom experience. Where have we gone so wrong?

In talking with teachers from elementary through high school, I am told of the struggles these disillusioned educators are faced with daily.

Even in affluent suburbs, many students show little interest in learning anything. They complain bitterly if they are asked to do original work or to expend any effort at all. Several veteran teachers have told me that they have become resigned to raising grades across the board by at least half a letter grade above what they feel is deserved because of pressure from students and their parents. It is unfortunate that the teachers themselves have succumbed to peer pressure. Once they have agreed to this unholy deal, it is not reasonable for them to complain about the inferior results.

Rather than demanding higher performance of their children, the parents instead ask the school to lower its standards—for their child, who needs acceptance into a better college, and the teachers have relinquished their traditional position of power by giving in to parents' demands. Like the Apologist teaching Abusive values, these teachers have unwittingly taken the role of the indulgent parent, spoiling both parents and children in a downward spiral into Abusive values. Apparently, these parents also think colleges can be persuaded to give their untutored, lazy son or daughter a degree by the same bullying methods. Or perhaps they already have planned to buy research papers for their child from the industry which has grown up for this purpose.

Some time ago, I spoke with a 12-year old I will call Eric, whose mother consistently did his homework for him. Although he was subjected to hours of haranguing and bullying in the course of a night's homework, the child seemed to resist the idea of doing his homework by himself. When I asked why he didn't want to give it a try, to earn the sense of accomplishment he would deserve, he said he wouldn't want that because he might not get an A every time. He could be sure his mother would always earn an A. He could get into the college they wanted him to go to that way. Pursuing this line of reasoning further, I asked him if he would rather do the work if he knew he could get a B+, or if he would rather cheat and get an A. He said he would absolutely rather cheat. When asked why he needed to get into such a college, he said it was because then he could get a better job and make a lot of money. Like Egil's mother, this supposedly helpful parent was raising a criminal, and the whole family resisted any suggestion that their materialistic focus was destructive to the child's moral development.

In the examples above, the children were being force-fed Abusive Personality values by their parents: Cheat and lie to get ahead of others, garner prestige, and above all make a lot of money. This is all that matters. Meanwhile, teachers stand by feeling overwhelmed, unable to stem the tide of mediocrity and ignorance. They too have been raised in this corrosive value system, and have been weakened in their resolve as well as their self-esteem.

At the other end of the scale, loving and supportive families who raise exemplary students may find their children the mockery of their "cooler" schoolmates. Often, the "popular" ones model themselves on the celebrated selfishness and criminality of their Wannabe elders.

Meanwhile, educators who learned of the link between low self-esteem and poor performance launched a program to try to boost the self-esteem of their students by praising them. To this end, children were told things like, "You're great. You're wonderful, just the way you are." Unfortunately, praise without accomplishment is another very effective way to encourage irresponsible behavior. This led to an extremely distasteful result: children are still lazy, but now felt entitled to be arrogant and boastful.

The "dumbing down" at all levels of the educational system has shown up in standardized test scores, even after the tests themselves have been radically simplified over the past 50 years. The dismal truth is that, on the whole, our students are no longer world-class. Our future capability to excel in the world is in question.

The law called "No Child Left Behind" has created a system which allows government overseers to deny funding to "underperforming" schools—many of them in poor urban areas. It has had the effect of threatening the entire system of public education by denying the individual needs of students, and instead favoring children from wealthier and better prepared families. Schools which are most effected are those which serve disadvantaged children, whose only opportunity to thrive might have been in the warm, vibrant atmosphere of a creative and innovative classroom. Those classrooms are becoming a thing of the past. Today, kindergarten children are likely to be refused recess and nap time in favor of sitting at their desks doing drills. Teachers are required to force-feed students what they supposedly need to score higher in math and sciences, but it does not work. They no longer teach children how to think and reason for themselves, so it is impossible for them to achieve anything meaningful. The effect on children is insidious. They are bored, restless, and eager to drop out. They have no input or participation in the decisions about what they will study, so they have lost interest in learning. It has had a more devastating effect on children's attitudes toward school than the hickory stick ever did.

Existing programs in art, music, and even sports have been curtailed, thereby removing the most civilizing influences a culture has. Being drilled in your times tables will never inspire a love of learning the way writing an original poem, producing your own play, or playing an instrument could.

Even caring teachers and students have become dispirited by increasingly oppressive rule-bound policies. At the same time, violence, alienation and bullying are on the rise. As a result, many of our schools have become the secondary breeding ground for Abusive ideals. Teachers who once hoped to inspire students to greatness now find themselves besieged and outnumbered by disrespectful students and parents. At the same time, they are overseen by administrators who are toadies to political and corporate bosses.

Educators have known for decades that the most effective way to teach children is through play and movement, not by sitting in a chair. Measure a six-inch hole in the ground to plant your tulip bulb, and you will never forget what six inches looks like. Throw three beanbags three times, and you will learn your multiplication tables effortlessly. Study a musical scale or bake a cake and you will know fractions. Why have we made it so hard for our children to enjoy school?

Stuffing endless amounts of memorized content into the brains of our children is not "education." This fundamental flaw in our thinking pervades every area of our lives. Being a Head Person does not make you a successful person.

In every area of education, we have added the element of divisiveness and competition. The infamous bell curve which was the educator's magic tool in the 50's and 60's automatically divided students into categories which we suspected were really the measure of our worth. We were superior, inferior and everything in-between, which was really mediocre. As the little boy Eric and his mother believed, if you were not in the highest percentile, you failed.

Competitions in which one wins and others lose lead inevitably to the kind of thinking that possessed Eric and his parents. "If I don't win, I lose. That makes me a loser."

Some reading this may be thinking that life would not be fun, or no one would be motivated without our competitive spirit. Although there is an important place for demonstrations of skill at the highest levels, there is no need for competition as we know it to inspire those skills. Human beings thrill in the experience of performing beautifully. Composers, dancers and musicians require no competitive challenge to motivate them. Excellence is its own reward. Athletes with the fire to excel would do so without crassly promoted professional athletics. The opportunity for the athlete to demonstrate her skill to an appreciative audience is more satisfying in the end than beating an opponent. Our insistence that winners must create losers is unjustified and inhumane to all who compete. By adding the element of competition, we lose the greatest opportunity for peace-building among communities and nations. Gaining power over another is an Abuser's game. Performing beautifully for all the world to see is a soulbody's dream.

It is encouraging and motivating for the athlete in training to compare his own progress against previous accomplishments, the way runners keep track of their own increasing stamina and speed. Without the anxiety of a possible humiliation and loss, an athlete is free to focus on developing excellence. As for fun, we need to look to our children for guidance. Children are very adept at structuring games to include all levels of expertise. If you have ever witnessed a neighborhood game of tag or hide-and-seek you have probably seen the way the youngest and least sophisticated players often provide the most hilarity and good fun.

Children have been learning what they needed to know to carry on life on the planet for eons, by playing, listening to stories, singing, dancing, watching, participating and experimenting. It doesn't need to be such a painful struggle. In our myopic focus on commerce, law and science, we have veered away from the very activities which make life richer and more interesting, and which open the senses in a way that only wholehearted participation encourages. Cut-throat competition destroys the sense of belonging and unconditional acceptance all children need in order to thrive.

In the *Ringing Cedars* books by Vladimir Megré, we are presented with a radical Humanist vision of raising a child in the most creative way possible. Anastasia, the Siberian woman who lives alone in the forest with her young son, gives us a future glimpse of what might be possible if we were to truly adapt our childrearing and education practices to the actual needs of an individual child. Volume Three, *The Space of Love,* offers a view of sex, childbearing and parenting based in unconditional love, tenderness and respect for the child's soul needs. Although Anastasia is described as being aided by the attention of several wild animal nannies, which modern parents may not have access to, there are fundamental truths which ring out from the pages. Her view on breast-feeding is that the mother's gaze while the child is feeding transmits to the child all the wisdom of the ages, in addition to the love and comfort of the mother's smile.

In book 6, *The Book of Kin* we are introduced to a 5-year-old child whose development would be unthinkable in our "civilized" societies. If we were able to achieve even a quarter of what is vividly portrayed in these lovely volumes, we would change the world. There is no reason to assume that we could not begin to view our children as the strong and intelligent souls they are, even from birth. Just that would change the way children think of themselves, and therefore the way they behave.

Under the loving eyes of a parent who offers a child freedom and respect, along with access to all the wonders of the natural world, the child has no need for toys, artificial games, or disciplinary practices of any kind. A child who is encouraged in his fascination with real life, real objects and real people has a dramatic advantage over one who is raised by technological gadgets, inanimate objects, and inattentive caregivers. The single habit of giving a child dead things to play with (plastic, squeaking, whirring and mechanical objects) takes the child's attention away from reality, to develop an interest in artificiality. By playing with a bug in the grass, a child explores the wonders of the Universe. By crawling and exploring without restraints, the infant discovers his strengths and his limits. A child who is free to indulge his curiosity and his physical needs for physical closeness, nutritious food, physical challenges, and quiet sleep whenever he needs them will have no conflicts with the parents who lovingly oversee his explorations.

This picture of attentive care is far from the American Dream version of parenting, in which both parents are preoccupied for most of every day with career-building rather than child-care. It requires that childrearing be accepted as a full-time job for at least one of the parents (most naturally in infancy, the breast-feeding mother) for a period of at least six years, preferably more. The same level of freedom to explore the natural world must then continue throughout school years if the child is to develop fully. It would require that parents reorder their priorities when it comes to deciding between nurturing their child or making money. Many parents will argue that money is the important element in getting their children into the best schools, and providing them with the best tools for learning. It is simply not true. A child raised close to Nature is better prepared for any advanced intellectual work than one which has spent his childhood in a chair, or being taught organized games. Originality, creativity, problem-solving—all are developed in the interaction between the child and the natural world.

As a first step, we must separate our selves from the safety and comfort of our well-appointed living rooms to explore the real world with our children. Planting, collecting wild herbs and foods, being close to wild animals in their natural habitat, and feeling the wind on your face is the beginning of a brilliant soul-expanding education.

Arts in the Schools

It has been well-known to educators for some time that art, poetry and music in the classroom allow the child to remain excited about learning beyond their sixth year. In 1975, the study titled "Coming to Our Senses" was published under the auspices of David Rockefeller, who convened a panel of experts from many fields and geographical locations around America. Their work drew together the findings of interviews and wide-ranging studies concerning attitudes and approaches to teaching art in the schools. Included as a part of the published report was the following eloquent and persuasive "Manifesto of a School Superintendent: The Arts and the Full Meaning of Life," by former Superintendent Charles E. Brown of Newton Public Schools, Newton Massachusetts. I have included it here in its entirety because I have never heard a more clearly stated argument for the inclusion of arts in the school curriculum:

"There are many things that I want my children—and yours—to gain from education.

"I want them to know something of beauty—the form it takes, the many ways in which it is revealed, the sometimes unexpected places in which we find it, the art of expressing it.

"I want them to be sensitive to the world around them—to feel the wind, to see—to really see—the stars, and the moon, and the trees, to hear the sounds of nature, to live as one with their environment.

"I want them to develop a sense of aesthetic taste—to have a feeling for and about the things in their lives, to be something other than a passive recipient of someone else's sense of what is aesthetically appealing.

"I want them to be discriminating—not only in their intellectual tastes but in their artistic and cultural tastes as well.

"I want them to know, in full measure, the wonder of being human—I want them to be sensitive to the human condition, to know themselves and to see themselves clearly in relation to others, to know that we have struggled since the beginning of our existence to express our thoughts, our convictions, our fears, our dreams—and that we have done this in a variety of ways.

"I want them to realize that history is a human story in the sense that in this story are found many examples of people's attempts to liberate themselves from the limitations and restrictions imposed upon them by the society of which they were a part—to know that some people have never made this attempt—that they have in Thomas Wolfe's words remained in the "unspeakable and incommunicable prison of this earth."

"I want them to realize fully that every person, as long as he or she lives, must make some kind of response to certain fundamental experiences of human life, ranging from birth to death and all that lies in-between; each of us, in our own fashion, must respond also to such aspects of our search for meaning as trust, compassion, authority, discipline, freedom, hope, beauty, truth, love.

"The question, 'How shall I find the full meaning of life?' has reference to every individual, and the answer, or more accurately, the parts of the answer, come from many sources.

"My strong conviction is that the schools must provide part of the answer, and that in the arts, we have one of our richest resources for working toward this end."

Mr. Brown wanted to train Heart People. He had the recipe for doing just that. The findings of the Rockefeller committee were both optimistic and worrisome. A trend toward burgeoning growth in the arts was apparent in the culture; theaters and concert halls. Performing arts groups of every kind were being newly established and expanding rapidly. At the same time, programs in the schools were dwindling. The return to a Nineteenth Century emphasis on the three basic skills of reading, writing and religion was beginning to be felt, with fewer public funds being allocated for school-based arts programs. In spite of clear evidence that participation in the arts had a significantly positive effect on the ability of students to learn, create, and reason effectively, robust arts programs were rarely found outside specialized schools. Now, 35 years later, those arts institutions which saw growth in the 70's have begun to dwindle and die out at a rapid rate, even before the 2008 economic downturn. Well-known institutions which had been fixtures in our culture are seeing economic hard times. Institutions we have taken for granted, like the New York Metropolitan Opera, the Seattle Symphony, the Detroit Opera, the Minnesota Museum of Art and three Oregon City, Oregon museums report severe difficulty in meeting their basic expenses. The large numbers of children who have been deprived of a cultural background in school and at home are now the adults who do not support the fine arts. It does not appear to be simply an economic issue either, since blockbuster Hollywood movies and sporting events are enjoying enormous financial successes.

The dumbing down of the American culture has had its effect in the quality of the arts as well. Dance schools teaching hip hop and gymnastics have supplanted classical ballet training, and dance training in general is seen as self-improvement or exercise rather than a fine arts discipline. A similar trend in singing encourages pop artists to perform exhibitionistic vocal and sexual gymnastics rather than develop their skills at storytelling, emotional expression or musicality. All over the country, small cities are losing their orchestras for lack of interest or funding. Since the Reagan era, government funding for the arts has been overseen almost exclusively by financial managers and bankers rather than artists. This has put the emphasis on making non-profits financially viable entities, rather than seeing them as a resource to be supported and funded by our government for the sake of our own hearts and souls. We have truly become the modern equivalent of the Philistines—powerful, gigantic, materialistic and uncultured.[15]

Field trips, student internships and artist-in-the-classroom projects have thrived in the past because of support from nonprofit arts organizations, which in turn were largely supported by government grants. As these resources dry up, so do the rich and enlightening experiences they afford our young people.

We could prevent these profound losses. Many of our greatest cultural institutions are still mostly intact, and a fair number of artists, actors, musicians and dancers continue to struggle to achieve excellence although they often are working in a void, with little recognition or financial support. Public radio and television is a small bright spot. It continues to fund and produce excellent programming for public consumption, but limited resources encourage safe programming. This provides a stage for already-recognized stars and well-known institutions. These public resources are now under attack by "fiscal conservatives" who would prefer to eliminate public support for the arts entirely. These same present-day Philistines who vote eagerly to fund an unlimited war machine have fought to deny support to publicly funded arts projects. Our greatest cultural treasure will not be safe until we are willing to accept that supporting the arts, like the preservation of wild spaces, is a matter of nurturing our humanity, and thereby transcends financial concerns. We have much to lose if we continue blindly to allow our artistic heritage to die or be reduced to

---

[15]   The Philistines were a group of invaders who counted Goliath as their most famous member and who were in direct competition with the Israelites for centuries. They controlled iron supplies in the area, and were known as materialistic and uncultured.

gaudy imitation. It will be tragic if we are too cheap to recognize that a country's people are ultimately measured by the quality of their arts, not just by the size of their GDP or their armies.

Politics

"Find out just what a people will submit to, and you have found out the exact amount of injustice and wrong which will be imposed upon them; and these will continue till they are resisted with either words or blows, or with both. The limits of tyrants are prescribed by the endurance of those whom they oppress."

—Frederick Douglass

By the time the Bush presidency ended in 2008, American political discourse had devolved into emotional manipulation and skillful name-calling. Scientific and intellectual activity was under attack, and we were descending once again into the kind of oppressive, fascistic society which seems to surface in waves every fifty years or so. As those citizens who suffered under the McCarthy inquisition are dying off, we have found ourselves once again struggling with government wiretapping, policies which allow illegal investigations, secret torture interrogations and arrest and detainment without legal justification or recourse. There had developed a pervasive feeling of fear and uneasiness toward the world at large, and toward each other. Divisiveness and political combat had risen to a fever pitch. Meanwhile, we were constantly reminded of the imminent danger of attack by terrorists. At every turn, our previously free-flowing lifestyle had degenerated into scanning, searching, and probing to root out terrorists.

The talents of these illusive terrorists seem to be mostly limited, worldwide, to car bombs and suicide vests, except for one sophisticated technological feat in which our entire country's defense system was taken over for several hours by mysterious and exceptionally talented international masterminds. Neither perpetrators nor accomplices have ever been brought to trial, so the American people may never know what actually happened, but we might consider the popular adage: "Follow the money." The U.S. treasury has been dumped wholesale into the pockets of private contractors. Trillions of taxpayer dollars have been spent on war machinery, scanning equipment, battalions of privately hired inspectors and "police presence." What has this bought us but a state of fear? Have we been duped?

In my travels I have witnessed search-and-confiscate tribulations involving ancient old ladies, harried mothers with babies, and large families traveling together. Are these really the sort of people we need to deprive of their water bottles and the gifts of perfume they are bringing home? What dangerous acts, exactly, could we expect them to perform on an airplane? In one airport inspection line, the scene had become so tense as we all took off our shoes that I couldn't resist muttering Jay Leno's joke to the passenger behind me: "Thank heavens Richard Reed didn't hide the bomb in his underwear!" Little did we know then that the next would-be airplane terrorist would hide explosives in his underwear. Like Richard Reed, most of the would-be terrorists we have encountered in the media seem remarkably inept and mentally unbalanced, troublesome but not terrifying.

As a result of these oppressive "Homeland Security" policies, citizens of every stripe have felt beleaguered and under attack. Perceiving dangers from without and within, we have allowed and even welcomed dangerously restrictive policies (the so-called Patriot Act), disregarding the long-term consequences. Although the tensions have eased a bit at the time of this writing, many of the previously instituted laws remain in effect. Prosecution of those who ordered and oversaw acts of torture and murder has stalled. Only time will tell whether healing must precede investigation, so that we can get on with the business of governing, as Obama has suggested. The festering destructiveness that lingers just under the surface of the American political system may destroy anything that is being built.

The film, "The Economics of Happiness," has presented us with a birds-eye view of what has really happened to our planet as a result of the merger of economic and political interests, and what we will need to do to fix it. Every administration since the Second World War has ascribed to the philosophy that economic growth is the route to prosperity and therefore happiness. Globalization has been accepted in international political circles as the beneficial next step in the march of "progress". This has resulted in an unwieldy and destructive global market in which the same items of food and other products (wheat, for instance) are both exported and imported by the U.S. in equal numbers.

In the process, enormous amounts of fuel and human resources are wasted, and environmental degradation has become a way of life. The resulting competition between workers on opposite sides of the world has lowered the standard of living among workers everywhere. The beneficiaries are those multinational corporations which have become most skillful at exploiting employees, natural resources, and the planet's over-stressed ability to absorb environmental toxins.

On every continent, indigenous cultures previously lived happily on the land, preserving rather than abusing the natural resources. They have been shamed and displaced because of their simpler lifestyles, and their lack of legal clout. Many have been seduced into leaving their land, or have been forced off it by sweetheart deals between corporate land-grabbers and dictators intent on lining their own pockets. This has sent millions of poor migrants into overflowing cities around the world. At the same time, there are also hopeful signs of growing movements around the globe of people who are working, farming, trading and connecting with others on a local level.

There is evidence all around us for the absurdity of our present system. Hawaiian grocery stores are filled with fish from Thailand, while New Zealand butter is cheaper in New York than New York State butter. Government-subsidized transportation systems around the world have created the nonsensical situation in which factory farmers in North America are bankrupting family farms in Hungary, while Chinese fish farms sound the death knell for small fishing boat captains in New England. How will it be possible to stop the insanity we have created when there is no international government to legislate common sense? Looking at the big picture of what we have designed as "commerce," one might think we humans had completely lost our minds. Why did this impossible mess ever make sense to anybody, anywhere?

Somewhere along the way, in the pursuit of profit and "rationality," we have learned to argue, persuade, and rationalize, but we have misplaced our common sense.

Descartes and the Rise of the Head People

The world has never been the same since Descartes. He viewed the human mind as a separate, superior faculty from the body or the emotions. This sent us down a six-generation path of near-worship of the intellect, as if it could be trained and used as a separate entity. Rationality was seen as the highest good, to be achieved by excluding any information which could not be measured by the laws of mathematics, physics, geometry and mechanics as they were understood in the Nineteenth and Twentieth Centuries. Science was to be practiced as a controlled study of the world around us.[16] However ambitious those studies might become, they must always be tested by a rigorous adherence to the scientific method. Information must be gathered and measured using the tools and measuring devices of our three-dimensional experience—that is, those things which can be seen and touched and therefore manipulated. Human emotion or intuition were not to be trusted. This approach has brought to light many interesting bits of knowledge, but it has also spawned an almost messianic search for ever smaller and smaller units of information. We have pursued the dividing and measuring of ever tinier elements in our world as if reducing a thing to its smallest components could tell us what that thing really is.

Enormous machines have been developed to measure particles whose presence can be detected only by their minuscule but still visible effect on other particles. Yet, we still do not know how life begins, or where we humans came from, or why the world is made up of irreducible energy forms. We cannot measure God, although the majority of people can feel the presence of a Higher Power. We can accurately measure the beneficial effects of prayer, but we do not know why it works. In spite of the apparent limits of the scientific method, we cling to the hope that science will one day find all the answers we need, and we continue to worship the cult of rationality, (a brain functioning separate from the body or heart), as the source of all accurate and reliable information.

The belief that things can be measured and therefore understood, and that everything that is "real" can be measured "rationally" has led us to become a race of opinionated, judgmental Head People.

Even some scientists have become narrow-minded and rigid in their defense of all things scientific and measurable. This has created a rift

---

[16] See *Descartes' Error*, by Antonio Damasio for a readable and illuminating assessment of the problem.

between those who adhere to strict forms of measurement and those whose creative inspiration leads them into uncharted, and sometimes unchartable, terrain. This closing of the ranks in scientific circles has had a stultifying effect on original thinking and research which pushes against the bounds of what we have learned using the traditional scientific method. Meanwhile, new discoveries await us in the areas of quantum physics, parapsychology, spirituality and the mysteries of intuitive perception.

Increasing our knowledge of the Universe in a meaningful way will require brand new methods of exploration. For example, how is it that we know when someone is looking at us from behind? How is it that we can walk on hot coals without getting burned (I have done it myself)? How is it that so many people see the same ghosts, and how do I know who is calling me before I pick up the phone? Even when scientists have shown through traditional scientific means that psychic ability is real and measurable, the results are largely ignored within the scientific community.[17] By denying the possible validity of psychic information, we silence the voice of the bodysoul, our most eloquent and expansive creative force, and the source of Universal knowledge.

Much has already been done to explore these mysterious phenomena, but it has been done mostly without it being publicly acknowledged. The U.S. government has traditionally denied any knowledge of such things as UFO's, global magnetic shifts, or the existence of paranormal activity while millions were spent studying these phenomena. Meanwhile astronauts, airplane pilots and well-grounded citizens continue to report experiences with beings or forces beyond what we generally accept as "real."

The attitude of scientific rigidity has filtered into the mainstream as well. Some people would consider me "crazy" if I profess to know what my brother is feeling or thinking five hundred miles away. However, these same people unquestioningly accept that radio waves can travel invisibly through the air and be captured by their bedside radio.

Resorting to the power of our brains is not enough. We must be willing to reach deeper, make contact with the age-old truths we carry in our hearts, and overcome our fear of using our emotional and intuitive strengths to solve our problems, whether they be in the area

---

[17]   See Gary Schwartz's book, *The Afterlife Experiments*

of education, psychology, politics or technology. In the undertow of a Wannabe society, we must consciously hold out against the divisiveness which threatens to sway our thinking toward oppression of originality, daring, uniqueness, and radical thought. We are being reminded that forces which may initially feel emotionally dangerous and unfamiliar may also hold the possibility of progress and change, as Socrates, Copernicus, Galileo, Leonardo and others taught us.

Here is author and historian Malcolm Hollick's take on the problem in his book, *The Science of Oneness:*

> "Like me, you probably grew up in a culture dominated by the worldview of science. And, like me, you probably absorbed its tenets into the depths of your subconscious as part of the way things are. But, as we have seen, science has its limitations like all human knowledge. Despite its success at unraveling the mysteries of nature, science is based on unprovable beliefs, is riddled with subjectivity, cannot illuminate our inner experience, and has a dark side.
>
> "Science must shoulder its share of responsibility for the problems we face as a civilization, as well as accepting accolades for the benefits of technology. Perhaps the most deep-rooted harm comes from the bleak classical vision of a lifeless, uncaring, mechanistic universe at the mercy of blind forces; of a world of separation and alienation of mind from body, person from person, and human from nature; and of a world of unbridled, ruthless competition that lacks consciousness, spirit or love. Is it any wonder that it has given birth to a society of alienated, despairing, lonely, powerless people?" (p.55)

Hollick has captured the sense of science as bleak and lifeless. I would go even further, to emphasize that it is not just the separation of mind from body, but also the separation of mind from heart and soul which is the basis of our current miseries.

Science alone is not the problem. Using science to pursue ends which have nothing to do with Heart has brought destruction. Technology used primarily for the sake of luxury leads us away from each other and from the Earth as the source of abundance and comfort. Science used to dominate Nature rather than work with Her brings environmental disaster. Science in the service of Heart brings creativity and further abundance, as for instance when new methods to improve organic farming are developed. This benefits the planet and the people who are able to consume nourishing food, produced with love and reverence for the Earth. Technological advances in the design of musical instruments and the reproduction of great performances for all to share brings inspiration and further creativity into our lives. The possibilities are infinite, as we may learn by further study of what the Egyptians and other advanced cultures knew.[18] It will take courage and determination for us to turn away from the uses of science which are based in greed, power and wealth, to evolve toward a Heart-centered way of life, but the alternative is becoming too horrific to ignore.

The Slide Into Darkness

Fearing that increasing personal freedoms might lead to private (legal) teenage abortions and other challenges to parental control, fundamentalist religious organizations have pressured the U.S. government into adopting policies which would ultimately reinstate the oppressive and dangerous custom by which children are seen as the property of their parents and women the property of their husbands. Ironically, Christian Fundamentalists who would fight to the death to prevent Sharia law from taking hold in America would heartily approve similar conservative practices restricting the freedom of women (minus the burka) to be reinstated here. There has been a slight change in our social attitudes toward children, in that we pretend we no longer accept the torturing and starving of children by their parents or their employers, except when a powerful corporation makes a fortune exploiting children in some other country's sweatshops. Then we call it "business."

Our preoccupation with mind over matter—Descarte's legacy—has left a huge vacuum in our day to day lives. Into the void have flown

---

18 For eye-opening discussions of metaphysics, sacred geometry, and their connection to ancient traditions, I refer you to the works of John Michell, Fred Alan Wolf, Drunvalo Melchizedek and the references they cite.

the Abusive opportunists, peddling their toxic products and their toxic ideas. Kindness and generosity have been set aside in favor of a system which rewards greed and selfishness. The term "fellow humans" has been nearly lost from our vocabulary. The overriding goal has been to obtain more material possessions than everyone else, and more than you had last year. Reverence is out of the question for creatures that interfere with our need for comfort and convenience. We prefer to bring on the poison, the lethal traps, and the chain saws. Interconnectedness with all the earth's systems is soft-minded gibberish to profit-minded capitalists. We make war on nature and believe our actions probably don't have anything to do with world poverty, diabetes, asthma, rising cancer rates, and the upheaval we are witnessing in our weather cycles, or if it does, there's nothing we can do about it. Our faith in science leads us to believe that someone—the scientists—will learn how to control it, and save us from ourselves.

The above description is of course a caricature of the worst of what our society has to offer, but these ideas, which may contain the seeds of destruction for our civilization and our planet, bombard us and our children daily, especially through television and the internet. Drenched in the constant stream of propaganda for the Dark Side, we have been shaped and molded, little by little, into an entire civilization dedicated to Abusive values. Numbed by the utter weight of it, and lulled by the sense of logical consistency in the message, (science is the Holy Grail) we fail to notice the constant, steady drift toward Darkness in all its forms. This is inevitable, of course, when one has reference only to ideas. When one idea is compared to any other idea without reference to the heart, the more it is repeated, the more we tend to believe it. It doesn't matter whether it is true or not.

Thus, we have been lulled into behaving robotically. The more innocuous actions came first: sitting in front of the television rather than talking to one another. Fast food and artificially grown plants and animals replacing nourishing food. Driving rather than walking two blocks. Then the temptations: big, fast cars feel deliciously powerful, regardless of the damage they may do to air, land, and other humans. Then came the siren song of prosperity, luxury and wealth, if only we compromise a little about polluting our air and water. Then the press of population this siren song attracted must be accommodated by ever grander houses, larger cars and shinier gadgets; and we now need to take over the world to supply our ever-increasing appetites. In the process, we have become a giant devouring monster, destroying everything in our path, unapologetic and unwilling to change, even when we are given the opportunity to do so.

Does this sound familiar?

As a cultural group, do we behave as if we have no conscience, no empathy, no kindness or generosity, no respect for human laws, and no respect for the environment or the health of the planet? In other words, are we Heart-less? Are we arrogant, lacking in real passion, and more interested in power than we are in truth? Are we selfish with our earnings and our belongings? Finally, are we voracious in our sexual appetites but uncommitted in our relationships, and unable or unwilling to love fully or care deeply?

Now go back to the list of classifications in the earlier chapter on Children of Darkness. The list included lack of empathy, selfishness, insensitivity toward the feelings of others, irreverence for the environment, and so on. You decide whether you are a Wannabe, and if all your friends and neighbors, and your children and your elected officials and their friends are either Abusers or Wannabe groupies, and whether our cultural attitudes and political inclinations make us a whole country of Abusers and Wannabes.

Here's where the difference matters. If we are Wannabes or kinda-Wannabes, we can change. If we are full-blown Children of Darkness, it's probably too late. But of course, if you're an Abuser you're probably not reading this book.

We have seen how being raised in an Abusive home leads to self-hatred and its corollary, an over-tolerance for abuse and abusive activities. Still, this does not completely explain the shift in cultural values which promoted the post-World War II materialistic frenzy. I have pointed to the possibility that television was the primary medium for spreading the acceptance of greed and materialism as a way of life. However, I believe there was another deeper and less obvious source.

Once we took Descartes' path to living in our heads instead of our hearts, the downhill slide into Darkness became inevitable. Without the corrective influence of a bodysoul and heart to guide us, we are completely vulnerable to believing absolutely anything, including ideas like science is the answer, or there is only one true religion. Religious fanatics who preach that you must read and memorize a book—their book—to find the true way to God are simply affirming the Abuser's stance, which ironically, is similar to the rigidly scientific approach. Both entail head before heart, mind over intuition, but have nothing to do with Spirit or spirituality. It is a game of memorized dogma, opinion and judgmental attitudes. By contrast, a spiritual path leads first to love, with the accompanying creativity, kindness and compassion toward others. No rigidly programmed system of beliefs is necessary for an individual on the path of the Heart.

As for our country and our civilization, it's up to all of us to stop the mindless drift toward everyday meanness, corruption and Darkness. We have been sleeping while the most powerful and outspoken Head People lulled us with their hypnotic suggestions and mind-numbing entertainments. Perhaps in reading these descriptions, you have come to the inevitable conclusion: The ultimate extreme of being a Head person is an Abuser.

We can change the direction of our lives. First we must find our hearts, and from there the connection to our bodysoul. If you can't tell which impulses come from your heart, then start with your intuition. Breathe into your bones, feel your heart beating, and calm the chatter in your head. This will allow the true feelings of your bodysoul to come forward. It is the only way out. Only a heart can know truth, and only a heart can feel compassion. Only a heart can trust, and only a heart can love.

The Limits of Learning Through a Book

Of course, you cannot learn to live in your heart by reading a book. By writing about these things and sharing ideas with you, I am appealing to you through your head. This can lead you to greater "understanding" by giving you the illusion that you (and I) have all the answers, but this is not a Heart path. It is understanding with your brain. You must take it further, to open the pathways to your bodysoul.

My ideas are a compilation of anecdotes and stories which offer a certain perspective—my own—which I hope will help you to loosen your grip on your own certainties enough to allow you to move toward a deep and profound heart connection from which you can discover your own truths.

With this in mind, let's look further at the Abusive tendencies which have seeped into our social, religious, financial and political institutions.

In the following chapter about the historical roots of the politics of greed and power in the U.S., I will explore the philosophical underpinnings of our current culture of divisiveness, competition and materialism gone wild. Perhaps this will help to identify some of the Head-without-Heart tendencies which lead us toward the Dark Side.

THE UPWARDLY MOBILE PRINCESS

I can't sleep on just any mattress,
I can't put on any old clothes.
I can't eat at diners or pushcarts or taverns
My digestion's so fragile, Lord knows.

It has to be gourmet, the finest
Or I'd rather stay home on the couch.
Don't ask me to shop at a discount
I just can't abide all those crowds.

Don't try to allure me with fakes and paste baubles
Gold, rubies and diamonds for me, nothing less.
I'd be very insulted if you were to give me
Anything less than the best.

My car's a Mercedes, my clothes from Chanel
The Ritz is my favorite hotel.
I've no cares about money—my lover's a banker
He knows I'm a high maint'nance gal.

Everything's custom; they know that I've earned it
You're judged by the objects you keep.
You might think that love will sustain you forever,
But my money never sleeps.

COMMANDANT

I am a rock., I'm granite and steady,
A sentinel you can depend on
To keep you from harm, I'm stable and ready
To guard you, I am the best one.

.

I'll be unbending, an anchor unending,
I'm here for your own protection.
So be quiet and docile, there's no way you're leaving
Restraint is a form of perfection.

I am an island in the storm
I suffer in silence, I choose it
Withstanding the waves is my duty, my pride,
And you'll never see me loose it.

I ask for nothing; you'll learn to love me.
You see, I'm saving your life.
I am a rock, you can count on me, Honey
Just kiss me, I'll put down this knife.

Don't try to escape it, you're safe in my tower
I'll never be caught with my guard down.
Just live with it, Sweetie, you don't need to fly,
We're here till the final bells sound.

CHAPTER TWENTY-THREE

AYN RAND AND MACHIAVELLI: APOLOGISTS FOR GREED AND POWER

> "In general, the art of government consists in taking as much money as possible from one class of citizens to give to the other."
>
> -Voltaire, *Dictionnaire Philosophique-*

With the end of the first decade of the millennium, life in the U.S. has accelerated to a crescendo of volatile economic forces and conflicting philosophical arguments which seem to be meeting head-on with enormous energy. Discussions about proposed changes in healthcare and the economy have stirred the most intense battles, with little reference to fact. Meetings designed to gather facts and encourage discussion were disrupted by screaming demonstrators whose objections seem to be focused mostly on fear of change, fear that they will lose something, but most of all fear that the program in question will benefit someone other than themselves. How did Americans become so selfish, so unapologetically unwilling to consider other people's needs? The most vociferous objectors seem to have little grasp of the problem, or any knowledge of the possible solutions. Their objections take the form of hatred toward "government," "socialism" and "communism," and the terms are apparently used interchangeably to mean "bad." The loudest cry seems to be, "Every man for himself!"

The Chicago School

Every other developed country in the world has managed to provide healthcare for its citizens, creating a sense of shared security and community that is lacking in the U.S. There are outstanding historical differences in philosophy and tradition in the U.S. which did not exist in other parts of the world and which might explain the dramatic difference. Along with the frontier spirit of rugged individualism, there is the Chicago School of Economics, which has had a pervasive and far-reaching impact on attitude and policy for nearly four generations.

Milton Friedman, the economist whose ideas became the foundation of the Neoconservative movement, was also the inspiration behind the writings of Ayn Rand. While Friedman influenced economic and social policy, it was Ayn Rand who won the "hearts and minds" of millions of American students with her frequently required readings, *Anthem*, *The Fountainhead* and *Atlas Shrugged*. Each of these convincingly told stories carries with it the philosophy Ayn Rand passionately espoused, which she called "Objectivism," a loosely conceived social and economic adaptation of Descartes' brain-without-heart orientation. Her promotion of unfettered individualism has had a universal appeal in the American consciousness where a lone-cowboy version of the frontier spirit remains alive, long after the frontier, its native peoples and wildlife have been decimated.

Ayn Rand came by her fierce rejection of all things resembling socialism in response to her early life in Europe. There she saw the corrosive effects of a despotic Soviet system which diminished personal ambition and increased resentments in its members. She passionately argued that the policy of "From each according to his ability, to each according to his need" punishes initiative, creativity and individual thought, while rewarding incompetence and sloth.

Her warnings helped to create the pervasive American fear of communism, as well as the confusion by which capitalism is linked with democracy, as if the two were inseparable or identical.

The credo of Ayn Rand, as represented in the person of John Galt, the hero of *Atlas Shrugged*, is captured in the large-type motto over his doorway:

"I SWEAR BY MY LIFE AND MY LOVE OF IT THAT I WILL NEVER LIVE FOR THE SAKE OF ANOTHER MAN, NOR ASK ANOTHER MAN TO LIVE FOR MINE."

His logo is a dollar sign.

Galt was determined to convince all the great industrialists, manufacturers and creative minds to go on strike, to teach "the looters" and "incompetent leeches" a lesson about who really provides the sustenance they steal in the name of "social progress" and "brotherly love."

Rand's stated premise is that greed and self-interest are valuable and necessary because they fuel enterprise and ambition and that these qualities are the expression of the ascendancy of the rational mind. Altruism, on the other hand, is a corrosive state of the spirit, an emotional weakness which encourages coercive, slovenly dependence on others, sapping the lifeblood of all concerned. Rand reiterates her philosophy of life in Galt's ringing pages-long soliloquies. Here is a sample:

> "This is the age of the common man, they tell us—a title which any man may claim to the extent of such distinction as he has managed not to achieve. He will rise to the rank of nobility by means of the effort he has failed to make, he will be honored for such virtue as he has not displayed, and he will be paid for the goods which he did not produce . . . We are on strike against the morality of cannibals, be it practiced in body or in spirit. We will not deal with men on any terms but ours—and our terms are a moral code which holds that man is an end in himself and not the means to any end of others."

The flaw in Rand's reasoning lies not so much in the system itself, but in the basic ideological premise that we can be highly evolved human beings without addressing our emotional and spiritual needs directly. Given the duality of Head versus Heart, or mind versus spirit as Rand describes it, only the ascendance of the rational mind, completely isolated from human feeling, can sustain a world in which creativity and industry in all its forms can blossom. Her heroes are all successful captains of industry and commerce, shining examples of honor and integrity who succeed by their merits and their considerable wit. Their sense of entitlement seems to create no hardship for others or noticeable environmental damage. Her villains are consistently described as unprincipled, stupid, misguided, incompetent and weak, small-minded failures. Out of jealousy and pettiness they become apologists for the insatiable groveling masses who want only to steal the profits of their betters by way of social laws and "directives."

Rand's heroes are, in reality, psychologically impossible creatures. Their creativity is supposed to spring directly from the rational (left-brain) mind, without reference to feelings of any kind. They are people who are completely devoid of the quality Daniel Goleman called Emotional Intelligence.[19] We now know, through extensive scientific analysis of right and left-brain functioning, that Rand's ideal of cold rationality being the source of creativity and inspired productivity is not only illogical, it is neurologically impossible. Human creativity of all sorts relies on the play between emotion and reason, form and meaning. We are organisms in which thinking and feeling, intuition and creativity are intended to be integral, inseparable functions. The more integrated with heart and spirit the person is, the greater their creative contribution will be.

In glorifying rationality and ego above and separate from feeling, Rand unwittingly encouraged what has turned out to be the worst kind of selfishness and greed: the self-righteous Head Person's belief in the absolute entitlement of the individual over the group. John Galt's motto might be paraphrased: "I will not help others. Don't even ask."

Here is Rand's picture of what she has described as the "ideal man," her hero, Howard Rourk, as he appears in the opening pages of *The Fountainhead*:

> "His face was like a law of nature—a thing one could not question, alter or implore. It had high cheekbones over gaunt, hollow cheeks; gray eyes, cold and steady;

---

19   Daniel Goleman, in *Emotional Intelligence,* makes the case that the most effective leaders actually function at the highest levels of empathy and awareness of the needs of others.

a contemptuous mouth, shut tight, the mouth of an executioner or a saint.

"He looked at the granite. To be cut, he thought, and made into walls. He looked at a tree. To be split and made into rafters. He looked at a streak of rust on the stone and thought of iron ore under the ground. To be melted and to emerge as girders against the sky.

"These rocks, he thought, are here for me: waiting for the drill, the dynamite and my voice; waiting to be slit, ripped, pounded, reborn; waiting for the shape my hands will give them . . ."

A few paragraphs on we get an inkling of the way other people feel about Howard Rourk:

"People turned to look at Howard Rourk as he passed. Some remained staring after him with sudden resentment. They could give no reason for it: it was an instinct his presence awakened in most people. Howard Rourk saw no one. For him, the streets were empty. He could have walked there naked without concern."

Rand unwittingly paints the picture of witnesses' normal responses to a darkly selfish being. Far from being a model citizen, Howard Rourk is completely oblivious to the environment or the impact of his grand plans. He is self-aggrandizing and self-absorbed, in love with his own vision, without regard for others. Howard Rourk is a modern day environmentalist's worst nightmare.

This might be a fitting portrait for a James Bond character, but would you really want this man as your husband, father, or neighbor? Given his attitude toward the earth and its riches, would you want his factory in your town? Would this man even care if his manufacturing process poisoned your water or rained soot on your baby's carriage?

The ethic of rugged individualism, while seeming romantic and bold in its conception, does not account for these gnarly issues. If we are to continue as a race, we will need to make room in our individualistic philosophies to address issues of our common survival. If your neighbor's house burns down, do you stand by and respectfully admire his heroic attempts to save his family and his belongings, or do you pitch in and help?

In an era of environmental catastrophes, do we let whole cities drown and starve, or do we take a "socialist" approach and send tents and food when we have more than enough? When an oil company defiles thousands of square miles of precious resources, are we surprised when they cover up the truth to avoid full responsibility? Why wouldn't they? They are a profit-driven enterprise, and it is in their own best interest to lie and avoid prosecution. It is not their job to protect the environment. It is their job to extract oil as cheaply and quickly as possible.

Safety precautions are expensive. It is naïve for anyone to think that for-profit corporations will "police" themselves. If it causes them to lose profits or forfeit their competitive edge, why would they, unless they were certain of severe and very expensive penalties? In her effusive admiration of industrial and technological advancement, Ayn Rand became the spokesperson for Milton Erickson's belief in the deregulation of industry, which remains the overall inclination in the U.S. today.

Rand felt that the pursuit of profit was a higher mission than any religion. It is said that on her death, friends presented a floral wreath in the shape of a dollar sign. Hers was indeed the anthem for the capitalist system and the "free market" economy.

Rand holds that there is one common psychological basis for the character traits she holds as sacred. Her hero states it clearly at the end of the slim book, *Anthem*:

> ". . . And the day will come when I shall break all the chains of the earth, and raze the cities of the enslaved, and my home will be the capital of the world where each man will be free to exist for his own sake.
>
> "For the coming of that day shall I fight, I and my sons and my chosen friends. For the freedom of Man, For his rights. For his life. For his honor.
>
> "And here, over the portals of my fort, I shall cut in the stone the word which is to be my beacon and my banner. The word which will not die, should we all perish

> in battle. The word which can never die on this earth, for it
> is the heart of it and the meaning and the glory.
> "The sacred word: 'EGO'"

Given the time this was written, it is probable that Rand was using the term "ego" as Sigmund Freud did, to mean the rational intelligence which controls and overrides instinct. In this sense it describes perfectly the attributes of a Head Person.

We have come close to her ideals in the U.S. system where corporations and their captains control the government, the economy, the military, the healthcare system, much of the educational system, the prison system, and more. It has not led to a glorious state in which freedom of opportunity lifts all boats. Instead, it had produced its own forms of debauchery, abuse and greed. This has presented itself in shocking clarity in recent years in the U.S., where politicians publicly and unashamedly make their arguments denying healthcare to children, or a living wage for poor working people on the basis that it is not an "economically sound" policy. Meanwhile, trillions of dollars have been borrowed for the war machine, much of it going "unaccounted for" into the pockets of wealthy military industrialists—the robber barons of the 21st century.

Around the world, enlightened people everywhere ask themselves, "Have they gone mad?" The land of the free and the home of the brave has a black heart—a dark secret at its center. Whatever the intentions of the Founding Fathers, our "freedom" has been reinterpreted to justify lack of concern for anyone but ourselves.

Money Can't Buy you Love

The Chicago School, Ayn Rand and their cohorts and followers have been remarkably successful in setting the tone as well as the principles guiding how we live our lives. Of course, their ideas are not new to the world—there have always been proponents of self-interest—but they have been implemented in a culturally homogenous way that is new in modern times. As a result, there is a fundamental flaw in our U.S. culture which can be deduced by looking at the scale we use to assign payment for work. There is a remarkably consistent relationship, which moves in inverse proportion to the amount of time and energy devoted to activities which engage the heart and spirit. The greater the distance from heart-centered action, the higher the pay scale.

We have come to the unconscious agreement across social classes that the business of every aspect of life will be conducted in such a way that those who have the greatest responsibility for the physical, spiritual and emotional well-being of others will be paid the least. The lowest pay scale of all involves anything having to do with children; the more tender the age of the child, the lower the pay. Artists, the only profession which cannot be authentically practiced without constant and unquestioning heart-centered action, are not even considered "workers" and are paid accordingly.

Inversely, the money workers—those who keep track of it, watch over it, count it, manage it, trade it, store it and lend it—are paid the most. This includes executives of corporations and brokers and traders of all kinds. None of them build or produce the products they oversee, but rather follow the flow of money to and from their business activities. All of this, which is generally performed for private individuals or corporations, takes place outside of any concerns about the welfare of the society as a whole. The conduct of commerce under a "free market" capitalist system, as practiced by the neoconservatives of the Chicago School of Economics, explicitly excludes any concern about the impact of its conduct on social or environmental well-being.[20]

I am not making any judgments about the people who perform high-paying jobs—they have diligently pursued success as the culture defines it. It is simply the way our culture has evolved. Unfortunately, it works to encourage Darkness, because it removes the most powerful and influential among us from any connection with their hearts for long hours each day. Those who perform the "Head work" as opposed to "Heart work" will have the most difficult challenge in restoring their heart connections. On the surface, it will appear to them that they have the most to lose; they may not realize that they therefore have the most to gain by moving to a heart-centered way of life. This is also a difficult shift because as Americans we spend so much time and devotion to our work that there is little time for anything else.

---

[20] See Naomi Klein's book, *Shock Doctrine*, for a comprehensive and revelatory compilation of the global actions of "the Chicago Boys" in the name of free markets.

It is a characteristically American idea that the ideal goal is to try to make one's work the fulfillment of life, while providing maximum wealth. Thus, the wealth itself has become synonymous with fulfillment. As a result, people in all sorts of jobs are feeling frustrated and confused when their chosen career does not bring them fulfillment—it just saps their energy and leaves them depressed. "Being of service" then becomes spending an hour a month at a volunteer center, or writing a check to a charity you have never met.

You are probably trying to think of exceptions to the upside-down value system. At first, there seem to be a few. Doctors are well paid, but of course, the specialists who have the least involvement with the patient, and who practice in the most mechanically precise or intellectual way are paid the most. People who perform personal services for others, like doctors, psychologists and teachers are all put through training programs to accentuate intellectual objectivity, scientific analysis, and a detached demeanor to qualify as "professionals." This does not mean that blue-collar jobs will necessarily lead to greater heart involvement. This is an equal-opportunity epidemic. Everyone operates in a Head-centered way, but those who can demonstrate their ability to remain untainted by any reference to Heart or intuition are paid the most, by virtue of adhering to the completely irrational notion that "It's not personal; it's just business."

Successful entertainers in the U.S. are paid exorbitant amounts of money, especially if they appear to perform from the heart. The cult of celebrity, and the constant gossip and voyeurism which has arisen around famous performers might be explained by the need Americans have to vicariously identify with those who presumably live exciting and passionate heart-centered lives. There is an especially prurient obsession on the part of gossip magazines, bloggers and tattletale internet sites to focus on the love lives and reproductive habits of famous entertainers. Celebrities' love, sex, anger and betrayal are discussed openly in the public forum. In our top-heavy judgment-centered Head configuration, the majority of the population is starving. In an effort to fill the hunger for real heart connections, Americans seem to be settling for observing (via the internet or TV) the appearance of passionate involvement—a long way from tasting the real thing.

Athletes are also rewarded with an out-of-this-world pay scale. Perhaps a similar dynamic applies here as well. Sedentary and in our

344

heads, we long to experience the heightened physical sensations of the well-trained athlete, but are not willing to put in the effort. Organized sports allow the media spectator the thrice-removed vicarious experience of the body. Studies of "mirror neurons" have shown that watching another perform an action creates a firing response in the observer's body and brain which mirrors the original activity. This would encourage the illusion in the spectator that they are taking part in the action. Of course this is not the only effect with people who are athletically inclined and who appreciate and admire watching other athletes perform. They are identifying with the athletes from the point of view of their own body knowledge of the sport and experiencing a sense of camaraderie with fellow athletes, adding to the pleasure of playing a sport themselves. Without actual experience in some kind of demanding physical activity, the experience is completely empty. Picture the way sedentary sports fans will cheer and shout at the television, as if the players could hear them. They are immersed in a fantasy, as if they were a participant in the artificially recreated game being played at a distance. The players, of course, have no awareness of the fan. The entire experience is imaginary.

After centuries of evolving toward the unspoken agreements which make our imaginary Head-centered value systems seem sensible, we have ceased to notice that nearly everything we do is upside down and backward. If you wish to pursue a spiritual path, you will need to right yourself, and shake off these unspoken values. In doing so, you will be taking the first step toward returning to your true nature as a Child of Light.

You need not fear that developing your connection to feeling—especially the natural attraction you feel toward nurturing and helping your fellow creatures—will make you irrational or weak, or will deprive you of your own sustenance. Just the opposite. Searching within to reconnect with that most precious of resources, the heart and bodysoul, will help each of us evolve toward a more enlightened and encompassing vision of human life and human governance. We will need much more than rationality to lead us in the difficult times ahead. We must search our hearts and our souls for deeper guidance.

Machiavelli: 15th Century Spin Doctor

In politics, the Abuser candidate or leader needs an army of Wannabe apologists to make the candidate's inhumanity and selfishness look like charity. This tactic has been labeled "spin." A skillful spin doctor (of which Karl Rove is known as the modern-day master) can redefine a leader's most glaring callousness or neglect of duty into highly valued human qualities. Thus, coldness becomes strength, selfishness becomes tough-minded adherence to moral values, war crimes are defined as patriotism, and refusal to admit wrongdoing becomes the courage to stick to one's conviction. Political spin doctors are in charge of creating such a barrage of personal attacks, counterintuitive misinformation and inflammatory emotional fear-mongering that the Abusers' victims and would-be detractors are left confused, befuddled and isolated. Although these strategies are not new, television and internet have increased the spin doctors' effectiveness and their reach.

For more than five hundred years, Abusers and their Wannabe supporters have had a readily accessible handbook on how to be a successful dictator. It is Machiavelli's book, titled *The Prince*. Machiavelli was an ambitious Florentine diplomat, born in 1469. Although history has made his name synonymous with "the power behind the throne," he never achieved the influence he coveted. It was his book which led to his being known as a scheming, ruthless strategist who believed that extreme tactics could be justified in the name of consolidating and maintaining power. The Prince is required reading in many college political science programs.

There are volumes of scholarly works which have identified Machiavelli's approach to politics as a radical—and questionable—separation from ethics and morals. However, some modern-day historians, in an interesting Wannabe apology for Machiavelli's "seeming" cruelty have redefined it instead as a remarkable achievement. They argue that it is a brilliantly objective way of describing history, unhampered by ethical or moral concerns. Thus, they unwittingly take the extreme Head Person's position that Abusive values are simply more objective than the emotionally driven ones which most of us humans hold. In this light, Machiavelli becomes the misunderstood and much maligned "brilliant strategist and political philosopher" whose "pioneering text . . . stands among the most original and lasting achievements of Italian Renaissance thought." It can be understood not as a "blueprint for tyranny" but rather as a "patriotic (albeit pragmatic) attempt to engender political unity . . . during an age of civic chaos."[21] Could this not be said about any dictator's attempts to subdue his minions, in almost any era?

Let's look at a few of these "brilliant" strategies Machiavelli promoted as a practical way to gain power and keep it.

In a flattering portrait of Cesare Borgia, Machiavelli describes the Duke as having "used every effort and practiced every expedient that a prudent and able man should," showing conduct which "merits both attention and imitation." Having inherited great influence from his father, Borgia managed, through quick-footed shifting alliances, military campaigns and political favors, to expand his power into the area called Romagna. There, Machiavelli notes,

> ". . . (H)e found it necessary, with a view to render it peaceful and obedient to his authority, to provide it with a good government. Accordingly he set over it Messer Remiro d'Orco, a stern and prompt ruler, who being entrusted with the fullest powers, in a very short time, and with much credit to himself, restored it to tranquility and order. But afterwards . . . knowing that past severities had generated ill-feeling against himself, in order to purge the minds of the people and gain their good-will, he sought to show them that any cruelty which had been done had not originated with him, but with the harsh disposition of his minister. Availing himself of the pretext which this afforded, he one morning caused Remiro to be beheaded, and exposed in the market place of Cesena with a block and bloody axe by his side. The barbarity of which spectacle at once astounded and satisfied the populace."

Thus, to demonstrate that "the cruelty did not originate with him," he beheaded his minister! Could the people truly have been so naïve as to think this was a reassuring humanitarian act? Not likely. It would,

---

[21]   Note in the Dover Thrift Edition, 1992, Philip Smith, ed.

however, strike fear into the hearts of any potential dissenter. Borgia was a past master at Shock and Awe.

Remember, this is the Duke who deserved "attention and imitation." The brutal murder of his own minister, who by Machiavelli's own account had served him well, is considered a skillful and expedient move. This is not a value-free assessment. It is an endorsement of cold-blooded cunning, a perfect Head game. Machiavelli goes on to trumpet that against great odds Borgia accomplished much.

> "Taking all these actions of the Duke together, I can find no fault with him; nay it seems to me reasonable to put him forward, as I have done, as a pattern for all . . . Whoever, therefore, on entering a new Princedom, judges it necessary to rid himself of his enemies, to conciliate friends, to prevail by force or fraud, to make himself feared yet not hated by his subjects . . . can find no brighter example than in the actions of this Prince."

Perhaps his apologists are swayed by Machiavelli's "moderate" approach to cruelty. He warns in the next chapter, "On Those Who By Their Crimes Come to be Princes" that success or failure can hinge on the Prince's good timing and judicious use of cruelty, its being "well or ill-employed." That is, it's not the cruelty itself which is unacceptable. It is unacceptable to fail at the project of winning hearts and minds because this is what is required to consolidate power. These arguments in favor of cruelty carry a familiar ring, in an era when our own Vice President Cheney and Attorney General Gonzales and others made the case for torturing prisoners. Those arguments could have been taken directly from the pages of Machiavelli's treatise.

Here, Machiavelli gives us his take on the use of military force:

> "A Prince . . . should have no care or thought but for war, and for the regulations and training it requires, and should apply himself exclusively to this as his peculiar province, for war is the sole art looked for in the one who rules . . . so to be proficient in it is the surest way to acquire power."

Like Machiavelli, American political strategists know that the surest way to increase power is to be a War President. When acquiring and keeping power is the ultimate goal, going to war is the best strategy.

On relationships,

> "(M)en are less careful how they offend him who makes himself loved than him who makes himself feared. For love is held by the tie of obligation, which, because men are a sorry breed, is broken on every whisper of private interest; but fear is bound by the apprehension of punishment which never relaxes its grip."

This is a truly chilling restatement of the attitude described earlier as "no feelings." It teaches the cynical Head approach to human nature and what we can expect from our fellows: Greed, betrayal and self-interest will always take precedence over loyalty and love.

Machiavelli clearly has no understanding of the true bond which love can create. His understanding of feelings includes only the experience of obligation or fear, and he presumes, as we humans are wont to do, that everyone else is just like him, and whatever feelings he may have are universal in human nature.

Finally, Machiavelli's utter contempt for the truth baldly reveals his allegiance to the Dark Side:

> "Princes who have set little store by their word, but have known how to overreach men by their cunning, have accomplished great things, and in the end got the better of those who trusted to honest dealing."

If you weren't paying close attention, you might be lulled into thinking his solutions make justifiable sense. Torture can be effective in achieving your short-term ends; therefore it is acceptable to use it. Chaos in the state is a bad thing, therefore cruelty is warranted. Cunning trumps honesty. This is the Pragmatist's—and the Abuser's—way. Like Machiavelli, these historians make the age-old "context" argument that he was living in a chaotic and difficult time, therefore extreme measures were warranted and acceptable.

It is alarming to find that any historians at all would be redefining Machiavelli's utterly dishonest and inhumane approach to governing as legitimately "pragmatic." His arguments have had a powerful effect on modern thinking, but by giving Machiavelli a legitimate place in history, scholars have unwittingly come down on the side of Darkness, in their attempt to be "objective." This is not simply a pointless exercise; it is dangerously misleading. Unfortunately, they have not accepted that there is no action without meaning, and that by expunging human values and ancient spiritual truths from your perspective, you cannot but espouse Darkness.

We have traditionally interpreted our world according to our human values. This is not a bad thing, nor is it "irrational." To imagine that there is such a thing as a philosophy without feeling or a reasonable system of governing without reference to basic human needs or values is inviting tyranny, by aggrandizing and normalizing the Dark Ones' cold-blooded attitudes.

Machiavelli did us a favor. In his little book, he has given us a truly revealing, abbreviated rendition of what could be subtitled "The Abusive Personality Type's Political Code of Ethics."

A system of government which nurtures the best of its members' human qualities—the qualities of the Heart, such as compassion, love, creativity and trust, will have to be built on a solid foundation of humanitarian values. Head People just cannot grasp the importance of these values, and so are the first to do away with the programs and protections which sustain all the people, whether princes or paupers.

Steeped in the Head-centered philosophy of the larger culture, our parents and teachers have passed on this thinking to us. We absorb the ideas presented above as we absorb the air we breathe, before we have encountered any other emotional and intellectual language to describe the world. These ideas combine with our own emotional responses to our earliest experiences in the family. Whether we are treated kindly or cruelly, our way of thinking will be filled with the symbolic references to power, competition, materialism and rationality as it is understood by our culture. Although we may be completely unaware of the connections, most of us will become judgmental, rejecting of others whom we see as weak or different from us, and indifferent to the living Earth and her needs. The melting pot of ideas since Descartes has created the pervasively single-minded attitude we live with today. That is the "rational" approach to life which excludes sensory or intuitive information if it does not emerge from a strictly three-dimensional (scientific) experience. Accepting those limitations to our existence means accepting a life without spiritual experience.

We may choose different intolerances from our parents, and we would shudder to think our strong beliefs and convictions might be the unrecognized inheritance of a painful childhood experience. It is even more difficult to accept that we might be crippled by culturally-imposed blindness or brainwashing. However, it is inevitable that we must carry on the Darkness that is our personal and cultural legacy until we consciously resolve to open our hearts, our minds, and especially our long-silenced souls, to be completely free of it.

GOD'S MESSENGER

I am God's Messenger
Sent here among you
To save you and
Show the true way.
And how do I know this,
You ask, Unbeliever,
He speaks to me every day.

I know it; I feel it
He gave me the secret
God saved me, He chose <u>me</u>
He knows <u>me</u>, He loves <u>me</u>;
He told me to say this
To save thee.

I am the shepherd who knows
How to save fornicators and fools,
So give up your soul
And your mind
And your thinking
Be one of our own precious jewels.

You never were happy
You have no worth
Be meek,
Be weak
You'll inherit the earth.

Turn over your wealth
And your worldly possessions
We'll spare you the sin
And the wages.
Now put down that textbook
That newspaper's Godless
The devil himself wrote those pages.

We'll turn back these laws,
And roll back the clock
It was better when girls
Knew their places.

The Infidels hate us
They try to destroy us
We'll fight for Allah
And his virgins.
Just blow up this bomb
Be a hero, a martyr,
Forgiven for
All of your sins.

We offer you friendship,
Eternal salvation,
The peace and goodwill
You've been after.
So throw down the gauntlet
And take up your weapons!
We'll slaughter and maim
For our Savior.

Christians, your past sins
Will all be forgiven
God blesses the ones who thrive
Abundance will come
To the righteous check-writers
The party-all-nighters
As long as you know
How to tithe.

As long as you come back
And pray once again,
Do it loudly
And often,
With feeling.
So come with me,
Follow me
Spread the true message
I'll put in a word
For you, Brother,
For I am God's Messenger
I know his way
And trust me,
He'll do as I say.

THE SHEEP'S SAGA

I am a sheep (a grownup lamb)
I grovel, beseech and wallow,
I have no mind, I gave it away
To my leader, now I must follow.

I am a good follower,
Perfectly loyal.
I add to his glory and laughter.
His glory is mine, I bask in it too,
As long as I'm following
After.

He's smarter than I am
He'll lead me away
From the dangers that lurk round the edges,
And all that he asks, the small bit he demands
Is my life and my loyalty pledges.

My friends in high places
Hold me in good graces
They need him to keep them in power.
They wine us and dine us and send a few gifts
While we build the great Ivory Tower.

Some call him a charlatan, faker
They don't know just what I have learned.
"Show his tricks," they say, why would I?
I'm comfortable here in the herd.

I'm no crusader, no barnstorming raider,
It's just too much to ask
I might lose my friends or my place at the Club
For a pointless, impossible task.

I'm concerned for my life
And my long-term investments,
My comfort, my safety, my hide,
I don't need a purpose, a cause or a passion,
I'll just go along for the ride.

What, church funds are missing?
Investigation?
How shocking: I don't know a thing.

Well, of course I'm the deacon
A pillar, a beacon,
I'm trusted far and wide.
Yes, the pastor's my friend
He's an upstanding man
I'm often at his side.

What? He's told you I stole it?
That m-f-ing liar
I'll get him for this
With the lawyers I'll hire.
Down to the station?
In handcuffs you say?
With cameras, reporters,
The perp-walk array?

How could I have known
I'm a worker, a drone,
Well, yes, I did ride in the limo
And the luxury flights, yes, I did go along
To the golf weeks in Puerto del Primo

But I had no idea
That thousands had come
From the till and the loans
And collections.
I'm a victim, I say,
At the end of the day,
I just followed my pastor's directions.

The Reverend has framed me,
Besmirched and defamed me,
His followers want my hide.
How could I have known
I'd end up here alone
When I just went along for the ride?

CHAPTER TWENTY-FOUR

VIOLENCE IN THE STREETS

> "The more uncivilized the man, the surer he is that he knows precisely what is right and what is wrong. All human progress, even in morals, has been the work of men who have doubted the current moral values, not of men who have whooped them up and tried to enforce them. The truly civilized man is always skeptical and tolerant."
>
> —H L Mencken, Minority Report (1956), quoted from_
> James A Haught, ed., *2000 Years of Disbelief*

Skeptical and tolerant. These are the very qualities religious and political fundamentalists of all stripes find unacceptable.

Just as in politics, advocates of a liberal approach to life hold the belief that individuals are capable of moral behavior whether they are policed into doing it or not, and that people will learn to thrive and to live a moral life under a more accepting, tolerant regime. This is the belief that humans are basically inner directed, and that moral behavior emerges from the individual's own will, value system and sense of self.

Adherents to more extreme fundamentalist sects (and those who follow the teachings of Paul) have an opposite philosophy. Their belief systems are based on the assumption that human behavior is outer directed, subject to influence and temptation from external sources, and must be held in check by a rigorously imposed system of controls and sanctions. This is the adult version of the child-rearing philosophy described in Chapter One—that humans are basically bad and in need of constant control in the form of punishment or threats of dire consequences.

Anyone who holds these negative beliefs about their fellow humans is bound to feel fearful and under attack, and the accompanying activation of brain channels for fight or flight on a daily basis can lead inevitably to a full-blown Ego/survival state of mind. In that state, militancy is a natural outgrowth of fear and distrust.

My God is Bigger than Your God

"Belief in a cruel God makes a cruel man."

—Thomas Paine

As the country newly under Democratic leadership is leaning slightly toward a more open approach to membership in the human community, leaders of the Christian Fundamentalist movement have been loudly stoking the fires of fear and paranoia—fear of domination by unknown others, fear of loss of control, and fear of unpredictable change. In his packed Texas church every week, preacher John Hagee titillates the passions of his followers with lurid images of apocalyptic violence and death. As part of a coordinated, aggressive political movement, members are warned that anyone outside the movement will try to destroy Christians, and will legislate their social values out of existence. Thus, the argument that marriage between gays will destroy the tradition of heterosexual marriage. Perhaps these angry tyrant/preachers are afraid their wives will leave them for the comfort of a sweet and accepting woman, or perhaps they fear homosexual impulses in themselves. One explanation for their objection to gay marriage was that it would open the possibility that people could marry their pet goat. If nothing else, these preachers should be charged with the offense of having no sense of humor.

Chris Hedges, in his book, *American Fascists, The Christian Right and the War on America*, cites the case of General William Boykin who revealed in a 2003 interview, ten years after leading American troops in a battle against Somalian warlords, that "I knew my God was bigger than his. I knew that my God was a real God and his God was an idol." Boykin was not reprimanded for his insanely inflammatory statements; he was promoted by then-Defense Secretary Donald Rumsfeld.

Reading this story in the news reminded me of a time many years ago, when my children were in primary school. It was a balmy day, and a group of little boys had gathered on our hillside deck to play. I monitored their goings-on by listening through the nearby kitchen window. The littlest member of the group was several years younger than the rest, not yet in school, but eager to keep up and earn the respect of the others. After much giggling and hooting, I overheard him protesting in a loud voice, "My Daddy can pee farther than your Daddy!" Apparently he had lost the contest for long-distance peeing over the side of the deck.

Perhaps this primitive need—the desperate search for self-worth through association with an awesome and powerful God/parent—lies at the root of religious wars through the ages. In the competition to prove MY DADDY is better than YOUR DADDY, winning means I am better than you.

It no doubt takes more than losing one peeing contest to drive a person to militancy and hatred, but we can imagine the potentially slippery slope. A person who has suffered years of humiliation and loss of dignity during childhood and adolescence would be exceedingly vulnerable to being told they are God's chosen warrior. The only requirement is that you believe it. This is the adrenaline-fueled fast track to feeling better about yourself: Turn all the self-doubt and self-hatred outward.

This vulnerability has been ruthlessly exploited in the cases of abortion clinic attackers. Followers of militant so-called "pro-life" activists were convinced that murder (and prison time) was a necessary tool to protect what they believe to be the highest possible value—that of making sure every pregnancy be carried to full term, regardless of the consequences to the mother, the child or the overburdened planet. They see themselves as martyrs and heroes, not terrorists and murderers.

Whether a cause is honorable and therefore justifies violence is a matter of personal values. Arguments which inspire panic and violence in the current Right Wing ranks have to do with allowing individuals to make their own decisions about life or death, either at the beginning of life or the end. Ironically, "social conservatives" who agitate for legislation to control the most personal and intimate areas of life are the same people who decry "too much big government" when they think their own pocketbooks are threatened. The massive contradiction in these positions can only be explained in emotional terms. People who are insecure about their slipping social and financial status can turn mean when they believe taxes (or changing social mores) will threaten their survival, freedom and hard-won prosperity. Ironically, these are not necessarily people who are stingy with their time and energies when a neighbor or family member is in need. They simply want to have absolute control over where their money is spent. If they believe that black people or immigrants or gay people or women are undeserving, they will fight to prevent their resources from being channeled to the people they (secretly) feel are inferior to themselves.

Reactionary and militant ideas can have great appeal to anyone who has been made to feel vulnerable and less-than. Humans who have lost contact with their own bodysoul are prone to feelings of inadequacy and loneliness. There are few among us who have not suffered self-doubt and fear at some point in our lives. The emptiness and alienation of our culture has left most of us yearning for meaning and solace. Through the ages, religion has served this purpose for millions of people, offering a sense of belonging, and a chance to pledge fidelity to something beyond present-day mundane existence. How leaders respond to these basic needs, and the path they offer to fill them has varied through the centuries, but there are themes which resurface repeatedly. Most organized religions as they are presently practiced (not necessarily as their book prescribes) can be categorized according to a few basic tendencies which their followers demonstrate. Roughly speaking, they can be seen to emphasize and promote ideologies along the following lines:

1) Those whose actions toward others shows a tendency to define their membership as exclusive, divisive, and emotionally territorial, as opposed to those who teach and express inclusiveness and acceptance of others, including a reverence for all life.

2) Those who strive for ascendancy over others, and whose sense of superiority is linked to their membership in a particular religion, as contrasted with those who strive for a sense of humility and dedication to service, regardless of religious affiliation.

3) Those who see their God as an angry and often punitive father figure to be feared and strictly obeyed, as opposed to one who

is less definitively male, and who is an inspiring source of compassion and love.

The differences are in the way people behave, not in what they say they stand for. In each of the above scenarios, the contrast is between Paulist ideas and the gentler, kinder teachings of Christ and his followers.

In the following section, I will place these ideological differences in the context of the discussion of Cartesian intellectualization (the Head/Ego orientation) as it applies to religion, compared to the spiritual values of the Heart orientation.

Self-righteous Morality

In the U.S., as political extremists advocate for laws which would require Paulist values to be the basis for the law of the land, we are again faced with the threat of religious oppression by those who see themselves as having a God-given right to control other people's destinies. This struggle has surfaced repeatedly in our relatively young life as a nation, in spite of explicit Constitutional laws guaranteeing separation of Church and State. For almost two generations, we have been in the midst of a tidal wave of Darkness; it can no longer be dismissed as a laughably insane and egotistical bit of comic theatre when a political leader says something like, "I will decide what is best for you, because I was told by God that I should be in charge; therefore, I make the laws. In fact, I am the law." Atrocities from religious wars to slavery have always been justified this way.

Human history tells us story after story of false prophets who claimed to be sent by God, but who misused their influence over others for personal gain—Abusive power-mongers whose damage to individuals and societies lives after them. There is a similarity in all those stories.

The false prophet will always cajole and manipulate to persuade his followers that he is the legitimate heir who should be given power over others. He typically shows a weakness for accumulating great personal wealth and/or power, usually procured through the sacrifice of his followers. Vengeance and superiority are defining themes in his "spiritual" teachings. His or her influence creates or encourages

360

divisiveness and discord, and it usually encourages aggressive militant action and separation from mainstream society as a way of life. These are the ideas which {Paul promulgated when he created a new and separate religion, "Christianity," which he insisted did not need to be based in the laws of Moses and the traditions of Judaism. This was the beginning of two thousand years of anti-Semitism and divisiveness between the world's existing religions.

On the other hand, genuine prophets through the ages have seen themselves primarily as teachers and equal participants in the flow of life, promoting and effecting peacemaking and inclusiveness wherever possible. While they may have professed to have valuable information from God passed through them to their followers, they did not encourage their disciples to subjugate or torture any group, nor did they encourage a divisive us-versus-them mentality. This does not preclude military action when necessary. History tells of great military leaders who, in fighting to defend their people against subjugation by others, have conducted their battles with fairness and dignity.

Descriptions of the great prophets, of whom there have been many, always suggest a demeanor of calm benevolence and generosity of spirit, which the leaders themselves often described as consciously cultivated and hard-won.

These gentler qualities were sadly lacking in Paul and in the media evangelists of today, who appear to be arrogant, emotionally overwrought, and intellectually lazy. Perhaps this too is a sign of our times. In Chris Hedges words:

> "The triviality of American popular culture, its emptiness and gossip, accelerates (the) destruction of critical thought. It expands the void, the mindlessness that makes the magic, mythology and irrationality of the Christian Right palatable . . . (T)he bizarre double speak endlessly repeated on cable news channels and the huge spectacles in sports stadiums have replaced America's political, social and moral life, indeed replacing community itself. Television lends itself perfectly . . . to the narcissism of national and religious self-exaltation. Television discourages real communication. It's rapid frames and movement, its constant use of emotional images, its sudden

shifts from one theme to an unrelated theme, banish logic and reason with dizzying perplexity. It too, makes us feel good. It, too, promises to protect and serve us. It too, promises to lift us up and thrill us. The televangelists have built their movement on these commercial precepts. The totalitarian creed of the Religious Right has found . . . the perfect medium. Its leaders . . . have mastered television's imperceptible, slowly induced hypnosis.

". . . The message being preached is one that dovetails with the message of neoconservatives who want to gut and destroy federal programs, free themselves from government regulations and taxes and break the back of all organizations, such as labor unions, that seek to impede maximum profit."

Devoted followers, many of whom may genuinely want to believe in the goodness of their leaders and their mission, seem to have been unconcerned about the misuse of their loyalty, their money, and their votes. A constant barrage of propaganda alone cannot have swayed so many people so completely. There must be a deeper, more compelling need which is fulfilled by inclusion in the group of "believers."

Earlier chapters explored the connection between fear, survival, and Ego. As a child is threatened, she is forced back on strategies to survive physically and psychologically—to save her unique identity as a self. This struggle strengthens her tendency to rely on a reptilian fight-or-flight response and its sergeant-at-arms, Ego. As a child under duress struggles to protect her fragile hold on her self, she must devise strategies to deal with her bigger, more powerful adversaries. She learns to calculate, predict, analyze and detect danger. As love and trust toward others slowly dies, Ego gains ascendance, along with the conviction that this is a necessary, life-preserving way to live. At the same time, the strategies she develops to protect herself are based on the model of strength and power she witnesses in the adults around her and in the religious principles they teach. If their God is angry and vindictive, then they will become angry and vindictive toward each other. If they were critical and unforgiving, she becomes critical and unforgiving, turning these attitudes against herself first, and self-hatred is born as the accompaniment to Ego. This is the orientation many of us, across numerous cultures around the globe, have been indoctrinated into when we enter adulthood.

Self-Hatred Is Lonely and Painful

The promise of rapture and salvation is held out to modern-day believers as the ultimate orgasmic triumph. Whipped into a frenzy of exaltation and triumphant self-righteousness by skillful preachers and mullahs who are experts in the manipulation of mob psychology, followers are guided into highly charged states of emotion in which they are told they—and only they—are God's chosen warriors. Militant leaders proclaim that followers will be called to vilify, punish, and celebrate the deaths of those they deem unworthy.

The high-pitched tone of these religiously inspired group meetings is cathartic. Participants revel in the release of pent-up feeling, made more intense by the affirmation of the crowd. Tears, writhing and exultant screams are a common feature of many Christian gatherings, all accompanied by assurances of love—from fellow worshipers, and from the powerful father/preacher who offers absolution and acceptance.

Anyone who has suffered self-hatred feels an unremitting level of emotional pain, made worse by the fact of its not being openly acknowledged. We have healing traditions to help victims of crime, warfare or natural disaster. Neighbors and friends offer help and solace in time of need, but there is little help or comfort other than drugs for the emotional toll exacted by years of self-imposed disapproval and shame.

Since our common culture has devolved toward the lonely and meaningless narcissism described earlier, our capacity for public celebration has also devolved to a paltry smattering of weddings, funerals, Super Bowl and New Year's Eve in Times Square. Even those shared moments have become circumscribed by artifice and commercialism. How is a person to really laugh, dance, cry or grieve? Intuitively, leaders of radical Fundamentalist movements around the world have rushed in to fill a real human need for connection, relief, and above all, absolution of the pent-up feelings of hatred and despair. Unfortunately, they have deliberately channeled those feelings into a tidal wave of aggression which surges outward toward others. As the American Religious Right's power builds to a frenzied crescendo, Christianity's original message has been turned inside out to proclaim, "My God Hates You!"

Self-Hatred Fuels Nationalism

AGAINST THE WALL
— By Aline Kilmer

If I live till my fighting days are done
I must fasten my armour on my eldest son.
I would give him better, but this is my best.
I can get along without it—I'll be glad to have a rest.
And I'll sit mending armour with my back against the wall,
Because I have a second son, if this one should fall.
So I'll make it very shiny and I'll whistle very loud,
And I'll clap him on the shoulder and I'll say, very proud:
"This is the lance I used to bear!"
But I mustn't tell what happened when I bore it.
"This is the helmet I used to wear!"
But I won't say what befell me when I wore it.

There have apparently been wars for as long as humans have lived on Earth. Throughout the ages, humans have been inspired by their leaders to organize crusades and conquering offensives, claiming self-righteousness and honor as they attack and subjugate their neighbors. Many, like our warrior above, stoically accept that he and his family will sacrifice themselves. It is understandable that groups might war and squabble over land and food if they are in sort supply, but these issues cannot begin to explain the fervor with which humans attack each other.

In his classic work, *The Mass Psychology of Fascism*, Wilhelm Reich makes the point that we can understand the rise of a dictator such as Hitler only by understanding mass psychology, for it is the psychology of the masses which explains the attraction of a "fuhrer," not simply politics or economics. The psychology of the masses, in turn, is primarily a creation of one's experience in the family. In his words, "(T)he decisive factor in the formation of the human structure, is to be traced back to their family ties. The fact that the family tie is the most intense and the most emotional, cannot be overrated."

In a section entitled "Nationalistic Self-Confidence," Reich draws the connection between the popularity of the fuhrer and the family psychology of the lower middle-classes who became Hitler's political base. In our own United States, we can see the resurgence of the same "family values" as those of Germany in the 1930s.

Reich cites the remarkably passive acceptance of Hitler's followers who ultimately participated in policies which we today refer to as "acting against their own self-interest." When Hitler betrayed his stated populist policies by favoring corporations and wealthy industrialists, (by outlawing strikes, for instance), his followers' passive acceptance was expressed in the sentiment that their leader undoubtedly knew better than they, and "he would manage everything all right."

> "Here we have a clear expression of the child's need for the protective attitude of the father. In terms of social reality it is this need for protection . . . that enables the dictator 'to manage everything.' This attitude . . . impedes social self-administration, i.e., rational independence and cooperation. No genuine democracy can or should build upon it.
>
> ". . . The more helpless the 'mass-individual' has become, owing to his upbringing, the more pronounced is his identification with the fuhrer, and the more the childish need for protection is disguised in the form of a feeling [of being] at one with the fuhrer. This inclination to identify is the psychological basis of national narcissism, i.e., of the self-confidence that individual man derives from the "greatness of the nation." . . . On the basis of this identification he feels himself to be a defender of the 'national heritage' . . . Other concerns are so overshadowed by the exalting idea of belonging to a master race and having a brilliant fuhrer that, as time goes on, he ceases to realize how completely he has sunk to a position of insignificant, blind allegiance." (p. 59)

The above passage could also accurately describe the passive acceptance of the large majority of Americans as successive administrations since Ronald Reagan have pushed through laws favoring powerful corporations and wealthy individuals, while our Presidents have increasingly represented themselves as the epitome of the common man, "one of us," "someone you'd like to have a beer with." Meanwhile, personal freedoms were curtailed, and social programs which benefit mostly the middle and lower classes were ridiculed as "socialist" in order to discredit and dismantle them. "Tea Party" organizers, backed by wealthy individuals and corporations, have spread the word that working class individuals will be victimized by taxes to pay for social programs. The facts show that it is wealthy individuals and corporations who contribute a greater share to the community pie, and it is those very working class people who benefit most from social programs like public education, unemployment compensation, Social Security and Medicare. The drift toward "corporate welfare" and corporate propaganda is not new, nor is it any longer the province of either political party.

It has always been in the self-interest of the wealthy to find justification for keeping their greater share of the wealth, regardless of the needs of poorer folk. As soon as bailouts and benefits to huge financial institutions and their executives succeeded in slowing the slide into a second Great Depression, the same executives whose rapacious practices caused the financial collapse were back at the trough, brazenly demanding huge bonuses, paid for by working American taxpayers. Congress, mostly indirectly on the payroll of the same institutions, has been reluctant to pass legislation to regulate dangerous but lucrative financial schemes, leaving the disaster-waiting-to-happen still largely in place.

It appears that the moral tradition of "noblesse oblige," the obligation of the wealthy to honor their responsibility to provide for others and to lead honorably, has mostly fallen by the wayside in the rush to accumulate wealth as an end in itself. On the bright side, there is a movement among billionaires to shame each other into giving more. Non-profit fundraising has taken a creative psychological twist. An email recently arrived in my inbox with the heading, "People won't like you if you don't give back."

During these same years of enormous wealth accumulation in the hands of the few, policies allowing illegal wiretapping of individual American citizens were surreptitiously carried out. In ensuing discussions in the media concerning the invasion of individual privacy, many references were made to the supposed explanation that "after September 11, everything changed." No mention was made of the fact that just 40 years ago, one of the articles of impeachment in the case against Richard Nixon was illegal wiretapping. Later revelations that the recent wiretapping had begun long before September 11, 2001 were met with a collective shrug. Even persuasive evidence that Administration officials had deliberately deceived the American people in order to build a case for war in Iraq[22] was not met with the outrage one might expect at finding out one has been utterly hoodwinked. Here we can draw a parallel to the many stories cited earlier of abused lovers who continue to love the object of their affection, even after revelations of unspeakable betrayal.

Egos on the March

The invasion of Iraq and Afganistan has turned out to be the largest Ponzi scheme in the history of the world. Although numerous expert sources (and common sense) contradicted the Bush Administration's story that Saddam Hussein was somehow involved in the 9/11 attacks, a majority of Americans believed that our leaders "must know something we don't know." These same rural and middle class enthusiasts for war are similar to those Germans who were particularly vulnerable to the appeal of an authoritarian father-figure.

A nationalistic strategy was used to whip up support for the attack on Iraq, a sovereign nation, contrary to international law. It allowed the enormously lucrative corporate takeover of the country which will be paid for by the misused and overburdened middle—and working-class American taxpayer for generations to come. As Senator Edward Kennedy said, if we had just two years worth of the money we spent in Iraq, we could have rebuilt every school in our country.

The constant drumbeat of "We are the greatest country in the world" was repeated over and over, while "brave and honorable young men and women" were asked to serve "in harm's way" for the greater good of the greatest-country-in-the-world. Like Madoff's scheme, the lure was membership in a most exclusive and desirable club, the honorable ranks of those who give their lives and their treasure for

---

[22]   See Fiasco, The American Military Adventure in Iraq, by Thomas E. Ricks

their country. If military might were the sole measure of superiority, we could accurately make that claim. Numerous empires before us have believed the same, and are no longer here to boast of their power.

When the "flawed intelligence" pointing to Saddam Hussein was completely discredited, the rationale was suddenly switched to an even higher purpose. We would fight the "war on terror" by "bringing democracy" to the Iraqi people, as if democracy were something one could package and present to others as a gift. By baldly appealing to our nationalistic pride and superiority as members of a superior nation charged with a superior destiny, the Administration defined the attack on Iraq as honorable, while labeling any resistance to the invasion as unpatriotic or even treasonous. The American people hardly noticed the bait-and-switch sales pitch, as the president's ratings soared ever higher with every exhortation to bravely serve "the greatest country in the world."

Thus, the neoconservative wing of the Republican Party has been able to forge an alliance between wealthy constituents who benefit directly from the extralegal consolidation of power in the hands of the wealthy, and lower and middle class religious fundamentalists who yearn for the psychological security of an authoritarian patriarchy, because it appeals to the familiar Paulist traditions they were raised with. The appeal to a sense of superiority and righteousness was seamlessly presented from the church pulpit to the presidential podium. In both arenas, the arguments made perfect sense to Head People who had traversed the path from childhood danger to Ego ascendancy, leaving bodysoul, heart and intuition behind as sacrifice to survival.

Once the transition has been made, from heart to head, arguments that defy compassion or sympathy for humanity do not ring bells of alarm. They are simply weighed as any other argument is weighed: in light of one's own self-interest. The march toward fascism is neither new nor mysterious, but American leaders are aided by the fact that the majority of Americans are unaware of the glaringly obvious historical precedents and are too self-absorbed to bother to learn.

Deliberate blindness has also accompanied reports of hideous acts of torture, performed by Americans in secret prisons, presumably to extract information from "enemy combatants"—a term obviously designed to allow inclusion of any enemies of the state, including American civilians. These reports were not met with universal outrage or horror, although some activists loudly sounded the alarm. The discussion quickly turned to the question of whether the torture served a valuable purpose in prosecuting the "war on terror," thereby providing further security for the American people. In other words, self-serving justification for the lawless abuse of power.

The inclination to turn a blind eye to the abuse of others held sway over the American public as they watched the massive bombings of Iraq (called Shock and Awe). Hundreds of thousands of innocent civilians were inevitably maimed and killed and the infrastructure of Iraq laid waste, while the propaganda machine trumpeted phrases like "surgical strikes" and "bringing democracy" to Iraq. Why has it been so easy to convince the American people that what you see is not what really is? Could it be that a lifetime of being taught that suspension of reality-processing is good (a Virgin birth can be made to make sense,) and that man is born evil, and therefore should probably be wiped out, especially if the people in question are not legitimate "Christians."

Reich's explanation of the attraction to an authoritarian father-figure was based on the assumption that lower middle-class families tend to adhere more closely to an authoritarian patriarchal structure than upper-class families. This still leaves us with an unexplained phenomenon in the U.S., where political polls repeatedly reported that upwards of 75% of the population strongly supported the Bush/Cheney Administration's Constitution-dismantling policies—clearly more than could be explained by Reich's lower middle-class numbers.

This is where the self-hatred dynamic comes in. It does not require an authoritarian father figure to crush a child's sense of self-worth. It can be accomplished by a negligent, harried single mother who has neither time nor inclination to gaze reassuringly into an infant's eyes, and to be empathic with the growing child. It also happens in middle-class families where both parents are working, and the child is at the mercy of neighborhood bullies, day-care indifference, and incessant television watching. Children of ambitious, wealthy parents may have their own issues with exhausting, overly structured and highly demanding schedules which leave little room for contemplation or individual expression. Although cruelty and authoritarian attitudes generally go hand-in-hand, family structure and social class are not necessarily relevant today. Any child, of any social class, is unhinged by humiliation and abuse or neglect. In Chapter One I suggested that love and cruelty eventually merge into identification with the powerful, destructive caretaker, whether they be mother or father, grandparent, older sibling, nanny, or the culture at large in what ultimately becomes a romance with The Dark Side. As Reich suggested, as it is in the family, so it is in politics.

As power struggles in the U.S. threaten to upset the balance between haves and have-not's, a wave of rebellion has swept across the Middle East, where graft and oppression have left millions of people with barely enough to buy food. Perhaps the courageous protesters will provide enough of a wake-up call to Americans to save us from ourselves. We have become soft and complacent, lost in a world of fantasy and denial. Should the food shortages spread to the U.S., we too may begin to feel the results of the profligate greed which has inspired Wall Street to gamble with global food supplies, starving millions around the world for profit.

Anyone who has suffered the secret prison of childhood abuse knows the temptation to turn the tables, to become the observer or even the perpetrator of abuse in a move toward power and control. This is something we all need to acknowledge and guard against, in ourselves, in our business leaders, and in our warrior/representatives.

Like other forms of government, Democracy is as much a psychological state of mind as it is a political structure, but Democracy is unique in that to function effectively, it requires its members to rid themselves of childhood inclinations toward destructiveness. That destructiveness later devolves into Ego-based feelings of religious and cultural superiority, racial prejudice and hatred in all its myriad forms. In an era when ignorance and negativity are given expression and nearly unlimited air time through the internet and television, Darkness is given inordinate power. This ultimately undermines the essence and purpose of the egalitarian goals of Democracy, just as it undermined the message of love and kindness which Jesus taught.

We must also find ways to eliminate the influence of money in the election process. Our current system has devolved into buying seats in Congress. How is this different from dictatorships around the world where the strongest arm becomes the law? To succeed, Democracy needs the leadership and nurturance of Heart People and a constituency made up of people who are willing to forgo the inclination toward material excess and self-serving Ego responses. These self-referential responses were forged out of fear and childhood insecurity, and have set the tone of uninformed and emotionally overwrought public discourse. Democracy is an institution of the Heart, based in the faith that humans are capable of decency, generosity and trust. Without an adult sense of trust in each other and in the goodness of a life lived in harmony with the planet and with our neighbors, it cannot succeed.

Liberals have often fallen into the trap of presuming that equality means that everyone is the same, or should be treated the same. There is a vital place for excellence in our lives, and for acknowledging the necessity of recognizing the elite group of individuals who serve as leaders in every field. Some among us develop expertise as a result of hard work and exceptional talent. They deserve to be honored for their achievements, and elected to public office because of their exceptional abilities if they agree to serve. This is not "elitist." It is simply true that we are not all equally accomplished. The best among us inspire us all to climb our own personal lofty peaks, to reach as high as we can on our own paths to fulfilling the unique potential we were each born with.

In the following chapters, I will offer a view of the brighter side. Darkness is, after all, the absence of Light. Banishing your attraction to the Dark Side requires that you turn toward the Light, toward the Heart and Spirit. In doing this, you will begin to strengthen and develop the qualities we know as character virtues—empathy, kindness, courage, compassion, honesty, temperance, appreciation of beauty, love and creativity. The more you open your heart, the more you reconnect with your bodysoul, the stronger these qualities will become in you. Once you turn toward the Light, darkness disappears, and you will find you can truly become the positive person you always wanted to be.

CHAPTER TWENTY-FIVE

THE CHRIST WE NEVER KNEW

The Man Who Stole Christianity

There is a deep cultural and religious divide which the world has suffered with for the last two thousand years. It began with the earliest teachings of Paul, the self-proclaimed Apostle, who took it upon himself to reinterpret the teachings of Jesus, against the wishes of the Jerusalem Council, the group of true disciples who had studied with Jesus and who knew him and his original teachings first-hand. Unlike them, Paul had never met Jesus, and had newly been "converted" from his crusade to persecute and kill Christians.

For a detailed and carefully referenced discussion of the few Biblical references which refer to the relationships between Paul and the disciples, I refer you to the websites of Scott Nelson and Sherry Shriner concerning Paul's as a liar and false prophet, as well as Edgar Jones' book, *Paul, the Stranger* These researchers and many more have questioned Paul's legitimacy as a representative of Jesus' teachings, as well as his honesty. Here, I will summarize the teachings of Paul and their profound influence on the development of religious thought, and the destructive effects we see today in the practice of what has come to be called "Christianity."

The trouble began only three years after Jesus' death, when Paul, by his own report, saw a vision of Jesus on the road to Jerusalem, in which Jesus asked Paul, "Why do you persecute me?" Paul was struck to the ground by the power of this experience, and henceforth forswore his persecution of Christ's followers, proclaiming himself an

Apostle instead. Nowhere in the Bible does it suggest that Paul was invited to spread the word of Jesus, or that he was in any way trained for the job. In setting himself apart from the original Jewish apostles who followed Christ, Paul created the idea that Christ's teachings were the basis for a new religion.

Jesus had no intention of setting up a new religion with himself as figurehead. He wanted to expand on Jewish teachings. He attempted to loosen the grip of rule-bound rabbinical thought which had created a conservative, authoritarian and dogmatic system emphasizing the role of an angry, vindictive God.

Jesus looked through the prism of religion and saw the spectrum of kindness, love, equality and generosity which had been missing from earlier teachings. He shifted the perspective to a more progressive, open and accepting one, eliminating the need for priests, rabbis and religious "authorities" of all kinds. He was liberal, open-minded and inclusive in his life and in his teachings. He excluded no one, regardless of their sexual practices, social status, or religious background. His intention was to elevate Jewish teaching and practice to an individual, Heart-based philosophy of living in which every soul has free and equal access to God's love.

Paul took it upon himself to travel extensively throughout the Middle East to preach to Gentiles about Jesus. His great influence to this day has been in the fact that he wrote extensively, and often boastfully, about his travels and his opinions. He claimed to have been the acclaimed Apostle to the Gentiles, although the designation seems to have been of his own creation. As Scott Nelson has aptly pointed out, his writings reveal a unique quality. Alone among the writers of scriptures, Paul frequently used his own name, and sprinkled thousands of passages with the pronouns I, me and myself. The other writers either remained anonymous and did not discuss themselves or their personal activities. This alone presents a picture of a man of questionable character, since his writings appear to aggrandize himself as the most important and influential Apostle, while none of the other writers except Luke, his side-kick, ever referred to him as an Apostle, and only once in all Luke's writings did this title appear.

The problem of having a renegade "Apostle" blanketing the countryside with writings and opinions would not have been so serious if it had not been for the insidious distortions Paul created and codified for future generations. Here are just a few of the most damaging ideas which came directly from Paul's teachings and writings, unauthorized by either Jesus or his legitimate disciples:

1. Jesus died for our sins. Because of our evil doings, Jesus died.
2. Jesus' life represents the suffering and persecution of all people on earth.
3. Jesus was God's only Son. The rest of us don't belong to the family.
4. God is in Heaven, sitting on a throne passing judgment on those of us far below. We humans do not have individual relationships with him. He puts in an appearance every few thousand years.
5. Jesus' resurrection was a result of his special relationship with God. The rest of us can't expect eternal life as a general rule.
6. The trinity is made up of the Father, the Son and the Holy Ghost, a mysterious specter who symbolizes death.
7. Christianity's God is the one real God, because Jesus was his only real Son.
8. Jesus should be worshipped because he is God, not a real man.
9. Because Jesus was a God, his day to day life was not like ours. We can't really be like him.
10. Jesus bestowed miracles on people. They were healed by magic, not because they grew into health because he inspired them to.
11. Jesus asked his followers to abandon their family farms and go with him, leaving their families to starve.
12. Jesus kicked the money changers out of the temple because they were cheating people, not because he objected to commercial business being carried on in the temple.
13. Christianity is a new religion, separate and apart from Judaism.
14. Christians do not have to follow the Laws, including dietary and health laws and traditions which had been the foundation of an ethical and practical way of life, based on the teachings of Moses and earlier prophets.

15. Moses' Ten Commandments are no longer relevant. They can be reduced to one: Help the poor.
16. Jesus' teachings can be reduced to one: Help the poor.
17. Dietary laws are not important. Pork and other unclean animals and fish are okay if you like them.
18. Wine represents the blood of Christ, therefore it's okay to drink a lot of it.
19. Man has dominion over everything else on earth. We own the Earth. Everything on it is there for our use and convenience.
20. Man is born with Original Sin, the essence of evil in his being. He can only be saved by adhering strictly to the teachings of Paul.
21. The purpose of religion is to frighten people into avoiding evil. The Devil is always among us, attempting to lead people away from God.
22. Anyone not baptized in the Christian faith cannot go to Heaven, or be granted eternal life.
23. God is an angry disciplinarian who sits in judgment over all human activity, meting out punishments, especially to those who do not obey him. Sinners will go to Hell.
24. Adam and Eve were kicked out of the Garden because they had sex, not because they had begun to rely on their heads rather than their hearts.,
25. Sex is dirty. It should be avoided except for the purpose of reproduction.
26. Homosexuality is a crime against God. So is masturbation.
27. Jesus was not married; he was celibate. Priests and other teachers of God's word should be celibate, because sex is dirty.
28. Priests must be relied upon to interpret God's word, since people cannot find faith on their own.
29. Women are inferior to men and should be excluded from decision-making of every kind because their judgment cannot be trusted.
30. Mary Magdellan was not Jesus' wife or one of his closest disciples. She was a prostitute.
31. Mary Magdellan washed Jesus' feet because she was beneath him.

32. Loose hair means a loose woman. Women should cover their heads to avoid seducing men.

33. Children belong to their parents, and are indebted to their parents for giving them life.

34. God rewards Christians with material wealth and other worldly success. Anyone not following these (Paul's) doctrines will be punished with poverty and disease as a result.

35. The proper place of worship is in a church, preferably a very grand one.

36. Christian doctrine should take precedence over civil law. Governments should bow to Church leaders.

37. Churches should be allowed to own property and should not be subject to taxes. It is appropriate for a church to be a center of wealth and power.

38. An Apostle is anyone who feels the urge to teach in Jesus' name. No credentials required.

Out of the dark imaginings of Paul's paranoid mind came a story of a magic, fantastical being, Christ, whose lineage and purpose here on Earth bore no resemblance to our own everyday lives. Under Paul's massive editing campaign, little is left of the true and simple message of love and creativity which the small shreds of original writings impart.

Paul's themes are foreboding, threatening and fearsome, and mostly predictable. He relentlessly preached his message:

God is angry, judgmental and holds ultimate power over all of us. A legitimate religion is made up of unbelievable tales of magic and supernatural feats, bearing no resemblance to normal human life. Sex is sin; sin is sex. Homosexuals and women are lowly, unclean creatures. Faith is born of fear. Fear leads to obedience, and to the denial of one's free will. Fear makes people more submissive, and this is a good thing for those in charge.

With very little training in psychological personality testing, one could easily deduce from Paul's rambling and self-referential writings that he was delusional, paranoid and extremely narcissistic. His history of bloody persecution of Christians adds to the picture of a man who was anything but a benign and well-meaning follower. He was a full-blown Child of Darkness, cloaked in the trappings of piety and religiosity. His malignant deeds echo down through the centuries, misleading, seducing and terrifying millions of unsuspecting followers. In creating a religion of pain, suffering and fear, he has increased the level of human misery on the planet a hundred-fold, leaving no one untouched. Even adherents to other religions find their doctrines measured against the backdrop of darkness and fear which Paul created.

Paul could not have accomplished the highjacking of Christ's message alone. Letters and books of scripture denouncing Paul's false teachings would have to have been destroyed or hidden. Why would the priests and scholars who assembled the Bible three hundred years after Christ's death have chosen his version over that of the genuine disciples? Perhaps because it was a more interesting drama, and required an enormous suspension of reality-based thinking to accept it. Perhaps it was the cynical attitude that controlling the masses controls the power and resources. Certainly Constantine, who commissioned the first Bible, had reason to encourage a body of teaching which could solidify his power as Emperor. Priests of all stripes would have their own reasons to applaud a message which gave them ultimate power over their parishioners.

Perhaps it is time for a courageous Pope to open the vaults of the Vatican and reveal to the world what happened to the many sacred writings that were not included in the Bible. Only then will we know the truth of what was hidden and what was changed.

And as for sex, well, who wouldn't be titillated by the constant covert discussion of sexuality and its ever-present dangers? It would be especially appealing to those who feared the intimacy and closeness which Jesus' message encouraged.

The contorted message as it is taught today should be called "Paulism," not Christianity.

Christ's True Message

Christ came to this life to teach these things:

> Love one another, be kind, be forgiving,
> and live with integrity in everything you
> do.

Create a child with love and you will have accomplished a holy act.

Love the Earth and her beauty as you would your own precious child. Express your gratitude for her nurturing love in all you do.

Share your bounty. With love in your heart, you will always experience abundance, regardless of the fare on your table.

We are all God's children. God loves you, one and all equally, just as he loves me.

You will all experience eternal life, as I do. You will go on after death, and we will meet again.

"Christianity" as it is taught today bears little resemblance to the teachings of Jesus Christ. The teachings above are the basis for what Christ preached, and for the way he lived.

He did not wish to be worshipped, nor did he try to frighten anyone into behaving well by threatening God's angry punishments. He had two loving parents, and a wife and child of his own. His own life was a model of how to live lovingly and well, in the company of family and friends. He did not teach that celibacy was preferable, or that man was born in sin. He did not claim to be God's only Son, or that life is suffering. His true disciples did not preach that Jesus died for our sins. All these ideas are nonsensical and directly contrary to his basic message of inclusiveness, love, compassion and forgiveness. No extensive study of doctrine or dogma are needed to understand the true teachings of Jesus. They are all addressed to matters of the heart, and encourage each of us to follow a Heart path rather than succumb to the darkness of a life as a Head Person.

PART VII

TRANSCENDING THE PAST

Chapter Twenty-Six

START A PEACE MOVEMENT

> "How can we heal the wounds of the world if we cannot heal our own . . . Where does this peace on Earth begin if not in the home . . ."
> —*Peace on Earth*, Rachelle Ferrell, 1992 album

P eace of mind flows from a state of acceptance and self-love. Knowing and embracing your own divine best qualities and you divine worst qualities allows you to use all of what you are made of in your day to day life, as you move toward fulfillment. It is impossible to reach peace of mind or fulfillment if you are harboring the dark force of self-hatred.

The downward spiral into Darkness begins with shame and self-loathing. The emotional flow chart would look something like this:

Shame—> Self-hatred—> Rage—> Denial—> Superiority/ inferiority >
Judgement > Self-righteousness > Blame > Repeat.

Living life with a perpetual backdrop of shame carried forward from childhood feeds feelings of hopelessness and depression, which in turn create a pervasive mood of impotence. No one can live with impotence very long before it degrades into resentment, jealousy, and an inevitable pull toward destructive action of some sort. What form that action will take depends upon the social and cultural influences surrounding the individual at that moment.

Let's assume the person in question is a troubled teenage boy who has spent many hours playing violent video games, and whose psychological balance is further destabilized by a paradoxical reaction to prescription antidepressants. His equally troubled friend arrives on the scene with a handgun and a plan to take revenge on the bullies who teased them at school. The rest of the story is all too familiar.

A less obvious connection can be seen in the example of a middle-aged man whose job has been out-sourced, whose wife expresses her disrespect for him daily. He feels ashamed that his life has not turned out the way he had hoped when he was young. As his self-esteem sinks toward suicide, a local meeting of the Ku Klux Klan or the Neo-Nazis offers him an outlet for his Dark feelings.

In the progression from shame to blame, the intervening denial is a crucial step. It allows the self-delusion that all bad things are coming from the outside world, and that the "victim" is helpless in the face of overwhelming odds. It is this denial of one's own part in the misery that allows a person to take a gun to a shopping mall and murder innocent strangers, for instance. For someone who is operating in a full-time Child Position, reliving past insults, the denial makes it all seem sensible.

Not all descents into severe self-loathing lead directly to physical violence, of course. There are more "socially acceptable" outlets available in our culture. We have already seen the connections between shame, self-hatred and addiction. The previous chapter illustrated how self-hatred acts as the wellspring for angry fundamentalism and extreme nationalism. The same dynamic fosters racism as well.

How Self-Hatred Fuels Racism

AN APOLOGY
By Oscar Brown, Jr.

I apologize for being black
For all I am plus all I lack,
Please Sir, Please Ma'am
Give me some slack
'Cause I apologize

I 'pologize for bein' poor
For bein' sick

And tired and sore;
'Cause I ain't slick
Don't know the score
I must apologize

I 'pologize for all I've done
For all my toil
Out in the sun;
Don't want to spoil
Your white folk fun
So I apologize
I 'pologize for all I gave,
For letting you
Make me your slave;
For goin' to
My early grave
I do apologize

I 'pologize and curse my kind
For bein' fools
For bein' blind,
For bein' tools
Without a mind,
Yes I apologize

I 'pologize and curse my fate
For bein' slow
For bein' late;
Because I know
It's me you hate
Why not apologize?

I 'pologize and tip my hat
'Cause you're so rich and free and fat
Son of a bitch!
That's where it's at!
And I apologize!

Oscar Brown knows what he's talking about. In one short poem, he captures the corrosive self-doubt, the rage, the irony, and finally, the acceptance of things as they are. He rises above the injustice, and the whirlpool of rage and superiority, ultimately, by not taking it personally. There is no self-hatred, denial or self-righteousness in his world-view.

(See Chapter 29 for more on not taking it personally.) The initial development, from being hated to self-hatred to hating one's own kind is vividly traced here. It is this dynamic which has devastated minority communities, destroyed families and whole neighborhoods—first from outside, with the legacy of oppressive colonizers and slave owners, then from within as self-hatred and contempt for one's own kind.

It has been said that bigotry hurts the oppressor as much as the oppressed. Perhaps we are just beginning to see the ultimate effects of this dynamic in the larger picture, in our behavior toward all living things. In the Western world, a form of "racism" extends not only to races other than our own, but also to any species not our own. We are just starting to notice the extent to which we have raped and poisoned our planet. Not a single plant or animal, not a single island or forest has been spared as Western "civilization" has marched across the globe, proclaiming it "progress" when smokestacks and asphalt cover the landscape where forests once supported indigenous people for millennia.

Modern civilizations have assumed that military might and technological sophistication determine the superiority of a culture, but our arrogance does not end there. History books of the Western world reveal the ever-present assumption that whatever habits or preferences we have developed automatically make us superior. This self-referential smugness set the stage for four hundred years of unapologetic conquest of native peoples across the globe.

Western colonial powers have even presumed that the inclination toward "fashion" rather than going bare-breasted was a mark of intellectual and cultural superiority.

Jared Diamond, in *Guns, Germs and Steel* offers an alternative to our entrenched ethnocentric view of ourselves as "civilized" to the "primitive" people we Anglo-Europeans have subjugated in the colonizing march across the planet. In his words,

> "The objection to such racist explanations is not just that they are loathsome, but also that they are wrong . . . Sound evidence for the existence of human differences in intelligence that parallel human differences in technology is lacking. In fact . . . modern "Stone Age" peoples are on

the average probably more intelligent, not less intelligent, than industrialized peoples."

As a result of his work with Papua New Guinea's indigenous people, Diamond has concluded that "primitive" people are smarter than their Western counterparts in most of the areas that really matter in life, like survival skills and the ability to use ingenuity and creativity to solve problems. He suggests that they may be genetically superior in intelligence because their survival strategies require greater resourcefulness than their counterparts in industrialized nations. In more "developed" nations, infectious epidemics were the major cause of death; therefore, passing on ones genes depended more on immunity than intelligence or resourcefulness.

The second and probably more important effect on intelligence is the issue we have explored here previously:

> "Besides this genetic reason, there is also a second reason why New Guineans may have become smarter than Westerners. Modern European and American children spend much of their time being passively entertained by television, radio, and movies. In the average American household, the TV set is on for seven hours per day. In contrast, traditional New Guinea children have virtually no such opportunities for passive entertainment and instead spend almost all of their waking hours actively doing something, such as talking or playing with other children or adults."

Whether we have become more stupid because of our medical advances and genetic immunity, or whether we have simply become stupefied by long hours of TV watching, Americans have become a lethargic lot, depressed, discontented and disconnected from ourselves. The constant flight into fantasy that television watching encourages leaves us in a perpetual Head-centered state. From there it is an easy jump to proclaiming ourselves superior in every way, when there is dwindling evidence to back up these beliefs. Remember, a Head Person does not require that something be true for them to believe it.

The truth of our human equality is in the heart. Since time began, lovers have crossed the artificial divide of cultural and ethnic prejudices to find each other, defying the long-standing hatreds of their less open-hearted elders. Racism will die a sudden death when people discover what children have always known: In our hearts, we know that all the others on the planet deserve our acceptance and love, whether they speak our language or look like us or not. This is not a fuzzy, idealistic idea. It is simply a fundamental heart-truth you will discover if you make the transition from being a Head Person to living in your heart.

The Difference between Prejudice and Bigotry

We all come out of childhood with a certain amount of prejudice. Our personal experiences and our formal education lay the groundwork for misconceptions and misunderstandings of all sorts. Simple ignorance of others' strengths, belief systems and ways of life may enforce tendencies to interpret their actions inaccurately and to draw conclusions about our own "superiority." While this is unfortunate, it is not hatred. It is possible to be open-minded and also prejudiced, if we use the term to mean a tendency to believe what you have been taught. Bigotry, on the other hand, implies an undercurrent of hatred and an inclination toward violence. While an encounter with prejudice is unpleasant for the recipient, bigotry is shattering. Its effects linger in the victim's consciousness for years, and if the bigotry is an everyday event, the imprint on the victim's psyche can last a lifetime, being handed down to younger generations in the air they breathe and the stories they hear from their elders.

In my twenties, I was told a story which touched my heart so deeply, the pain was palpable at the time, and has remained in my consciousness ever since. It was the late 60's. I was a young mother of three small children, without extended family support or help. I was fortunate to find a woman who could come for a few hours a week to help me with childcare and housekeeping. Delaney was poor, Black, and responsible for the care of her retarded nephew. Her earnings were barely enough for their survival and to keep her old car running to get her from the inner city to the suburbs where her employers lived. After we got to know one another, she told me this story.

As a young girl in Alabama, her parents struggled to provide enough to eat for their five children. They worked as sharecroppers near the place where Delaney's grandparents had been released from slavery into desperate poverty. The bigotry festering around the edges of the Black community was omnipresent and terrifying. Since the family could barely afford clothing for the children, and shoes were a luxury, Delaney's education was limited. The family's hopes for some relief rose when Delaney's uncle landed a job in a nearby store, working as janitor, stock boy and general handyman. An intelligent and ambitious man, he worked hard to prove himself to the owners of the store, a White man and his attractive young wife. As his efforts began to make a difference in the general appearance of the store, and customers commented on it, the husband became paranoid and hostile toward the young Black man. Returning from an errand one day, the owner found his wife praising the man's work and flew into a rage. He loudly accused Delaney's uncle of making advances toward his wife. Although Delaney did not know the details of the accusations or how the sheriff became involved, she was a witness to the gruesome outcome. Her uncle was lynched by a white mob, hung from a tree with his penis cut off.

Those horrifically violent, widely condoned events in our country's past began to subside only about 60 years ago, with the first advances of the Civil Rights movement, while the bigotry and fear have diminished only gradually.

To minimize the lingering prejudice in our midst, schools and businesses have instituted courses in "diversity training." In the process, these attempts at "teaching diversity" have had their own ironic impact on how we currently manage our mindless prejudices. In the following poem from his book, *Zapata's Disciple*, Martin Espada gives us a creative perspective on how to manage the banal everyday racism which passes for "appreciating our differences." In his words, "(S)ometimes a belly laugh is infinitely more revolutionary than the howl of outrage that would have left me pegged, yet again, as a snarling, stubborn 'macho.'"

MY NATIVE COSTUME
By Martin Espada

When you come to visit,
said a teacher
from the suburban school,
don't forget to wear
your native costume.
But I'm a lawyer,
I said.
My native costume
Is a pinstriped suit.

You know, the teacher said,
a Puerto Rican costume.

Like a guayabera?
The shirt? I said.
But it's February.

The children want to see
a native costume,
the teacher said.

So I went
to the suburban school,
embroidered guayabera
short-sleeved shirt
over a turtle-neck
and said, Look kids,
cultural adaptation.

While the out-of-touch teacher in this interaction may not be expressing hatred, she is insensitive and self-absorbed. Her attitude is disrespectful, thinly disguised behind her supposed advocacy for appreciation and tolerance. We still have a long way to go.

Beyond Racism and Intolerance

It is always easy to insist that someone else ought to forgive and forget and get over it, especially if you have never witnessed firsthand the atrocities they suffered. Victims always have a longer memory for abuse than their perpetrators; it's a matter of survival for them. When it comes to forgiveness, it is up to the victims to decide whether they are able to leave the injuries behind to move forward together. Only by offering genuine feelings of respect toward our fellow citizens, for as long as it takes, can we heal the hatred that came before us. Kindness and the spirit of generosity alone can earn forgiveness and absolution for the crimes of our ancestors. We will need to cultivate a culture of healing and reconciliation as it has been attempted in South Africa, for instance. Without the Peace and Reconciliation activities which accompanied the end of apartheid, the country would have been destroyed in revenge and counter-revenge for generations to come. In such a spirit, we need to wholeheartedly accept the responsibility (not the blame) for healing, and for building a culture together in which everyone can have the pleasures and the benefits that come with being color-blind.

This process of acceptance and forgiveness is the same as the healing which must take place after a difficult childhood. We must learn to forgive ourselves for the weakness and vulnerability we felt as children. By developing empathy for our own humanity and our own foibles and failings, we learn by extension to accept others with all their gifts, strengths and weaknesses.

Behind the ravings of a bigot or a hate-mongering political partisan (Rush Limbaugh, Glenn Beck and their counterparts come to mind) is always the echo of the screaming child, raging against those who remind him of his own past weaknesses, and especially those who represent Heart. Like children in a deadly game of "Hot Potato," they pass on the insults, berating others who represent the weaknesses they have felt in themselves. Through the Shock and Awe process they have come to adopt the very tactics which left them broken in childhood. They express their bile especially toward the weakest among us, like longtime welfare recipients, who openly show their inability to adapt to a competitive culture because of injury or disability. Often, it is evident that the disability these people live with was a result of emotional injury to their self-worth and competence, brought on by childhood abuse or the pervasive bigotry they have lived with. The hate-mongers refuse to recognize this sad fact. Without compassion or empathy, they rail against human need—yours, mine, and theirs.

With the shift of power in Congress and the election of Barack Obama in 2008, a new and unexpected wave of virulence and hatred swept across the land. Perhaps this is because the sharing of power directly threatens the Head People's belief in their own racial superiority. Should he persevere, the scaffolding upon which their identities have been built will be proven wrong. Without the fantasy of superiority, they will be thrown back into the whirlpool of shame, denial and blame, in danger of being reminded it is they who are lacking—in awareness, subtlety, humility and compassion.

There is the uncomfortable possibility now that an entire population might be forced to acknowledge that bigotry is a Head Game, the self-aggrandizing obsession of Children of Darkness.

DEPRESSION

It's no use; life sucks
You can't win for losing.
It's useless, depressing,
My company's moving.

My TV broke yesterday
Kids have the flu.
The boss hates me; job stinks
So how's it with you.

My sugar's up lately
I'll probably die.
It just doesn't matter
Here's mud in your eye.

That bartender's surly
It's always like that;
It rains at my picnic,
My tires go flat.

But I keep on going
In spite of life's trials
I can't give up now,
Have to think of the girls.

One's ugly, one's stupid
I guess I'm just stuck
I sure got the short stick
When God gave out luck.

OBSESSIVE-COMPULSIVE

Look out!
You'll trip, Dear,
You can't be too careful.
I know a boy
Who put out his eye
Running with his pencil.

Your friend is driving?
I'm worried sick
You never know what's out there.
Wrap your muffler around you,
And don't forget Kleenex,
Just call us as soon as you get there.

It said on the news there's a killer afoot
Yes, I know he's in Sascatchewan,
But I fear for your safety
You're always so trusting,
I can't sleep whenever you're gone.

You heard about Sadie's boy,
Drown in the river
Jumping off 30-foot rocks.
Yes, I know you're not swimming
But rain has been falling,
The river could rise
By the way, did you wear your wool socks?

What will you do
When I'm not here to tell you
The world's overflowing with dangers?
Those people will rob you
You'd better stay here
Where we never speak kindly to strangers.

CHAPTER TWENTY-SEVEN

HOW CAN I GET OVER IT?

I was running a group for middle-school children in a town near where I live in upstate New York when one of the most important learning experiences of my career took place. The group was made up of nine children who had been hand-picked by the school administration for intervention because they were causing disruption in their classes, doing poorly in their studies or because the school psychologist saw a need for them to receive intensive psychological support. Most of them were from middle class or working class families, and all the families were in some kind of crisis due to loss of jobs, alcoholism, drug addiction, or divorce.

It was the fifth meeting of the group, and the children were beginning to know me well enough to speak out. Their initial fear of revealing feelings to each other was beginning to subside. Several incidents had occurred in previous sessions where one member had reached out in a very supportive and friendly way to another. This was a new idea for these children who were deeply immersed in the hostile culture of middle school where taunts and insults were more common than compliments, and cooperation occurred mostly when a fight broke out. They were the very age at which children need to learn that physical violence has become a serious offense. More sophisticated verbal skills must be substituted for fists or name-calling.

During the previous weeks of the group, they had had some success with managing anger, learning to negotiate, and they had even begun to notice the change in each other. On this day, several of them began to talk about conflicts at home, and their inability to use their new skills to make anything better there. One boy described how his parents screamed and fought with each other. The night before, he had been in his room playing video games and trying to stay away from them. A younger brother came in and demanded to play the game. A small disagreement between them had barely begun when the father came into the room, smashed the game, and struck the older boy hard enough to send him across the room. The worst part, he said, was that his father cursed at him and accused him of being selfish, although he often let his brother play with his game. He had tears in his eyes as he spoke. Unlike previous emotional incidents, no one stepped in to mock or blame him. Instead, they became very quiet and attentive, murmuring sympathetic comments. Together they were learning to open their hearts and feel compassion for one another.

Another boy then described how he had moved into a shed in the woods behind his parents' house. He could not stand to live with them because they frequently beat him when they were drunk. He had a wood stove which he kept stocked himself, and his uncle brought him meals from next door. Apparently the parents did not intervene to retrieve him, even during subzero weather. The children saw my horror at the extreme neglect he was suffering, and they reflected sympathy toward this boy who had felt like an outcast at home and at school. The girl next to him put her arm on his shoulder, and his mask of toughness began to soften.

One girl acknowledged sheepishly that although her family did not beat her, she felt ashamed. Her father had finally gotten a job as a pizza delivery driver, after years of drug abuse and neglect of his family. She described her parents' drunken parties during which all the adults passed out on the floor, and she was left to put her younger sister to bed. As she talked, she became aware of how she had taken over the position of parent in her family, since no one else was available to fill the role.

Other children spontaneously began to describe horrific and violent scenes in which they had been either physically or verbally abused. They acknowledged having done things their parents objected to, but any attempts at negotiation or reparation were in vain. Usually their "crimes" were small infractions like not taking the garbage out fast enough or leaving something on the floor. Their parents' actions were, from a reasonable adult standpoint, entirely out of proportion.

For the most part, these children expressed little anger toward their parents. What I heard instead was a reluctance to acknowledge how truly irresponsible their parents were. They were deeply ashamed and acutely aware of the way the community associated them with their parents. The boy who lived alone in the shed spoke despairingly about how his life was hopeless because people always said things to him like, "Oh, you're one of those Barker kids." His imitation suggested someone looking down his nose as if he had just smelled something revolting.

"You're not responsible for what your parents do," I said. Suddenly, the room full of jumpy, fidgety children snapped to attention.

"What???" What are you talking about? My parents always say
    it's my fault when they hit me or scream at me!"
"It's because I do things that drive them crazy!"
"My mother cries all the time because I make her unhappy."
"My father left us because I was bad."

They were all talking at once, all of them taking the blame for their parents' irrational behavior.

"No," I responded. "They may disagree with something you do or say, but no parent has the right to beat up their children, or scream or go out of control. They are having trouble controlling their feelings, and it has nothing to do with you. They were grown up, all of them, before you were even born."

There was a long moment of stunned silence, then suddenly, mayhem. Two of the boys began pole vaulting over desks; notebooks and pocketbooks went flying. Joe pretended to sock Mike in the arm, and Andy started hooting at them both. The girls yelled at them to stop, increasing the bedlam, and Melanie, the girl with the pizza delivery-father, put her hands over her ears and started to cry, loudly.

I had long since learned that any stern command would only increase their hyper-reaction, so I began very calmly to put myself in the middle of the fray, hugging Melanie, then gathering in a few boys, touching as many of them as I could, putting my hands on their heads as I had in a calming exercise the week before, reassuring them. Little by little, they started to come around, and by the end of the session, they were mostly back in their chairs, looking very young, and still somewhat confused. I pointed out that what we were discussing must have upset them a lot, given their reaction. They were not used to having someone listen carefully to their feelings and acknowledge that they were not to blame for their parents' problems.

It appeared from the stunned looks on their faces, they had not even made the connection between what I had said and their volcanic reaction. This time, I saw it coming, and because our time was up, I sent them out moments before another eruption would have occurred.

The frantic reaction of these children demonstrated just how completely they had accepted the idea that the painful events at home were their fault. The alternative would have been unbearable. They could not accept that their parents really were as irresponsible and irrational as they seemed. How could a dependent child accept that kind of truth? I had been very careful not to blame or comment on the parents' specific behaviors at all, but had focused instead on the children's coping skills and self-control issues, helping them to find more productive ways to handle difficult situations. It had been the implication of what I said that unhinged them.

Adding to their difficulty in absorbing the information I offered was the dilemma the group itself presented. The "zero-tolerance" rule I had established in the group from the beginning had taken hold. Not once in our weeks together had anyone been mocked or harshly criticized. Friendly, problem-solving suggestions were freely given, but humiliation of any kind was absolutely forbidden. None of them was used to such compassion or sympathy. Even at their young ages, they had become inured to criticism and violence, and had closed their hearts in order not to be hurt.

The group took a dramatically productive turn after that. They continued to explode into hyperactive energy every time something really positive or warm transpired with me or between the members themselves, but they began to learn how to recognize it and monitor themselves. Melanie, the child of alcoholics, appointed herself monitor in charge of noticing when group members did something kind, and how the others reacted to it. A few of them told of incidents where, instead of battling with their parents, they had just walked away, or avoided an argument by being especially friendly and cooperative. They were amazed at the calming effect it sometimes had on their parents. Mostly, however, they began to take their focus off their parents and turned toward their school activities and studies. By the end of the year, four of them were on the honor roll, and everyone had found some creative ways of handling their predicaments.

The turning point was "It's not your fault"

It's Not Your Fault

... that your parents didn't love you
... that nothing you did was good enough
... that you were constantly being corrected or ridiculed
... that you were not as beautiful or smart or athletic as they wanted
... that they were so often disappointed or angry with you
... that you were not happy as a child
... that you were anxious and fearful
... that they liked other children better
... that you got into trouble at school
... that you didn't rebel
... that you didn't make them stop
... that you didn't like them
... that they were unhappy.

It's not your fault. Your parents were already grown up before you were born, and if they were not happy it was not about you.

If this discussion makes you want to jump out of your chair, then we're onto something. The first step in "getting over it" is to learn to love yourself, and that requires that you begin by exonerating yourself for all those awful, painful things that happened to you before you were of the age where you could truly understand enough about the world to make your own choices. You were not weak, in the sense of character weakness, nor were you defective. You were a child.

Remember a childhood incident in which you felt humiliated or castigated. What was your offense? Was it a truly serious moral lapse, or was it a trivial infraction blown out of proportion, or worse yet, a bullying attack brought on by your own uniqueness? And what did you learn about your own uniqueness as a result of it? Did you feel yourself losing your grip on yourself, letting go because the effort of holding on was too much? Perhaps you felt the half-formed thought that if only you could be something else, something less ... hateful ...

less unlovable, if only you were not *you*, then maybe it would be better. This was the beginning of the war with yourself, the wish to disengage from your bodysoul, the essence of the *you* you were meant to be. This was the beginning of the end.

Look into your heart of hearts and absolve yourself of all the "crimes" of your childhood—yours and your parents—because you will never be truly happy and free as long as you are still concerned with what they thought, what they said, and how they felt about you. It doesn't matter. Once you are an adult, you begin anew, with your own intelligence, and your heart and soul to guide you. You have the ability to assess what you choose to believe, how you choose to behave, and how you feel about yourself in your heart.

Bullying as a Competitive Sport

An extended visit with my grandchildren left me stunned at the culture of bullying our children are immersed in. In the recent past, a single perpetrator or a gang of toughs might have terrorized a schoolyard or neighborhood. Programs to discourage "bullying" addressed these conditions, with the assumption that the majority of children were victims or by-standers. Things have changed. The balance has shifted to a culture of pervasive psychological bullying—redefined as "teasing." This makes it sound innocuous, but in reality it is even more destructive than physical attacks.

Trading insults has become a stylized, ongoing competitive sport. By the time children reach high school, they can expect that every encounter between friends and enemies alike, every phone call or passing comment, is likely to carry with it a verbal barb. Like their television counterparts, the "popular kid" is the one whose skill at insult and innuendo earns the biggest laughs from the crowd. Bystanders must join in the game or show "weakness" and risk becoming targets themselves. Most of the participants—especially the skillful ones—do not think of what they do as bullying. It is just a game, just for fun, just kidding.

Recent studies with adults who report having been picked on verbally shows that verbal abuse is actually more damaging to a person's sense of self-worth than physical abuse, especially when it occurred during the middle-school years. These childhood victims showed greater life-long difficulty in social adaptation than their more "popular" peers.

We owe it to our children—both the victims and the perpetrators—to teach them a new, more powerful Golden Rule. "Belittle and humiliate others and prove to the world what an insecure fool and weakling you are." Or for the less intellectual crowd, "Dissing others shows you're scared."

For all parents and teachers who are coping with this tsunami of verbal abuse among middle and high school children, I recommend Patricia Evans' book, *Teen Torment*, a guide to raising awareness of what verbal abuse really does to young people.

Parents must rally to create a zero-tolerance atmosphere for their children, beginning at home. First, they must honestly apologize to their own children for disparaging remarks they may have made in the past, to each other in the presence of the children, and to the children themselves. They must also apologize as a group to any child who has been teased or ridiculed by other family members. Perpetrators and by-standers alike must identify their own roles and vow to each other to protect and cherish, rather than destroy other family members, no matter what may have transpired in the past. It is often the case that even the youngest victim may object to the new standards out of reluctance to forgo the anticipated revenge he or she might have been savoring.

This is not a project of getting Them to stop bullying your innocent kids. It is more a matter of teaching yourselves and your own children a new kind of respect for each other's most sensitive—and therefore most precious and valuable—feelings. Any comment which irritates another person because it is an attack on their being, their soulbody, shows a lack of sensitivity, and therefore a lack of character, on the part of the attacker.

Any incident in which you do or say something which deliberately causes an innocent person emotional pain becomes a black mark against your own soul. You may not be reprimanded or punished in this life. In fact, you may garner influence or prestige because of it, but at the end of your life, you will be required to relive these moments, this time in the victim's shoes. Eventually, you will feel the sting of the arrows you have launched toward others in a callous attack.

Do not wait until you die to review your own actions and examine your intentions. Do it now, in the company of your children and your friends. Create an atmosphere in which everyone can own up to their own tendencies to tease or ridicule others. That attitude is compassion and forgiveness. First, forgive yourself for having become insensitive in your treatment of others. It was the way your were taught. Then, work to change your legacy, by changing the way you speak to your children and by teaching them to treat each other with respect. Create a new standard of attentiveness, in which any genuine objection is carefully considered, and remedies are immediately found to repair the damage between the abuser and the victim. These remedies must include apologies, recognition and consideration for the one whose feelings have been hurt. Perhaps even more importantly, acknowledgement must be given that the abuser must have been struggling with issues of self-worth, or he would not have initiated the attack in the first place. He must then be helped to heal and go on with an open heart, which will be easier after a kind handling of his own injured bodyself.

If every incident is handled immediately in this way, the round-robin of attack-and-revenge will be nipped in the bud and will eventually give way to an atmosphere of respect and its natural accompaniment, self-worth for all the members in this circle of respect and love.

Revising Your Own "Identity"

Here is an exercise. In it, you will imagine yourself at an age before you began to doubt your self-worth. Perhaps it was infancy or toddlerhood. Try to do the exercise fully, filling in as many details about your true nature (before "civilization") as you can. Above all, be truthful, nonjudgmental and empathic.

Imagine this: As a child you lived in a quietly loving community where everyone was delighted to have you around, where your parents were curious about you and appreciated your growing talents. You were gladly included and respected for the age-appropriate contribution you could make to the important work of helping your family live happily and well. What would your normal everyday emotional state have been? What would have interested you? What work or creative activities would you have been especially drawn to? How would you have related to the people around you? It will take some mind-expanding to imagine yourself in a life with character-building challenges, but without severe disrespect, humiliation or shame. Keep trying. Go back in age far enough to make sure you're not transposing your later life experiences, or your parents' attitudes toward you. Do not go on reading until you have learned something new about the child you were.

When you have finished, you should have an emerging picture of the child you actually were, at the core of the person you can now begin to be. You can do this exercise as often as you need to, to rid yourself of your early misconceptions and self-condemnations. Starting with a clean slate does not mean you're going to be without structure or direction. It simply means you have to stop blaming yourself, and accept that all children are weak, confused, and legitimately in need of much loving attention. Early deprivation incubates the desperate feelings of neediness, loneliness and self-doubt, but what continues the misery into adult life is the conviction that you are defective, and the self-hatred that follows. Then begins the repeating cycle of hungrily pursuing love and affirmation from the very people who are least likely to offer it to anyone, including you.

So stop it. In your quiet moments with yourself, you deserve to have yourself as good company. You will find that little by little, the feelings of stress, anxiety and depression will melt away, along with the need for a "fix" to make life worth living.

Here's how. Imagine the connection between you, the you that is your body mind and heart, and your bodysoul. The electrical connection is like the plug on an electric dryer—big, sturdy, solid teeth fitting into a receptacle made to hold it firmly. Plug in, and never let go. Not for anyone or anything, not ever. Feel the surge of electrical power course through your body. Now you are alive, and you are whole. You have everything you need.

As you practice these techniques to strengthen your trust and partnership with yourself and your whole body's systems, you will find there is no such thing as a mind/body split. You are no longer at war with yourself. You operate as a single organism, whole, dynamic, and ongoing.

If you were one of those children who felt welcomed and loved, surrounded by a circle of competent, comfortable adults who were highly developed in their capacity to manage your care and their emotions, you were rarely blessed. Most children have a difficult time of it. Our society is generally not child-friendly. Children are forced to adapt to the unnatural demands of an unforgiving culture which requires that children behave and think like adults, until they reach 13, and then they are expected to be rude, incorrigible and irresponsible.

Early on, exuberance and boundless curiosity are labeled "hyperactive" and stifled by a Sit Still, Don't Ask, Don't Cry policy which continues through all their school years and beyond, until they finally comply by becoming depressed teenagers. In the process, they are likely to overuse their reptilian brains. Most of us manage to grow up with at least a modicum of our human capacity to feel warmly toward others, but we tend to enter adulthood with our channels still programmed for a fight-or-flight reaction to almost any strong emotion.

Once the overused fight-or-flight channels have been laid down, it is inevitable that difficult challenges in life will trigger a headlong plunge into a reptilian adrenaline rush, followed by an emotionally intense, infantile stress reaction. This is how many people describe it: "primitive." It is the basis for such irrational responses as fear of commitment to someone who truly loves you, and whom you love in return, or an irrational preference for someone who makes you heart go pitty-pat (fear). Relationships are not supposed to hurt, and they shouldn't take all that much work, if you have previously reconditioned yourself to feel at home in an environment of love and appreciation rather than conflict.

Fortunately, if we managed during childhood to lay down even a thread to the deepest human power in our hearts and our bodysoul, we can build stronger and better connections now. It does take some determination and practice. Before we go on to further exercises for taming the fight-or-flight response, let's look at anxiety and depression, and how they can be tamed for good.

The Anxiety Trap

Living with anxiety takes a tremendous toll, especially because of the way many people experience it—as low-level gnawing worry that lingers even in sleep. It wears out the physical structure, drives your friends and family and coworkers crazy, and precludes joy. So many people are desperate to find a way to rid themselves of it that anti-anxiety medication has become a billion-dollar industry. Like depression, treating the symptoms without addressing the underlying causes is self-defeating.

The psychiatric/pharmaceutical industry has not been helpful with their advertising campaign to treat anxiety "disorders" as if they were diseases. Anxiety is not a disease. It is a feeling. No matter how intense the feelings might be, they are not generated by our bodies alone, or by a disease of the brain (except possibly in extremely rare cases of brain injury or *identifiable* disease). Anxious feelings are a response to the idea that there is danger present.

Here is the good news: Anxiety (or panic) is not something that happens to you. It is something you do. Therefore, you have a choice. You can continue to do it or not. Of course, this sounds simplistic, but it is true nonetheless. We are all biologically designed to respond to our environment in life-preserving ways, and the anxiety response would be life-preserving if it helped to protect us from danger, but ongoing anxiety or worse yet, a panic attack, hardly makes you a more effective defender.

A panic attack is nothing more than an extreme anxiety reaction to a situation which you interpret as life-threatening, whether it actually is or not. For instance, fear of leaving the house, of taking airplanes or crossing bridges are not what we would call rational fears, since most of us would agree that these things are sufficiently safe to warrant doing them without a second thought. Nevertheless, many people's lives are reduced to paralysis by such fears.

In the case of either chronic anxiety or panic, the person experiencing it has convinced herself that fear is an accurate, or at least understandable response to the circumstances at hand. However, we would not label it an "anxiety attack" if it were a reality-based reaction. We acknowledge the reasonableness of being afraid of a mugger with a gun or a rabid raccoon in your yard. We would not refer to that fear as an anxiety attack. It is just fear.

We have agreed as a society to give fantasy-based reactions polite double-speak names like "stress." This has lulled us into thinking there is little difference between these idea-based reactions and fear of real life-threatening situations. There is a difference, and that difference can set you free. Stress is a Head response. Patience, forbearance, tolerance and courage are Heart responses.

Negotiate with yourself. Get out of your head and into your heart, and insist on real responses to real events. Refuse to allow fantasy and fear-mongering to ruin your life and spoil your fun. Airplanes are not terrifying—they are transportation, safely used by millions of people every month. Insist on living your day-to-day life on the basis of probabilities, where they are known. If there is a 10-million to one possibility that the activity in question will injure or kill you, go for it. Eating a sandwich could be more dangerous.

If you insist that life should present no danger, no variety, no challenges, no heart-racing excitement, then there is no hope for fulfillment. Life is an adventure, and adventures involve risk. Some risks are well worth taking because life would be insufferably boring without a large element of joie de vivre. This is not a pull-yourself-up-by-your-bootstraps suggestion. It requires only that you go to your honest and compassionate heart and acknowledge your actual adult strengths. After all, you are suffering every day because of your anxious way of life. You can change it.

Stress Is in the Eye of the Beholder

Here is the irony. The very people who suffer "uncontrolled" anxiety attacks when they are on vacation or at home with their families are often the same ones who are excellent in a crisis. Calm and competent under pressure; paralyzed by anxiety on their day off. This is the picture of a basically responsible person who only succumbs to the throes of anxiety when all actual life-threatening events have been adequately handled. How could this be—cool under fire; a basket case when there is nothing crucial at stake? Perhaps anxiety, like 5-star accommodations or box seats, is a modern-day luxury. Our day-to-day lives in America are truly not life-threatening unless you are a member of a SWAT team, or you live in a violent drug and gang-infested neighborhood. It is rare to hear of a person who starved to death in the U.S. We are not generally in danger of death. Therefore, "stress" as we experience it in Twenty-first Century America has more to do with the fear (or memory) of emotional trauma than with physical survival.

This is not to say that anxiety should be dismissed as silly or crazy or weak. At least, it is a flashback to an earlier terrifying experience. Ironically, the people who are experiencing these traumatic reactions to life may actually be the canaries in our virtual mine. Things are not right. The emotional state of affairs is out of balance, too harsh, too inhuman, too far from what we need to fulfill what we came here to experience. Where in our everyday lives is the compassion, the forgiveness, the warmth and kindness which sustains a human heart? In order to change our environment, we need to change the energy we create ourselves, because that is the atmosphere we breathe, moment by moment. Begin by generating a state of calm, and surround yourself with it, using the exercises you have learned so far and the ones which follow. As you practice, you will become stronger and less vulnerable to the chaotic energy around you, building your own version of a force-field which nourishes and protects you.

The Two-Week Cure for Depression

If you are a walking-around depressed person, you can shake off a long-term struggle with depression and its regular companion, sleeplessness. These strategies are not designed to replace medication for bipolar or schizophrenic disorders, but they will be helpful. They work best for people who have lived with misery and depression, but are still managing to function in some areas of life. The cure is simple, but not necessarily easy. It will take courage and determination on your part. Your ego will probably try to trick you into saying things like "*MY* depression is different," or "but I've felt this all my life!" Probably neither one is true. I have never seen a depressed baby, have you? Calling it *MY* depression suggests ownership, something that belongs to you or defines your identity. In this case, that something is Darkness, misery. Embrace it and continue to suffer, or consider a radical path to freedom. As you work your way through this discussion, be on the lookout for any hint of pride or possessiveness. It will trick you into giving up before you have a chance to change anything.

First, the hard part. Call it by its least attractive name: self-absorption, even self-pity. It is the All-About-Me preoccupied focus, thinking about your own bad feelings. Don't beat yourself up. You didn't set out to be miserable, and you probably had good reason for feeling anger and despair—the backdrop for depression—in the first place. The issue is not whether your feelings are justified or not. They probably are. The question is whether you want to go on like this or not.

It seems to be a well-kept secret that depression begins with unexpressed anger. If you are dealing with depression in yourself, it is fair to assume you are carrying around a whole lot of resentment. That resentment may be layered over with an equal amount of what you would think of as self-control, but it seethes just under the surface, creating the sickness of spirit we call "depression." Actually, there is no such thing as the entity, depression. It is always a combination of anger, resentment, and fear. The fear prevents expressing the anger, resentment results, and there you are, sunk in a black hole of despair. The black hole deepens as you argue endlessly with yourself about how you can't possibly express your feelings—*these* feelings—or something terrible will happen.

The arguments go something like this: You couldn't possibly express how you feel or you will be fired immediately from your job, your partner will leave you, your children will hate you, and your parents will disown you. Of course, some of these fears might be realized if you expressed your objections to the way you have been treated in a violent, screaming rage or a full-blown kicking, flailing tantrum. These tactics would be unwise for an adult. However, a calm, measured statement requesting respect and fair consideration from another has the best chance for success in any environment.

Now, listen to yourself arguing, "That wouldn't work, they wouldn't even hear me," or "It would start World War Three." Of course, the World War Three argument is nonsense, since a war requires at least two combatants. If you aren't one of them, no war. You might hear angry objections, but if you listen to them respectfully and ask intelligent questions about why your "opponent" is angry, you are likely to learn some astonishing truths. One of them is likely to be that they feel *you* are a disrespectful and inattentive listener. Before you dismiss this out of hand, consider the effect of your abiding conviction that you will not be heard. Your resentment precedes any conversation, and is likely to set up a wall of negative energy toward the other person, creating or reinforcing the barrier between you. The first argument, that they won't hear you, is probably also untrue, but you won't know it unless you try. If the other person is truly as deaf and dumb as you say, they are a living monument to insensitivity. As such, it is unwise for you to continue in a relationship with them for even one more minute. If it is your boss, make every effort in your power to leave. No amount of money is worth spending half your waking life with a cold-blooded Abuser.

You probably learned this silent-treatment response as a child. The adaptations we adopt in childhood have a way of turning dark and miserable as we get older. Silent resentment in a child takes the form of a pout. Most children are incapable of sustaining a pouting match for very long before they are distracted by life's wonders. Not so for adults. An adult can remain in a pout for years on end. *This is depression.* In a child, it is usually recognized for what it is—an angry response to something that displeased the child. In an adult, it is called a disease, and medication is prescribed.

So, unless you are looking for the prize for the longest living pout, stop it. Stop thinking about your resentments, you troubles, your worries and your pain. Get up from your psychological sick-bed and venture out into the world in search of an opportunity—any opportunity—to do something to help someone else. Ignore the objections you hear in your mind. It's your ego tricking you into maintaining your sit-down strike, for your own "protection."

Walk out your door with the clear intention of finding a need you can fill. Put it in the form of a prayer if you're willing: "Please send me a need to fill." Then, reap the results. Help a struggling senior to get on a bus. Walk around your neighborhood, or any neighborhood, with your eyes and ears wide open. Pick up some litter and carry it to a garbage can. Shovel the snow from your neighbor's walk when they're not looking. Volunteer at your local library. Use your best acting skills to read a good novel to a senior whose sight is failing.

Don't let your age or your physical limitations stop you. There is *always* someone who is worse off than you are. Do this every day, for as many hours as you possibly can, until you are tired, fulfilled and exhilarated. Keep doing it until your own spirits lift and your soul soars, then do it some more. Keep going until the idea of taking anti-depressants depresses you. Get rid of them, as quickly as an enlightened doctor agrees, and run barefoot in the grass, or make angels in the snow. Swim. Walk. Breathe. Live. Celebrate. If you still have any time to think about your own feelings, or you need more tools as insurance against relapse, do the following exercise.

Taming the Tiger

The pathway to change is through our hearts to our soulbody. We need not rely solely on the traditional approach to therapy, working through the feelings and ideas which are the response to our early environment, as we have done in much of this book. We also have powerful additional tools which speed and deepen that process without drugs. Along with the exercises and brain focusing practices presented earlier, there are additional techniques which are especially helpful *before* the fight-or-flight response turns to rage or its dark companion, depression. The HeartMath Institute teaches a technique called Freeze-Frame™.[23] I have found it so helpful in working with people who truly desire change that I will summarize a few of the basic elements of it here.

You can probably think of an incident in the past month which triggered your most troublesome response, whether it is anger, anxiety, depression or some other pet neurosis. Begin by pinpointing the circumstances which most often trigger your problem reaction. Now make a brief list of those conditions for yourself. Write them down. They might include the experience of having someone cut you off in traffic, or a disagreement with your colleague or your spouse, or the holidays with your parents. Place a mental red flag on these events, a big one, and don't forget it. Now you are prepared to take it on. It is better to start with easier challenges, until you get the hang of it. First, imagine a situation which would normally get you riled up. Then, instead of going into the fight-or-flight reaction, stop yourself. Freeze. Do not allow yourself to dwell on the negative emotions you would normally cultivate. Instead, take a breath, redirect your focus, and imagine a time when you experienced a genuine feeling of appreciation, one where the appreciation originated in you, where you felt warmly toward someone or something. It can be as simple as a sunny day, or a delicious meal, or a friendly greeting from someone you care for. Breathe deeply, and absorb that feeling into your heart. If it helps, put your hand on your heart, and concentrate on sending the feeling of warm appreciation. If you can think of an incident where you felt unconflicted love, use that.

---

[23]   For a full description of these techniques, see *The HeartMath Solution*, by Doc Childre and Howard Martin.

Keep concentrating on your heart and the feeling of appreciation until the irritation of the moment melts away.

Done regularly, this procedure has a dramatic and immediate effect. Instead of the toxic cascade of stress hormones, your body begins producing healing, life-giving DHEA and related hormones. Many people are familiar with the endorphin effect which results from physical exercise. The sensation here is similar, but more complete and long-lasting. It is also extremely reassuring because you create it yourself, and with practice confidence builds around the knowledge that you are managing your own emotional reactions, and doing it effectively. It is helpful to have more than one pleasurable incident at the ready, and to practice before an emergency strikes.

Like any good learning tool, this is not a quick fix. We are talking about literally reprogramming your brain circuits, so you can't expect to change a lifetime groove in an hour or two. Keep reminding yourself of the benefits you will achieve when you eliminate "stress" from your life.

As your skill at stopping the fight-or-flight response increases, you will find you may be able to maintain your focus on the problem situation while you find something in the moment to appreciate or admire. You may even begin to feel generosity or a kind of sympathy toward the people who had previously driven you crazy, even if you still don't appreciate their behavior or their attitude toward you. Eventually, you may find that you experience a warm glow of pleasure much of the time, regardless of what is going on around you. Ultimately, your environment really doesn't matter very much when you are directing your own feelings and responses through the powerful energy of your heart.[24]

These methods are effective because they retrain our brains on the most fundamental level, bringing emotions, thinking and feeling into what HeartMath researchers call "coherence." You can see why

---

[24] Recently, scientists have developed energy scans which can measure the relative energy we emit, and they found that our hearts generate about 5000 times more energy than our brain, so it makes sense to start where the real power is, and use that energy to bring your body processes and your thinking into alignment with it. See Joseph Chilton Pearce and work by the HeartMath Institute.

this state of harmony can fill up the hunger and longing which may have led you to compromise your integrity and your safety by involving yourself in Darkness. It is not a quick answer, but healing yourself from the wounds and unfinished development in childhood can accomplish what no amount of arguing with yourself could ever achieve.

A Note About Suicide

It is generally believed that suicide is a tragic act of hopelessness and suffering. This is not true, except perhaps in rare cases of extreme physical pain or impending death. It is most often an act of vengeance, designed to punish those closest to the suicidal one. It is the ultimate "You'll be sorry when I'm dead." The evidence lies in the results. Partners and children of a person who commits suicide are marked by feelings of regret, despair and self-condemnation for years, even generations to come.

Suicide is a violent rejection of the value of human life. As such, it is a denial of meaning, of faith and of any acknowledgment or hope of God's love. If one's own body is not precious, then nothing is. This nihilistic attitude is a result of deep and profound rage. Treatment for anyone contemplating suicide must begin by addressing the underlying rage, not the feelings of helplessness. It is an act of determination and will, not weakness. The suicide can be prevented only if the person is convinced that whether the vengeance is warranted or not, suicide is not the most effective resolution of the problem.

Most people who consider suicide are angry at God, presuming that God is as angry and judgmental as they are of themselves and of others. This is a dead-end belief system which justifies killing yourself and everyone else in your life. Should the people around the candidate for suicide play into this belief system by being overly indulgent, or taking undue responsibility for the person's rage, they will encourage the person in their vengeance, making the suicide more likely. While medication may be a temporary palliative, it is no replacement for dealing with the underlying feelings of rage and self-pity.

A sensitive handling of the problem does not preclude addressing these thorny issues. It may be a matter of life or death for the person who has sunk into the darkest of moods: the belief that murder is the only solution to dealing with life's emotional problems.

Breathing Inner Peace

Here is an exercise you can do to strengthen the connections between mind, body, heart and soul, opening the channels between you and your soul, and between you and the world, while you remain safe and comfortable in your own internal environment.

This is a three-part exercise. Initially, you will practice each part separately, then you will put them together in a sequence. Sit comfortably in a quiet place. Breathe deeply and slowly, creating the feeling of plenty. Be aware that you are a part of the Earth, that you generate electromagnetic energy, just as the Earth does, and that you are compatible with the Earth's energy field. Now, as you inhale, concentrate on your own energy, your engine, and as you exhale, send that energy downward, beaming it down into the earth, making a connection so that you experience yourself as grounded in the earth. With that energy, send your feelings of love and gratitude for the sustenance Earth provides for us and for the natural beauty you have witnessed whenever you find yourself in a park or a forest. Feel the energy flowing through your whole body, down through your legs and feet into the earth. When you feel the sense of being "plugged in" to the Earth, you can draw on the constant and steady flow of energy which flows back to you, Mother Earth's love returned to you tenfold. Feel it radiate up through your feet, into every cell of your body, nourishing and replenishing you. Concentrate on doing this part of the exercise until you feel deeply peaceful, alive and connected.

Next, as you inhale, concentrate again on your energy, and this time as you exhale, send it upward, through your body up into your brain, and out through the top of your head. Beam your energy, which has your signature on it, (like Batman beaming his Bat-signal into the sky). Send it out into the universe. Imagine the expanse of a night sky, with stars, moon and planets glowing and sparkling down on you. Send your message of gratitude and wonder to Father Sky, with love from one of his children. Open your heart to receive the love which comes pouring down on you, the unconditional love from Spirit, which will sustain and comfort you through all your life. Communicating this way with Mother Earth and Father Sky will not only offer you comfort and nourishment. It will also help you to develop your psychic powers, your sensitivity to the world around you. You may ask your deepest questions about life on Earth and the mysteries of the Universe. Listen quietly for answers, which may come from outside yourself, or deep within your heart.

Third, concentrate again on your energy, but this time as you exhale, instead of beaming it outward, gently send it into your heart, nourishing and warming your feelings toward yourself. Allow feelings of love and acceptance from the Earth below and the Universe above to surround your heart and then emanate outward, like the ripples on a pond. The first ripple surrounds you, enveloping you in feelings of warmth and appreciation. Then, allow the ripples to continue outward, creating a loving environment for anyone else who comes within your circle, which may extend outward up to 10 or 12 feet or more.

Continue doing this exercise now, one breath down, one breath upward, and one to your heart, for at least twenty minutes or longer.

You may need to practice this every day for some time before you really begin to feel the inner glow of fire which warms, comforts and inspires you, and a new sense of belonging, to yourself, to your world, and to the planet. You are taking possession of your bodysoul.

About Your Soul

As you become accustomed to doing this exercise, you will begin to feel more comfortable in your body, less dependent on figuring things out, and you may begin to feel your inner voice becoming stronger. That inner voice is the voice of your soul. It is the unique amalgam of body and spirit which has united for this lifetime, this adventure on Earth. It is your soul which will carry the lessons you have learned in this life back to the Greater Soul which awaits you "on the other side" when this life is done. There, in the realm of unconditional love, you will discover what God really is, and we will all learn what this life was really meant to accomplish.

These exercises are intended to stir and awaken that bodysoul which has been waiting for your attention and love. As you begin to recognize the presence of your soul, which is usually seated somewhere between your throat and your genitals, you will be able to experience it as a living part of yourself, as much so as your stomach or your liver (and more). As you recognize and admire it, you may begin to feel joy.

Walt Whitman was a deeply spiritual and abundantly joyful poet, the self-proclaimed bard for America, Democracy and Faith. In his day, he called his spirituality "religion." I will use the more current term "spirituality" to describe the profound sense of joy and belonging you will feel when you forge deep connections with your body, your heart, your soul, the Earth and the Higher Power(s). All these things are a part of the experience of being fully human, fully alive.

In *Leaves of Grass*, Whitman celebrates the connections between body and soul, Earth and Spirit: His first lines describe what has been referred to here as bodysoul.

> "I have said that the soul is not more than the body,
> And I have said that the body is not more than the soul,
> And nothing, not God, is greater to one than one's self is,
> And whoever walks a furlong without sympathy walks to his
> own funeral drest in his shroud,
> And I or you pocketless of a dime may purchase the pick of
> the earth,
> And to glance with an eye or show a bean in its pod confounds
> the learning of all times,
> And there is no trade or employment but the young man
> following it may become a hero,
> And there is no object so soft but it makes a hub for the
> wheel'd universe,
> And I say to any man or woman, Let your soul stand cool and
> composed before a million universes.

In "Song of Myself" he describes the sense of abundance and trust in the goodness of life which strong faith brings:

> "Why should I wish to see God better than this day?
> I see something of God each hour of the twenty-four, and
> each moment then,
> In the faces of men and women I see God, and in my own
> face in the glass,
> I find letters from God dropt in the street, and every one is
> signed by God's name,

And I leave them where they are, for I know that wheresoe'er
    I go,
Others will punctually come for ever and ever."

Whitman felt the intimate connection with the God in all things, and the sense of being one with the Universe in a very direct and immediate way. This is our goal here, to forge deep connections to the source of all things, by living as a complete and sacred being—the whole, aware human we were meant to be.

The exercises you do to make connections with your heart and soul are best done in private, until you begin to get the hang of it. Most of us have been distracted by the hubbub around us, so at first it is important to create a place of solitude for yourself, however small, to concentrate on your journey inward.

However, this is just the first step. Faith is not a sentimental emotional fog, centered on pleasant bodily feelings. It is action. Use your newfound sense of security within to reach out with camaraderie and good will to others. You will be a welcome breath of fresh air and Light to those around you. They too have souls, and the need to fulfill the promise of a life well-lived. For each of us, that need is to love, and to create. If our love is filled with compassion and kindness, we will come close to the unconditional love which is Light, or Spirit. If we create beautifully, whether it is in the act of creating and loving a child, or planting a garden in synchrony with Nature, or building a beautiful building in harmony with the Earth, or carving a sculpture which reminds others of their tender feelings, we are doing sacred work. In the act of creation, our souls will sing with fulfillment.

Do not do this work in secret. Introduce it to your children, your partner, your sister, your friends, your hairdresser and your yoga instructor. They will help you, or it will help them. Nearly everyone has forgotten their sacred promise to come to this life not to earn or accumulate material possessions, but to love and to create. Some will hear the resounding truth in your words, and in your work. They too may catch fire with the forgotten need to fulfill the life they came here to live. It is never to late to begin living that authentic life. We are given complete free will, to succeed or fail, to stumble or soar. What you live, you teach. Do your own meditations with a sincere and open heart.

Then, tell your doctor. Teach an exercise to your neighbor or your kids' teachers.

Keep on doing these exercises, trusting your heart and quieting your mind, until your soul, freed from the destroyer within and without, is free to learn, to develop, and to rejoice.

THE WINDS OF FATE
By Ella Wheeler Wilcox

One ship drives east and another drives west
With the selfsame winds that blow.
    'Tis the set of the sails
      And not of the gales
Which tells us the way to go.

Like the winds of the sea are the ways of fate,
As we voyage along through life;
    'Tis the set of a soul
      That decides its goal,
And not the calm or the strife.

Chapter Twenty-Eight

LEARNING FORGIVENESS

When it comes to an encounter with a Child of Darkness, or anyone who has wronged you for that matter, forgiveness is a complicated issue.

Let's first define what we mean by forgiveness. The Oxford English Dictionary defines it as "to grant free pardon and to give up all claim on account of an offense or debt." Like other dictionary definitions of the concept, this leaves a lot to be interpreted, or misinterpreted. It does not tell us what will ensue in the relationship between the offended party and the offender.

The Role of Forgiveness in Racial Relations

On a large scale, forgiveness has been a tool for bringing peace to areas of the world where civil conflict tore countries apart. In some cases, it has been the route to peace, as in South Africa. It is also being attempted in Rwanda. The peace pacts rely on international exposure and a combination of rebalancing power and inspiring forgiveness on the part of the victims. This process is considered successful if it reaches its intended goal of a state of rapprochement in which all parties can feel secure in their safety and can go on with their lives in civil cooperation with one another. They can cooperate because they have laid down their weapons; the danger they presented to one another has passed, and the prospect of endless revenge has been forsworn. This would not be possible without the reciprocal type of forgiveness—making peace, and agreeing to be friends again, in spite of the past. The presence of powerful outside parties encourages compliance.

In the U.S., affirmative action programs began in 1965 to encourage employers and educational institutions to provide opportunities for minorities based on population percentages. These programs were designed to rebalance access to economic and social opportunities for the large population of Black citizens who would not otherwise have been accepted at higher levels in the job market, in politics, and in higher education programs. The results were dramatic. Blacks began to climb the economic ladder in larger and larger numbers. Although these programs have helped to some extent, the U.S. has never officially apologized to Black people for its part in accepting and promoting slavery.

Without this offer of reconciliation, there is no opportunity for the Black community to come forward to accept an apology and to offer forgiveness for the crimes they suffered at the hand of our white ancestors. Without openly accepting responsibility for the policies and laws which supported slavery and subsequent discriminatory practices, the American people remain in the stage of denial which does not allow for relations between the races to evolve toward forgiveness, and then reconciliation.

Native Americans have been treated just as badly, with the added insult that history books still crow triumphantly about Columbus "discovering" America, as if no one of consequence lived here before the white conquerors. Battles between settlers and "Indians" are still reported as if the settlers were somehow entitled to invade and take over other peoples' lands. Armed resistance on the part of the native defenders is generally described as more brutal and vicious because it involved murder with hatchets and arrows rather than guns. Given our history of massacre and abuse of power in our earliest relationships as a newly forming country, it is remarkable that the concept of democracy was able to rise at all from the ashes of destruction.

Relationships of all kinds tend to evolve and change. Relations between and among the settlers of the United States, including recent immigrants from South America, present new opportunities for either virulent racism or new levels of cooperation and forgiveness. Our foreign policies have helped to create the misery many of these people are escaping from, and again we have yet to apologize for our imperialistic corporate practices which have helped to impoverish the countries from which they come.

The United States is in need of forgiveness. Unfortunately, we are still stuck in the denial, self-righteousness and blaming-others phase in a downward spiral into Darkness. Unwilling to accept responsibility for our own Abusive behavior and the misery it has caused, we have spread our Abusive practices and values across the globe. We have proudly encouraged the growth of "developing" Wannabe nations who now imitate our aggressive form of capitalism with its accompanying environmental destruction. And yet, Americans are prevented by arrogance and denial from seeing any resentment toward us as warranted. We will not apologize, therefore we cannot expect forgiveness.

As a country, we have behaved heartlessly, showing the characteristics of a Child of Darkness. If we were to apply the same techniques for change presented here to our country as we have used for our own growth, we would need to reach deeply into the spiritual and philosophical roots of our beginnings as a democracy—to the soulbody which was the original best of what we are. At its heart, democracy stands for equality and fairness, the political version of compassion and empathy. With compassion and fairness comes humility, and the ability to acknowledge your own divine best and worst qualities and to ask for forgiveness for the times when our worst qualities turned Dark.

It is a strength to ask for forgiveness and to accept forgiveness when it is offered. Perhaps if our leaders are too belligerent and arrogant to ask for forgiveness and make amends to those we have injured, we can do it as a society of strong individuals. We can begin to treat everyone we meet as if they really mattered, and do our best to create real opportunity for people whose ancestors suffered as a result of our country's institutionalized racism. We can begin the conversation about how sorry we are for what our country did in the past, and we can apologize. Then, together with the people we have injured, we can begin to forgive ourselves. As we turn together toward the Light, we will once more begin to grow.

Forgiveness Up Close

There is another less common definition of forgiveness: one which involves a deep kind of resignation and acceptance. Miriam-Webster defines it as "to cease to feel resentment against (an offender)." It requires no action from the perpetrator. Everywhere, from talk shows to yoga magazines we hear advice promoting the idea that forgiveness is health-giving for the forgiver. This has frequently led to the assumption that forgiveness should therefore be applied across the board, whenever and wherever a person has been wronged. In other words, since "living with anger" or "carrying anger around forever" is unhealthy and bad, the only alternative is to forgive the abuser. This leads to a serious dilemma when the abuser is someone who viciously molested you as a child and is still close at hand, or someone who murdered your parents and is still roaming free.

There are cases where prosecuting a criminal is a pressing necessity, when society at large would be endangered otherwise. Letting a dangerous criminal go free and forgiven is not a higher level of spiritual development for the victim if it would put the criminal's or the victim's preferences above the larger community's safety. We must always refer to the "greater good" principle when these difficult moral questions come up. Pursuing justice for a crime done to you is often far more demanding and courageous than just "dropping it," and it helps to protect others who might be future victims. Legal prosecution and forgiveness are not mutually exclusive.

There are other important issues to consider besides the practical need to protect others. Often the most heinous of crimes, like the sexual abuse of a child, leaves the victim feeling shamed and guilty. These victims are likely to be inclined to forgo protecting themselves in favor of exonerating the abuser. This risks leaving them forever in the grip of reenacting the original abuses, either with the same abuser or others. Applying a blanket definition of forgiveness—assuming that the only righteous or "spiritual" way to resolve these issues is to reconcile with the abuser—is fundamentally unfair to the victim.

Forgiving the perpetrator in cases of personal abuse, while continuing a relationship with him or her requires an effortful suppression of natural instincts—to fight or flee—when one is attacked. It also requires suppression of a related lifesaving strategy, which is to be very cautious and wary around someone who has already shown himself to be dangerous.

To resolve the dilemma of forgiving an abuser who may still be threatening to the victim, it has been suggested that forgiveness has nothing to do with the other person—it is only a feeling or an idea which one can accomplish without reference to the actual person, even though that person may be alive and well, nearby and unrepentant. It is often assumed that this kind of forgiveness means absolving another for an offense done to us, without mending the relationship. This is incomplete unless we specify how the victim is to behave in relation to the abuser or how to deal with the day-to-day aftermath of the abuse. Otherwise, the whole exercise bears an eerie resemblance to the Humpty Dumpty scene in Alice in Wonderland, in which he says, "A word is whatever I say it is!" Any time we try to simply change our feelings without addressing the source of those feelings, we are denying intuition and the needs of the heart.

Now, let's get back to the difficult moral dilemma of trying to find peace when you have been victimized, and the abuser is either unrepentant or out of reach. First, we must accept—in the sense of absolute resignation—that the perpetrator really has committed the inhuman acts you experienced, and you really were the innocent victim of those actions. It happened, and it is over. Accept also that their actions are simply an extension of who they are. You did not personally make them the way they are, you did not cause them to commit their crimes, and it is not your responsibility to change them.

If the perpetrator's actions are abhorrent and relatively consistent, then that is the kind of behavior they are likely to show in the future. For example, many perpetrators of sexual abuse of children have been extremely resistant to reform, and therefore need to be monitored carefully by the authorities. In the case of religious figures who preyed on children, the reluctance to address those crimes and to appropriately restrain the abusers led to generations of pain and heartache for victims. Only when the scandal was brought to light and to the courts were the victims publicly acknowledged to be truly innocent, and truly wronged. At last the criminal actions were identified for what they really were.

Focusing on the attacker, and not taking personal responsibility for someone else's crime absolves the truly innocent victim (as in a rape or child molestation), and helps them to accept that it was not their fault. It does the same for someone who suffered verbal abuse, especially when it began in childhood. This includes repetitive experiences in which the child is made to feel inadequate, insecure, or seriously emotionally disrupted.

To forgive others, you must first forgive yourself—for your own mistakes, for not having been stronger or wiser or more loving, and even for not having been able to forgive. Acknowledge your own innocence, and let go of the anger and shame. You no longer need it to justify your own self-worth. This will take you a long way toward feeling inner peace.

The next part of the challenge involves complete acceptance of what happened. In addition to forgiving God, we must also forgive what might have been, what should have been, and what was lost. To do this, we must adopt a radical, absolute form of acceptance, completely absorbing the following truths:

1. It happened. (Not: "Maybe I was just too sensitive," or "Maybe I made it up")
2. It was heinous. (Not: "She couldn't help it. She had a bad childhood" or "He didn't really mean it.")
3. Many heinous acts are not reconcilable. There is no reason or rationale by which to explain it away or make it better. (If you have used the experience to become stronger, more empathic, that is a good thing, but it is not the reason it happened.)
4. It was what it was. It cannot be changed.
5. Forgiveness as radical acceptance is unconditional, requiring nothing of the other. It is an action of the heart, not an economic transaction.

We need not absolve the attacker. What they did was wrong. We must instead work to make peace with the losses, the scars, and the regrets for what we lost. Having experienced severe trauma leaves its mark, like a warp in the personality, which shapes how we see the world, what matters most to us, and how we will respond to it. This is not a bad thing. Once healed, we can become effective and empathic champions for kindness and compassion. We can use our resultant knowledge and strong will to help prevent the abuse of others.

In this way, victims of abuse have the option to go on with exceedingly productive lives, knowing that the abuse is not punishment for some inner defect or unrevealed crime, but rather an example of one of life's great challenges. It offers the opportunity to grow by finding the way to healing, restoring a sense of equilibrium, and going on with an open heart. This is a great hurdle for anyone who has suffered severe abuse. Remaining angry and bitter toward the abuser keeps you in a closed-down, preoccupied state which prevents the freedom to love wholeheartedly. It also keeps you in a closed-loop relationship in which the abuser is the most important person in your life.

Here is where a little "behavior therapy" works very well. Do not wait for your healing to happen to you. Get back on the horse. Invest in feeling. Do something that will bring fulfillment to your sore heart by taking action to be of service to others. Forgiveness opens the door to the feelings which naturally follow. As you turn from licking your wounds, look outward for ways to express your increasingly expansive feelings. You may even begin to feel differently toward your Tormentor, who is so utterly without any route to genuine happiness or fulfillment in his or her own life. Eventually, you may find yourself feeling a kind of impersonal human compassion for a being who is so bereft of the pleasures of being a human among other humans, unable to join in building and creating with others.

At the same time, you may feel a renewed commitment to take action in some larger way to change your family dynamics, the culture or the world at large which has allowed so many of us to be treated so badly, so young. An act of service which benefits a child is the greatest contribution you can make. Singing a song to a child who is disturbed and can't sleep, for instance, teaches the child that someone cares about their well-being, and that the world is a friendly place. Hearing a soothing song introduces the child to the experience of music and its healing properties, opening a channel for life-long satisfaction and pleasure. Experiencing the comfort of sleep teaches the child to accept his or her body processes as natural and pleasing. Being of service to an adult is important, but a simple act of kindness toward a child has a formative effect on that child's experience of life and their ability to love and to forgive. As the old saying goes, "First teach your children to forgive, because you're going to need it."

Begging Forgiveness

The most important relationships in life evolve and change over time. Partnerships may grow and flourish, or dissolve in bitter rancor, depending on whether the people involved are capable of asking for and offering forgiveness. Most long-lasting relationships will at some point encounter severe storms in which one party may feel deeply wronged.

What if you are the one who has committed the offense that left a loved one in pain? How will you overcome your guilt, shame and defensiveness enough to reach out to the one you have hurt? This is perhaps the greatest of all challenges. Denial, pride, self-pity and righteous self-justification all stand in the way of simply acknowledging your wrong-doing and begging the one you have wronged for their forgiveness. What if they refuse? What if your crime has turned their heart to ice? What if you can't restore your love to its former comfortable trust and companionship? Would you rather suffer in guilt and conflict than to lose the structure of the partnership you built? These questions most often arise when one partner has had an affair or a brief fling, or when one has betrayed the other's trust by unilaterally making decisions which affect the family's well-being in a profound way. Gambling, drug addiction, financial recklessness, arguments in which one humiliates or belittles the other, even an extreme preoccupation with one's work, all risk leaving the partner feeling deeply betrayed.

Now it is the opportunity for the guilty one to make the decision to turn shame into love. Deep in our heart of hearts we know when we have done wrong. Our initial reaction would be remorse, if it were not for our Ego and its accompanying feeling, pride. Instead, we convert the pure feeling of remorse—genuine regret—into guilt. Guilt is a problematic combination of anger, shame, and fear which leaves us unable to reach out in a creative, constructive way to heal the rift.

The opposite of guilt is humility. It is opposite because of the large component of self-hatred and anger embedded in the guilt which lead to blaming and escaping blame, denying the importance or the wrongness of the action while simultaneously blaming the other for some feeling or action which may have been a precursor to the guilty act. All these maneuvers disguise a secret sense of denial based in superiority. The result may linger as resentment on both sides—the perpetrator who has been caught in a destructive act, and the loved one who feels injured by it. This gnarly dead-end can only be undone when the one who has committed the glaring wrong is able to truly acknowledge their destructive actions, while humbly searching their own heart and soul for the darkest of dark intentions. It is only when we are able to admit to ourselves, and then to others, that we really were acting out of selfishness or fear or both, in a blind act of self-indulgence, that we are finally able to put down the burden of shame and denial.

At the turning point where we accept our own destructive impulses and beg forgiveness of those we have hurt, we can start over new, with resolve and hope which grows out of the humility. Finally, in the act of acknowledging our own failings, compassion and love can begin to grow. This creates the fertile ground which makes it possible to change. When self-blame and denial dissolve into compassion for yourself and your partner, the energy of love rekindles hope, and the possibility of an entirely new sense of strength and resolve. In the light of loving yourself, weaknesses and all, you can begin to see others more kindly as well.

Of course, begging forgiveness is the same as offering an apology—it means you will never, ever do it again. If you cannot find it in your heart to honestly change your ways, then asking forgiveness or offering apologies is nothing more than a manipulation. Going down that path will quickly qualify you for Abusive Personality status. Do not beg for forgiveness of a loved one unless you have discovered in yourself the strength of character to make your promises stick.

As with other Dark inclinations, like depression and self-hatred, turn outward to those you have harmed to try to make it up to them in any way you can. Do something to make their lives better. Change your energy from hang-dog guilt to Light, and they will do the same. Service to others does not simply mean helping strangers or giving to charity. Here is the application for the old adage, "Charity begins at home." Be the generosity and good will you wish to receive, and keep it up until the ones you love learn to trust you once more, and are able to forgive you without fear of being hurt again.

Forgiveness, like love, is an action, not simply the internal experience of a sentiment. Once you have healed the rift in your own family, continue by taking action to help others who have been victimized. Create an environment for a child so that his humanity will be nourished in a way that yours was not, allowing both of you to grow. With greater understanding and an open heart, a new kind of forgiveness, born of the amalgam of radical acceptance, humble accountability and soul-lifting service to others, can begin to grow.

Chapter Twenty-Nine

ALL YOU NEED IS LOVE

The Beatles were right, of course, but most people interpret their wonderful lyrics—all you need is love—to mean that you only need someone to love you, and you will be just fine. This is not true, and it is a dangerous ambition to pursue. It gets you into the kinds of relationships we have been talking about here. If you're pursuing love, you're liable to pursue it in all the wrong places, and all the wrong people. That project is fruitless, frustrating, and endless, as we have seen. Instead, let's turn it around: We all need to love. Let's look at what expectations would be reasonable, and what conditions we need to embrace in order to learn to love *happily*.

Love in Action

First, we must acknowledge the following simple truths:

1) Love doesn't hurt. If you are feeling anxious or depressed or hurt on a regular basis, something is terribly wrong. Look deeply into your heart of hearts to make sure you're not being unreasonably demanding or needy. While you're there, make sure this is not a family tradition. If not, you're dealing with an Abuser, or at least someone who is working hard to make you miserable. Save yourself, and don't look back.
2) Loving someone who is reliable and kind is not dangerous. If you are feeling a powerful gut-wrenching adrenaline surge in anticipation of seeing your lover, it is probably not love, it is fear.

3) Loving someone who is kind to you is not boring. You would only be tempted to think that if you are used to the kind of relationship described in 2), above.

4) A good relationship does not "take work," at least not much of it. If you are constantly struggling with each other, something is dreadfully wrong. Get help immediately, especially if children are involved, or give it up.

5) A long-lasting happy relationship is based on one elemental principle: mutual respect and decent treatment, both ways. You need only one simple rule to govern all your interactions, your arguments or disagreements: Never say or do anything to your partner which will humiliate or diminish them, or deprive them of their personal freedom, and they must do the same. No exceptions.

6) No fair complaining. If you find you are tempted to frequently grumble and whine to friends, relatives and confidants about your relationship, or you can see yourself on a battling-couples TV show, ask yourself what sort of martyrdom you are aiming for. If that doesn't interest you, go back to 4), and take action, now.

And most important of all:

7) The person you love is not responsible for your happiness, your mood, or your psychological well-being. You are. If you are not happy, do something. This does not mean you should try harder to change your partner. Assume they will remain pretty much as they are for the duration. Either accept and love them wholeheartedly as they are, or move on and stop the torture.

Here is Elizabeth Barrett Browning's plea for unconditional love:

SONNET XIV

If thou must love me, let it be for nought
Except for love's sake only. Do not say
"I love her for her smile—her look—her way
Of speaking gently,—for a trick of thought
That falls in well with mine, and certes brought
A sense of pleasant ease on such a day"—

For these things in themselves, Beloved, may
Be changed, or change for thee,—and love so wrought,
May be unwrought so. Neither love me for
Thine own dear pity's wiping my cheeks dry,—

A creature might forget to weep, who bore
Thy comfort long, and lose thy love thereby!
But love me for love's sake, that evermore
Thou mayst love on, through love's eternity.

   —from *Sonnets from the Portuguese.*

CHAPTER THIRTY

LEAD WITH AN OPEN HEART

When we suffer too many blows to our young selves, we learn not to rely on what our hearts tell us, not because it is inaccurate, but because it tells us what we do not want to know. When the one we love is also a threat, we must turn away from our best instincts, discredit the heart's truth, relying instead on our ability to figure out, calculate, rationalize, and argue with ourselves. As a culture, we have become severely top-heavy and out of touch, after long years of training as Head People.

The brain is in charge of ego functions that helped us survive. It then becomes the faculty we rely on as a replacement for heart-intelligence if we have been overly stressed in early life. We become talking Heads, preoccupied with fancy intellectualizations, proud of our prize-winning analyses, and certain in the conviction that if we can just know everything, we can control everything. Then we will never be hurt again. Wrong. This approach is not only life-consuming and fruitless. It separates us from the power of our emotional intelligence. We got this way because of fear.

Most people think that having an open heart means you'll be vulnerable. It has become a popular term in New Age coaching-type counseling methods, where "making yourself vulnerable" to another person is considered a good and generous thing. Why would anyone want to do something that is so emotionally dangerous? It sounds less appealing than being asked to stroll through dark alleys at night with your eyes closed, or to relive all the terrifying elements that made childhood unbearable. It was just that feeling—vulnerability—which made most of us want to close our hearts and bury our heads under the covers in the first place. Let's call it having an open heart and an open mind. It does not make you more vulnerable, because you are an adult. It does make you more loving and friendly.

Keeping your heart closely guarded may prevent you from becoming deeply involved with another person, out of fear of being hurt (again). It also leads to a lonely life. Should you decide to venture into a love relationship, you will bring distrust and fear into the encounter, causing the other person to feel frustrated and unappreciated. The good news for those people who have responded to the trials in their past by shutting down is this:

The thing you fear already happened. It's over, in the past. You survived. As long as you are here, breathing and alive, with even a tiny connection to the capacity for warmth and love in your heart, you can recover and go on, whole and loving and joyful, because your soul is intact, ready and waiting to join you. As you reclaim your heart and bodysoul—your true self-system—you will become stronger.

Remember this: Since you are no longer small, you are no longer "vulnerable." Unless you persist in a state of time-warp reenactment of childhood emotion, you will not feel devastated or broken. Of course you can be disappointed, but it will never have the same overwhelming effect it had when you were a child. Paradoxically, when you weather the troubles life sends you with an open heart, it has the opposite effect. Each time you pick yourself up, brush yourself off and go on, you become sturdier, like metal that has been forged in fire.

Combine this strength from having been forged in the crucible of life with your well-developed radar, and you can quietly and calmly read the environment the way a dog sniffs the breeze. You will be as close to invulnerable as a human being can get. Of course, this does not mean that henceforth you will never have a problem. The Universe determines the external things, not us. You might find your life becomes even more like a roller-coaster, but you will find the ride exhilarating and fulfilling as well as challenging.

Heart Truth

Let's redefine what it means to live with an open heart. First, it implies the capacity to love another person or people, without unreasonable fear of disappointment or hurt. For anyone who has been severely hurt in a previous relationship, it means being willing to put the past where it belongs, and not bring forward earlier feelings and impose them onto present relationships. It also means having the capacity to live truthfully and authentically, without need for deception, manipulation, shame or shyness when it comes to dealing with others. Living with an open heart means creativity and intuition are a way of life; passion, conviction and resolve flow organically from the center of your being. These are human qualities, available to anyone who is open and free.

If you were lucky enough to come out of childhood with your creativity and freedom intact, good for you. Carry on, but be compassionate toward those who were not so fortunate. For even the strongest survivor these qualities are not easy to sustain when you have been raised with the constant barrage of well-meaning childhood reminders to "Use your head," "Be careful," "Be polite" (in other words, lie when someone doesn't want to hear the truth), and above all, "Don't take risks." Once we are adults, these admonitions evolve into "Don't wear yourself out," and "Slow down. You'll have a heart attack." The fact is, when you're doing something you love, you will probably be filled with energy and enthusiasm. If you learned to be shy and fearful, shake it off and be the bright light you were meant to be. The endorphin-charge will not kill you. In fact, it's good for you, so go on, throw caution to the winds and create something beautiful.

The following sections will offer some basic suggestions to help you restore those free-flowing qualities in yourself.

Having an Open Heart Does Not Make You Vulnerable

First, let's look at why everyone thinks that having an open heart, or allowing themselves to love another person, makes them vulnerable. All children are at the mercy of all adults—parents, teachers, babysitters, neighbors, ministers and priests, older siblings and extended family members, the bus driver, the crossing guard and the coach, to name a few. We are dependent, helpless, and utterly without the resources to take care of ourselves. We feel vulnerable, because we are. That vulnerability is the result of being small, in a world where almost everyone is bigger and more powerful than we are. At the same time, young children face the world with an open heart. We love our parents no matter what they do. We look up to the people who take care of us, because it is in our nature to follow them, listen carefully to what they say to us and about us. We turn over our hearts and our selves to them, trusting because we have no other choice.

Because children think associatively, if they are mistreated they conclude: being loving and being hurt go together. Because they happened at the same time, the child concludes that loving equals vulnerability. (This is similar to the correlation fallacy in logic. If the door slams and the phone rings, we cannot accurately assume that one caused the other.) Suffering severe disappointment and pain in childhood leads us to conclude that being open is what led to being hurt. Nothing could be farther from the truth. Being open or not, loving or not is hardly relevant. It is being small that makes you vulnerable.

Now that you are no longer small, you could continue to generate the feeling of vulnerability if you insist on it, but you are not vulnerable the way a child is. So go ahead. Tell her you love her. Give him flowers. You'll never know how wonderful it might be unless you give it a chance.

When you begin to open your heart, you also open yourself to a sense of wonder at the mysteries of how our paths meander through complex and varied interactions with other people. The events of our lives seem to be tailor-made to offer the challenges we need to grow. Flowing with life's currents while you steer your own course through good times and bad allows you to accumulate skill and faith. The Universe will not deal you a challenge you cannot eventually manage. In the process, you will provide opportunities for others to grow as they interact with you.

Look back over the course of your life so far, and allow yourself the satisfaction of knowing that however difficult the events behind you might have been, you are here now, able to learn and grow. That in itself is a triumph. Do not criticize yourself for not having done better, or for having made mistakes, or for taking too long. We do the best we can with what we know at the time. Demanding more of yourself than you were capable of is a futile exercise in self-hatred. Use your current strength and knowledge to rise above the judgmental disapproval you might be inclined to inflict on yourself. It is the only way to move on.

Intuition Is Your Inner Guide

Living with an open heart as an adult gives you greater abilities to protect yourself from being hurt because it acts as a working companion with intuition. You won't find the intuition system in an anatomy book, but it is there in us, in the connection between heart and bodysoul. Here I am taking liberties with the biological details. I am using the term "heart" to include our capacity to love as well as the intuitive capabilities we have, whether they express themselves in our heart, our gut, our brain centers or our bones. Probably it is a combination of intricately balanced and interconnected physical and metaphysical abilities. When people are asked where love comes from, they always point to their hearts. When asked about intuition, many people point to a place on their chests, near the bottom of the rib cage. If you look, you will find it. It is what makes it possible for us to experience faith, and to know when something just "feels right." This is our trusty soul-guide, the lifelong companion which will help protect us through the most difficult times if we allow it.

It is one of the tragedies of our culture that we are relentlessly trained to disregard our powerful intuitive abilities in favor of arguing with ourselves in our heads. Make a list of pros and cons, we are told. Then add them up to make the important decisions in your life. You will thereby leave out the very sources of information which are most reliable: your "gut feelings," and what you know in your heart. We have become so enamored with "rational thinking" that we have lost our ability to trust in our own senses. We dare not put our faith in the things we perceive on our own. Instead, we have been taught to rely only on scientific "evidence," or barring that, we prefer to rely on corroboration by others. Here is an everyday example: Even though almost everyone has had the experience of knowing when someone is looking at them from behind, we persist in describing such abilities as weird, occult, or magical, as if it could not possibly be reliable information. Never mind. You know when your intuitions have been accurate, and if you stop to credit your own good senses, you will notice how reliable and protective they really are.

The capacity for intuition in humans is like radar in bats; we can detect emotional vibes at a distance, using our bodysoul as our guidance system. See trouble ahead, and you will automatically swerve to avoid it. A person whose emotional orientation is primarily malevolent will make the hair on the back of your neck stand on end. The kind of "bad boy" so many people find attractive would repel someone whose heart/intuition radar is online and sensitively tuned. A "femme fatale" would appear as just that: a deadly, transparent mockery of genuine attractiveness and love. Neither would inspire attraction or love, unless your heart is shut down. Walking around with your heart closed is as safe as walking around with your eyes shut and your ears plugged. You will not sense danger when it is coming, and you will not protect yourself. You are then much more likely to blunder into a disastrous relationship where disappointment and pain are inevitable, but which would have been prevented had you noticed and believed your initial muffled warning signs.

The True Self System

You will find as you begin the journey of leading with your heart that you will often be confused about whether the information you feel emerging in yourself comes from your heart or your head. Here is a rule of thumb which helps in the beginning: If you hear yourself repeating something that sounds like a rule you may have absorbed in childhood, like "You shouldn't be lazy.", or "Your messy room (or your addiction to chocolate) is a reflection of lax morals," put your foot down. Refuse to be distracted and depressed by old strictures and moralistic pronouncements. Generally, anything that sounds like an argument or self-criticism is a Head-game, designed to focus your judgmental attention on *you*. The ultimate goal, a challenge for anyone raised in our mind-obsessed culture, is to get out of your head.

Being "in your head," the state of thinking-without-feeling which has been so lauded in our educational system as "rationality" is in fact a state of being which goes hand in hand with an over inflated Ego. Instead of tying yourself in knots worrying about yourself, turn your attention outward, and just feel your way, listening quietly, tuning in to your heart's and your body's signals. This is a learning process. Just as with the exercises to dispel anxiety and depression, the more you practice, and the more you increase your awareness, the easier and the more fulfilling it becomes. You will begin to notice and appreciate emotional nuances in the people around you, and you will be free to respond accordingly.

Here is a way of picturing the True Self system, embodying the qualities of heart and intuition discussed above:

1) Heart, the commander, is in charge of guiding us through life. In concert with our intuitive sensors (our bodysoul), our heart makes contact with others on a deep emotional level, resonating with the electrical energy from other people, animals, the Earth, and Spirit.

2) The bodysoul, second in line, and most in danger of being ignored, is the source of intuition and the connection to Spirit. It is the well-spring of creativity, ancestral wisdom and Universal truth.

3) The body, third in line, allows us to experience this material existence. In charge of satisfying the heart's yearnings, it implements what the heart wants and needs, carrying out the acts of service to others, performing the dance, painting the picture, celebrating sex, and so on.

4) The brain (in service to the other three) is fourth in line, our information-storage tool. It records and remembers the useful knowledge we need to find food and shelter, drive the car, and procure the necessary materials to build, create, and accomplish what the heart and bodysoul desire. Here is where education is of great value. A broad understanding of the world and what it offers is invaluable when we want to create something meaningful. We must learn the steps, master the language, draw up the plans, write the proposals, gather the team, contact the appropriate experts, then act on what we know. None of these abilities makes the brain an effective decision-making tool. It is the computer, not the designer.

Returning to the Light

Now let's add a very basic approach to the world which will allow you to flow through life without being defeated by "the slings and arrows of outrageous fortune," as Shakespeare put it. As you breathe deeply and gently, feel the energy you produce in your own body engine, flowing through your veins, nourishing you and sustaining you. Feel your way back to the center of your brain where you can position yourself in the channel where the energy of Spirit flows through you, down through your brain, through the center of your heart, through your bodysoul, and into the Earth beneath your feet. Anchor yourself to the Earth, solidly, comfortably a part of the energy you share with all other life forms. Allow the Light of unconditional love to flow down through your entire system. Feel your heart pumping the love through your arteries to every cell in your body, nourishing every part of you. Breathe that love, and as you do, you will begin to emanate the light energy in ripples outward, soothing and calming others in your presence. This alone is a gentle positive contribution to the environment around you.

This higher energy vibration, the combination of inner peace, breathing light and unconditional love, produces a powerful force-field. It is at once the greatest protection against Darkness and the greatest creative force for Light an individual can generate. The more individuals combine their energy to create a high-vibration environment, the less power or attraction Darkness has.

Light one candle in a room, and darkness is dispelled. Light 100 candles and Darkness completely disappears.

As your connection becomes stronger, you will be able to direct the Light energy through your body, nourishing and healing the people, animals and plants you touch, and they can heal you as well. Practice this every day, clearing your channels and increasing your ability to channel Light as you learn. You have the rest of your life to enjoy perfecting this skill.

Don't Take It Personally

An active modern life does not allow us to spend long hours every day in meditation, practicing our strength and balance before we enter the fray that is everyday life. We must also have skills to help us ride out mundane frustrations, personal attacks, and unforeseen blows. We need a perspective from which to view those challenges which will allow us to maintain our dignity and our equilibrium.

As you meet others along your path, be aware that each one you meet is also traveling along their path, learning their own lessons, responding to their bumps in the road. You can never know the whole of what makes another person respond to you, or to life, in a particular way. Each person is unique. No two people will respond to the same event in identical ways. We may reach some agreement, but that does not mean our experience is the same. Keep this in mind when you assess the other person's reaction to you. You are not the center of their experience. They also have a self, and may be struggling to keep an open heart even more than you are. Perhaps they have been so bruised and battered in life that they are not able to see clearly, or to be generous. Perhaps they have not had access to help along the way, or certain advantages of time, place, or economics you have had. Emotional scars do not appear on the outside.

Don't take it personally when someone else behaves badly, even if it is toward you. Breathe, move back into the center of your brain where you are surrounded by your own intelligence, breathe into your heart, and anchor yourself downward, putting your roots down into the Earth, where you will feel welcomed and embraced.

Many arguments and misunderstandings begin with someone lashing out at another person for no other reason than they are having a bad day, or the person reminds them of their mother. It could even be because the other person makes them feel jealous or inadequate because of their obvious success or generosity or goodness.

It is not a reflection on you if someone else behaves in a hostile or angry way. It is about them, their perceptions, their feelings, and their decision to respond in a certain way. Knowing this, you may even find yourself feeling surprisingly compassionate toward people who eliminate themselves from your good graces by attacking you or betraying you. They will behave toward others in similar ways, and will destroy friendships and opportunities for real contact in their lives, until they learn to approach others with greater understanding and generosity. It is not your problem, but you may feel sorry they are creating such chaos and loss for themselves.

If you find yourself saying, "I would never do something like that," or "How could they do that to me?" you are actually saying they should be like you. They are not like you, and most people will not take it kindly to be told they should not be who they are, but should be more like you, no matter what the issue is. We must each find our own way, in our own time. Therefore, when someone does something insulting or disappointing or cruel, it is important to keep your balance, breathe, and tell yourself, "It's not about me." Of course this assumes you have been scrupulously honest in your dealings and have not done anything unfair or unreasonable to cause this reaction in the other person.

If you are completely comfortable in the knowledge that the trouble did not start with you, then let it be. You do not need to argue, justify, or defend yourself against something that is not about you. You will probably want to respond if it is a serious insult, but keep it simple, direct, and without fanfare. A statement like, "This incident convinces me that I no longer want to have anything to do with you," or "I can no longer respect you or trust you because of what you did to me" is far more powerful than a screaming match filled with accusations and recriminations. Walk away with your dignity intact, and you are free to move on to more satisfying relationships.

You may meet people who flatter you with compliments about how wonderful you are when they hardly know you. It's nicer than being inexplicably attacked, but it is just as inappropriate. Do not assume that just because someone professes to love you, or is attracted to you, that they truly see you for who you are.

Not taking things personally does not mean that you care any less about what is happening around you. It is not about feeling less or refusing to express anger when it is appropriate. It is simply a shift in ascribing the source of volition in an interaction. It is a way of accurately acknowledging that you are not the source of all things, even all the things that happen to you. You are not the cause of everyone else's feelings, any more than you are the cause of the weather. This does not mean you are without impact on the events of your life. Far from it. We are free to interact and respond to others as we see fit, but it is helpful to know the limits of our power. Just as children need to know that they are not responsible for their parents' moods, we must also learn that we are not in charge of any one else's feelings. This does not make us less responsible for our own actions or our own feelings. Just the opposite. It frees us to be completely aware and considerate of the impact we have on others. It requires a delicate sense of balance to take full credit for your own impact on others without usurping their own responsibility for theirs.

A warning: Do not use this approach as an excuse to say to someone you care about that they are crazy or that their feelings are without merit, or to discount a heartfelt point of view by smugly proclaiming that since we each have our point of view, it's all relative anyway, so their personal opinion doesn't matter. This would be using a powerful tool to humiliate another.

If an argument is the result of a momentary lapse on the part of someone who truly does care about you, you will avoid a serious rift by remaining calm and asking them if there is something wrong, or if there's been a misunderstanding of some kind, rather than going into battle stance. Remember: It's not about you.

If you have even a slight suspicion that you might have played some part in the misunderstanding, ask. Be genuinely curious to know the other person's take on the incident. Do not let pride or stubbornness prevent you from exploring the misunderstanding further. In doing so, you demonstrate respect for the person you are dealing with. If you have done something which you now realize was thoughtless or unkind, apologize. Building a meaningful relationship takes courage and character, not pride. It matters not at all who is right and who is wrong. We are all in it together, in the end.

So, a basic program for surviving life's unpredictable relationship conflicts goes like this:

Lead with your heart, rely on your intuition, and don't take it personally.

OVER THERE
A hymn for John Lennon
by Makarta

When my short days on Earth are done,
I'll be going with Jesus to meet the sun.
O'er Earth's blue oceans we will fly
Like two comets in the sky.

Refrain:
>   Heartstrings play their lonely song
>   When parting early seemed so wrong.
>   Flying high over oceans blue,
>   Like an eagle with vision true,
>   I send my song back home to you.

Long nights alone I searched my soul
To understand how I could be whole,
Memory flooded my lonely heart and
The sins of my days took a heavy toll.

Refrain

Soaring thoughts lift my soul to God.
My poor body's gone now, beneath the sod.
Finding my voice in a new kind of way
Lifts my Earth-weary heart at the end of the day.

Refrain

Finding my way to the Light with regret,
Reluctant to leave, I wanted more yet,
Loving hands held me gently as I passed away
To the place where I now live from day to day.

Refrain

Over the rainbow where angels fly
There's a land that you've heard of where souls never die,
Where love and creation inspire each soul
Abundance and friendship are ever the rule.

Refrain

It's over, that lifetime, but much lies ahead
I'll raise up my song for the living and dead,
To help them find Light when they've come to an end
To lift their sore hearts and calm their dread.

Refrain

For life does not end with this one time on Earth.
We go on, far beyond, in our search for the truth
Meeting challenges still when our souls walk the path
Finding meaning and purpose and learning our worth.

Refrain

CHAPTER THIRTY-ONE

AWAKENING

"Destiny is not a matter of chance, it is a matter of choice; it is not a thing to be waited for, it is a thing to be achieved"

—William Jennings Bryan

Often people who have suffered pain or adversity try to explain the trauma in terms of God's will. The assumption is that you somehow deserved the misfortune. In this view of God, it is his business to reward and punish us directly, on the basis of his somewhat arbitrary and mysterious requirements for Man. Evil and sin are God's primary concerns, and it is his job to watch our every move and respond with vengeance when we step out of line. His punishment may be swift or delayed; we have no way of knowing when the axe will fall. Once this belief is in place, it is the ultimate trump card, of course. No argument to the contrary will override God's will. God's will is absolute, therefore punishment is inevitable. If this is truly the basis of your view of God, then no matter how often you are reminded of your own innocence, or your goodhearted actions, you cannot find peace if you truly believe God is punishing you.

My experience in working with hundreds of traumatized victims is that large numbers of those who are most embittered and depressed, unable to forgive or move on, are the same ones who hold ideas about divinely inspired punishments. In New Age language, it translates to karma as punishment for some past transgression. Regardless of how it is shaded, these foundational religious ideas create a backdrop for hopelessness, despair and (again) self-hatred. The same people who complain of depression and hopelessness acknowledge they are angry with God, and who could blame them, if God were the angry sadist many of us were taught to believe he is?

Until recently, psychologists have been reluctant to take a stand on any political or religious issue, especially where one might come into conflict with a client's closely held religious beliefs. Some psychologists have entered the arena of religious counseling, but challenging anyone's moral or religious beliefs has been considered beyond the pale.

However, in recent years it has become abundantly clear that moral people of any profession cannot remain above the fray where issues of human suffering are concerned. In 2008, a scandal appeared in the news concerning a number of psychologists who have held offices in the APA, the American Psychological Association. It became known that psychologists working for the government were closely involved in situations where the FBI was holding prisoners and interrogating them. These interrogations included the torture of "enemy combatants" whom the FBI felt might have useful information. The same psychologists were instrumental in discouraging a proposed APA resolution denouncing torture of every sort and prohibiting APA members from taking part in it in every case. (It has since been passed.) Their rationale for being there was that their presence provided an element of safety for prisoners. However, these same psychologists have been paid large sums for their services, by the very people whose behavior they were supposed to be overseeing. This would be completely contrary to the psychologists' Code of Ethics, which forbids working under conditions where a conflict of interest might sway one's judgment.

The psychologists in question not only violated the ethics code. They clearly did not provide the element of safety they claimed to offer, since the prisoners were tortured on their watch. If we pursue their contorted reasoning to its logical conclusion, we could allow that they might have prevented the prisoners from being killed, but should any psychologist, or any helping professional, be voluntarily taking part in a program where there is any likelihood of people being killed? Are they not providing a veil of legitimacy by their very presence? These are moral questions which resonate far beyond the present issue, echoing the same questions which were raised by Nazi concentration camp atrocities in which psychiatrists were central to providing expertise and legitimacy for illicit "research."

The conflict of interest rule is a good one, covering many situations where trouble might arise. We can apply it in our approach to religious issues. If the professional involved has some personal stake in the outcome, they should excuse themselves from the project. Otherwise, it is the responsibility of psychologists, teachers and other concerned adults to actively uphold standards of fairness and decency, whether this conflicts with a religious practice (or government program) or not. Recent examples include the U.S Congress taking a stand against the practice of genital mutilation, which has caused untold suffering to women across large areas of Africa and the Middle East. Any practice which inflicts long-lasting harm on vulnerable victims should be exempted from religious protections, and needs to be addressed as the abuse it is.

What about the traumatized and embittered people described above, whose belief system is apparently a cause of their current psychological pain, and who learned that belief system under the name of a religion? How are we to discuss healing from early wounds if we do not address the organized belief system—and the God in whose name those wounds were inflicted?

I have found that by the time an individual is aware of the connection between their own suffering and some of their early religious teachings, they are usually open to the possibility of seeing a kinder, gentler Spirit. We do not need to attack the traditions or beliefs themselves. Every major religion has imbedded in its teachings a positive view of love, charity, and good works in the service of sustaining the family and community. From there, we can tease apart the family and cultural traditions which may have promoted a punitive, authoritarian attitude, while highlighting the more benign religious teachings.

I have used the term spirituality throughout this book to describe a philosophy or way of life which is based in a positive view of a Higher Power (called, in various traditions, Great Spirit, Creator, God, or simply Spirit). It is a way of life which focuses on love, creativity and service to others. It implies an inclusive, egalitarian attitude. No dogma or specific traditions are implied by the term spirituality. The most basic premise in this kind of spiritual stance is that God represents the energy of unconditional love, is basically accepting and kind, has something mysteriously to do with this adventure we call life on Earth, and has our best interests at heart (our spiritual growth), even as we struggle with the many difficulties in our lives.

My Own Awakening

As you read along with me, perhaps you will find information that you can use in your own search.

Like many of us, I was raised in the tradition which encouraged church going, but it resulted in a mostly shame-ridden view of myself and the world. I did sometimes enjoy being in a church, especially an old stone one, where the stones echoed with the feelings of devotion and calm from generations past. I enjoyed the services, especially the singing, but I never found a sense of lasting peace from the teachings I met there. I especially disliked the emphasis on suffering I encountered in the many denominations I visited. I could not accept the Judeo-Christian view of an angry, punitive God. As a teenager, it occurred to me that many people seemed to develop a picture of God that bore a striking resemblance to the way their parents—especially their fathers—behaved. If God were as angry as my parents, we were all in trouble. I was able to distract myself from these depressing thoughts by immersing myself in my studies, but always I searched for greater understanding, and wondered if "faith" was just another form of delusion, or wishful thinking.

From time to time after that, I would experience inexplicable moments of clairvoyance, but because there was no "scientific" explanation I knew of, I disregarded it until a trip to France in the early 80's. On my first night in a ski resort town in the Alps, I was literally shaken awake in the middle of the night by the presence of a being who was not visible, but who was clearly transmitting feelings of great anguish and desperation. I awoke with tears streaming down my face, sobbing. The feelings I was experiencing were so intense and heart-wrenching, they could not possibly have come from within me. I was on vacation, delighted to be skiing and making new friends in a beautiful place.

Moments before, my dreams had vividly depicted a car plunging off a cliff in the small town where I was staying. Other information came through vividly as well—names, dates, pictures of people and places. I reassured the anguished presence, whom I somehow knew was a man, that I would try to learn about what he was showing me. I went back to sleep, only to see and feel more vivid, troubling images, including the words "deux ans" (two years), "chez Michael," "suicide," and the face of a man who was Chinese experiencing some kind of sexual mutilation.

In the morning, I asked my skiing guide if she knew of anyone who had committed suicide there. Her eyes grew wide and fearful. With much coaxing, and the help of others who had worked at the resort at the time, I finally was able to piece together the story: Two years before, a man whose son worked at the resort had come to see him, they had argued, and the father impulsively went up to his car and drove it off the side of the mountain. Apparently he had lived in a nearby town named Chinoise (Chinese), and his wife had left him for a woman (which apparently made him feel castrated). All the while, I felt the man's presence. As before, he exuded a feeling of desperation.

The second night of my stay, I again felt his intense sorrow, along with a pleading urgency. I told him I would try to find his family and tell them how sorry he was, but that he must not keep me awake because I had work to do the next day, and besides, he should have come to me before he drove off the cliff! The feelings stopped. I did try to search the official records, and was given the name of the wife and children, but I was never able to locate them. Her name was Janine Choucroux. I was told they had probably moved to England. I turned over the project to a young woman I had met who was very curious about the story, but I had the definite feeling that he had breathed a great sigh of relief when I said I knew he was sorry and wanted to apologize for the pain he had caused his family. I never heard from him again. I believe that the compassion I expressed allowed him to pass over.

As I was leaving the resort, on impulse I went to the upper level of the town to see how it might have happened. As I got out of my car, a man appeared from a doorway and came over to me, and I asked him if he knew of the incident. He showed me the place where the car went over. It plunged down more than 300 feet (a lot of time to think about what he had just done, I thought) and the driver was killed instantly. The man had been at the gas station below and saw it all. He had been the only witness. He did not know where the family had gone, but knew they had moved away shortly afterward. As I turned my car around to leave, I noticed the sign beside his doorway, "Michael's taxi." The shivers ran up and down my spine as I drove away, feeling lightheaded and strangely off balance as I considered the "coincidences" I had experienced in the past three days, and how remarkable it was that my conversation with Michael had been conducted entirely in colloquial French without a single misstep.

The experience left me oddly changed. It was as if the lens had been replaced in my telescope, allowing me a glimpse of something beyond this life to the feelings of responsibility and anguish a person could feel after death. I felt compassion for this man who had suffered so much, and whose rash action had undoubtedly caused great harm to the people he loved. His torment was far beyond anything I had ever experienced in my life. I hoped that I might have helped him to move on, to finally find peace. Later, I chuckled at the idea that it was the first time I had ever had a spirit as a client.

I have since learned from experienced psychics that this sort of "visit" is fairly common, but need not be a problem for us here as incarnate humans. Contrary to popular TV programs in which shivering and screaming researchers sneak through basements and attics searching for "ghosts," there is nothing to fear from the spirit world. Those who have remained here in the earth realm, demanding attention from the living, are usually lingering because of unfinished business. They may have experienced a sudden or violent death and are looking for justice, or they are worried about someone they left behind. I have recently experienced contact from souls who wish to help us to create and to thrive. They are souls of special talents who are working to redeem themselves from some mistake or failing in their own past lives. If you ask them to desist or send them away, as I did with the Frenchman, they will generally comply. If they persist, you only need to turn off your transmitter and refuse to communicate. (Turn your attention elsewhere, and they cannot come through.) However, knowing there is a reciprocal assistance program available to us and to those who have passed over, you might prefer to try to discover what the entities who make contact might have to offer, or what they might need to fulfill their own destinies. Either way, when we too leave our bodies, we too will travel beyond the Earth realm with its time and space constraints, back to the place we come from, to review and continue the work we came here to accomplish.

The experience in France was important for my spiritual development because of the mind-expanding effect it had on me. There were so many details in my dreams that checked out, I had a firsthand experience of the best kind of scientific documentation. There was absolutely no way I could have known anything about the man and his suicide before my encounter with him. I had never been to this area of the world before, and even the people at the resort were reluctant to talk about the event. After that kind of proof, I have found it hard to be disbelieving about information involving life in other dimensions.

I began to read as many books as I could find on "the occult" (an unfortunate term in that it is often used to imply something kooky or weird). I compared my experiences with others to explore what might be learned about the world beyond our five senses. I also began searching for alternative views of religion and spirituality. My search was richly rewarded. I read or reread books by Carlos Castaneda, Sylvia Browne, and Brian Weiss' *Many Lives, Many Masters*, which has now been the introduction for millions of people to the concept of past lives. I especially enjoyed Michael Newton's *Destiny of Souls*, which inspired me to learn deep hypnosis techniques and begin using past life and between-lives regression with my clients. It has answered hard questions and brought healing to many who could not have achieved it any other way.

One of my favorite ground-breakers is a book by Gary Schwartz called *The Afterlife Experiments*, because of its original use of scientific methods to study psychic mediums. In it he reports the results of a number of studies he conducted with several well-known mediums, including John Edward, Laurie Campbell and Suzane Northrop, who risked their careers to be studied in the laboratory. Great effort was made to completely ensure that the mediums had no way of knowing who they were "reading." Double blind measures were used to prevent any "cheating" from the mediums or the experimenters. During the tests, the experimenters did not know ahead of time who they would be studying, and responses were transmitted in such a way that the medium could not receive any feedback from the subject which might allow him or her to be led to a correct answer.

The results were remarkably reliable and consistent. While each medium's success rate varied with the type of test they were given, results were greater then chance, and in many cases, showed success rates higher than 1,000,000 to 1. These famous intuitives, working under the most difficult conditions, were apparently able to pick up information they had no way of knowing through any of our "normal" means. They repeatedly demonstrated their ability to reach willing friends and relatives who have "passed to the other side," bringing reassurance and comfort to many of their clients.

The fact that they are able to get accurate and very private information for people they have never met is remarkable in itself, but even more interesting is the quality of the information they receive. If you have ever watched a session with a medium, you may recall that the spirit entities often begin by reassuring their loved ones that they are doing well, having a fine time, and looking forward to seeing them again one day. They may send apologies or messages of love, but the overriding tone is one of humor and playfulness. Apparently, life on the other side is a joyful affair, at least for those who come through to talk with their relatives. There seems to be no mention of punishment or hellfire.

These spirit beings who have left their bodies behind after their Earth life have experienced resurrection, just as it was demonstrated to us by Jesus. They are not specially privileged or honored. This is the benefit available to all of us when we leave this life. We will all ascend to what is known as the Fourth Dimension—that place close-by, right here beside and around us, where souls first alight to make their re-acquaintance with God in person, and where we review the life we just finished. Once we have finished that process, we will move on to higher vibrational levels. The length of time we spend at the fourth dimensional level, whether it be days or years, depends on the need to address what impact we had on the people, animals and the natural world during our stay here on Earth. Acts of service, love, and creativity speed our journey. Actions which have hurt or diminished others will require reliving and reviewing until deep understanding is accomplished.

This process is a gift for the growing soul. Each of us needs to learn greater empathy and love on our way to becoming Light. What better way than to spend as much time as we need studying our own actions and attitudes in great depth, in the company of other spirit-students and Master teachers and guides? There could be no finer justice, nor a better opportunity to expand our soul consciousness than to study our past actions under the benign eye of a caring God. There may be painful or difficult moments when we truly realize our past sins against others, but the goal is laid out carefully before us. We are all on a path toward enlightenment. It is up to each of us to work toward it, as God and our Guides and Angels cheer us on.

The research cited here and my own channeled information, presented above, will not convince anyone who insists they do not believe anything unless they can touch it or see it. It is not intended to convince anyone who wishes to remain in darkness. They too will encounter their work to be done when they arrive in the Fourth Dimension after this life is done. Those who begin now to open their hearts and souls to a higher vibrational level will find the transitional flight gloriously exhilarating, without fear or dread. Others will learn to adjust as they go. The difference can be a speedy and joyful leap into a higher plane of existence, and with it more exciting challenges and cosmic assignments, or a slow and plodding student life, filled with many repetitions and demotions. The choice is ours.

Presented with the research information above, "skeptics" will insist there must be some trick in the way the information was received, implying that either dozens of researchers and subjects must have colluded to "fudge" results of a study, risking their professional credibility for no motive other than to prove themselves right in a particular prejudice, or the mediums are receiving telepathic wish-fulfilling information from the subjects. Although it is always possible that insanity or self-indulgence might lead a professional researcher or two astray, in this case there is little to gain, either monetarily or otherwise, for the scientists involved. They were risking their credibility in their own fields by even pursuing such a study. Therefore, the former seems highly unlikely. If it is the latter—that the mediums were receiving telepathic information from living subjects, then this would be an extremely interesting finding in itself.

To all those who consider themselves "skeptics:" A genuine skeptic is someone who is open to any and all information and will not make a decision until extensive exploration has been done and all kinds of evidence has been gathered, not just the simplest sort which can be gathered in a controlled laboratory experiment, evaluated with our five senses. A true skeptic is not closed-minded or resistant to change or revelation, no matter how non-traditional the methods of gathering the evidence might be.

In my own transition to becoming a genuine skeptic, once I had decided to explore the unknown, information came to me nearly every day. Here is an anecdote from Ellen Messer, a friend and co-author of my previous book, *Back Rooms*. Several years ago, a conversation between us turned to Ellen's interest in parapsychology. I described to her a prime time TV special about a two-year old boy who had been telling his parents about being shot down by a Japanese plane during the Second World War. Eventually, they were able to trace crucial facts like the unit he served in, and the aircraft carrier's name. They even contacted a friend and living member of the pilot's unit who corroborated the story, including the exact place, time, and details of the event.

By the time he was four, the memories had faded, along with the nightmares of crashing in a plane. This could be interpreted as evidence for reincarnation, or it could be seen as an example of a human consciousness carrying the images and feelings which are present in the cosmic Unconscious, available to all of us, if we are open to it. Perhaps we resonate most strongly to those stories which offer the potential for learning or teaching about particular challenges we came here to resolve. Certainly the child's parents were deeply moved and profoundly changed by the experience of living with a child who was tuned in to other dimensions.

I was fascinated, not only by the story, but also by the fact that a major TV news program had aired it. I asked Ellen if she had ever had the experience of a past life memory. She said, "No, but I do remember before I came here. I remember being in a big room, like a huge library, and I was talking to someone who was God-but-not-God. That's the only way I can explain it. We were looking at my book—the record of everything about me. This was where all the information about everyone was. We were talking about something I was going to do in the future. I remember they were giving me choices, and I was saying, 'Oh, no!', and then 'Oooh, no . . . well, maybe. Oh, okay.' And then I came here. That's all I remember."

Our legal system acknowledges firsthand accounts as admissible evidence in our courts. We share the intuitive understanding that the things other people see and hear can have relevance to our experience, and we rely on others' experiences to instruct our choices and decisions in all kinds of practical real-life situations. Why not look at personal accounts when we are looking for "scientific" evidence of spiritual truths?

I was beginning to accrue a great deal of information about other people's experiences with psychic phenomena and otherworldly encounters. In this spirit, I determined to go further toward understanding some of the mysteries of where we come from, and why we are here. Spiritual teachers of all stripes have referred to the Library of all thoughts and events, commonly called the Akashic record, which Ellen was referring to. Thousands of people who have lived through near-death experiences report they felt and saw inexplicable and profoundly moving things in their brief journey into the Beyond. Many others have pursued this exploration, with the attitude that if you really want to know what "Heaven" is like, forget about ancient writings. Why not ask someone who has been there? As intriguing as firsthand accounts are, I wanted to know for myself, but of course I didn't want to die to get there.

I began a journey to explore what might be learned from making contact with beings who are "on the other side," but available to us through contact with skilled mediums. In the process, I was privileged to learn some things about the way the Universe works, and our part in it as humans working toward enlightenment and understanding. It has given me comfort to have it confirmed that we are part of Spirit's great project, even though much of it is unknowable for us as the humans we are at this time. I will share an important part of what I learned.

"I've Learned a Lot Since I've Been Dead"

My first individual session with Joey, the psychic, was astonishing.[25] He conducted a reading which he calls "Cosmic Court," in which he called upon the guides and helpers of some of the people who are currently alive and had been involved in my life. I was given suggestions and reassurance about how to proceed, and what strategies would be most effective in achieving the goals I had set out for myself before I came here, including writing this book. Then our exploration took a startling and completely unexpected turn. I had planned with Joey to do an astrological chart, which he calls a "life reading." Never having done this before, I was unaware that I needed to know the hour of my birth. I asked Joey to contact my mother, since I suspected she might remember a detail like this. Although he was doubtful, since most mothers are too busy and involved in childbirth to remember anything,

---

[25] Personal communication, Joey Mergatroid, of Littleton, Colorado

I encouraged him to ask. The answer came back immediately (and I later found, correctly): 2:32 am. We both laughed, and Joey continued, saying, "She says she doesn't want to be bothered right now. She is just waking up, and she is still kind of confused. They are waking her up slowly. There was a problem with her brain (she had had a stroke), so she is still recovering. We will contact her later."

At this point, it had been four years since her death, and five years since my brother Tom had found her on floor next to her bed, as I described earlier. I was very curious about what she would have to say about her experience of life and her treatment of me and my siblings. One thing had already been confirmed for me: if there is a Hell, she apparently wasn't there.

Later that day, in the process of doing my astrology reading, Joey again made contact with my mother. He told her, "Kathryn wants to ask you some questions." Joey replicated her very definitive tone: "*I* always called her Katy." I could not help but laugh at the impossibility of this: Here I was talking to my dead mother, and she sounded just as uppity as ever. It was confirmation for me that this was real, since Joey had no way of knowing my childhood nickname. We had just met, and had not exchanged any personal information at all. Here are some of the high points of our encounter, with Joey transmitting the information as she gave it to him:

> "She says she's learned a lot since she's been dead. She is asking for your forgiveness. She can see now that she was always trying to control you, and she tried to hold you back. She says she now sees that you are a responsible woman, but she thought she had to control you because she thought you were wild. She was afraid of your big ideas."

> (A hilarious moment, in retrospect: her use of the term "big ideas" sounded so like her pejorative attitude toward anything she didn't understand.)

> "She couldn't even think about the things you were saying because she was so shut down. She thought she was being a good mother by controlling everything you did, and she

didn't beat you every day with a belt the way they were beaten."

(This was completely new to me. She had never revealed these things about her own family. It explained a lot.)

"She is saying you shouldn't speak ill of the dead."

(and here I have written about her, calling her an Abusive Personality Type. Well, I will use the information to help others. That way, there is some good in the generations of suffering.)

"She is showing me . . . a square ring. (I looked at the ring on my finger, the one she had left me in her will.) She is saying she is honored that you are wearing it, and she sees this as the beginning of forgiveness. You are helping her that way, and she really enjoys your dreams as well. (?!!!) She says she can help you too. She will come to visit you when you are on that exercise machine you have—the one that steps. She says she will give you inspiration too."

In that moment I remembered an incident from the previous day, when I got up from my desk to stretch my legs. I stepped onto the machine she described, then stopped to watch a blue jay putting up a huge ruckus. It screeched and chattered, looking directly at me the whole time from about fifteen feet away on the branch of the maple tree outside my window. I could not recall ever having heard a blue jay making such an extended statement, without reference to the calls of other birds. It continued screeching and screaming, never taking its eyes off me, for a good three or four minutes. I smiled, and said aloud, "Yes, blue jays are important too," and reached to open the window so I could answer in person, but my movement scared it away.

In my session with Joey, I remembered this incident, and was again struck by the familiar tone of it. Among the few acts of caring my mother had consistently performed in her life, she had always fed the birds in her yard, and she showed real interest in their habits. Had she been able to express love, she would have said those words, "Yes, blue jays are important too." It must have been one of the few points of real contact she had with life, the appreciation of the small creatures that came to visit her feeder, which she kept supplied all winter long. This, apparently, was her offering of inspiration to me. Joey continued:

> "She says there are things she can't talk about yet, because they're too difficult and she's still learning."

> Joey was not deterred by her refusal. He asked what things she didn't want to talk about.

> "She says there may have been sexual abuse, as well as the beatings . . . and she says that losing a husband is really painful, almost like losing a child."

> I responded, "Yes, but you drove him away!"

> "She says yes, she understands that now, but it's still painful. And she says to remind you to remember that the difficult things that happened, even the things she did to you, are lessons, and they have taught you what you know now . . . . She's leaving now."

Later, thinking of that conversation, I wept. If only we could have had this talk when she was alive! Years of pain and confusion were brought to the surface again, but this time I had answers to explain why my brothers and I had suffered, and a new understanding of the person who had been my mother for more than 60 years, but whom I hardly knew. This time, I wept for the suffering she must have endured, and for the emptiness she must have felt all her life. She had so little to give, and so much resentment and anger toward everyone around her, misdirected toward the children she could not nurture and the husband she could not really love. In life, her days were consumed with acts of jealousy, rage and contempt. She cut a swath that left lasting wounds and destruction behind her, but in death she sounded mostly childlike and confused. She was able to apologize and ask for forgiveness, something she could never have done in life.

I am grateful for the experience, and the opportunity to make peace. I have felt the comfort of finding forgiveness in a way I had never expected. Not only could I understand, and in that understanding be free of the regrets about what might have been. It even became possible to imagine a new kind of relationship with my mother: Me, here on Earth, and her, somewhere on the other side, learning and growing along with me. It's not the same as working it out while you're both alive, but it does add new dimensions to what is possible in this life.

The Universal Law of Flow

Much attention has been paid in recent years to the idea of creating abundance for yourself through the power of intention. It is called the Law of Attraction. The film, "The Secret" created a stir by appearing to promise, in some people's interpretation, that one could receive the gift of a new Jaguar by willing it. This God-as-Santa-Clause approach to spirituality is misleading because it only tells half the story—the part about asking for what you want for yourself. By itself, that would be a celebration of self-centeredness and greed. The other half of the story is about what other people need, and how others' needs can be met.

Most of us have experienced the feeling of deep satisfaction when we meet another person who needs something, we provide what they need in an unquestioning way, and then both people go their own way, warmed by the experience. The key here is the simple, immediate and direct response, without questioning what this will cost you, or whether you will be late, or what anyone will think. The gesture may be large or small: stopping to give good directions to someone who is lost, running after someone on the street who has dropped something, anonymously writing a check to pay a young person's tuition to medical school, or giving your neighbor a ride to the store. Any such action, done without expectation of getting anything in return, sets something in motion. You can feel it. In the aftermath, you are suddenly swept into a sensation of being directly in the flow of life, alive and present, exhilarated and reassured: Life is good. When we set something in motion through a selfless act, we cannot know what the results may be, but we do sense that something has just happened, and that something is a good thing.

The Universe takes care of the rest. You have started something, and more will come of it, like ripples on a pond moving outward from the splash of a rock thrown into the water. Go about your day, enjoying the positive glow of fulfillment, and be on the lookout for another opportunity to be of service.

Now let's apply this to being a parent of a young child, or being an informal teacher of any kind—activities which offer constant opportunities to be kind, compassionate and loving. Begin by addressing each need the child presents as a unique opportunity, living in the moment. This eliminates the cumulative feeling of being burdened by the "insatiable demands" children present. You will be experiencing the lingering fulfillment from the earlier moments of being of service.

You may want to try to answer the screaming objection from Ego: "But what about ME?" "When do I get something?" You are getting something. You are experiencing the precious opportunity to be in the presence of a young child. You are being freed from the endless demands of trying to satisfy your own Ego, and you are experiencing your own relevance in the bargain. Not a bad trade.

There is another benefit to this way of operating. You have needs too. Every time you ask for help, you give the other person the opportunity to practice being of service, and feeling the fulfillment of being a part of the Universal Law of Flow. Notice there is no mention here of being owed something, or "karma" as it is popularly interpreted (I caused this, therefore I deserve that). This is a simpler, more immediate way of living. Part of expressing healthy self-esteem is being able to ask for what you need. Every incident creates a dynamic result; every need is an opportunity.

Living in the moment, seeing each incident as a new opportunity also helps parents to turn away from feeling entitled to expect their children to fulfill their needs, since they did it first. We do not own our children, nor do they owe us, quid pro quo, for having brought them here or for having cared for them. Caring for a child is a precious opportunity to learn and to grow. If you live this way, the child will probably grow up to behave similarly, and for a time you will gain a young comrade along your own life path. The child will probably not be like you, or necessarily agree with your opinions, but will nevertheless be an interesting and unique companion.

Any environment or relationship can be an opportunity to be of service and thereby put yourself directly into the flow of vital energy which is the lifeblood of a society, a family or a partnership. Remember—if you are "on the clock" at work, and you are doing something kind, you are being paid for it, so don't convince yourself that your helpfulness at work counts toward putting yourself in the flow, unless you can truly answer the following question to the affirmative: "Would you still do it even if you were not being paid, and you were absolutely certain no one was looking?" If so, it is a really good thing, and it stirs up the kind of reverberative action which comes with a selfless, freely expressed act of kindness, *providing it fulfills the other person's need as they explicitly define it.*

Keep at it, always reminding yourself that doing something for another is not to accumulate points for you. It is putting you into a flow of Light and good energy, and that alone would be enough to try it. There are other adventures in store. When you take the action which is like pushing your canoe away from shore, out into a free-flowing river, you never know what will be around the next bend, but there will be something interesting or exciting or challenging in a growth-inducing way.

I am now fortunate to count among my good friends and teachers a few people of exceptional integrity, spiritual knowledge and development. In their company, I have had the courage to continue to explore and grow. As they say, "As long as you're still here and you're still breathing, your work is not done."

Here are wise words about the spiritual path to fulfillment from teacher Makarta:

> "The greatest, greatest power in the Universe is the power of love. The greatest feeling any individual can possibly have is the feeling of fulfillment, not the feeling of love. The feelings of love we share with our human partners are part of the emotional network that will last for a certain amount of time, and then they are gone. Feelings of love are one of the great teachers. What does it teach when you have loved someone absolutely and then lost them? It teaches you that when love comes, fulfill it.

"If you have fulfilled your love when the opportunity came, when you experienced it, then when you lose that person to death, it is natural and healing to grieve for the loss, but if you have been fulfilled in that love, then even in the worst moments of grief there is no suffering, and no regret.

"Pleasure is certainly to be encouraged, but pleasure and fulfillment are distant relatives, because fulfillment is lasting. Look back on everything you have done that truly helped someone, the feelings from those moments are as rich and alive and as beautiful and wondrous and light-filled now as they were at the time it happened, and will always be.

"Fulfillment goes beyond the conditions or the sentiments of love. It is when you, exactly as you are, are able to be put to work for the good of someone or something outside yourself. There is no greater feeling than to be the one who has the talent, the education, the experience, the craft, to provide something someone needs, to bring fulfillment to a state of desire, to bring to fruition a concept or an idea or a passion or an ambition.

"Fulfillment is taking that which you are and using it for the highest good of the other—as long as it is not for yourself.

"In each moment, be fulfilled. It is not an inward thing that you acquire, it is an outward thing you do, and it doesn't matter if it is removing snow from the branch of a tree that is about to break under it, or providing water for an animal, listening to a fellow human going on about themselves—they just want to be heard. Whatever it is, look to the part of yourselves that is unfulfilled. For it is my wish for each of you, that in your moment of discarding the body, you are able to look at your life and see fulfillment, not regret, not terror at what is to come, but the tranquility and inner peace of fulfillment.

"Where there is a lifetime of fulfillment, then the moment of death, like the moment of grief for love fulfilled, is something that can be happily met, for all of life has been fulfilled. You are not leaving something undone, some part of you undeveloped or undernourished or unexpressed, and everything about you has come to some useful purpose in this world. There is your heaven, and that fulfillment is eternal."[26]

---

[26] Makarta, personal communication, January, 2011

THE HAWK AND THE HUMMINGBIRD

As I sat by my window overlooking the lake, a spotted hawk came to perch on the porch railing just outside. He sat there, contented to listen and watch, slowly turning his head in that circular way that large birds do. I hoped he would turn toward me, but our eyes never met. He was scanning his view of the trees near the lake. I had never seen a hawk at such an intimate distance before. His colors shone white, tan and chocolate brown in the sun. He was curiously calm, nonchalant in his demeanor, with no hint of the hungry predator about him. Long minutes passed before he flew to the birches just across the small clearing, nearer the edge of the lake. He sat quietly in the birch tree, perched high above the path, then, satisfied with his quiet meditation, he flew on down the lake.

A moment later, a hummingbird flew directly toward the window, then pulled up and halted mid-flight just before colliding with the glass. Seeing she couldn't penetrate the glass, she flew off. The nights have turned cool. Perhaps it is time for her long journey south.

It is late summer, and Hurricane Irene has just passed, veering off to the east to continue its path of destruction, aiming for all the large cities from North Carolina to Newfoundland. It wasn't interested in us. Here in the Canadian woods we were spared its fury. After a day of rain and dark clouds, it departed without incident. Today, big white cotton clouds float across the blue sky.

Buzzing on the inside of the sunny window, an enormous wasp tried to press against the glass to free himself to the outdoors. He must have come in through the open door. He made his way up the glass, then dropped suddenly to the windowsill to begin the ascent upward again. In the corner next to an abandoned bud vase he seemed to become entangled in a cobweb. He buzzed furiously as he pushed against the glass, struggling to free himself. A small fly flew from across the room, landed on the window and walked purposefully toward the wasp and the invisible thread which seemed to be holding him back. As the wasp wobbled and pushed, the fly walked directly into the path of the troublesome web, within millimeters of the struggling wasp. Suddenly, the wasp was freed and flew to the top of the window. The fly, now wobbling and struggling himself, spent a few moments untangling and cleaning himself before he too flew away.

It is time to swim in the glorious lake. The ripples have died down, as the sun moved across the sky toward the opposite shore where it would set behind the hills. Low in the sky, it lights up the birches here on the Eastern shore. They glow silver-white, like fluorescent light sticks of white neon. When the sun is briefly obscured by a cloud, they return to being regular grey and white-trunked trees. The hammock hangs quietly alone between the spruce trees overlooking the lake. It stirs and rocks gently in the breeze. The birches were glowing again as I walk down to the lake.

The water is cool now after the rain. It will not return till next year to the welcoming warmth that made swimming such an easy pleasure. In July and August the lake invited hours-long leisurely paddling to opposite shores. Now it is bracing, exhilarating. I swim and sip the clear clean water.

As the sun sinks lower in the sky, small ripples break its reflection into glittering diamonds on the lake's surface. It is quiet. I am the only one on the two-mile lake. The wind dies down completely until the surface of the lake is like glass, reflecting the sky and the shoreline, where the trees are reflected upside down on the mirror-lake. I swim gently, trying not to break the mirror around me. My small ripples barely reach the loon that suddenly pops to the surface 30 feet in front of me. I stop to watch as the beloved loon, one of the pair which claims our lake as home, cranes to look around him into the water, ignoring me. He spots something interesting and dives, disappearing deep into the water for long minutes, then reappears far out across the lake.

I turn for home, floating through the silky water, aware of my own buoyancy and the effortless motion of gliding, supported lightly by the water. Near the shore, paddlebugs dash around me. Do the paddlebugs with their tiny oars exult as they skim across the water at top speed, just for the fun of it? Do they arrange sculling races on warm September afternoons to demonstrate their exquisite craft?

At the edge of the lake, sand, rocks and water meet the porous, soft earth, built up over eons of falling pine needles, leaves and the interplay between insects and soil. There are no sharp edges here, no imposed boundaries. The lake's level rises and falls at the whim of beavers, wind and rain. As the water claims inches of shoreline, the trees adapt, sending roots upward to firmer ground, or sacrificing their bodies, like bridges into the water, to be turned into soil at the constantly changing border between water and land.

Here there is no warfare between species. They simply adjust, sending seeds a little further inland, or reaching taller for their share of sunlight. The spruces line much of the lake edge, but just behind them rise hemlock, birches, white pines, maples and oaks, and behind them on the first ledge above the water, majestic lodge pole pines and an enormous arching elm.

A perfect, tiny white pine tree perches alone on the surface of a huge shore boulder, sending its tiny thread roots deep into some unseen crevice in the great rock. Its presence has attracted a collection of leaves, pine needles and moss which surround and protect its small trunk. Even in difficult conditions, alone with the resources at hand, this small being thrives, well into its third year. Nature has provided sun, rain, the company of its mother ten feet away, and the competent help of plants and insects of many other species. Perhaps the sturdy humans among us are like this small tree, expressing the will toward life and growth. If only the help we give to our children could be as appropriately nourishing as Nature's is to her young.

Darkness brings profound silence, and deep, nourishing sleep. The earth breathes a deep slow rhythm that rocks all her creatures to sleep. Perhaps they all dream, as I do, of the sunlight on water, soft earth under my bare feet, and the feel of warm rain on my face.

In the morning, the lake is still and calm, a perfect arena for the loon to practice his calling, diving, and motor-boating along the surface, creating an enormous racket, compared to the quiet movement of other birds and insects. It must be the one baby loon, doing loon-calisthenics to prepare for his upcoming trip south. His parents beep occasional responses from the far ends of the lake while he races at top speed, just skimming the water, for a quarter of a mile or more before landing with a flourish in the turbulence of his own wake. In the distance, the calls of other loons on nearby lakes echo over the hills.

All of nature is exulting in the triumph of a luxuriant summer. At the same time, the energy rises in expectation. Preparations for winter have begun all around me. Bees dash about with uncharacteristic speed, flies and small wasps zoom by on a mission, and another hummingbird whizzes past my head. Where does it find sustenance for its long trip? Perhaps her attraction to bright colors leads her to gardens like my neighbor's, luxuriant with red and yellow this time of year. I wish her godspeed.

Here, everything is in harmony. The sense of abundance and cooperation fills the air I breathe and the water I drink.

How did the little fly feel when it risked its life to free the giant wasp? Did its little heart beat fast with the thrill of performing such a heroic, selfless act? Was the hawk content to have eaten just one of the numerous mice available around the edge of the woods? Did he worry about tomorrow's meal, or was he happy with his lot, confident in Nature's ability to provide for him too? Did the mice resolve to work harder and multiply, to store more grain and soft nesting fluff, even as they mourned their lost brother?

Were the hummingbird and the loon thrilled to be setting off on a long and challenging journey, perhaps for the first time, with their parents and friends, or possibly with only their own internal GPS system to guide them for thousands of miles? Do they telegraph, "Are we there yet?" to their parents whenever they feel tired or hungry?

How will I return to the city of anguish and desperation? There, Earthlings crowd together, separated from Nature by concrete barriers, fences and the help of steel girders which keep them in orderly boxes high above the ground, like the hawk, but never looking down, never touching the earth with their feet or their hands.

There, everything has sharp edges and defined boundaries. The curb keeps the rain from encroaching on the sidewalk. Locks and steel keep neighbors from opening each other's doors, or even seeing one another for weeks on end. Nature's softening effect is long gone there. Harmony, cooperation and the sense of abundance have given way to separation, division and want.

The mind responds accordingly, shaping itself to the necessity of thinking in defined, carefully controlled categories. I'd rather my mind meandered along winding pathways, flowing with the terrain, open to surprise and adventure, like the loon and the paddlebugs.

Here at the lake, God speaks to me all day long. In the city, the din and the crush of anxious energy overwhelms and eventually deadens my receptors, leaving me feeling off-kilter, disoriented. When I look around me on the crowded streets, everyone seems to have sunk into a state of dazed indifference, except when they rouse themselves to flash a strained smile or a glare of irritated impatience.

How will we ever find our way back to the state of grace where we comfortably adapt, fitting into the flow of life around us, in harmony with Earth and her other living things, rather than commanding, ordering, changing and killing everything we encounter?

I pray for a way home for all of us, with all my heart.

Chapter Thirty-Two

EARTH AS MOTHER

> "It seems reasonable to believe that the more clearly we can focus our attention on the wonders and realities of the universe about us, the less taste we shall have for the destruction of our race. Wonder and humility are wholesome emotions, and they do not exist side by side with a lust for destruction."
>
> —Rachel Carson, *Silent Spring*

As weather patterns change in dramatic and unforeseen ways, more people are acknowledging deep, intuitive feelings that come over them at unexpected times. In New Jersey, the spring of 2009 brought a record string of twenty-eight out of thirty rainy days. People who had never considered themselves in tune with Nature found themselves saying things like, "Mother Nature is crying," or "Mother Earth is trying to cleanse herself." Many felt oddly unsettled, others downright unstrung. Some seemed to be awakening for the first time, newly questioning whether this money-obsessed lifestyle we have been seduced into is really the only way to live, or the only way to be "successful," given the toxic effect on our air, water, and the planet.

We have been asleep, completely hypnotized by our mindless entertainments and self-indulgent fancies, while the Earth lay beneath our feet, alive and evolving. It is easy for us in the Western World to imagine we are descendent of some special, civilized race, unrelated to the "primitive" indigenous cultures like the Mayans, the Hopi, the Iroquois, the Koji, Maori, Kuaian, Zulu, Tibetan, Egyptian and Celtic. All these cultures trace their origins, through myth, cave painting, pyramids, carvings and songs, back thousands of years. Throughout those thousands of years, many of these cultures have quietly kept alive the traditions which celebrated our sacred connection to the Earth as provider of all our earthly needs. They have also understood, with far more sophisticated knowledge than we currently possess, (as demonstrated within the structures of the Egyptian and Mayan pyramids, Stonehenge, Easter Island and others) the intimate interactions between the planets, the stars, and the forces of Creation we have only begun to glimpse. Deep within our DNA, we share that ancient knowledge. It has been drowned out by the noise of the modern world, and disparaged as less "civilized" than our brain-centered way of life which has been based on conquering Nature rather than working with her.

The Living Earth

Ancient traditions refer to the Earth as a living, conscious being, the Mother of all the living creatures on the planet, of whom humans are just one. We are loved as her children, but we are not superior over the others, and we are not superior over her. It is by her bounty that we are able to survive and prosper here. There are many names for her, but the most familiar in our culture is Gaia. Rather than moving beyond what these ancient traditions taught, we have lost the ability to truly understand the simplest acts of daily life. The planting and harvesting of food and the slaughtering of animals are sacred acts which must be accompanied by prayers of gratitude to the animal, and thanks to the Mother for providing for us. The establishment of settlements, the preparation of food, the training of children—all invite us to savor a sense of humility and gratitude for the gift of life we humans enjoy. Ceremonies for every important facet of life were practiced and passed down for thousands of years, serving to strengthen close bonds and organize life around the most intimate knowledge of Earth's seasons, her relationship to other planets, the Moon, and the stars. These were not whimsical pastimes, like celebrating your yearly birthday, or scientific pursuits designed to encourage further domination of the Universe. They were as necessary and meaningful to our ancestors as their own heartbeat. Every action, every relationship, every creative endeavor was infused with the deep knowledge that those actions would affect their Mother and the hundreds of generations to come after them.

Food

We will need to completely reevaluate our methods of food production if we are to sustain life on the planet for more than one more generation. What sort of culture would allow the institution of factory farms, as if animals and food products could be manufactured to our specification, like automobiles or computers, with less direct knowledge of how our food is being grown than we have of the inner workings of the computers we buy? [27]

A recent chance meeting with an earnest young man left me scratching my head in wonder. I came across him fishing, as I paddled by in my canoe on a pristine, sparsely populated Canadian lake. Casting from the shore, he was clearly enjoying what he was doing. I asked him if he had caught anything, and he said, "Yes, two big ones. About two or three pound bass." I marveled at the catch, and said something about the incomparable dinner they would have, but he informed me he had thrown them back. Since he was the only fisherman on the entire two-mile long lake, it seemed highly unlikely that his small catch would have any impact on the bass population. I asked why he was doing that. He said, "Well, I don't like to kill them, you know." I tried to encourage him to experience the taste of real food, caught and cooked the same day himself, but I suspect he could not stand the idea of seeing how a fish is prepared. Later I noticed that their campsite was empty. I mused that they probably had gone into town for a burger. In spite of his fishing, his attitude echoed that of so many of the young people I have spoken to about this issue: "I'll eat it, I just don't want to know how it got to my plate," or, "I'll pay somebody else to kill it. I couldn't possibly do it myself."

This willful blindness about the source of our food is worse than short-sighted. It is the only thing that really matters for our survival. We have moved so far from the reality of what sustains human life that we hardly give it a passing glance. What were we thinking? We have become so blinded by our way of life that we have been convinced

---

[27]   *Food, Inc.*, both video and book, has covered these issues masterfully.

that food, water and air are less important than say, economic profits, or technological advances. Let's be honest about it. Perhaps anyone bringing a toxic or environmentally costly product to market should be required to place a label on their product: "It's more important for us to get rich and for you to have this thing than for you to breathe clean air (have clean water, etc.) Please justify our greed by buying this product."

Polluters need to be held responsible for their environmental damage, swiftly, and expensively. But there is little hope for that presently. As long as polluting corporations fund Congressmen, and Congress funds the Environmental Protection Agency, we can expect to eat and breathe toxic waste as a steady diet. It will be up to individuals to educate ourselves, and to refuse to buy the products which poison our Earth. We must learn to count the costs in the way food or consumer products are grown, manufactured, packaged, shipped, sold, and disposed of, and act accordingly.

Perhaps if we had known the true environmental cost of the things we have bought—if anyone had even mentioned it—we might have made different choices. We can now. Organizations like the NRDC, the Sierra Club, Greenpeace, The Nature Conservancy and others produce carefully researched publications which can educate and inform all of us on the current state of environmental issues. We now have better ways of estimating the real cost of the things we make and do, so there is no excuse for continuing the environmental sins of our past. This does require being awake, aware, and living in your heart, where life and breath matters.

Fortunately, the problems have not gone unnoticed. Increasing groups of "foodies" and farmers have joined ranks to encourage the use of locally grown, clean organic food. Farmers' markets in cities and towns are beginning to replace aging, travel-weary supermarket produce. A resurgence of home gardening is inspiring even apartment dwellers to try their hand at window-sill gardening. One of the most hopeful developments of all is the Transitional Networks[28] movement, which has inspired entirely new forms of community activism to deal with dwindling oil, climate change, and economic hardship. In

---

[28]   Transition Towns are springing up all over the globe. Go to TransitonUS.org for information about how to do your part.

many places, going "back to the land" may mean a struggling young suburban couple uses their retired neighbor's land to grow produce for both families.

Russian families from all walks of life have found a new way to insure "food security." Under Putin, every family who wants to grow their own food has been allotted a hectare of arable land (about 2.5 acres) on which to grow their own produce and other agricultural products. All products from this family plot will remain untaxed, thereby providing a sustainable living from the land for every family. This visionary approach will insure that poverty and hunger will eventually disappear, as urban populations gradually transition to their own family domains to build and work together. Small plots, sustainably farmed, do not require artificial pesticides or fertilizers, insuring a return to richer, more fertile lands, and clean air and water.

Gardening as a Spiritual Act

Growing your own food is more than a practical issue. It is a way of experiencing a sacred connection with the Earth. Planting a seed you have held under your tongue, as Anastasia suggests,[29] transmits your own unique body needs to the seed, which can then create a fruit designed to nourish and heal you. Information absorbed by the seed concerning your particular physical needs becomes the medical treatment which can cure disease and slow the aging process. She reintroduces us to age-old knowledge—that every disease has its cure in the natural world. We only need to look around us, with an open mind and a sense of discovery, and the wisdom to help us thrive will be laid out before us.

Organic gardening has reached new levels of technological expertise, and ancient traditions have been rediscovered which blend a knowledge of astronomical influences, water systems, crop interplanting, and respect for Nature's cooperative intentions. A new approach to co-creative gardening has been practiced and described by Machaelle Small Wright, who has developed a research garden, called Perelandra, in Virginia. Her beautiful workbook for those who wish to learn a completely new approach to gardening in harmony with

---

[29] *Anastasia,* Book I, *The Ringing Cedars* Series.

nature, is called the *Perelandra Garden Workbook: A Complete Guide to Gardening With Nature Intelligences.* In it, she teaches the method called kinesiology which, when practiced well, gives everyone the ability to communicate with Nature spirits and others, in a conversation which allows the gardener to gain intimate information about garden design, seeds, planting, soil building and pest control, none of which requires any toxic chemicals.

Using her methods, I have redesigned and planted a large organic garden in Upstate New York. The initial stages required intense preparation of the soil and building walkways and beds. Planting was done as the nature spirits' directed, each plant carefully planned for and balanced with its neighbors. No watering and little weeding is required, once the layers of straw are in place. The plants I planted myself have mostly thrived beautifully, in spite of weeks with little care, while those of an assistant, whose attention often wandered, never even sprouted. Apparently, this was the gardening lesson for me. The plants that I grew from seed are producing bountiful, as attentive to my needs as I am to theirs, in equal proportion. The garden feels like a friendly place, with circular pathways and flowers interspersed with the lush green foliage of asparagus, squashes, tomatoes, beans, chard, kale and native fruit bushes.

Combining the gardening methods from Machaelle Wright and Anastasia, a family of four could live well and stay healthy from the crops they could grow on a plot in the suburbs. As more and more people are becoming aware of the dangers and pointlessness of eating factory-raised produce, the home gardening movement is growing exponentially, and the tools for making it possible are readily available. If each member of a family, from toddlers on up, get involved in the growing, the plants will respond accordingly, growing nourishing and healing fruits for each member individually. The key is the heart connection you make with the plants, and the sense of pleasure and gratitude which is shared, from plants to people and back.

The Arts as Lifeblood

It would be impossible to feel alienated or alone if you were a part of a culture that sings, dances and celebrates life all around you. How different it would be from our lonely, self-conscious lives in which singing and dancing is the exclusive province of professionally trained performers, while the rest of us just sit and watch, fearful of being judged and compared with the best. Even singing in the shower seems to be a lost art. Perhaps today's vestige of these celebrations is still carried forward in the raucous, celebratory rock concerts and religious gatherings where everyone dances, sways, and claps with the music. What we now think of as "audience participation" used to be the reason for making the celebrations a community affair rather than a solitary and sedentary experience.

The celebrity madness which has overtaken the Western world involves an insatiable curiosity for details about our "stars'" personal lives and personalities. It is certainly an expression of the Cult of Ego gone wild, but perhaps it is also based in something deeper: an ages-old longing to be closer to the most talented among us, and to be more like them. We all long to witness soaring talent, exhibitions of artistry so far above the norm that it takes our breath away. It inspires us to strive for our own excellence, in whatever arena that might be. It also makes us want to sing, dance and be a part of the music and drama in our own way, as an expression of our need to be part of the community that celebrates together. Unhappily, we have become used to the paltry substitute of sitting in a darkened living room, watching commercially-hyped mediocre performances, silently distant from the energy and excitement of a truly exceptional live performance.

Fortunately, since the 1960's some young Americans have participated in gatherings which were designed to allow audiences to sway, clap, jump and stomp in unison and in collaboration with the performers. This form of entertainment seems to be growing exponentially, as producers strive to bring great performances closer to the people. Outdoor venues with magnificent sound and video systems have allowed huge gatherings of people to witness and participate in person. Hopefully, this is just the beginning of an explosion of creativity and participation in the arts.

New levels of expertise and diversity have been reached in opera, dance, music and the visual arts. We now have access to great performances from around the globe via television and internet, but this is not enough to truly inspire large numbers of people. Participation is essential. Professional artists can be inspiring, but what will they inspire us toward if we don't get out of our chairs?

Where will the aspiring young artists of the future come from, if not from among those who have been there, witnessing excellence firsthand? Who will be the patrons who support and nourish the artists among us?

In the 80's, the shift toward seeing art as a commercial enterprise changed the way we have approached art. Insisting that artists should make a living by selling what they do—and that if it does not immediately gain commercial support it must not be valuable—has put an impossible burden on artists. Many human civilizations going back as far as cave people have apparently provided sustenance for their artists, who must spend their time and energy in the training and practice of their art. Picture the cave communities which created the beautiful wall paintings thousands of years ago. Do you think the artist's family and friends said to him or her: "Put down those useless colors and get out there and hunt with the real men," or can you imagine the end of the day when the hunters came home with their prize, and the community stood awestruck before the artist's creation, and quietly and respectfully handed the artist his dinner? Through their artists' eyes, these early people must have seen the wonder in their everyday life, their relationships to each other and the plants and animals who sustained them. They must have understood, even as they struggled to survive, that there is more to life on Earth than material success.

Why shouldn't we have block parties or village gatherings to celebrate the changing of the seasons, the rising of the full moon, the harvest of the corn, or anything else which celebrates our own unique connection to the plants and animals, Mother Earth, the Great Spirit, and All That Is? We could all sing, dance, perform rituals and dramas, while also admiring and celebrating those among us who are wonderfully gifted in the Arts. There could be a place for every person's creative abilities, whether it takes the form of organizing, building, writing and composing, or performing for others. It will require that we overcome our fear and self-centeredness to reach new levels of creativity and community involvement. Only then can we satisfy the hunger for creative expression which is innate in our human beingness. If our ancestors could do it, so can we.

Can You Count the Ways

We have seen repeated devastation caused by invasive species like zebra mussels, kudzu, and caulerpa taxifolia, a hybridized aquarium plant which has choked acres of shoreline around the Mediterranean, and which has spread to threaten oceans all over the world. Yet, we permit corporations to genetically engineer plants and animals which will inevitably create upheaval by upsetting the balance, beginning a struggle between natural and engineered life forms. Who can possibly predict what monstrous results await us?

Unfortunately, profit-driven ingenuity has been given practically free reign, since the legal system as it stands in the U.S. requires the government to demonstrate that the products brought to market are dangerous, rather than putting the onus on the producers to prove the safety of their products. Corporations using questionable toxic processes to produce their products or mine their resources, for instance, have only to convincingly claim that the ingredients in their chemistry are patented, and therefore proprietary and secret. In this way, they are able to avoid strict oversight or public knowledge of the dangerous potential for environmental damage their activities present. The result is that tens of thousands of toxic chemicals have entered the ecosystem, pervading the soil, water and air to such a degree that not a mother alive on the planet today can produce breast milk uncontaminated by such toxins as DDT. It was banned in 1972 in the U.S., but it continues to be used for mosquito control in many areas of the world.

In the U.S. a controversy rages about the relative dangers of "fracking," the process by which the earth's surface is violently fractured in order to extract shale oil. Whole towns in Pennsylvania have experienced poisoning of the water supply, to such a degree that some residents near the shale fields find that their drinking water can be lit on fire as it comes out of the faucet. Yet, New York has agreed to proceed with permits to allow fracking of the Marcellus Oil Sands, against the objection of hundreds of thousands of New York residents.

A newly discovered threat is the halogenated fire retardant chemicals, or PDBE's, which have been required by law in the manufacture of cribs, strollers, car seats and other children's furniture.

They are known to be highly carcinogenic, linked to birth defects, cancer, thyroid disruption and mental retardation, but have continued to be required by law even after the related chemical, known as TRIS, was banned from use in children's sleepwear in 1977. PDBE's are now commonly found in extremely high levels in children—even those children of parents who consider themselves to be health-conscious and environmentally aware. Is it surprising then, that brain cancer and leukemia, along with other environmentally induced diseases like asthma, have risen dramatically in children?

Medicating Ourselves to Death

We have been warned—too late—of the dangers of overusing antibiotics, since the very organisms they target will eventually mutate to become stronger than the antibiotic designed for them, resulting in a Cold War arms race against germs. Perhaps the entire philosophy—one drug for each bacteria or virus—is fundamentally flawed. It has been enormously profitable for drug companies, but the result is that major cities all over the globe are finding antibiotics and antidepressants in their drinking water. Thus, people who are neither ill nor depressed are being constantly medicated.

It is only a matter of time before a version of avian or swine flu, born out of the unspeakable conditions of a pig or chicken factory farm or the laboratory of an ambitious vaccine manufacturer, wreaks its havoc on a population already weakened by an overload of environmental toxins, inferior food and sedentary habits. Rather than build our immunity by strengthening our bodies to fight off disease, we have done the opposite, weakening our ability to fend off new and unforeseen biological anomalies.

In the U.S. Northeast, where Lyme disease is rampant, we already have a situation where half the population in some communities has contracted it, and many of those people have lingering symptoms. It is finally getting some recognition as the serious illness it really is. A month of antibiotics often does not eliminate the complex bacteria, which hide in joints and muscles out of reach of circulating white blood cells.

As I personally struggled with repeated infections, I was led, by a persistent vision, to investigate a contraption I had relegated to the closet. It is a dome-shaped tunnel which emits far-infrared heat, providing soothing, stimulating warmth which has been effective in the past for aching muscles or injuries. I spent a timed session under the tunnel, as I was inspired to do by an encouraging but very insistent intuition or presence. By the following morning, all symptoms of aching muscles and bones were gone. I have since learned that the infrared treatment was effective for early-stage body symptoms, but not a complete treatment for the presence of the disease in the brain.

There are many treatments available for serious illnesses which use the natural effects of heat, light and sound, and of course herbal remedies, to defeat even the most persistent of modern diseases. As one long-time sufferer said, she felt Lyme disease was a "dark force" which feeds on anger. Others have said the same about cancer and heart disease, the illnesses most often linked with emotion. A crucial element in the treatment of any persistent disease is the willing and dedicated cooperation of the patient. The well-known placebo effect is real. It is created by the strong will to recover which super-charges the person's immune system to fight the disease, with or without medication. Visualizations which help to direct the body's natural defenses to fight the disease directly have been demonstrated to have a powerful healing effect, and has been used to shrink tumors, defeat viral infections, and heal quickly after surgery. We must begin to seriously consider the possibility that there are more effective ways to get well than taking a pill.

A recent experience with the brilliantly effective spiritual healer called John of God provided further confirmation that we have been perversely single-minded in our adherence to present-day limited medical treatments. Surrounded by healers living and in spirit, the man who has given his life, day in and day out to free medical treatment to the people who come to his clinic in Brazil, accomplishes "miracles" by helping people to accept healing by the expert "entities" who are his medical team. I personally witnessed several tearful moments of relief in people who had traveled many miles to experience a medical intervention, and was present to hear Wayne Dyer, the well-known inspirational teacher, tell of his complete spontaneous cure from leukemia as a result of his treatment with John of God's team. I myself was dramatically helped to recover the feeling in my back and leg which had been lost 25 years ago as a result of back surgery.

In the clinic in Brazil and in the venues where he visits for healing sessions, miracles are an everyday occurrence. There is no conflict between the spiritual treatments and regular medical care and supervision by private doctors. It is seen as a powerful addition to standard medical care, or a life-saving alternative where modern medicine has failed. John of God himself refuses payment or credit for the healings which are accomplished through him. He insists that he has done nothing; the help comes from God, and from God's helpers.

At the sessions I attended in Rhinebeck, NY, more than 1500 people a day attended the efficiently-run healing clinics. Numerous volunteers and staff members from the Omega Institute and John of God's team were warm, comforting and available in a way that no American doctors office could begin to match. In our current system, the doctor and her helpers must satisfy first the insurance company, and second, if there is time left over, the patient. If our way of treatment was truly working, there would be no need for thousands of people every year to travel to Brazil and elsewhere to find the healing they need—without cost, and without side effects.

In our nearly messianic efforts to be safe, healthy and well-fed, we have inadvertently poisoned everything which might have provided for our health and well-being. If it were not so tragic, the ironies would be downright funny. Our fanatical cleanliness has wiped out the very germs which might allow our children to build immunity by exposure. Colds and flu flourish in winter, not because of our exposure to cold weather but because we are all confined in climate-controlled spaces in an effort to avoid any small chill which might cause us to get sick. Constant washing with antibacterial cleaners has probably been instrumental in the development of flesh-eating designer bacteria for which we have no antidote. Factory machines wash our produce, eliminating the possibility that any soil might remain on our food. That very soil would contain beneficial bacteria to aid in our digestion and immune building, if it weren't for the fact that the soil itself is so devoid of life because the acid rain has destroyed the life-giving organisms which once sustained our ancestors.

Thus, with each new "modern" innovation we have created a problem larger than the one we intended to cure. It is inevitable that a people who live in their heads rather than their hearts will make such monumentally arrogant mistakes. We have tried to outsmart

Nature, instead of working with her, and we are being humbled for our errors.

The Oceans

An internet search of "The Great Pacific Garbage Patch" reveals the astonishing facts about where all those plastic bags, toys, water bottles and Styrofoam cups have gone. Covering an area of thousands of square miles, two enormous floating "islands" of debris have concentrated in the Pacific Ocean, swept along by circling ocean currents which can carry a plastic water bottle from the storm drains of Los Angeles thousands of miles to the Hawaiian Islands and beyond. Similar plastic dumps have been found in the Atlantic and Indian Oceans as well.

Two vast areas, one between California and Hawaii, and the other off the coast of Japan, remained unreported until Charles Moore "discovered" the massive collection of garbage on a return trip from competing in a transpacific yacht race. His shock at the enormous extent of the garbage problem led him to establish the Algalita Marine Research Foundation. He is now an active spokesperson who has dedicated himself to educating the public and searching for solutions to the growing problem.

It is estimated that two million plastic bottles are used *every five minutes* across the planet, and only five percent of those are recycled. Every day, millions of those bottles are swept off beaches, down streets to storm drains, ending eventually in massive floating islands of plastic in various stages of disintegration. Much sinks to the bottom of the ocean, creating a separate toxic waste problem, while the rest is floating, several feet deep in places, providing toxic synthetic "food" for sea birds and fish. Many die tangled in plastic bags, 6-pack soda carriers, and errant plastic netting. Others simply die of starvation, with their stomachs full of trash. None of the larger species of fish is free of significant amounts of plastic-based toxins which collect in their tissues as they grow.

The floating garbage is not visible from the air, since it lies mostly just beneath the surface, and is translucent rather than solid. Weather and wind conditions have made these vast uninhabited areas unfavorable as traffic lanes for boats, so the extent of the damage has only begun to be recorded. The problem becomes worse with every rainstorm, since cities around the world expel the trash directly into the oceans to be added to the trillions of pieces of plastic already floating there. Since plastic does not degrade in the landfill, but it does degrade in sunlight, the problem is made worse as smaller and smaller particles drift toward the ocean floor, to be consumed by smaller and smaller species of fish, leaving nothing untainted.

Learning to be a Conscious Non-Consumer

As I read of the unimaginable devastation of our precious oceans, and I watched Charles Moore's documentary video of the floating detritus, I was overcome with the horror and senselessness of it. Nausea swept over me as I saw the photographs of disintegrating bodies of sea birds which had died with their bellies full of bottle caps and shreds of plastic. The killing plastic remained intact on the shore, ready to be consumed by another victim, as the bird itself returned to dust. I vowed then that I would never buy another piece of plastic, no matter what.

I have remained true to my vow, almost, but it has been extremely challenging. I have been forced to concede to buying a few food items wrapped in cellophane, and I am required to wrap my small amount of garbage in a black plastic bag, but I console myself with the knowledge that at least it is going to the landfill and not into the ocean. I am fortunate to have an organic garden where I can recycle all food scraps, so my garbage is minimal. It has long been my practice to refuse to buy produce, fish or meat if it is packaged on Styrofoam trays. Most stores still have a person who can wrap your purchase in deli-type paper, or unwrap your produce and reuse the containers. Any plastic bags that have found their way into my kitchen are washed and reused indefinitely. I am fortunate in having a local food co-op where none of the produce or grains are wrapped; spices, coffee and tea can be bought in bulk, and I can take my own storage containers and fabric carrying bags with me. However, I was dismayed to find that even there, at the most conscientious of all natural food stores, it is not possible to buy shampoo or dishwashing soap in anything but plastic bottles, many of them proclaiming themselves to be natural, biodegradable, and good for the environment!

I have solved the dishwashing problem by carving bars of Fels Naptha or Ivory or other bar soap into the old plastic squirt bottles, which will probably outlast me. It works just fine, and has even helped ward off poison ivy as a bonus. I have found some really good shampoo in bar form from a specialty soap store. It seemed expensive at first, but the suds are endless, the bar lasts indefinitely, and the intoxicating smells of the shop where it is made is a treat in itself. Toothbrushes may prove to be an insurmountable problem.

As for water in plastic, there is nothing good about it. The idea of someone in New York buying water from Fiji which has been transported using enormous amounts of fossil fuels is beyond ridiculous. When a simple faucet attachment or carbon filtering pitcher can put the finishing touches on municipal tap water, why should we drink water that had plastic toxins leeching into it over a long, environmentally expensive journey? For millennia, our ancestors drank from clear streams and springs which could still provide for us, with sensible protections. No one should be allowed to poison the well, not for any amount of profit.

I have pursued this experiment with the simple guideline: What did my grandmother use? She managed to have a fully operational household without plastics, and with little waste of any kind. Why can't I? I have found there is little I can't do without, since I already own more "stuff" than my grandmother could have imagined. I have rediscovered the advantages of glass, pottery and stainless steel as all-purpose containers, and am increasingly amazed at how utterly trivial and useless most (although possibly not all) of our uses for plastic really are. Even rubber duckies are made of plastic. Unfortunately, so are the bumpers on my car, but they are not likely to end up in the ocean.

Packaging—or rather the over-packaging—of breakable items is a serious problem. For a past renovation project in my home, I made the mistake of ordering lighting fixtures over the internet. The small fixtures arrived embedded in extra-large custom-molded Styrofoam boxes, which were then packed in shrink-wrapped cardboard boxes. The residue was overwhelming. I resolved to buy locally made or reused items from then on. If I can't bring it home in a blanket, I probably don't need it.

These small gestures will not erase my footprint from the planet, but it will reduce waste, and I, for one, will not strangle or poison one sea creature with my personal refuse. If everyone who reads this does the same, and teaches their children about the Seven Generations rule, we could all stop the problem in its tracks. For those who may not be familiar with it, the Seven Generations rule is a Native American tradition which says that no decision or action should ever be taken without considering the impact for seven generations to come. We have strayed far from the simple, generous consideration that there will be others to follow us, and they deserve to live too.

Fish Stories

I went in search of answers to how we might begin to correct some of the worst problems concerning our relationship to the environment, and especially to the oceans. I spoke at length with Phaedra Dukakis, PhD, a marine biologist who has worked and traveled extensively studying sturgeon and their precious product, caviar. Sturgeon is a species which is especially significant to humans. Because of its long life span, it is a bellwether indicator of the health of the oceans, and by extension, of the planet. I asked her what her research has shown about the possibility of finding new or better ways to feed the planet, and what part fish might have in that process. Her answers were at once disturbing and hopeful. On the problem of feeding our enormous numbers, she was circumspect.

> "It used to be a problem of distribution, but we have reached the point where the population has grown beyond our capacity to provide for everyone. It's complicated by the wasteful methods that are used to produce what people want. It takes three pounds of feed to produce one pound of farm-raised salmon, which is far inferior nutritionally to wild salmon. The feed is made from ocean-caught krill and other small fish, so it deprives wild fish of their food source. The feed is then laced with antibiotics to prevent diseases and parasites, because the crowding in ponds breeds disease, and the ponds tend to create pollution problems.

"The ocean pens are the worst, because they interfere directly with wild fish populations. There are ways to make fish farming environmentally sustainable, but people would have to be willing to change their preferences. For instance, carp is a fish that takes far less feed to produce a pound of protein (one-to-one). It isn't popular.

"Huge profits and consumer demand are a big part of the problem. For instance, many countries still do not control shark fin harvesting. Because they are so valuable as a self-indulgence in China and Japan, they are caught, stripped of their fins and the huge carcass is thrown back. The U.S. at least requires that they use the rest of the fish. It's similar with sturgeon. It takes twenty years or more for a sturgeon to reach maturity. The caviar makes up only ten percent of the fish's weight, but it is the profitable part, so the rest is often discarded.

She became quiet, thoughtful for a time. "It's really a matter of self-control. We will have to learn to use more self-control when we make choices about how we live."

Phaedra used the familiar term "self-control" to describe where we need to go, but I sensed she was referring to something even deeper.

Temperance is Honorable

Everywhere we look, the facts point to the same urgent requirement: If we are to survive as a race, we will need to learn Temperance. Perhaps, after all, it is one of the most fundamental of positive human character traits. It requires a higher level of consciousness than exerting what we usually think of as self-control. It is not the rigid application of rules and regulations to impose restrictions on our "liberties," nor is it self-imposed deprivation. Temperance requires a balance between inner and outer needs, self and others. It also requires a greater dedication to a spiritual path. It combines the qualities of generosity, care for others, and the actions which demonstrate those traits. It is based in the deep acknowledgement that our fancies are not more pressing or more imperative than the survival needs of others, and that self-indulgence at the cost of the planet and the other creatures on it is not justified, ever.

Earth will go on, with us or without us. It is time we returned to our indigenous roots, to the ancient origins we all share if we are to begin to repair the damage we have done. We will need to wean ourselves from many of the destructive institutions we consider necessary and good, like money, partisan pride, manufactured food, and the Army Corps of Engineers, whose job it has been to bring military might to the construction of projects which frequently create monumental environmental destruction.[30]

For nearly 300 years in the U.S., we have lived like greedy toddlers, as if profit and self-indulgence were our exclusive God-given right. We have conquered, laid waste, and moved on, sated, self-satisfied and oblivious to the cries of the indigenous people, the animals and the lands we have dishonored. It is time for us to learn temperance, sensitivity and generosity of spirit.

For this time, in this era, less is more.

---

[30] See John McPhee's description in *The Control of Nature* of governmental efforts to do battle with the mile-wide Mississippi River.

EARTH MOTHER SINGS
A Love Song to Mother Earth
by Makarta

A hill cloaked in gold where bold courage was taught,
Where children were born and bright painted braves fought,
While Earth Mother changes his corpse to soil,
Farmers plant, till and seed and go on with their toil.

Refrain: Sing your song, Earth's children, before it's too late.
             Our Mother is dying; arise from your sleep.
             Sing your song, Earth's children, before it's too late.
             Find your way to God's heaven, before it's too late.

Red rocks of the Holy Land rise to meet the sun
Where the plains of the desert knew the Holy One.
People gather there to pledge their hearts to God
As they dance with joy where the Holy One trod.

Refrain

A blue tropic island where music fills the air
Where the palm trees sway and the women are fair,
A feast is prepared to honor the gods of food,
While the young people swim and the elders feel good.

Refrain

A forest green where the animals roam,
And the people build the earthen homes,
Silence descends in the waning light
As all of God's creatures welcome the night.

Refrain

Sky scrapers crowd closely to block out the sky,
The children breathe poison and never ask why.
Will people join hands to help one another
To nurture and save our precious Earth Mother?

Refrain

CHAPTER THIRTY-THREE

CREATING A NEW SOCIETY

I dream'd in a dream I saw a city invincible to the attacks
of the whole of the rest of the earth;
I dream'd that was the new city of Friends;
Nothing was greater there than the quality of robust love,
it led the rest;
It was seen every hour in the actions of the men of that
city,
And in all their looks and words.
                                    —Walt Whitman, Calamus

The world is changing. As I write this in 2011, there is a worldwide flow of money upward into the hands of the few, and a global consolidation of sociopolitical power previously unknown on the planet. This is happening to such an extreme that the foundations of democracy, as well as our financial institutions, are resting on little more than good faith and illusion. At the same time, there is a vast spiritual resurgence. Rebellion is spreading against dictatorships across the Middle East. Large numbers of people are questioning the values they were raised with, opening their minds and hearts to new ways of understanding relationships between individuals, communities and nations. As some struggle to construct a vision of how it might be possible to end genocide and border wars, and to change the patterns of distribution and ownership of global resources which currently leave whole countries starving, there is a simultaneous counterforce which argues for the status quo.

Toward a Spiritual Civilization

Wealth and luxury hold a seductive attraction. Most of us in the Western world were raised to strive for material wealth as a measure of success and personal value. Most religious traditions have long held that spirituality is the direct opposite of materialism, which has been seen as the indulgence of greed and excessive bodily pleasures. In Twentieth Century America, however, the "new" Christianity adopted a philosophy which openly espoused the idea that God bestows wealth on the worthy.

The largest Christian church in the U.S., led by the Reverend Joel Osteen, has attracted a following of tens of thousands of people who fill a sports stadium while thousands more watch on TV. The religious fervor appears to focus largely on issues of personal advancement and material gain. Sermons laud the right of every believer to celebrate Jesus Christ by claiming their rightful share of the abundance. Perhaps Mr. Osteen does not intend to reinforce the American obsession with material wealth, but his message has been interpreted in interviews with parishioners as something like the following: God loves you; therefore He wants you to achieve your due—a generous piece of the American Dream. This version of the Dream seems to have evolved far beyond FDR's modest vision of "a chicken in every pot" to an SUV or two in every circular driveway.

The pursuit of The American Dream as it is currently conceived ignores the simple truth that there are just not enough resources on the planet for everyone to pursue the kind of self-indulgent consumer lifestyle that Americans have become accustomed to. This is especially true since the developing countries of India and China are fast on the heels of "progress," which promises to deplete and pollute the planet at an even faster pace. The free-market rugged individualist-as-worshipper creates an untenable problem for the planet. The philosophy behind it has been: If man has "dominion over" the planet and all its plants and creatures, then we are entitled to toy with the Earth without a wink of recognition that our activities have utterly poisoned our own life-sustaining resources of food and water in favor of luxury, convenience and economic "progress." The sense of entitlement combined with righteousness has fueled the headlong wreckage of the planet's fragile balances.

The earth does have abundant resources; there might be enough food and water to sustain us if we take responsibility as a world of nations and individuals to reduce our global population rather than increase it, and to share the wealth of the planet as it was intended: for all humans, everywhere. We have the technology to make life livable for many, if we had the will to organize in the spirit of community the way we do after an environmental disaster. We will have to be willing to completely reorganize the structures of ownership and distribution and the power which results, if we are to accomplish a more equitable and more sustainable way of life on the planet. As it is, the degradation and depletion of food, water and energy resources have brought us to a tipping point.

A Time for Change

A system which is controlled by clandestine alliances, government officials elected by the contributions of interested parties and unregulated international corporations cannot be considered a valid test of "capitalism" any more than the U.S.S.R. could be considered a valid test of "communism." Both have been imposed on society from without, one by stealth, the other by brute force. Both communism and capitalism are based in the unproven assumptions that all human beings are innately selfish, and therefore must be forced to share (communism) or allowed free rein as Ayn Rand proposed, because selfishness is linked to creativity and "progress" (capitalism). Except for short-lived shining moments during the 200-year process of establishing the democratic system in the United States and other European democracies, the modern world has not seen genuine democracy in action on a large scale over long periods of time. Europe has mixed socialist economic policies with democracy in ways which create greater stability among the general populace, but many of these are fairly new experiments which have taken place within the past 50 years.

It is probable that The Five Tribes of the Iroquois Nation achieved a more balanced and egalitarian system than our own. It probably was a model our Founding Fathers referred to in designing our Constitution. It would be worth our efforts to study the way the Five Tribes governed themselves. There are written versions of their

Constitution showing remarkably well worked out traditions of laws.[31] They show a deep appreciation for the necessity of providing a careful balance of power, while also maintaining the ability to take immediate action when circumstances required it. For instance, representatives from the tribes were elected by the women, for time-limited council meetings and negotiations. It was also understood that anyone who had experienced a severe trauma within the preceding four years would be exempted from serving. Their sensitivity to the needs of the whole included recognizing the vulnerabilities and needs of the individuals involved, something which is sadly lacking in our current process.

We have dramatically departed from the Five Tribes tradition in our lack of emphasis on training our young people to serve the greater good, by developing their skills as negotiators, diplomats and lawmakers. If large numbers of our children were knowledgeable about the many options for organizing government at every level of community life, you would never see protesters with signs saying things like: "Keep the government's hands off my Medicare." (Medicare is, of course, one of the most popular of all government programs in the U.S.) An evolving, creative and problem-solving approach to government requires a citizenry educated to take an active part in their own governance, rather than leaving it to "politicians."

When serving in Congress is seen as a route to accumulating power and money, rather than an honorable but time-limited act of service to the community, we get what we pay for:—a system of institutionalized corruption and greed which serves only those in positions of power.

We must begin with the children, who need to be taught to govern themselves thoughtfully before they can be expected to be participating citizens. Children who are taught to treat their parents, their siblings and each other with respect will envision life systems which will consider the needs of all. A child who is asked to determine his own path of study will learn to search deep within himself to know authenticity, and will recognize it in others. When a child is given autonomy and responsibility for his own needs, in loving consultation with his parents and teachers, he will learn how to fulfill those needs and to take others' needs into account in the process.

---

[31] See the Constitution of the Five Tribes, at indigenouspeople.com.

Freedom to learn, experiment and grow in an environment which presumes that each child will make a valuable original contribution produces children who will surpass their elders in every way. If we continue to dictate everything a child does in school, according to an imposed system of demands, we can only hope to continue producing children who are dull, submissive and disinterested. It is up to us to determine which sort of society we prefer.

There are no simple answers or completely realized models for what structures and institutions will guide us in the coming years. It does seem clear that any political tradition which ignores a deep spiritual connection with the Earth and all her creatures cannot by definition create a sustainable system. We are as likely to be killed off by our use of bug spray and genetically engineered crops as we are by nuclear warfare.

Begin Here, Now

Do we really have it in us to rework the way we conduct our government, our schools, our religious attitudes and our family lives? I believe we do, but we must start with ourselves, and the way we treat our children. As I hope I have shown in the preceding pages, we are shaped by our earliest experiences, in every sense of the word. Our religious beliefs, our childrearing practices, the way we treat our employees, our neighbors and our friends, and even our attitudes toward other countries and their religions—all are forged and shaped during the first years of our lives. None of us is completely free of the profound influences which are registered in the deepest channels of our brains, where our definition of relationship is formed.

It was my purpose to reveal, in every way possible, the powerful currents of selfishness and greed (those influence we can attribute to "Ego") which underlie the many institutions and structures we defend with such pride. We can change them. Probably, all complex technologically top-heavy societies throughout the ages have made similar mistakes. We are not to blame for the culture we were born into, but we will be to blame for the future result if we do not change our behavior. We can do better. We must first heal ourselves, not only by examining our internal states, but by reaching out to heal each other. The inward journey is important, because it helps us to identify where in ourselves we harbor old fears and resentments and what our greatest strengths are, but it is just the beginning.

I have witnessed it in my clients and myself. Each startling revelation about the effect which childhood trauma has laid down in our thinking must be accompanied by action if we are to effect change. By breathing out the pain, while we muster our new strength, we must act, and then act again, to lay down new channels and new ways of being the shining selves we were meant to be. Where there was fear, we must move forward; where there was resentment, we must generate forgiveness, and where there was hatred, we must create love.

I have seen this process take hold in the people I know, and in others who are awakening around the globe. When we set aside terror of an apocalyptic future and the hopelessness and denial it inspires, we can begin to creatively address the pressing need for change. We must begin by simply accepting that our complete dependence on megalithic corporations using fossil fuels to provide for our every need is not only unsustainable. It is no fun. Transition United States has a brighter outlook for our future, although they do not prescribe any system or formula to get us there. Each community must find its own solutions to its own unique needs. As founder Rob Hopkins has described it on their web site: "Our vision is that every community in the United States has engaged its collective creativity to unleash an extraordinary and historic transition to a future beyond fossil fuels; a future that is more vibrant, abundant and resilient; one that is ultimately preferable to the present." Information is available there to support and guide anyone who is willing to take part, in any community in the world, in whatever way they are willing.

Once we have accepted that change is necessary and inevitable, and we have done the work of building our own internal strengths, the courage will follow to move forward into a completely new and unknown adventure with our fellow Earthlings. All the talents and abilities we collectively possess will be needed. People from every walk of life, with every imaginable skill can be put to use.

This is not an easy task, remaking yourself, fearlessly joining with your neighbors to remake your community, but it is a worthy one. Coordinating with your neighbors in order to help each other creates a new sense of belonging. With each action, you will grow. With greater understanding and a solid hold on your center, sensations of love, contentment and joy start to flourish. Remember: love is not a mere sensation. It is an action, and a joy that is meant to be shared.

If each person who reads this page begins to take creative, loving action each day, the world will change. Look first to your immediate family, friends, and coworkers. In the spirit of gratitude for what life has given you, reach out, do something to be of service, to make someone else's day a little easier, a little better. Offer your gifts and talents to a project that will improve all your lives. Ask others to do the same.

Turn especially to the children—yours or someone else's. Do something to make a child smile. When you do, that child will learn from you that the world is an accepting place, and they will become more loving, kind and cooperative, and less vulnerable to the myriad and omnipresent charms of the Dark Side and its proponents.

As for an ideal political or social scheme for the future—no one person will be able to envision and create that or lead us to it. Change will come as an evolving process, because we fashion it together out of moral, economic and emotional necessity, or because we are forced to do so by the earth's changing conditions. If Earth forces our hand, as seems likely in the coming years, then we could see it not as disaster, but as opportunity. If we prepare now, by reaching deep into ourselves for the source of greater strength which resonates within us, we will learn to evolve and grow, no matter what the Universe has in store for us. By seeing ourselves, each as a small but crucial part in the whole scheme of human life and beyond, our efforts take on new meaning. Each small change we fashion in ourselves ripples outward in ever widening circles, creating the possibility of a new kind of life for ourselves and our fellow travelers.

Let us begin.

BIBLIOGRAPHY

A.A. World Services, Inc. *Alcoholics Anonymous: The Story of How Thousands of Men and Women Have Recovered from Alcoholism.* (New York City, 2001)

Aris, Aziz, and Leblanc, Samuel, "Maternal and fetal exposure to pesticides associated to genetically modified foods in Eastern Townships of Quebec," *Reproductive Toxicology.*

Bancroft, Lundy. *Why Does He Do That? Inside the Minds of Angry and Controlling Men* (Berkley Books, New York, 2002)

Berne, Eric. *Games People Play.* (Ballantine Books, 1964)

Bolin, Inge. *Growing Up in a Culture of Respect.* (University of Texas Press, 2006)

Breggin, Peter, M.D. *Toxic Psychiatry.* (St. Martin's Press, New York, 1991)

Bronte, Emily. *Wuthering Heights.* (Classic Books America, 2009)

Brown, Oscar Jr. *What It Is.* (Oyster Knife Publishing, 1992)

Carson, Rachael. *Silent Spring.* (Houghton Mifflin, New York, 1962)

Chess, Stella, M.D., Alexander Thomas, M.D., and Herbert Birch, M.D., PhD. *Your Child is a Person: A Psychological Approach to Childhood Without Guilt.* (The Viking Press, New York, 1965)

Childre, Doc, and Howard Martin. *The HeartMath Solution.* (HarperCollins, New York, 19990

Cozolino, Louis. *The Neuroscience of Psychotherapy.* (W.W. Norton Co., New York, 2002)

Damasio, Antonio R. *Descartes' Error: Emotion, Reason, and the Human Brain.* (G.P. Putnam Sons, New York, 1994)

De Becker, Gavin. *The Gift of Fear.* (Dell Publishing, New York, 1997)

De Laszlo, Violet, Editor, *The, Basic Writings of C.G. Jung.* (The Modern Library, New York, 1959)

Diamond, Jared. *Guns Germs, and Steel.* (W.W. Norton & Co., New York, 1997)

Eadie, Betty Jean. *Embraced By the Light.* (Gold Leaf Press, 1992)

Evans, Patricia. *The Verbally Abusive Relationship.* (Adams Media Corp., Avon, MA, 1992)

_____. *Teen Torment.* (Adams Media Corp., Avon, MA, 2003)

Espada, Martin. *Zapata's Disciple.* (South End, 1998)

Fromm, Eric, M.D. *The Anatomy of Human Destructiveness.* (Henry Holt and Co., New York, 1973)

_____. *The Sane Society.* (Holt, Rhinehart and Winston, 1955)

Fromm-Reichman, Freida, M.D. *Principles of Intensive Psychotherapy.* (University of Chicago Press, 1960)

Goleman, Daniel. *Emotional Intelligence.* (Bantam Books, New York, 1995)

Hare, Robert D., PhD. *Without Conscience.* (Guilford Press, New York, 1993)

Hartmann, Thom. *Screwed: The Undeclared War Against the Middle Class.* (Berrett-Koehler Publishers, Inc., San Francisco, 2006)

Hemingway, Ernest. *For Whom the Bell Tolls.* (Scribner, 1940)

Hollick, Malcolm. *The Science of Oneness: A World-view for the Twenty-First Century.* (O Books, Hants, UK, 2006)

Hopkins, Rob. *The Transition Handbook; From oil dependency to local resilience.* Chelsea Green Publishing, White River Junction, Vt.)

Jung, C.G. *Man and His Symbols.* (Aldus Books, Limited, London, 1964)

Klein, Naomi. *Shock Doctrine.* (Picador, 2008)

Lakov, George. *Don't Think of an Elephant.* (Chelsea Green Publishing Co., White River Junction, VT., 2004)

_____. *Whose Freedom? The Battle Over America's Most Important Idea.* (Farrar, Straus and Giroux, New York, 2006)

Lash, John Lamb. *Not in His Image.* (Chelsea Green Publishing, White River Junction, VT., 2006)

Lykken, David T. *The Antisocial Personalities.* (Lawrence Erlbaum Assoc., Hillsdale, NJ, 1995)

Mahler, Margaret S. *The Psychological Birth of the Human Infant.* (Basic Books, New York, 1975)

McPhee, John. *The Control of Nature.* (Farrar, Straus and Giroux, 1990)

Messer, Ellen, and Kathryn E. May, PsyD. *Back Rooms: Voices From the Illegal Abortion Era.* (Prometheus Books, 1988)

Miller, Paul E. *Love Walked Among Us: Learning to Love Like Jesus.* (NavPress, Colorado Springs, Colorado, 2001)

Moody, Raymond. *Life After Life.* (HarperCollins, San Francisco, 1975)

Newton, Michael. *Life Between Lives*. (Llewellyn Publications, St. Paul, MN, 2004)

Pearce, Joseph Chilton. *The Biology of Transcendence*. (Park Street Press, Rochester, Vermont, 2002)

_____. *From Magical Child To Magical Teen*. (Park Street Press, Rochester, Vermont, 2003)

Peterson, Christopher, Seligman, Martin E. P. *Character Strengths and Virtues*. (Oxford University Press, 2004)

Radin, Dean. *Entangled Minds*. (Pocket Books, New York, 2006)

Rand, Ayn. *The Fountainhead*. (Bobbs-Merrill, New York, 1943)

_____. *Atlas Shrugged*. (Plume, New York, 1957)

_____. *Anthem*. (Cassell, London, 19346)

Reich, Wilhelm. *The Mass Psychology of Fascism*. (Farrar, Straus, New York, 1970)

Rockefeller, David, Jr., Panel Chairman. *Coming To Our Senses*. (McGraw Hill, New York, 1977)

Schore, Allan N. *Affect Regulation and the Repair of the Self*. (W.W. Norton & Co., New York, 2003)

_____. *Affect Dysregulation and Disorders of the Self*. (W.W. Norton & Co., New York, 2003)

Shahn, Ben. *The Shape of Content*. (The President and the Fellows of Harvard College, Cambridge, 1957)

Sheldrake, Rupert. 1999 *Dogs That Know When Their Owners are Coming Home*. (Three Rivers Press, New York, 1999)

Silverman, Debora. *Selling Culture*. (Pantheon Books, New York, 1986)

Stout, Martha, PhD. *The Sociopath Next Door*. (Broadway Books, 2005)

Szasz, Thomas. *The Therapeutic State*. Prometheus Books, Buffalo, New York, 1984)

Vonnegut, Kurt. *A Man Without A Country*. (Random House, New York, 2005)

Wallace, B. Alan. *Contemplative Science: Where Buddhism and Neuroscience Converge*. (Columbia University Press, New York, 2007)

Ward, Dan S. *Reincarnation is Making a Comeback*. (Whitford Press, West Chester, Pennsylvania, 1990)

Wolf, Fred Alan. *The Yoga of Time Travel*. (Quest Books, Wheaton, Illinois, 2004)

World of the Sagas, Ed. Ornolfur Thorsson. *The Saga of Icelanders*. (Leifur Eriksson Publishing, Iceland, 1997)

Wright, Machaelle Small. *Behaving As If the God in All Life Matters.* (Perelandra Ltd., Jeffersonton, Virginia, 1997)

_____. *Perelandra Garden Workbook, (second edition): A Complete Guide to Gardening with Nature Intelligences.* (Perelandra Ltd., Jeffersonton, Virginia, 1993)

Yunus, Muhammad. *Banker to the Poor.* (Public Affairs, New York, 1999)

Zinn, Howard. *Original Zinn.* (Perennial, New York, 2006)

_____. *The People's History of the United States.* (HarperCollins, New York, 1980)

Zukav, Gary. *The Dancing Wu Li Masters.* William Morrow & Co, New York, 1979)

_____. *The Seat of the Soul.* (Simon and Schuster, New York, 1989)

Videos and Films

Century of the Self. Dir. Adam Curtis. BBC Documentary 4-Part Series. (2002)

Food, Inc. Dir. Robert Kenner. (2008)

No End in Sight: The Story of the American Occupation of Iraq. Dir. Charles Ferguson. (2007)

Sailing the Great Pacific Garbage Patch. Dir. Charles Moore (2009)

The Economics of Happiness. Dirs. Helena Norberg-Hodge, Steven Gorelick, John Page. (2011)

The Greenhorns. Dir. Severine von Tscharner Fleming (2011)